JUDAISM [illegible] GE

An Anthology of Secular Humanistic Jewish Thought

THE LIBRARY OF SECULAR HUMANISTIC JUDAISM

JUDAISM IN A SECULAR AGE

An Anthology of Secular Humanistic Jewish Thought

Edited by
RENEE KOGEL and ZEV KATZ

Foreword by
SHERWIN WINE

Introduction by
YEHUDA BAUER

International Institute for
Secular Humanistic Judaism

Milan Press

International Institute for Secular Humanistic Judaism
28611 West Twelve Mile Road
Farmington Hills, MI 48334

Library of Congress Cataloging-in-Publication Data

Judaism in a secular age : an anthology of secular humanistic Jewish thought / edited by Renee Kogel and Zev Katz.
p. cm. -- (The library of secular humanistic Judaism)
Includes index.
ISBN 978-0-967-32598-9
1. Humanistic Judaism. 2. Jews--Identity. 3. Jews--History--Philosophy. I. Kogel, Renee. II. Katz, Zev. III. Series.
BM197.8.J827 1995
296.8'34--dc20 95-38081
CIP

Manufactured in the United States of America

Contents

Preface

This anthology is the creation of the International Institute for Secular Humanistic Judaism, the educational and intellectual arm of the International Federation of Secular Humanistic Jews. Making the basic literature of secular Jewish tradition available to the Jewish and general public is one of the chief aims of the Institute.

The first editor of the anthology was Zev Katz of the Hebrew University, the first Dean of the International Institute, who began the process of selecting appropriate thinkers and collecting their relevant messages. His achievement was continued by Renee Kogel, a faculty member of the International Institute, who completed the difficult task of assembling the necessary materials, writing the many biographies, and finalizing the text. The special devotion of Renee Kogel has brought this project to completion. In addition, the special expertise of Bonnie Cousens, the Executive Director of the Society for Humanistic Judaism, was invaluable. Ruth Duskin Feldman, creative editor of *Humanistic Judaism*, provided guidance in the initial stages of the project. The bibliography was compiled by Rabbi Adam Chalom, Associate Dean of the International Institute. We are grateful to them all for their work.

The publication of the anthology has been made possible by the generous support of the Milan Foundation of Detroit.

Yehuda Bauer
Sherwin Wine
Co-Chairs, International Institute

Foreword

This anthology is an important innovation. For the first time readings from the basic literature of Secular Humanistic Judaism have been assembled in one book.

Secular Humanistic Judaism has existed as an alternative in Jewish life for over one hundred years. For most of its history it was an informal option in Jewish life. There was no awareness of a single movement. Secular Jews participated in a wide variety of Jewish movements—Zionism, Yiddish nationalism, and Bundism. They created Jewish schools, reading circles, and cultural associations. They joined fraternal societies, community centers, and welfare agencies. They supported Jewish community life and fought against antisemitism. Some lived in tight-knit Jewish communities like the farm kibbutzim in Israel. Others lived unaffiliated lives in big urban centers, expressing their Jewish identity through family and social relationships, through reading Jewish newspapers and attending Jewish cultural events. All were uncomfortable with the institutions of the well-organized Jewish religious world, whether those institutions were Orthodox, Conservative, Reform, or Reconstructionist.

In recent years secular and humanistic Jews have coalesced into an international movement, with self-identified communities, national organizations, publications, publicly proclaimed statements of belief, and schools for training leaders of the movement. The name Secular Humanistic Judaism reflects two principal ideological strains. It could just as easily have been called Cultural Judaism or Naturalistic Judaism or Rational Judaism.

Secular Humanistic Judaism is a reflection of the enormous changes that have occurred in Jewish life over the past three centuries. From the perspective of the age of science and of modern Jewish life as actually lived by millions of contemporary Jews, it is quite conventional. From the perspective of traditional religion—and even the official ideology of liberal religion—it is a radical departure from established norms. There are four major differences from "official" Judaism.

1. Secular Jews do not view Judaism as primarily a religion. They see it as the evolving culture and civilization of a world people. This culture embraces many variations—Ashkenazic, Sephardic, Oriental, and Israeli. It includes many options—language, literature, music, holidays, and religion. It features many ethical styles—authoritarian, intuitive, and consequential. It provides many political and economic choices—theocracy, democracy, capitalism, and socialism. It allows many interpretations of the Jewish experience—theistic, pantheistic, and atheistic. Being Jewish may include any one of these options. What unites all positive Jews is an active identification with the history and fate of the Jewish people.

2. Secular Jews do not accept the authority of a supernatural God. Nor do they seek to "rescue" religious and theistic language for naturalistic purposes. Secular Jews do not believe that traditional religious expressions fit secular interpretations of Jewish history and the human experience. They want to say boldly and clearly what it is that they believe. They want their words to point easily to what they think and feel. A Judaism without "God language" is a radical departure from even the most liberal of existing Jewish religious options, including the Reform and Reconstructionist movements. It poses the challenge of framing Jewish aspirations in a secular language.

3. Secular Jews do not feel any need to be validated by traditional religious texts. They do not seek the "approval" of either the Torah, the Talmud, the Siddur, or the responsa literature of the rabbis. They find their authority in the evidence of Jewish and human experience. Conservative, Reform, and Reconstructionist Judaism

choose to justify their norms by appealing to sacred texts. In this respect, they resemble Orthodoxy. Secular Jews view these texts simply as famous Jewish literary works. They recognize that many important humanistic ideas and values appear in them, but do not attribute authority to these ideas and values solely because of their presence in the texts. These ideas and values would be equally significant even if the texts did not exist, and even if their earliest exprssion occurred in other Jewish texts.

4. Secular Jews deny that there is only one Jewish tradition. They do not accept the establishment rabbinic tradition as the only example of "Jewish roots." They recognize that there have always been counter-establishment traditions whether mystical or secular. These traditions are often known to us through denunciations in the "official" rabbinic literature or through popular cultural creations. Ashkenazic Jewish religion is pious. Ashkenazic Jewish humor is skeptical. There are "underground" and "folk" traditions which are just as rooted as the official ideology. Conformity and censorship prevented most of these traditions from ever being "published." Only the freedom of modern democratic societies has allowed Jews the opportunity to give open expression to them.

The implications of these four differences are very clear. The basic literature of Secular Humanistic Judaism overlaps the literature of religious Judaism. But it is essentially different and overwhelmingly modern. Most Jewish literature written before the Enlightenment is not suitable as inspirational and instructional reading for secular and humanistic Jews. It is historically interesting—and sometimes ethically elevating—but it does not easily fit into the secular perspective on the meaning of the Jewish experience and the human condition.

There is a large body of Jewish literature, written during and after the Enlightenment, that very explicitly articulates the feelings and thoughts of secular Jews. Much of it was written by famous people who were not comfortable with the ideas and institutions of the religious establishment. Most of it is unknown to the general Jewish public—even to most Jews who identify with or are sympathetic to a secular perspective.

The purpose of this anthology is to assemble the best of this alternative literature and make it available to the Jewish public.

This outreach includes the possibility of serving three sets of needs.

1. This anthology can be a basic reader for Secular Humanistic Jews who are seeking the inspirational and ideological roots of their commitment. Secular Jews do not need an alternative Torah. But they do need access to the writings of their teachers and heroes.

2. It can also be a journey of Jewish exploration for Jews who are searching for an effective way to express their Jewish identity, but who are not comfortable with the religious alternatives that are presently available.

3. It can certainly be an interesting opportunity for students of modern Judaism, even those who are religious, to understand an important development in modern Jewish life.

I hope that this unique reader will make an important difference in Jewish life by increasing the awareness of Secular Humanistic Judaism in the Jewish and non-Jewish worlds.

Sherwin Wine

Introduction

I.

Secular Humanistic Judaism is a relatively new idea with a long background and history.

First, a few definitions are in order.

What do we mean when we talk about Judaism? The traditional definition identifies Judaism with a set of theistic beliefs: fundamentally, belief in the existence of a supreme being who rules and regulates the universe, our planet, and humanity. Many people call such a set of beliefs religion, though others will argue that a religion is any set of beliefs and norms of behavior, theistic or not. We will return to this question later; in the meantime, let us use the term "religion" as it is popularly used, to denote theistic belief.

But which theistic beliefs constitute Judaism? The theism of Reform Judaism is hardly identical with that of the Lubavitcher sect, and a Conservative rabbi accepts different beliefs and norms of behavior than do scholars at Yeshiva University in New York, though theirs probably are closer to his than the beliefs of, say, the Satmar Hasidim (an extremist Hasidic sect bitterly opposed to the Lubavitcher).

Ancient Judaism was not a fixed, unchanging belief system. The very name of the one, universal, and invisible God in the Bible is *elohim*, a plural form that means "gods." This and other elements of polytheism survived in the biblical accounts, a fact religious commentators have to try to explain away.

For millennia, the Jews were both a religious group and a people. When outsiders became Jews, they accepted both membership in the people of Israel and the then-current interpretation of Jewish theistic religion. Their ethnic origin did not, and does not, matter. Their acceptance of the developing and changing tradition of beliefs and practices did. This applied also to those who were coerced into becoming Jews, such as the inhabitants of large parts of the land of Israel between about 140 and 63 B.C.E., when the Hasmonean rulers wanted to establish a unitary Jewish civilization in the land.

The Jewish people developed a culture, and religion served as the garb in which it was clothed. This was true, as well, of every Christian or Islamic culture, then and until the Enlightenment, more than two hundred years ago, when the various garbs began to be shed. If you look at the Bible, you will see that it is composed of such diverse elements as history, poetry, laws, and so on. Although the language is mostly (though not entirely) theistic, the content is economics, politics, personal and social problems, and moral issues. If you look at the Talmud, the point becomes even clearer. There is very little about God in the Talmud, but there are tomes devoted to the regulation of societal norms: who can be a witness; how interpersonal conflicts should be resolved; marriage, education, divorce, property matters; social and community life; and much more of this kind. Jews, in ancient times as today, were concerned with their everyday lives.

Bible is Judaism, Talmud is Judaism, everyday life is Judaism, Jewish history is Judaism, Jewish poetry is Judaism, Jewish customs are Judaism, Jewish food is Judaism, Jewish jokes are Judaism; just as religion is Judaism. But you cannot argue that Judaism equals the religious beliefs of Jews; first, because these beliefs were and are different, even mutually contradictory; and second, because religion was and is just one aspect of Jewish existence; today, for many Jews, it is not even that. Judaism, then, is everything that the Jewish people in their very long history have produced. Judaism is Jewish civilization, Judaism is Jewish culture.

Judaism historically includes Jewish religion; and, because religion was a strong binding force, until the Age of Enlightenment it was a positive element most of the time. The point is that from about two centuries ago, when the close identification of religion with peoplehood began to wane with the rise of secularized nationalism, Jews in increasing numbers remained Jews as people and ceased to be Jews by religion. Consciously or not, they ceased to observe the traditional customs and norms and ceased to believe in a God who was concerned about whether they ate their salami with cheese.

Judaism, then, is not equivalent to Jewish religion but is equivalent to the totality of Jewish experience, as Jews interpret it at different times and places. It is Jewish civilization as a whole.

Beginning in the mid-nineteenth century, more and more Jews, particularly those living in western European countries who were urban and were impacted by both the Scientific Revolution and the Age of Reason, began to alter their self-definition of what it meant to be Jewish. Increasingly writings began to appear that equated Judaism, not with religion, but with a culture, a way of life. The advent of socialism and then of Zionism added to the number of secular Jews.

What, exactly, do we mean by secular? The origin of the term is Christian—it refers to the real, present world in contrast with the "nether" world of religious beliefs, the world of God, Paradise, and Hell. This division is typically Christian because in religious Judaism it was blurred; Jews never had very clear notions of the next world, and their religion related very closely to everyday life. The reason for this was highly practical: as the psalmist sang, *lo hametim yehalelu yah* ("it is not the dead who will praise God"). Jewish religion was for the living. This-worldly and other-worldly concerns were closely intertwined. Jewish postbiblical literature was directed primarily toward commercial, interpersonal, or social matters. Yet, clearly, Jewish life until about two hundred years ago was traditional, religion- and custom-bound. At least outwardly, every person who belonged to a Jewish community followed rules and regulations that were part of a code of behavior organized by theistic beliefs.

Since the Enlightenment, European society has undergone radical change, and Jewish life has followed suit. The influence of religious beliefs declined—in Jewish as well as in general society—and Jews left the ghetto, as the saying went; not just the physical ghetto, but the spiritual ghetto as well. Critiques of religion ranged from moderate ones that still accepted theism in one form or another to radical rejections of belief in God. Many Jews left the Jewish people altogether; but most Jews, including most of those who no longer abided by religious norms and customs, remained part of the Jewish community and the Jewish people. Today they are termed secular Jews.

Secular Jews come in different shapes and forms: nonreligious Zionists, nonreligious Yiddishists, and those who do not choose to identify as either Zionists or Yiddishists but are acculturated to the host society—such as many North American Jews who are quite happy where they are, speak and think English, are at home in the American culture, but also feel their Jewishness quite strongly and wish to identify with Jewish matters and causes. Regardless of which of these categories they fall into, secular Jews seek an interpretation of Jewish civilization that accords with their own preferences, attitudes, and beliefs.

Secular can be defined most simply as "nonreligious." If you believe that the idea of a God is irrelevant to your life—either because you do not believe in a God, or because you think that even if a God exists, he (or she) is not the kind of being that controls the universe and your own life—then you are a secularist. Many Jews who belong to religious congregations are "closet" secularists. They may pay lip service to organized religion in its various forms because they know of no other way to express their membership in the Jewish community. They may believe that by keeping "something" they remain attached to the Jewish people, although what they do in the synagogue, if and when they go there (and most Reform and Conservative Jews do not attend regularly), has no intrinsic meaning for them.

It is one thing to read prayers when you believe there is somebody there who hears and cares; it is quite another thing to mumble words—especially when you do not really understand what you are reading—when you are convinced that there cannot possibly be anyone who listens and cares. It is one thing to follow ancient practices and obey ancient taboos (about food, for instance) because you really believe that they were ordained by a God who is intent on ensuring that you do not eat shrimp; it is quite another thing to follow the same habits and customs when you are quite certain that these are meaningless remnants of ancient taboos and superstitions.

To come out of your "closet," then, is a matter of personal integrity: to assert to yourself and to others that whatever you do, you believe in, and what you do not believe in, you do not do. At the same time, though, if you are like most secularists, you are the first to demand that those who do believe in the religious customs you do not observe should have every right to follow them. You are a pluralist, a supporter of a democratic and humanistic way of life. You believe in the right of all individuals to live their lives in accordance with their convictions, as long as their actions do not impinge on the rights and well-being of others.

There are secular Jews who call themselves religious because they define religion differently from the popular notion. They may say, for instance, that a religious attitude is a spiritual one: not just going beyond crass materialism, but relating to nature and to society in a way appreciative of beauty, external and internal; for example, experiencing, enjoying, and internalizing art, music, philosophy, and literature. They may view spirituality as a way to grapple with the many unsolved problems of human existence, without reference to a supreme being onto whose shoulders such problems can be unloaded. Secular Jewish religionists say that a belief system that does not acknowledge a godhead but fulfills the spiritual needs of individuals and communities by providing meaningful seasonal and life-cycle ceremonies that relate to the Jewish past is, by definition, religious. You may belong to a group of people who hold such beliefs and enact them in appropriate ceremonies. If so, and if you do not believe in a world-creating authority that supervises you throughout your life, you are a secularist, a religious secularist. You simply define the term "religion" in a different way from the usual one.

However, there are issues underlying this play with semantics that are of considerable importance. Do secularists "possess" spirituality? Do secularists "believe"? Are there things that are "holy" for them? Indeed, secularists believe: they believe in individual and social morality and do the best they can to build a slightly better society than we have now. Secularism's spirituality is of a different nature than the religion-induced kind, which depends on an external authority that has to coerce ethical behavior with threats of punishment in this world and/or the next. Secular ethics are autonomous, the result of personal decisions and personal responsibility, and therefore might tend to be more seriously considered.

Secular Jews believe in the holy—that is, inviolable—nature of certain things: the value of human life, the integrity of the human personality, the primacy of human dignity, the equality of men and women everywhere, the right of children to unfettered development. These and similar things are "holy" to us, as they are to many religious people whom we would call religious humanists.

On the other hand, some of the things that are holy to an Orthodox (or sometimes a Conservative) Jew are trivial in our eyes: separation of meat and milk, dressing in medieval clothing, obeying the prohibition of the use of money or engaging in sports on Shabbat, and so on. These and other issues are addressed and discussed in this anthology.

We secular Jews know that the Jews are a people whose civilization is the result of a very long and very impressive history. We have no problem in principle (though there are many practical problems of great complexity) in peeling off the religious component from the Jewish heritage. We have no need to impute to our ancestors attitudes that belong to our own times. We can read the ancient texts with new eyes and recognize that while we do not believe what their authors believed, we still can identify with them. Many of us will differentiate between a direct quotation (which must not be tampered with) and the changing of texts to fit our needs, in which case there is a new text that may use or adapt portions of the traditional wording. In the latter case there is a context of a festival or a life-cycle ceremony, which itself is the development of an older tradition, and within which the new text reflects our individual and/or communal needs in an innovative, creatively changing way.

What do we mean by humanism? You will find a number of definitions and descriptions in this anthology. Perhaps the simplest is that which says that a humanist believes in the centrality, inviolability, and, yes, sacredness of human life and human integrity. There are excellent grounds for saying that there can be a religious humanism, because people who believe in a godhead may still see human life as inviolable and may view human integrity as a supreme value. Secular humanism emerged out of religious humanism.

In Jewish religious tradition, the emphasis was on humans. Our old texts—not only the Bible, but the Mishnah and the rest of the Talmud as well—contain the wisdom of generations: the philosophical and moral insights, the caring responsibility for individual, family, and community, the concern for all human beings. This is part of what we understand as humanism. Of course, these texts also contain superstitious beliefs and calls for action that we do not consider moral: xenophobia and even genocide. But then, part of being a humanist is that you are free—free to make your own choices and your own decisions. You are responsible to yourself and to your fellow humans, and you undoubtedly will reject parts of your heritage even as you acknowledge that it is yours. Responsibility is both personal and social: it implies the absolute equality of all humans and an obligation toward a community of choice; an obligation that each individual decides upon and enters into by adhering to a community and defining her or his part in its development. Both individual choice and individual assumption of responsibility are intrinsic to what we mean by freedom.

For secularists, then, humanism means that we believe there is no God out there to take the responsibility for our lives off our shoulders. The moral values propounded by the Jewish or any other religion are not the result of divine intervention in human affairs but were conceived and pronounced by humans just like ourselves. Our attitude toward ourselves and the world around us is one in which the human being is the center of our endeavors.

While secular humanism emerged out of the religious variety, religious humanism is incomplete and contradictory. If human life, human integrity, and human existence are the central values, they must be independent of a God; otherwise it is God who is the central thing, not the human personality. The logic of humanism is secular, not religious.

Secular Humanistic Jews, then, are persons who wish to belong to the Jewish people and to carry on the traditions of the Jewish people free of dependence on supernatural authority. They believe in the sacredness of the human personality, its dignity and its integrity. They want the Jewish people to be a productive, respected member of a family of equal nations and are open to cultural influences of all members of the human race.

Secular Humanistic Jews have some other unique definitions. What, or who, is a Jew? A Jew, we believe, is a person who either is born a Jew or chooses to join the Jewish people. A Jew will be, in most cases, descended from Jews through either or both parents, and it should not matter whether it is the father or the mother who is Jewish. The matrilineal definition adopted by religious Judaism was very useful in days past, particularly to protect and legitimize children born as a result of rape committed during persecutions and pogroms. A child's mother was much more easily identifiable than the father; whoever the father was, the child of a Jewish mother could not be denied her or his Jewishness. Today these considerations are meaningless, unacceptable, or no longer relevant.

The child of a Jewish father and a non-Jewish mother who wishes to be Jewish is a Jew according to our definition.

What about a person without Jewish ancestry? Secular Humanistic Jews consider such a person a Jew if he or she wants to be a Jew and acts accordingly, by joining and participating in a group or community that defines itself as continuing the Jewish tradition in one of a variety of ways. Becoming a Jew need not include a religious conversion. If non-Jews who want to become Jews are not religious as non-Jews, why should we expect them to be religious as Jews? And why should we exclude them if they are not religious? Those who want to do so know very well that the Jewish people is a small people with many existential and other problems. Anyone who sincerely wants to be one of us, we should welcome with open arms. The question is, following a good old Jewish tradition, what you do and not what you say or utter. If you act like a responsible member of a Jewish group or community, you are one.

II.

Why this anthology? What purposes does it serve? What does it contain?

Let me say, first of all, what the anthology is not. It is not another definitive text, a sacred text of some kind, a final word on beliefs and ideologies. But, if you are a Secular Humanistic Jew, or a secular humanist who wants to learn about Jews, there is no readily available book that brings you in touch with Secular Humanistic Jewish thought. There is no book that collects the main names, and the thoughts and literary production of individuals whose basic approach was or is similar to ours. Nor is there a book that chronicles the thoughts and ideas of those Jews who paved the way for Secular Humanistic Judaism by challenging the prevailing ideologies and proposing alternative ways of thinking. While they themselves were not either secularists or humanists, they helped to prepare the ground where new beliefs could sprout.

Jewish civilization is probably the oldest continuously existing civilization: older than the Chinese, older than the Indian. Some of the products of Jewish civilization have come down to us in texts and traditions; many, most likely, have been lost. Best known, of course, is the Bible: a compendium of writings known as the Five Books of Moses, the literature of the prophets, and an assortment of other materials that were collected into one book sometime between the last two centuries or so of the pre-Christian era and the first century C.E. The separate books that make up the Bible were written at different times over a period of about a thousand years, by different people with different views and for different purposes, and were edited by others who struck out some passages and introduced others for ideological reasons.

Nevertheless, the Bible is a magnificent creation of the human spirit. It contains sagas and legends, poems and prose. It contains "prophecies": social, moral, and political analyses in the form of exhortations, warnings, praises, and predictions. It contains parables and prayers and philosophical treatises. The centuries in which the Bible was written were times in which people, Jews and others, believed in supernatural powers; they attributed their experiences to a god or gods who were responsible for what happened.

Not all the authors of the Bible thought so; the Book of Ecclesiastes is a clearly Greek philosophical statement, in which the Jewish God is introduced as an external factor, quite unnecessary from the point of view of the flow of the argument. It got into the Bible because the author (or someone who wanted to have it included) claimed that it had been written by King Solomon. With a recommendation like that, it could not very well have been left out! Of course, good old Solomon had nothing to do with Ecclesiastes; it was written probably about the third or second century B.C.E., perhaps even later, at least some six to seven hundred years after Solomon's time.

Then there is the Book of Esther, with the famous story of the rescue of the Jews of Persia from the evil Haman under King Ahasuerus, with the help of that clever old Jew, Mordecai. The problem is that no king by that name ever reigned over Persia, and the names of Esther and Mordecai are derived from names of pagan gods—the Phoenician Astarte and the Babylonian Mardoch, to whom human sacrifices were offered. Now, what is a nice Jewish girl with the name of a pagan goddess of fertility doing at the court of a nonexistent Persian king, her activities masterminded by a Jew with the name of a horrible pagan god? The answer, apparently, is that this was a parable, the background of which may well have been the struggles between Sadducees and Pharisees under Hasmonean rule in the second pre-Christian century. The name of God is not mentioned in the book at all.

Behind all these elements of fable lies a deep truth, I believe: a society developed; an economy and a social system arose, experienced crises, and tried to resolve them. Religion was the ideological form into which this experience was poured—not, initially, a monotheistic system, as was later developed in Jewish religion, but a polytheistic one. As I have mentioned, the Bible speaks of *elohim*—"gods"—as the name of the one God. It speaks of *terafim*, family gods that the patriarchs worshipped; it speaks of the struggle between the Jewish god and the other gods, assuming as a matter of course that these other gods exist and exercise influence over the Jews as well as over "their" nations. Only slowly, painfully, after the Babylonian exile in the sixth century B.C.E., and then increasingly with the reconquest of historic Eretz Yisrael, or Palestine, by the Hasmoneans (second century B.C.E.) did monotheism finally take over.

Again, religion was the ideological form, not all-pervasive but clearly there. The content, however, was social, moral, economic, political. The Bible contains the laws and the customs that developed and were followed, and reflects some very important concepts. The very idea of one God implies that all humans are "his" children and, therefore, as the prophet Amos says so eloquently, the fundamental equality of all humans.

Then there is the law that requires all Hebrew slaves to be set free after seven years. In other words, there is a statement against slavery, in a world in which slavery was the norm. There is the lex talionis—eye for an eye, tooth for a tooth; not two eyes for an eye, not two teeth for a tooth—in other words, equality before the law, a new and revolutionary concept that the Jews developed.

There are many more examples. There was no landed aristocracy, no very large landholders, no Hebrew slaves—though enslavement of others was still all right. Perhaps most importantly for us, there are statements legitimizing opposition to accepted authority when that authority is misused or when its bearers act immorally. The stories about King David, for instance, and the legitimate challenges that he had to meet from commoners and prophets, or the famous story of the man Naboth who challenged a king of Israel who had done him wrong, illustrate this concept of rights of citizens as against the authority of the state.

Above all, there is the story of the Exodus from Egypt, which is mentioned innumerable times in the Bible. It symbolized in ancient times, as it does today, the yearning for freedom—a yearning expressed in the name of the individual and also in the name of the community, of society, and of the nation. Slavery in Egypt, rebellion against that slavery, the struggle for freedom, the process of education that the Hebrews, according to this legend, had to undergo in the desert—all these are central biblical themes. The historical details may have been lost or overlaid with legend in the course of time, before they were written down, and some of these legends are very beautiful indeed. But there hardly can be any doubt that the basic facts were preserved: nomads were enslaved but managed to escape into the desert, finally arriving in the land of Canaan.

No wonder, then, that so many nations, so many traditions, took their inspiration from the Bible: downtrodden blacks, persecuted European minorities, poor and despairing people everywhere. But there is another side to the Bible, too. There are calls for genocide, as in the story about the Midianites in which Moses tells the Israelites that when they killed "only" the men, they sinned—they should go back and kill all the women and all the male children as well. There are scenes of depravity and injustice, because the Bible is a composite construction, reflecting different attitudes and social ideologies.

And then, of course, there was the editing. Writers who were not of the same mind as the editors were silenced, probably forever. It is highly doubtful, for instance, that the "false prophets" called themselves "false prophets." They probably saw themselves as the true prophets and viewed those who were included in the collection as the false ones. We do not have the opinions of the opposition figures. Nor do we have the writings of many nonprophets, though we know that literacy was widespread even before the Babylonian exile and, after the building of the Second Temple, became (probably by stages) more or less universal. Some "external books," not included in the collection, have come down to us (some only in fragments), as has the great collection of writings known as the Dead Sea Scrolls; but much of what was written in the nonbiblical literature has been lost.

Secular Humanistic Jews view the Bible as an essential part of our heritage because it is our people, many generations ago, who are reflected in those pages, who wrote and spoke in a language that is today spoken and written by many Jews. Even though we do not believe that there is anyone to pray to, we do believe in the people who prayed. The psalms, for example, are the outpourings of distressed, hurting, desperate souls, with whom we have a natural emotional bond. (Recent researchers claim that many of the psalms were literally taken over from earlier cultures of the Middle East; but even if this is true, the fact that they were translated into Hebrew and absorbed into the Jewish tradition means that Jews identified with what they contained.) None of this requires us to accept the views of people who lived thousands of years ago. A parallel might be that of the modern Greek who admires and loves and learns from the *Iliad* and the *Odyssey,* but of course without believing in the pagan gods that are an integral part of the story.

The traditions that are written down in the Bible have to be carefully sifted and analyzed. Some of them can serve as the basis or paradigm for moral statements, for demands for social justice, for political morality. Some of them are repugnant and unacceptable. A Secular Humanistic Jew analyzes them by the standards of her or his humanism, that is, with an attitude of personal and social responsibility. We do not deny that the portions we reject are part of the heritage handed down to us, but we choose not to accept them as valid for ourselves. So the Bible has to be studied and considered in a critical and discerning way, both on an intellectual and on an emotional level.

The further, postbiblical development of Jewish thought, philosophies, social systems, customs, folkways, music, poetry and prose, social organization, types of leadership and communal constructs—all of that belongs to the tradition of the Secular Humanistic Jew. Again, we will not accept everything—certainly not simply because it is part of the religious tradition—but neither will we reject anything just because the people who thought, uttered, or wrote it had beliefs we do not share. These people and the things they wrote are part of our past, our heritage. It could not be expected of them to arrive at the conclusions of Jews in the second half of the twentieth century.

Nor do we reject the achievements of others, be they Europeans, Asians, Africans, or whoever. Secular Humanistic Jews will happily integrate the intellectual and emotional achievements of other civilizations into their own tradition. This, indeed, is what our ancestors did throughout the ages. Almost all the great moral precepts in the Bible have precedents in the civilizations of the surrounding world, but nowhere were these put together in the way they were in the Bible. Jesus repeated the ideas of the sage Hillel the Elder, and then they were spread by the new Christian religion.

Hillel himself summed up the basis of his ideology in two sentences: "Do not do unto the other what you would not have done unto yourself"; and "Love your neighbor as yourself—that is the whole Torah standing on one foot." No mention of a God. These are the quintessential statements of a humanist. So, we not only do not reject Jewish tradition; on the contrary, we claim that we are its legitimate outcome and continuation.

Two other essential elements in our understanding of Jewish history are integral parts of our secular and humanistic Jewish commitment: (1) the perception that Jewish tradition is not monolithic and never has been, but is the result of a multitude of conflicting social and intellectual trends; and (2) the perception that there is no part of the Jewish tradition that can claim absolute authority over us, as distinct from serving as a possible source of inspiration.

The misconception of an immutable Jewish tradition is an intellectual construct mainly of Orthodox Jewry, one that stands in stark contrast to known historical facts. During the period of the Second Temple (roughly between the end of the sixth century B.C.E. and the first century C.E.), the Sadducees, representing the upper strata of Jewish society in Palestine, and the Pharisees, representing the intellectual elite of the lower social orders, were locked in bitter conflict over the correct interpretation of the Jewish religious and social tradition. While the Pharisees finally won out, this outcome was not preordained. There were additional groups—the Essenes, for instance, reputedly the main authors of the Dead Sea Scrolls—and they, too, claimed to be the only correct interpreters of the Jewish tradition.

More than a thousand years later, Maimonides, the great Jewish philosopher, born in Spain and living in Egypt, was the center of another controversy. His books actually were burned by Jewish communities in some European countries. Today he is revered, especially by the ultra-Orthodox, as an undisputed authority. In eighteenth-century Poland, Hasidism arose as a rebellion against the petrified state of Jewish traditionalism. The struggle between the Hasidim and their opponents, the Mitnagdim, went to such an extreme that Mitnagdim appealed to the Russian authorities to arrest and persecute Hasidim.

The story of Judaism, in other words, is the story of constant change and constant struggle between different interpretations of what Judaism is. Jews always have been a pluralistic people, though they never wanted to be. They were pluralistic in practice because, fortunately, they never could agree on only one interpretation of their tradition. There never has been unanimity. Today, with a variety of religious and nonreligious observance, pluralism is the only road to Jewish survival.

What does pluralism mean? It means the realization, first, that we are all human, and second, that while we are absolutely convinced that we are right, we know we might be wrong. It means that your view of Jewish culture and civilization has equal validity with other views, that Orthodoxy must renounce its claim to papal infallibility, and that all interpretations must compete for adherents among the Jewish people.

Halakha, Jewish religious law and the repository and source of the Orthodox way of life, was formulated in the Babylonian and Jerusalem Talmuds, which were completed about 500 C.E. Before that, there was no halakha but a slow, painful, development toward it, which lasted for at least a millennium and a half. Thus the Jewish people existed without halakha longer than it has existed with it. The judges, the kings, the prophets, even the rabbis of the post–Second Temple period managed without the Talmud, without the halakha in its completed form. Today's Orthodox and Conservative claim for an immutable halakha, or for a halakha that has to be readjusted only marginally to our times, is based on a misunderstanding of history. The Reform movement, which is slowly moving toward halakha without actually believing in its sanctity, is doing so, it seems, partly because some Reform leaders think that halakha somehow represents "genuine" Judaism. It doesn't. It is simply one expression of Jewish creativity, which fit the situation of Jews some fifteen hundred years ago and was then partially adapted to changing circumstances until it became hopelessly out of date during the past two centuries. This does not mean that we cannot or should not learn from it, as we would from any other part of our tradition. What we utterly reject is the claim that halakha (or, indeed, any other part of our tradition) is the authority for what we should believe and how we should live.

The Jewish people emerged from its halakhic shell during the modern period, from, say, the end of the eighteenth century—the age of Emancipation—and became transformed. The transformation took different forms in different places, in accordance with the historical development of the peoples among whom the Jews were living. Differences in cultural-social background gave rise to such varied movements as German Reform, American Conservatism and Reconstructionism, American Reform, Eastern European

Hasidism (which dates only from the 1760s), modern Orthodoxy, "Lithuanian" Orthodoxy (the non-Hasidic, Mitnagdic variety), and many other groups.

Secularism, as it slowly arose, was also dressed in a variety of clothes. Jews who were involved in political, social, and cultural movements that were by definition secularist did not really trouble to articulate their nonreligious attitudes. Other concerns seemed more important, like the Zionist political movement, some of whose mid-nineteenth-century precursors were religious people, but more were individuals who had abandoned religion as irrelevant. As Zionism spread from its original home in East-Central Europe and became a national movement of the Jewish people, it became largely secularly-oriented. Its Labor and General Zionist and Revisionist components were intent on developing a Hebrew-language approach that would distill from the old heritage that which could be useful in the new social atmosphere of a renascent Jewish peoplehood. These writers, philosophers, politicians, and literary figures represent one important tendency among the Jewish secularists included in this anthology.

Another important tendency, concentrated in Eastern Europe before the Holocaust and largely but not entirely socialist, was to develop a popular, secularist Jewish culture based on Yiddish, the common language of the Jewish masses there. The most important mass Jewish movement that propagated these ideas was the Jewish labor movement called the Bund (Allgemeyner Yiddisher Arbeterbund). Founded at the same time as the Zionist organization in 1897, this movement attracted very large numbers of Jews in Russia but was suppressed by the Communist regime after the Bolshevik revolution. It then gained tremendous popularity in Poland and, to a lesser extent, in other Eastern and Central European countries. Yiddishist writing was permeated by a love for the ordinary Jewish people in the cities, towns and villages.

A third tendency developed in Western Europe and in the New World. Jews, thinking, speaking, and writing in the languages of the countries in which they lived, developed a sense of Jewish community not necessarily based on religious beliefs. While some inclined toward Zionism or some other ideology, their main motif was the struggle for integration in their environment while maintaining Jewish specificity.

In North America, thinkers such as Horace Kallen, Max Rosenfeld, and many others—some of whom you will find included in this anthology—identified with the Jewish people as an ethnic group with a long tradition that they felt had to be interpreted in secular, humanistic, twentieth-century terms. This strain, based on a large body of thought, literature, and social action, reflects a growing need of very large numbers of Jews who do not feel they can participate in religious observance but many of whom do not accept the alternative of no Jewish life at all.

Secular Humanistic Jews may identify with any of the political or social tendencies that have developed among the Jewish people during the past couple of centuries, or they may be unattached to any of them. As long as they subscribe to the general principles outlined in the first part of this essay, they are, whether they realize it or not, Jews of the Secular Humanistic orientation.

There are two main organizations in North America that embody a Secular Humanistic approach to Jewish life; together they embrace nearly fifty communities across the United States and Canada. The Society for Humanistic Judaism (SHJ) was founded by Sherwin Wine in 1969 in Detroit. The Congress of Secular Jewish Organizations (CSJO), founded the same year, has some local groups of older vintage and developed from a Yiddishist-oriented secular humanism. The SHJ represents a community-oriented membership, seeks to develop a secular humanistic rabbinate (*rav* in Hebrew simply means "teacher"), and appeals to many people who have acculturated to middle-class North American life. The CSJO is, today, based to a large extent on schools where children receive a secular Jewish education and on adult groups connected to these schools, with a strong emphasis on the great traditions of the Yiddish-speaking Jewish culture of Eastern Europe.

These two organizations have joined together in a North American Federation of Secular Humanistic Jews, which in turn is affiliated with the International Federation of Secular Humanistic Jews. The International Federation, founded in 1986, currently consists of nine national organizations; in Israel, Europe, Latin America, Australia, and the former Soviet Union. The International Federation supports an International Institute for Secular Humanistic Judaism to train teachers and leaders and to serve as intellectual center for the Secular Humanistic Jewish movement.

Secular Humanistic Jews neither reject the traditions and the history of the Jewish people, nor do they follow observances they consider to be obsolete and antiquated. They choose, as free humans, out of their splendid and vast heritage that which is meaningful to their contemporary social, personal, moral concerns. Living in the present, they are committed to developing new concepts and ceremonies, looking toward the future, and grappling with the many unsolved problems in both the general and the Jewish community of which they are part. In this way, Secular Humanistic Jews develop their tradition and give new meaning to their Jewishness.

These are the foundations on which this anthology is built.

A serious problem that this anthology attempts to address is the decline of organized Jewry. About one-half or even more—no one knows exactly—of the Jews in the United States are not members of any synagogue or congregation. In part, this fact may be a function of age. As young people grow up and have children, some of them join synagogues so that their children can have some kind of Jewish education. Many of these people drop out after Bar/Bat Mitsva. Attendance at synagogues is meager, perhaps because the kind of service provided is not conducive to the expression of a deeply felt Jewish identity. Without being able to put their finger on exactly what is wrong, many Jews simply vote by their absence. This is true not only of Reform and Conservative congregations, but of some Orthodox ones as well.

Secular Humanistic Judaism, with its appreciation of Jewish peoplehood and its determination to identify credible Jewish ethnic, historical, cultural, and moral traditions and values, offers a viable alternative for Jews alienated by established religion. Without such credible answers, large numbers of people may well be lost to Jewish peoplehood. If an increasing number of Jews accept the answers of Secular Humanistic Judaism, they may remain within the framework of organized Jewry.

The anthology does not start with Secular Humanistic Jews but with Kindred Spirits: Jews who did not become secular humanists but went part of the way. This first part lends depth to our movement. We are heirs to pioneers who preceded us; we salute key figures of our own century or the past few centuries, whose thinking, while we do not agree with it fully, is close to ours in certain respects. The second part includes Pathbreakers whose views are more closely aligned with ours, who lived not long before our time but too early to be identified with our movement. The third part comprises leading figures in today's movement for Secular

Humanistic Judaism. Excerpts from each author's works are preceded by a short biographical and interpretive note.

Each of the three parts of the anthology includes ideals and ideology, prose and poetry. Why we include philosophical thought is probably obvious. But why literature? Because we want to appeal not only to rationality but also to emotions. Many Jewish writers and poets have beautifully expressed ideas akin to ours. The excerpts in this volume may inspire you to dip into it frequently, in quiet or troubled moments. You may wish to read some of them aloud in family or community settings. Or you may be motivated to seek out an unabridged source, or additional writings by a particular author. If so, this work will have achieved its purpose.

Actually, before our first part commences, we have included a thinker whom we have identified as a precursor, Baruch Spinoza.

But why Baruch Spinoza, who lived some three hundred years ago? After all, Spinoza presented himself as a believer in a kind of godhead. And, while rejecting atheism, he also rejected Judaism and Jewishness. So why should Jewish secularists see in him the first great precursor of our ideological position?

There are weighty reasons for our choice. Spinoza formulated, for the first time in Western thought, a principle of rational criticism: the right and duty of the human mind to examine sacred texts and analyze them for consistency, truth, historicity, and moral integrity. He began with the Bible and moved to other texts. Conventional religion became unacceptable to him. Knowing that he would never be heard if he denied the existence of God outright, and being a universalist, he developed a pantheistic philosophy according to which God was everywhere. God was, in essence, nature; and, perhaps more importantly, nature was God.

But if God is everywhere, he is nowhere. A God who is present in every blade of grass, who is within nature and not outside of it, is in no sense the all-powerful, omnipresent, moral God of Judaism or Christianity (or Islam, for that matter, though Spinoza did not deal with that). God then resides, among other places, within the human soul; thus, in a sense, he becomes the human soul, or, again more importantly, the human soul becomes God. Such a conclusion is very close, though not identical, to a secularist stance. True, Spinoza never uttered his beliefs in quite this way, but I would argue that the analysis just outlined is a legitimate interpretation of his writings.

To be sure, Spinoza had no great love for the Jewish community as he saw it in his native Holland. Still, although he was not at all concerned with Jewish peoplehood, he recognized the right of Jews to autonomy and specificity. Even though the community had turned against him, he upheld the principle of individual and communal responsibility. His principles of autonomy and moral responsibility can serve as foundations for a modern, secular Jewish communality.

Spinoza certainly was a humanist, though of course not a twentieth-century one. His abstraction of God into a general principle rather than the personal creator of the universe and of humankind was linked with his insistence on human autonomy. He believed in the essential equality of all human beings and their right to develop to the fullest their talents and possibilities. These considerations were underpinnings of his critique of classical religion and his attempt to build an alternative.

Kindred Spirits

The first part of the anthology deals with what we call Kindred Spirits, pioneers who were not secularists but whose work forms an essential background to a developing secularist outlook. These thinkers are part of the tradition to which Secular Humanistic Jews lay claim.

Why do we jump from Spinoza to the nineteenth century? Spinoza was a spiritual giant whose humanistic outlook had no immediate successors. Emancipation was very slow, and liberation from the rule of religious authority came slowly, too.

More than a hundred years after Spinoza, in the latter half of the eighteenth century, there arose in the Polish countryside a new, fervent, religious movement —Hasidism— which, with twentieth-century eyes, we might view as a predecessor to fundamentalism. Hasidism saw piety and goodness, not endless learning, as the main purpose of Judaism. It encouraged a return to nature as God's creation; and it demanded total devotion to religious observance. The Hasidic movement wrought a revolution in the Jewish world; certainly, given the situation of Polish Jewry at the time, a positive one. Unfortunately, it eventually declined into a formalized, senseless religiosity fortified by fanaticism and the absolute rule of the rebbe, a charismatic leader whose every breath had to be carefully noted and whose every word had to be obeyed. The rebbe, the holy man (*tzaddik*), whose post usually was inherited by birth, was the supreme authority. Corruption—spiritual, moral, and material—followed in many cases. Jewish secularism had to struggle long and hard against both Hasidism and the traditional yeshiva world.

In Central and Western Europe, where the often-painful process of modernization brought about the emancipation of the Jews, Jewish intellectuals were in the forefront of social and ideological change. One of these was Moses Hess, a forerunner of modern socialism, a one-time associate of Marx and Engels who broke with them and became, in their eyes, an idealistic reformer. Hess became convinced that only a regeneration of Jewish peoplehood would solve the problems that modernity posed for the Jews. His book *Rome and Jerusalem* was a harbinger of Jewish nationalism, especially its Zionist wing. Hess was a theist—no doubt about that; while he may not have followed Jewish religious customs, he saw Judaism as a religion. But he also said something new and important, which was later to become a basis for the Secular Humanistic outlook: he reclaimed Jewish peoplehood as a concept. On the basis of the universalist notion of what he called humanitarianism, Jews were as entitled as anyone else to freedom as a group, wherever they lived.

The Zionism anticipated by Hess was accelerated in response to events in the late nineteenth century. The pogroms in Russia in 1881-82 and the Dreyfus trial in France in 1894 shocked many Jews who had believed that emancipation had solved their problems. Theodor Herzl, the first of our Kindred Spirits, and the father of Zionism, was galvanized by these gross examples of anti-semitism to issue a dramatic call for the creation of a Jewish state in order to remove European Jews from an environment which would never accept them as equals. Herzl was a secular Jew who had no interest in the Jewish religion. Antisemitism led him to affirm the nationhood of the Jewish people. Herzl challenged the idea of the supremacy of religion as the main component of the Jewish people. For Herzl, nationhood was the supreme identifying factor of Jewish identity, and his goal was to make possible a Jewish state to concretize that vision.

We have included Martin Buber in our selection, though he undoubtedly must be turning over in his grave. Buber was a Kindred Spirit in quite a different sense from the others. He was a deeply religious person; his major works were designed to bring the Jewish religion, or his interpretation of it, closer to the people.

(He translated the Bible into German in order to make it accessible to the Jews of Central Europe, among whom he spent most of his life.) But what he considered to be Jewish religion was almost as far removed from traditional religion as is secular humanism.

In Buber's thought, the historical Jewish deity underwent a transformation. God ceased to be the heavenly father—the personal god of Abraham, Isaac, and Jacob—and became, to all intents and purposes, an abstraction, a "Thou" that dwells within a person and forms a kind of super-conscience which ideally is in constant and productive dialogue with the subjective "I." Hence Buber's radical attack on traditional religious concepts and observances. Kashrut (keeping kosher), the customary Shabbat (Sabbath) observance, even prayer, were nonissues for him; because the personal I-Thou relationship cannot be reached by these means, they became redundant, irrelevant.

For Buber, religion and religiosity were separate. His was an intensely individual, personal kind of religiosity—his students at the Hebrew University used to call it "Buberology"—which established a positive attitude toward the Jewish heritage and the necessity to learn about it, but not necessarily to follow its prescriptions.

What Buber saw as the principal content of Jewish tradition was its social message, the ideal interpersonal relationship as brought out by the prophets and by the best of the subsequent classical heritage. He most certainly would not have accepted Jewish secularism, though politically his relationship with the Zionist labor movement in general and the kibbutz movements in particular was not merely understanding but openly supportive. He probably would have declared himself a religious humanist who opposed established religion, and such a position would have placed him very close to our camp.

Buber was a Jewish nationalist in a very moderate form. He combined nationalism and universalism in a humanistic fashion. He advocated that a renascent Jewish people should seek brotherhood and understanding with the Arabs in Palestine and with all nations. He fought energetically against Jewish chauvinism. In sum, therefore, he was truly a kindred spirit to Secular Humanistic Judaism: a religious thinker who rebelled against religious observance and against all forms of organized religion, who removed the deity into a subjectivist abstraction, and who proved himself, during his long life, to be a defender of Zionism while opposing its more extravagant forms.

Albert Einstein was a theist, in that he believed some kind of supreme being existed. But he had no liking for organized religion. He did not think that God or religion had formed the Jewish people. Like a secular humanist, he saw religion as a historically conditioned product of human thought and human endeavor, which fulfilled certain social and psychological needs and served certain purposes in historical circumstances that have since changed. Like many of us, he recognized in the classical Jewish tradition important humanistic elements, which, though often clothed in religious garb, were the products of our people's culture. A number of them are mentioned in the selections from his writings in this anthology; indeed, they are among the parts of our tradition of which Secular Humanistic Jews are most proud. (Not that they are necessarily unique to Jews; other cultures developed similar or even identical traditions) But as Jews we feel a special identification with concepts that have been adapted or developed by our own group. If you are a non-Jew, you may find that you are sympathetic to Jewish culture and its way of adapting other peoples' ideas.

Was Einstein then a precursor of Secular Humanistic Judaism? I would say he was more than that. Despite his theism, which was even more abstract than that of Buber, he most certainly was a humanist. He probably would have given his (nonreligious) blessing to the ideas presented here.

Why is Mordecai Kaplan, the founder of the Reconstructionist movement, included in our anthology? For several reasons. First, Kaplan's theism was of a peculiar kind. He did not subscribe to either the Orthodox-Conservative belief in a deity who created the world and directs history, or the classical Reform notion of a God who gave the Jewish people universalistic ideals and a messianic mission to humanity. He wanted to use the old texts unchanged and to follow the liturgical traditions, not because he believed in what they had to say, but because they were Jewish, the product of the Jewish people's genius. His God was, on the one hand, abstract and very remote, and on the other, fulfilled a pragmatic function in symbolizing Jewish peoplehood. Indeed, Jewish peoplehood was Kaplan's central idea; he wanted to preserve it at almost all costs and believed that he could best do so from within the religious tradition rather than from outside it. The result was Reconstructionism.

Secular Humanistic Jews have very serious problems with this approach. If Kaplan's ideas are followed, we arrive at an irresolvable contradiction: either we do things (pray, observe kashrut, and so forth) that we do not believe in, or we believe in the content of all these observances, in which case we do not accept Kaplan's criticism of them. However, some of Kaplan's ideas are very productive from our perspective; his critique of traditional religion, his emphasis on the centrality of Jewish peoplehood—even his use of tradition to change tradition, in some of its aspects—can teach us something.

Kaplan was a Zionist—indeed, Zionism, or Jewish nationalism, was at the center of his thinking. We have included another Kindred Spirit who thought that way: David Ben-Gurion, founder of the State of Israel. In contrast to Kaplan, he was a pragmatic politician, though very knowledgeable about his Jewish heritage. Ben-Gurion came from a traditional Eastern European background and possessed a wide, if not deep, knowledge of Judaism, along with the important additions of classical Greek literature and Marxist socialism, which he tried to blend with a deep and genuine interest in biblical studies, both historical and literary.

Ben-Gurion was, in his own way, a product of Westernizing influences. He warned of the dangers of theocracy and advocated a democratic, secular state in which freedom of religion would be guaranteed. It is for this reason that we include him. We also include him because of his Aristotelian and Spinozist leanings. Although self-taught, his knowledge of Greek philosophy was considerable; he tried to create a bridge between Jewish and Greek ideas. He did not reject religion but reinterpreted it so that it became almost unrecognizable. There was something, he thought, behind energy that caused it to exist but had no impact on humanity—certainly no moral, personal impact. A nonmaterial, diffuse deity, irrelevant to human concerns, was hardly the God of Reform, Conservative, or Orthodox Judaism.

Religion, as Ben-Gurion defined it, embraced the whole history and all the aspects of Jewish peoplehood. Although he himself eschewed traditional observances, his Western, liberal inclinations led him to be politically tolerant of organized religion. He believed, as some secular humanists do, that Jewish traditional literature is eminently usable in our modern world by people who do not believe in its sanctity. He was an expert in modern, scientific biblical interpretation (though very respectful of the traditional interpretations he did not accept). His study circle on the Bible contributed to modern biblical scholarship. Philosophically, however, he was a humanist, and a nonreligious one, so he fits into our category of Kindred Spirits.

Aaron David Gordon was a different kind of Zionist labor thinker. Even more a Spinozist than Ben-Gurion, he developed a unique idea within modern Judaism: the religion of labor. If God was nature (and, in effect, nature was God), Gordon believed it was incumbent upon people to come as close to nature as possible. The only way to productively approach nature was through physical labor. And the purest, even religiously purest, form of labor was agricultural labor. Harking back to idealistic socialist thinkers of the nineteenth century, Gordon prescribed a total revolution in Jewish ways and work: away from the city, away from factories and offices and intellectual professions. Was Gordon, then, a nostalgic reactionary, who would lead us back to a non- or antimodern world? There are, indeed, some who see him in that light. Others believe that Gordon's message is important, emphasizing the centrality of human endeavor, the dignity of the working person (especially of those who work with their hands), and the quest for work that is not debilitating and does not contradict intellectual pursuit.

Gordon is one thinker who might fit the model of a nontheist (at least not a theist in the traditional mold) whose thought may be termed religious. It is a worked-out set of clearly humanistic beliefs; his God, like Spinoza's, is practically nonexistent. As a humanist and a moderate Zionist, Gordon sought to learn from other nations, at the same time emphasizing Jewish peoplehood. His great influence, especially in Israel, may well serve as a counterweight to antihumanistic tendencies there. He is a very important Kindred Spirit.

About one-half of the Jewish people today live in North America (Canada and the United States)—probably close to 6.4 million out of the nearly 13 million Jews in the world. During the past hundred years or so, since the Russian pogroms of 1882, which started the mass migration of Eastern European Jews to North America, North American Jews have not only maintained and developed ideas and traditions they brought with them from the "old country" but also have developed new cultural trends, new ideas, and new forms of social organization, which are having an increasingly important impact on Jews everywhere. We will have more to say about these trends in the remaining sections of this anthology.

Here, we want to bring to your attention one very important personality: Judge Louis Dembitz Brandeis.

As a Supreme Court justice, Brandeis was a great supporter of liberal principles, which he successfully advanced within the American legal system. His interest in Judaism was initially very limited, but when it became aroused he arrived at some interesting and unique (for his time) notions. Contrary to more recent American Jewish custom, Brandeis defined Jews as a nationality, the way they are usually defined in Europe. In Poland or Russia or Romania, for instance, Jews are neither Poles nor Russians nor Romanians—they are Jews. As Poles are a nationality (and so are Russians and Romanians), Jews, too, define themselves and are defined by others as a nationality. There are Polish Jews; that is, Jews who live or lived in Poland. But Jewish Pole is a construct that simply does not work; if you are the former, you cannot be the latter.

In the United States, on the other hand, citizenship and nationality need to be identical. If you are an American citizen, you are an American national, whether you are white, black, blue, or green, and whether your ancestors came on the *Mayflower* or from the Yangtze valley. If that were not so, America's identity as a nation of immigrants from everywhere under the sun would disintegrate into a host of incompatible fragments. Americans, therefore, use another term, "ethnicity", which means more or less the same thing as nationality, except that you can be an American national and yet have a different ethnicity and, of course, a religion you may adhere to. Thus you may be an American of Native American or Italian or Norwegian or Hispanic ethnicity, and be a Buddhist or a Moonie or a Catholic as well.

Brandeis, using the old term in the European sense, defined Jews as a nationality and saw no contradiction between that and American citizenship and/or nationality. On the contrary, he believed that by emphasizing their Jewish nationality, Jews would become better Americans, because their specific culture and their global interests would strengthen American culture and American liberalism—and liberalism, as he used the term, was equivalent to what we understand by humanism, that is, the supremacy of the concept of the dignity and integrity of the individual, and the obligation of groups as well as of individuals to respect each other's ways of life. Religion, to Brandeis, was a component of Jewish nationality; for Brandeis, a very non-Orthodox Jew, religion meant the observance of certain customs that emphasized his cultural identity, and not much more than that.

What is important about Brandeis is his rejection of the fear of "double loyalty"—as though being a Jew might stand in some kind of contradiction to being American, or, by the same token, being British or Canadian or French or Uruguayan. In other words, Brandeis was what we today would call a pluralist: a person who recognizes that an individual can have a number of identities, the more the better. In a humanistic, pluralistic, civilized world, you can be an American, a Jew, a secularist, a humanist, a baseball fan, an accountant, a mother or father, husband or wife, a lover of Bach and a hater of heavy rock (or the other way around); and all this—and more!—can be included in one person's identity. No contradiction. Clearly, Brandeis is a Kindred Spirit.

We have included in our anthology a group of writers and thinkers who lived and worked in Eastern Europe in the nineteenth and early twentieth centuries. They were the product of a great Jewish civilization that developed in Poland, Russia, the Baltic states, Romania, Hungary, and eastern Czechoslovakia; most Jews in English- and Spanish-speaking countries today are descendants of that civilization. The prevalent language there was Yiddish, a literary language derived from Middle High German of the medieval period, with Hebrew and Slavonic additions. Great literature was produced in Yiddish—prose and poetry, drama, philosophical and historical and sociological works.

Three major figures of this illustrious group are in the anthology. Mendele Mocher Sforim, Isaac Leib Peretz, and Sholem Aleichem were contemporaries in the second half of the nineteenth century and the first decade or so of the twentieth. They had in common a great love for the ordinary Jewish people and less than a great love for their "spiritual" and communal leaders. These three writers presented the ordinary life of ordinary Jews in all its poverty and degradation in an Eastern European environment that caused millions of them to flee to other parts of the world. Mendele, Peretz, and Sholem Aleichem translated the abstract idea of Jewish peoplehood into a powerful, personal identification on the part of the reader with the people they described so movingly.

Mendele's satirical descriptions were permeated with a deep hatred of the situation in which the Jews found themselves. His suppressed wrath against non-Jewish oppressors, against some of the Jewish rich and powerful, and against some members of the rabbinical establishment comes through in his stories.

Peretz is perhaps less a satiric writer than a wonderful storyteller—as is Sholem Aleichem. The tales of these two literary giants connect us to our peoplehood, not as we might like to see it but as it actually was in their part of the world. We live today in a nostalgic culture that picks up tidbits from the past, often without really understanding their relevance to our lives. We hope that the selections we have chosen avoid that pitfall. We believe they are relevant because they embody our immediate ancestors' search for a better future than the desperate situation in which they found themselves.

They also embody one of our two main principles: that of humanism, of Jewish humanism. The human person stands clearly at the focal point of each story. It is upon him or her that the reader's attention is fixed, not upon abstractions. Of course, part of the reality of those days was that most Jews were religiously observant, and that fact is, of course, reflected in these stories. But this observance, sometimes described by the authors as a result of superstition, sometimes as a result of a touching, naive belief, becomes part of a weft of folkways and folk customs with which we can identify because we identify with the characters in the stories and their personal joys and tragedies. While neither Mendele, Peretz, nor Sholem Aleichem was a secular humanist, all three were humanists, and all three described the Jewish people of their time and place as nobody else did. They, too, are Kindred Spirits.

Haim Nahman Bialik is probably the best-known modern Hebrew poet. If one can talk about modern poets as "classical," then he is the towering classical figure. Bialik was brought up in the traditional religious atmosphere of Eastern Europe, and in some of his poetry there is a strong nostalgic yearning, harking back to the Beth Hamidrash (house of study). However, the reference is as to something that is past, never to return. Bialik belonged to the nonreligious but slightly traditional middle-class Zionist intelligentsia, and his poems are permeated by a strong affection for the Jewish people and their everyday life. He wrote in both Hebrew and Yiddish at first, but later concentrated on Hebrew.

Bialik criticized traditional ideas and, as a member of the Tel Aviv City Council during the 1930s, advocated a modernistic line. His ideological commitments were limited to general Zionist views. He was not a secularist; but neither was he religious. He was a humanist, and he strongly influenced the younger generation of Hebrew poets—people like Avraham Shlonsky and Yehuda Amichai, whose secular humanism was or is unmistakable. Some of his lovely short poems, put to music, became, in a way, folk songs of the nonreligious Jewish population of Israel. So he does belong here, as a Kindred Spirit.

Pathbreakers

I have described what we mean by Kindred Spirits. The Pathbreakers are people whose attitudes and ideas were much closer to Secular Humanistic Judaism. Most of them were secularists (or close to secularists) and humanists in the sense in which I have defined that term. If they were alive today, they would be likely to identify themselves with contemporary Jewish secular humanism. There is a large number of candidates for inclusion in this group, and it is only because of lack of space that we present a limited number of them here.

There is, for instance, Max Nordau, an early and close ally of Theodor Herzl in the creation of the Zionist movement. A well-known writer of essays and novels, Nordau, like Herzl, was greatly affected by the Dreyfus trial in France, which caused him to rethink his assimilationist position. Distancing himself from religious Zionism, he called his own brand of Zionism "new": nonreligious, nonmessianic, directed against "mysticism," by which he presumably meant all religious belief. He was a humanist; he saw himself as a liberal, post-assimilationist Jew, avowing his peoplehood without giving up his universalist convictions. As he put it: "The Jewish nationalist does not suffer from egotism . . . he modestly recognizes the good qualities of other nations and diligently seeks to make them his own."

Nordau was a political Zionist, intent on translating his nationalist vision into the political reality of a Jewish commonwealth. He was totally opposed to the kind of spiritual nationalism advocated by Asher Hirsh Ginsberg, who wrote under the pseudonym Ahad Ha'am, meaning "one of the people." Ahad Ha'am was an important thinker who believed that Jewish nationalism had to be different from that of other peoples, that it could never achieve the kind of political power to which larger nations aspired. In an age of upheaval, Ahad Ha'am wanted to preserve the spirit of the Jewish people by creating a national-spiritual center, that would adapt the historical tradition of Judaism to the modern world. He envisioned Palestine as the spiritual center of a people most of whom would continue to live outside of it. (Practically speaking, they could not all live there in any case.) By spiritual center he meant the center of Jewish academic life, but mainly a center for spiritual regeneration and cleansing from Diaspora existence.

I am not sure that Ahad Ha'am would have liked to be called a secularist, because he probably would have regarded secularism as opposed to spiritualism. But, in fact, he clearly was a secularist: he regarded the putative existence of a God as irrelevant to the life of the individual. He maintained that the religious commandments were the result of historical developments and not actually commandments at all, because no one had commanded them. Some of them he regarded as important from the point of view of a national tradition, but most of them as inappropriate for a modern Jewish community. However, he regarded religion as having been of central importance for Jewish existence in the past, a positive historical force in the long history of the Jewish people. He was, undoubtedly, a nonreligious Jewish humanist. Like Nordau, he was far from chauvinism; while insisting on Jewish specificity, he regarded non-Jewish traditions with respect and a desire to learn from them.

In a very important way, Ahad Ha'am was a Pathbreaker for Secular Humanistic Judaism: he wanted to carry on Jewish tradition and Jewish history in a secular, or nonreligious, fashion. He sought to preserve what remained valuable in the traditional literature and thought, rejecting some elements completely, and consigning the rest to historical memory as a foundation for the present: not to be repeated for everyday use, not to be forgotten, yet not to be regarded as relevant or normative to our day and age. Like Ahad Ha'am, most Secular Humanistic Jews are not extreme nationalists but are strongly concerned with the preservation of Jewish peoplehood. Some of us would subscribe to Ahad Ha'am's version of secularism. We favor a continuity of Jewish history and traditions, not a break that would turn us into an ahistoric community with very little chance of survival.

Another Pathbreaker was the great historian Simon Dubnow, who died a martyr's death in the Holocaust in his city of Riga. Dubnow was not a Zionist, but an autonomist; he argued that Jewish survival could best be guaranteed if Jews organized themselves and were recognized by others as national-cultural communities within the host countries in which they lived. Zionism could not solve the problem of the whole Jewish people, and assimilation was both impossible, because of the enmity of the peoples into which Jews might wish to assimilate, and dishonorable, because it would mean giving up the valuable cultural treasures that Jews had developed over time. Cultural autonomy would continue a trend that Dubnow observed and analyzed in his monumental study of Jewish history: Jews had developed a talent for organizing themselves as cultural entities within non-Jewish host societies.

Dubnow, not unlike Ahad Ha'am, regarded religious tradition as an important and valuable part of the heritage of the Jewish people. He viewed religion as a historical phenomenon; it had a beginning and changed with time. Whereas in the past there had been an identity of religion and peoplehood, this was no longer so, and the two had to be separated. As a nonreligious Jew, Dubnow opposed messianic yearnings, notions of the intervention of a godhead in history, and a politicized religion (or religiously fanatical politics). He was a Pathbreaker for Jewish secular humanism.

Haim Zhitlovsky is another important Pathbreaker, who had a fascinating biography. Originally an assimilationist, he toyed with Zionism but then rejected both, to become an ardent Yiddishist and socialist. He was caught in the net of pro-Soviet, even pro-Stalinist, ideas in the thirties and supported the notion of Jewish autonomy in territories other than Palestine, including the settling of Jews by the Soviets in Birobidjan, a supposedly autonomous territory in the Far East.

Zhitlovsky differentiated between radical antireligious sentiment, which he rejected, and a secularism that could accommodate anything between atheism and a metaphysical-idealist concept of a spiritual force guiding the universe. While denying the existence of a God who intervenes in human affairs, he, like many other secularists, saw the importance of religious beliefs in the history of the Jewish people. His solution for the cultural and national problems of the Jews was the development of a secular Jewish culture based on the Yiddish language, the language of the Jewish people he knew. For him, Yiddish was not only the form which Jewish culture should take; it was also, in many ways, the content. It reflected the ordinary lives of ordinary Jewish people; it had done so in the periods when religion was paramount, and it would continue to do so. We should remember that Zhitlovsky lived before the rediscovery by Ashkenazi Jews of the great Oriental Jewish tradition, which has been preserved in languages other than Yiddish. Had he lived later on, he might perhaps have added those languages to his cultural concepts.

Zhitlovsky, like many secular humanists today, did not reject the traditional literature. Rather, he reinterpreted it and saw in it an inspiration for new, modern forms of expression. He introduced into it notions that may be quite foreign to the traditional religious mind, but that can legitimately be read into the ancient texts. Zhitlovsky did not want to leave the Jewish heritage to the rabbis and insisted that it belonged to the Jewish people as a whole.

No anthology of Jewish secular humanistic thought can do without the towering figure of Sigmund Freud. The scion of a Jewish family from southeastern Poland, Freud was raised in a nonreligious atmosphere and was in every possible way a child of the Enlightenment. He not only rejected theistic beliefs as based on imagination, but explained their origins as an answer to inner psychological needs. He would have agreed, no doubt, that while religion was a historical construct based on such needs, these can be satisfied by other means, such as spiritual or emotional experiences, particularly communal feasts and festival celebrations stripped of the link to theism. Interestingly enough, he defended rational explanations of metaphysical phenomena despite the fact that in his work he generally debunked the supposed rule of rationality over subconscious drives.

Freud's attitude toward his Jewishness was one of mild identification; it did not form a major element in his conscious makeup, but he identified as a Jew when challenged or questioned. Indeed, some of his statements suggest that he felt a very strong emotional bond with the Jewish people. In his controversial work on Moses, he tried to clarify elements of Judaism and of Jewish history from a psychoanalytic point of view, again denying the objective validity of religious belief.

There can be no doubt that Freud was a humanist par excellence, a man deeply concerned with human beings and their ultimate worth. He put people at the center of his world—not as the center of a creationist world-view, but as autonomous beings, responsible for themselves and for the community in which they lived. To Jewish secular humanists, Freud is a focal point of identification and admiration, a person who teaches us some of the foundations of human existence. Both his disciples and his opponents may have successfully challenged some of his analyses and conclusions, but his basic insights are still very much with us.

It is not necessary in this introduction to mention every single writer or thinker included in our anthology; rather, I want to touch on some of them, so as to paint a general picture. Horace Kallen is an important part of that picture, because he was both an important Jewish thinker of German-Jewish background and also a prototypical modern American Jew. Educated at Harvard, he had impeccable academic credentials. As an outspoken secularist and humanist, he was attacked for his cultural Zionism of the Ahad Ha'am school; to many American Jewish universalists, he was not universalist enough because he insisted on Jewish peoplehood.

In his wonderfully irreverent style, Kallen introduced the notion of Judaism as a culture with many faces—each in its own way a legitimate expression of it, and none able to claim to be the sole representative of an abstract idea called "Judaism." His own clearly stated preferences were formed by his humanist notions of right and wrong. He did not deny the fact that Judaism contained traditions that to him were absolutely abhorrent, but he picked from the vast range of Jewish possibilities those with which he could identify. While he, like Ahad Ha'am and Zhitlovsky, saw the vastness of Jewish civilization and refused to limit it to one-sided interpretations, his own view was very clear: he was an outspoken and convinced secularist.

Ber Borochov may be more familiar to older readers who were brought up in the atmosphere of the Jewish working-class movement. Borochov undoubtedly was one of the great thinkers of the Zionist labor movement, perhaps the most important of them; even those in the movement who rejected his teachings were strongly influenced by them. He was the ideologist of the Russian Poale Zion (Workers of Zion) movement.

A devout Marxist, Borochov tried to apply Marx's social analysis to the Jewish problem. He advocated a restructuring of Jewish society to develop a large working class, as in other nations. Such a basic change could be effected only in a new country, in a Jewish society that would include all the necessary elements of a healthy national structure. Obviously, he thought, this could happen only in Palestine; hence his Zionism. The working class in such a society, he expected, would be bound to effect a socialist revolution and to establish a new and better Jewish nation. To Borochov, such a society would have to be humanistic and secular, though of course there would be some people who would adhere to religious beliefs, and their rights would be respected. Borochov did not live to see Lenin's revolution or the way socialism was interpreted by the Bolshevik regime. He belonged to Western social democracy, albeit in one of its more radical forms. His secularism was certainly more radical, too, than that of Ahad Ha'am, for instance, or Dubnow.

I ought to introduce at least some of the literary writers included in this section, some of whom may be unknown to many American-Jewish readers. A prime example may be Saul Tchernikhowsky, one of the greatest Hebrew poets of this century. His powerful poems, which years ago were required reading in Israeli schools, are now on the way out because he was an unabashed secular humanist, and the way he wrote, in marvelous Hebrew, is anathema to many of today's Israeli leaders. He tried to bridge the gap between traditional Jewish culture, which he knew intimately, and Greek culture, which to him was a symbol of the beauty of the Gentile world. He was a Zionist who wrote beautiful poems (some of them later set to music) about the nature of the Land of Israel. He also was deeply concerned that future Jewish generations not backslide into superstitious traditions but be open to cultural messages from the Jewish past, while not giving up their contact with the non-Jewish world around them.

Another writer who may be unfamiliar to an American audience is Joseph Haim Brenner, who was killed in an Arab terrorist attack on nascent Tel Aviv just after World War I. Brenner was a severe critic of traditional Jewish life in the Diaspora. His secularism was strident, but his critique of the secular Jewish world around him was no less so. Basically, he was an extreme pessimist; he doubted that the Jewish revival could succeed, he saw rottenness everywhere, yet he nevertheless supported radical labor groups that sought to change the Jewish people and the conditions in which they lived. Brenner is an enigmatic personality, but one can feel in his writing a love for the Jews he criticized so harshly. He hoped for Jewish-Arab coexistence, and it was a tragic paradox that he should be killed by violent Arab nationalists.

The group we call the Pathbreakers represents a wide range of views. The differences between them are considerable—from Nordau to Brenner to Zhitlovsky to Borochov to Ahad Ha'am. And yet there is something that unites them: a pluralistic approach to Jewish peoplehood, beliefs, and traditions. They demonstrate that you can be a Secular Humanistic Jew and argue vehemently with other Jewish secular humanists, yet have common ground with them. Secular Humanistic Judaism is an open-ended philosophy, not a closed one. It provides options, rather than creating new canons. At the same time, it is rooted in Jewish peoplehood and an appreciation of the Jewish past, together with a goodly element of universalism.

Framers of Secular Humanistic Judaism

This last section consists of members of the movement for Secular Humanistic Judaism and some contemporaries who share our outlook and have contributed to the molding of our movement's principles. In the same anthology with Spinoza, Einstein, Freud, Zhitlovsky, Dubnow? Really, you may think, what chutzpa! But small as we may be in comparison with the greats of the past, we represent a living movement, a set of ideas that we hope will swell into an important stream among the Jewish people. Most Jews are not religious (again, in the usual sense). Our attempts to answer some of their concerns may provide—for some, and, we hope, for many—a satisfactory answer to their intellectual, emotional, and spiritual needs and a solution to their dilemmas of identity and commitment.

Again, I will not refer specifically to all those who appear in this section. We aimed for a balance between North Americans, Israelis, and Europeans; between thinkers, writers, politicians, and communal leaders. Most of the people we chose fit into more than one of the latter categories.

Haim Cohn was the attorney-general of Israel, a judge, and, to cap his legal career, a member of the Israeli Supreme Court. He abandoned theistic beliefs fairly early, combining a nonreligious outlook with intensive humanistic activity. He is a founding father of the Israeli Secular Humanistic movement (though, to be fair, he would prefer that we called ourselves simply "Jewish humanists").

Haim Cohn sees the Jewish humanistic movement as a natural continuation of Jewish tradition and history. He believes we should study the traditional sources, reinterpret them in the light of present-day knowledge, and choose those elements with which we can identify. He refuses to discard any of the traditional texts; for example, he studies and teaches the Rambam (Maimonides)—critically and historically, of course. He would argue that the Rambam is a centrally important Jewish thinker, part of our tradition and history. To ignore him, and others like him, would impoverish us. Armed with his vast knowledge of the sources, Cohn attacks rabbinical authority with its own weapons, citing authorities who in the past took stands completely contrary to what Orthodoxy permits today.

In his writings, Cohn demonstrates that Jewish legal tradition, though not always appropriate to contemporary issues, can be used productively in defense of human rights and in opposition to Orthodox attacks. Our movement's position on the "Who is a Jew?" question is largely based on his thinking.

Two other major thinkers and authors on our list are Sir Isaiah Berlin of England and Albert Memmi of France. Berlin is a convinced and active secular humanist. His interpretation of these terms may perhaps differ slightly from that of Judge Cohn—a typical Jewish trait, is it not? But he, too, believes Jewish tradition should be continued with a secular interpretation; and, like Cohn, he is an active and committed humanist.

Albert Memmi's origins are in Tunis, and his cultural traditions are a charming mixture of Arab, Jewish, and French. Memmi is a deep thinker and a writer of fiction, one of the most important in France. It is largely through his characters that he conveys his secular humanistic message; but he is also a polished journalist, and his statements in that medium are clear and logical, in the best French tradition. Memmi is the honorary chairman of our French Coordination Committee and the motive power behind the efforts in that country to bring together all the different strands of humanistic Jewish thought and activity.

A very interesting case of an original Jewish secularist thinker is that of Saul L. Goodman. A pupil of Horace Kallen, he is one of those who, using John Dewey's definition of religiosity, argue that we are most accurately identified as "religious secularists." That is, we are deeply committed to a spiritual and moral understanding of our Jewish and universal heritage, which we interpret in a secularist way; and as "religious" and "religiosity" are defined as expressions of deep spiritual commitment, they are perfectly appropriate terms for a nontheist to use.

Goodman, like Zhitlovsky and others, is a Yiddishist; that is, he favors the development of Jewish secularism within the framework of Yiddish culture. Goodman puts Jewish secularism in an American context, saying that those Jewish secularists who live in

North America are in perfect tune with the development of American civilization while preserving Jewish ethnicity. Morris U. Schappes is another thinker in the same mold, seeking to integrate Jewish secularism into both an American framework and a continuation of Jewish tradition.

We have included a number of writers of fiction. Amos Oz and A. B. Yehoshua, Israeli secularists whose works have in part been translated into English, are important because they represent different shadings along the spectrum of Jewish secularism. Oz is more traditional but politically outspoken in his struggle for a better and more humanistically oriented Israel. Yehoshua is less tradition-bound (though very much aware of Jewish sources) and much more critical of Israeli Jewish society. He constantly struggles with the Holocaust as a turning point in Jewish history and is extremely critical of Jewish behavior before and during that period. Both are internationally acclaimed writers representing the best of Israeli secular culture.

Last but not least, the leading activists of our movement: Sherwin Wine, Max Rosenfeld, Zev Katz, Hershl Hartman, Daniel Friedman, Uri Rapp, Yaakov Malkin, Shunya Bendor, Gershon Weiler, and myself—we all appear here. I am reminded of an uncle of mine who lived on the same Tel Aviv street as Ben-Gurion; he used to say that some very important people lived on his street and so did he. So, yes, we live on the same street, and yes, we have also given these matters some thought, and we believe that we have contributed to the development both of the movement for Secular Humanistic Judaism and of its ideological underpinnings. We differ among ourselves, of course; we are Jews, after all, are we not? Max Rosenfeld and Hershl Hartman come from a Yiddishist background. Sherwin Wine and Dan Friedman were ordained as Reform rabbis. Uri Rapp, Zev Katz, Yaakov Malkin, and I are Israeli academics who are deeply concerned about developments in Israeli society. The basis of our consensus is a pluralistic approach that allows us to compromise without giving up our differences.

We present this anthology not as a final word, but rather as a first attempt to state who we are, where we come from, and where we stand, so as to know better where we are going. Our goal is to assure Jewish continuity through a different interpretation of Judaism from the officially accepted one; an interpretation that is not entirely new, but that has to be renewed and rethought at each turning of the road, so that we remain one people with one civilization that we each may interpret in our own way, in freedom, with hope.

Yehuda Bauer

Acknowledgments

Excerpts from *Tractatus Theologico-Politicus* by Baruch Spinoza, edited and translated by A. G. Werham, Clarendon Press, 1958. By permission of Oxford University Press.

Excerpts from *The Jewish State* by Theodor Herzl, Dover Publications, 1988 reprint of 1946 publication. By permission of Dover Publications.

"Labor," "The Immortality of the Soul," "The Nation," by Aaron Gordon, from *Contemporary Jewish Thought* edited by Simon Noveck. Copyright 1963, B'nai B'rith Commission on Continuing Jewish Education. By permission of B'nai B'rith.

Excerpts from *I and Thou* by Martin Buber, translated by Ronald Gregor Smith. Copyright © 1958 Charles Scribner's Sons. Reprinted with the permission of Scribner, an imprint of Simon & Schuster.

"The Imperatives of the Jewish Revolution," by David Ben-Gurion from *The Zionist Idea* edited by Arthur Hertzberg. Copyright © 1959 by Arthur Hertzberg. Used by permission of Doubleday, a division of Bantam Doubleday Dell Publishing Group, Inc.

Excerpt from *The Social and Economic Views of Mr. Justice Brandeis,* edited by Alfred Lief. Copyright © 1930 by Vanguard Press, Inc.

Reprinted by permission of Vanguard Press, Inc., a division of Random House, Inc.

"Science and Ethics," from *Out of My Later Years* by Albert Einstein. Copyright © 1956, 1984, by the Estate of Albert Einstein. Published by arrangement with Carol Publishing Company.

"Just What Is a Jew?" and "Jewish Ideals" by Albert Einstein from *The Faith of Secular Jews* edited by Saul Goodman. Copyright © 1976 by Saul Goodman. Reprinted by permission of KTAV Publishing House, Inc.

Excerpts from *Judaism as a Civilization* by Mordecai Kaplan. Copyright, 1957, 1967 Reconstructionist Press. Reprinted by permission of the Reconstructionist Press.

"Shlomo-Reb-Khayim's" by Mendele Mocher Sforim and"But a Person has to Davn" by I.L. Peretz, translated by Max Rosenfeld. With permission.

"A Woman's Wrath" by I.L. Peretz, from *Yiddish Tales*, translated by Helena Frank. Jewish Publication Society, 1912, reprinted 1948. Reprinted by permission of the publisher.

"A Yom Kippur Scandal," from *The Old Country* by Sholem Aleichem, translated by Frances and Julius Butwin. Copyright © 1946, 1974 by Crown Publishers, Inc. Reprinted by permission of Crown Publishers, Inc.

On the Slaughter," by Haim Bialik, reprinted from *Modern Hebrew Poetry*, edited and translated by Bernhard Frank. Copyright 1980 by University of Iowa Press. Reprinted by permission of the University of Iowa Press.

"Wrecking and Building," by M. Berdichevski from *The Zionist Idea*, edited by Arthur Hertzberg. Copyright © 1959 by Arthur Hertzberg. Used by permission of Doubleday, a division of Bantam Doubleday Dell Publishing Group, Inc.

Excerpts from *Nationalism and History* by Simon Dubnow, Copyright 1961 by Jewish Publication Society. Used by permission of Jewish Publication Society.

"Death and Rebirth of Gods and Religion,"and "The National Poetic Rebirth of the Jewish People" by Haim Zhitlovsky, translated by Max Rosenfeld. By permission.

Excerpts from *The Conventional Lies of Our Civilization* by Max Nordau, reprint by Arno Press, 1975. By permission of Arno Press.

Excerpts from *The Future of an Illusion* by Sigmund Freud, translated by James Strachey, with the permission of W. W. Norton & Company, Inc. Copyright © 1961 by James Strachey, renewed 1979 by Alix Strachey.

"On Questions of Zionist Theory" by Ber Borochov, reprinted from *Class Struggle and the Jewish Nation*, edited by Mitchell Cohen. Copyright 1984 by Transaction Publishers. By permission.

"And This is Our Nationalism" by Joseph Brenner, translated from *Kol Kitve Joseph Hayim Brenner* by Dr. Edna Coffin. With permission.

Excerpt from Emma Goldman, *Red Emma Speaks*, edited by Alix Kates Shulman. Copyright © 1972 by Alix Kates Shulman. By permission.

"Was My Life Worth Living?" by Emma Goldman, reprinted from *The American Jewish Woman: A Documentary History* by Jacob Marcus. Copyright © 1981 by Jacob Marcus. By permission of KTAV Publishing House, Inc.

Excerpts from *Judaism at Bay* by Horace Kallen. Copyright, 1932 by Bloch Publishing. By permission of Bloch Publishing Co.

Excerpts from *Eichmann in Jerusalem* by Hannah Arendt. Copyright © 1963, 1964 by Hannah Arendt. Used by permission of Viking Penguin, a division of Penguin Books USA Inc.

Excerpts from "Creating a Cultural Atmosphere" by Hannah Arendt, reprinted from *Commentary,* November 1947 by permission; all rights reserved.

Excerpts from *Abraham Maslow: A Memorial Volume* by A. Maslow. Copyright © 1971 Brooks/Cole Publishing Company, a division of Thomson Publishing, Pacific Grove, CA 92950. Reprinted by permission of the publisher.

Excerpt from *Toward a Psychology of Being* by Abraham Maslow, Van Nostrand, 1962. Reprinted by permission of Van Nostrand Reinhold.

Excerpt from *Psychoanalysis and Religion* by Erich Fromm, Yale University Press, 1959. Copyright © 1950 by Erich Fromm. Reprinted by permission of Yale University Press.

Selected excerpts from pages 8, 47, 59-60, 72, 125, 133 from *The Art of Loving* by Erich Fromm. Copyright © 1956 by Erich Fromm. Copyright renewed © 1984 by Annis Fromm. Reprinted by permission of HarperCollins Publishers, Inc.

Excerpt from *You Shall Be as Gods* by Erich Fromm. Copyright © 1966 by Erich Fromm. Reprinted by permission of Henry Holt and Co., Inc.

Two poems, "Law and Order," and "The Covenant," from *Gleanings: A Diary in Verse* by Marie Syrkin. With permission from Nahum Guttman, editor of *Jewish Frontier.*

Excerpts from *Quest for Being* by Sidney Hook. Copyright © 1961 by Sidney Hook. Reprinted by permission of St. Martin's Press, Inc., New York, N.Y.

Selected excerpts from page 352 from *Out of Step: An Unquiet Life in the 20th Century* by Sidney Hook. Copyright © 1987 by Sidney Hook. Reprinted by permission of HarperCollins Publishers, Inc.

Excerpts from *A Peculiar Treasure* by Edna Ferber. Copyright © 1938, 1939 by Edna Ferber. Reprinted by permission of Edna Ferber Literary Trust.

"Here on Earth" by Rahel in *Modern Hebrew Poetry: A Bilingual Anthology,* edited by Ruth Finer Mintz. Copyright © 1966 The Regents of the University of California. By permission of the University of California Press.

"I Believe" by Saul Tchernikhowsky in *Saul Tschernikchowsky: Poet of Revolt* by Eisig Silberschlag. Reprinted by permission of the Publishers, Hebrew Publishing Company, P.O. Box 157, Rockaway Beach, NY 11693. Copyright © 1968. All rights reserved.

"They Say There is a Country" by Saul Tchernikhowsky in *Modern Hebrew Poetry: A Bilingual Anthology* edited by Ruth Finer Mintz. Copyright © 1966 The Regents of the University of California. By permission of the University of California Press.

"Toil" by Avraham Shlonsky in *Modern Hebrew Poetry: A Bilingual Anthology,* edited by Ruth Finer Mintz. Copyright © 1966 The Regents of the University of California. By permission of the University of California Press.

Excerpts from "Jewish Secularism" by Saul Goodman from *Judaism,* Vol. IX, no. 4, 1960. Reprinted by permission of the American Jewish Congress.

Excerpts from "A Secular View of Jewish Life" by Morris Schappes from *Jewish Currents Third Reader.* Copyright © 1966 Jewish Currents Press. By permission of Jewish Currents.

Excerpt from *The Crooked Timber of Humanity* by Isaiah Berlin. Copyright © 1991 by Isaiah Berlin. Reprinted by permission of Alfred A. Knopf Inc.

Excerpts from *Portrait of a Jew* by Albert Memmi. Copyright 1962, Albert Memmi. Reprinted by permission of Albert Memmi.

Excerpts from *Dominated Man* by Albert Memmi. Copyright 1968, Albert Memmi. Reprinted by permission of Albert Memmi.

Excerpts from *Jewish Theocracy* by Gershon Weiler. Copyright © 1988. Reprinted by permission of E.J. Brill, Leiden.

Excerpts from *The Slopes of Lebanon* by Amos Oz, translated by Maurie Goldenberg-Bartura, copyright © 1987 by Amos Oz and Am Oved Publishers, Ltd., Tel Aviv; English translation copyright © 1989 by Harcourt Brace & Company. Reprinted by permission of Harcourt Brace & Company.

Excerpts from *Between Right and Right* by A.B. Yehoshua, translated by Arnold Schwartz. Translation copyright © 1981 by A.B. Yehoshua. Used by permission of Doubleday, a division of Bantam Doubleday Dell Publishing Group, Inc.

"My Head, My Head" 13 lines from *Love Poems* by Yehuda Amichai. Copyright © 1981 by Yehuda Amichai. Reprinted by permission of HarperCollins Publishers, Inc.

"Great Tranquillity : Questions and Answers" 10 lines from *Great Tranquillity: Questions and Answers* by Yehuda Amichai. Copyright © 1983 by Yehuda Amichai. Reprinted by permission of HarperCollins Publishers, Inc.

"Sabbath Lie" 19 lines from *Great Tranquillity: Questions and Answers* by Yehuda Amichai. Copyright © 1983 by Yehuda Amichai. Reprinted by permission of HarperCollins Publishers, Inc.

"I Feel Good in My Trousers" 18 lines from *Great Tranquillity: Questions and Answers* by Yehuda Amichai. Copyright © 1983 by Yehuda Amichai. Reprinted by permission of HarperCollins Publishers, Inc.

"The Windmill in Yemin Moshe" 11 lines from *Great Tranquillity: Questions and Answers* by Yehuda Amichai. Copyright © 1983 by Yehuda Amichai. Reprinted by permission of HarperCollins Publishers, Inc.

"An Arab Shepherd is Seeking a Kid on Mount Zion" 15 lines from *Great Tranquillity: Questions and Answers* by Yehuda Amichai. Copyright © 1983 by Yehuda Amichai. Reprinted by permission of HarperCollins Publishers, Inc.

Articles by Shunya Bendor, Uri Rapp, Yaakov Malkin and Shulamit Aloni reprinted with permission of the Israeli Association for Humanistic Judaism.

Articles by Sherwin Wine, Dan Friedman, Hershl Hartman, Max Rosenfeld, Haim Cohn, Yehuda Bauer and Zev Katz from *Humanistic Judaism*. Reprinted by permission of the Society for Humanistic Judaism, Farmington Hills, Michigan.

While every effort has been made to trace and acknowledge all copyright holders, we would like to apologize for any omissions.

THE PRECURSOR

Baruch Spinoza (1632-1677)

Introduction

As the scientific revolution of the sixteenth and seventeenth centuries began to influence philosophical and religious thought, Judaism was bound to be affected by the scientific challenges to beliefs about the operation of the universe. Baruch Spinoza, a Sephardic Jew residing in Amsterdam, and one of the most illustrious figures in seventeenth-century intellectual history, manifests in his work the dilemmas that the new scientific thinking presented for traditional Judaism.

Spinoza was born in Amsterdam in 1632 to a family of former Marranos (Jews from Portugal who had been forcibly converted to Christianity). His family were prosperous leaders of the Jewish community in Amsterdam, and Spinoza was educated in traditional Hebrew studies. After he left school, he learned Latin, and this led him to the study of the natural sciences and contemporary philosophy, particularly that of Descartes. For reasons that are unknown, he chose lens-grinding as a profession.

The Spanish and Portuguese Marranos who had settled in Holland and returned to traditional Judaism included several persons who had begun to question Judaism on the basis of the new scientific knowledge. Spinoza grew up in an environment in which there were excommunications, recantations, and stories of doubts and persecutions. Because the Jews in Holland were not citizens, the leaders of the Jewish community feared that any signs of religious doubt or atheism in their ranks might threaten their tolerated status. When Spinoza began to discuss his critical views of the Bible within the community, the leaders of the synagogue were notified and he was offered a bribe to remain silent. Although

Spinoza had no desire to agitate or proselytize, he could not be persuaded to renounce or even conceal his skepticism. He was excommunicated and the Dutch authorities were notified that he had been expelled from the Jewish community. He was twenty-four years old at the time.

Spinoza remained in Amsterdam for another few years, grinding lenses, and discussing Descartes' new philosophy with enlightened Christians who had formed a small scientific discussion circle with Spinoza as their intellectual leader. In 1660 Spinoza moved to a quiet village near Leyden where he would have more time to devote to writing. He completed several of his early works there while maintaining a correspondence with eminent European scientists. In 1663 he moved to The Hague and there began to write his major work, the *Tractatus Theologico-politicus (Theological-Political Treatise),* which was published in 1670. In 1673 he was offered the chair of philosophy at the University of Heidelberg, which he declined on the grounds that as a philosopher he must remain without any official commitments that might hamper his independence of thought. He died at the age of forty-five from consumption, bearing a reputation as a serene man of courtesy and sincerity.

The *Theological-Political Treatise* was designed as a defense of the principle of religious toleration and of liberal principles in a modern, secular state, critical issues for him at that time. Spinoza rejected the belief that the Bible could be reconciled with philosophy and set out to demonstrate that the Bible was incompatible with the natural sciences and natural logic, making him a forerunner of modern biblical criticism. He described the prophets, for example, as men possessing moral insight but no theoretical truth, exhibiting ignorance of the natural causes of the events to which they referred. The biblical law code was necessary to maintain the political stability of the ancient Israelite state and was not divine in the true sense. Since the laws set forth in the Bible were suited only to the social life of the ancient Jews, they have no rational validity for postbiblical Judaism.

The function of religion, according to Spinoza, was to inspire a life of right conduct, particularly for those who were not philosophically enlightened and needed external pressure to remain moral. The attitude of the state toward religion must be to practice toleration, so that its inhabitants are free to think whatever they like so long as their actions remain peaceful and law-abiding.

In his *Ethics,* Spinoza develops a philosophical system which is known as pantheism. God and nature are simply two aspects of the ultimate unity of existence. God does not exist separate from the world but rather is totally immanent in it. The universe is eternal and is the immediate unfolding of God as order, carried out according to strict mathematical laws, in a deterministic mechanism of absolute necessity. Nature is fully rational and logical, and there is no possibility for free will. While Spinoza was not quite the atheist he was accused of being in his lifetime, he pioneered the removal of Judaism from the hold of traditional rabbinical thinking and postulated new ways of thinking about the Bible and Jewish tradition.

TRACTATUS THEOLOGICO-POLITICUS

Man's true happiness and blessedness lies solely in the enjoyment of good. Not in feeling elated because such enjoyment is his alone, and others are excluded from it; for he who thinks that his blessedness is increased by the fact that he is better off, or happier and more fortunate, than the rest of mankind, knows nothing of true happiness and blessedness, and the pleasure he derives from such thoughts, unless merely childish, arises only from spite and malice. Let me elaborate. A man's true happiness and blessedness lies simply in his wisdom and knowledge of truth, and not in the belief that he is wiser than others, or that others lack true knowledge, for this adds nothing whatever to his wisdom, i.e. to his true happiness. Hence the man who is pleased by such thoughts is pleased by the misfortune of another, is therefore spiteful and wicked, and knows nothing either of true wisdom or of the peace of mind which true living involves. Accordingly, when Scripture tries to encourage the Jews to obey the law by saying that God has chosen them as his own before all other peoples (Deuteronomy 10:15), that he is nigh unto them and not unto others (Deuteronomy 4:7), that he has given just laws to them (Deuterotonomy 4:8), and, finally, that he has revealed himself to them alone, preferring them to the rest (Deuteronomy 4:32 ff.), the words are merely a concession to the understanding of the Jews, who, . . . knew nothing of true blessedness. For would they have been less blessed themselves had God called all men equally to salvation? Would God be less gracious to them were he equally nigh to the rest? Would their laws have been less just, and they themselves less wise, had such laws been given to all? Would miracles have revealed God's power less clearly, had they been wrought for other peoples as well? And finally, would the Jews have been less bound to worship God if he had vouchsafed all these gifts to all alike?

(Chapter III)

. . . I must point out that since the laws of Moses were the civil laws of his country they necessarily required some civil authority to maintain them. For if everyone were free to interpret civil laws as he pleased, no state could survive, this alone would immediately disrupt any state, and turn public right into private. But with religion the case is entirely different. For since it consists more in simplicity and integrity of spirit than in outward acts, it is not subject to any control by public authority. Simplicity and integrity of spirit are not inspired in men by the command of laws or by public authority, and it is quite impossible to make anyone blessed by force or legal enactments, the means required are pious and brotherly counsel, a good upbringing, and above all, a judgment that is free and independent. Thus since everyone has a perfect right to think freely, even about religion, and cannot conceivably surrender this right, everyone will also have a perfect right and authority to judge freely about religion, and hence to explain and interpret it for himself.

(Chapter VII)

. . . For he who accepts everything in Scripture indiscriminately as the universal and ultimate teaching about God, and does not know precisely what has been adapted to the understanding of the masses, will inevitably confound their opinions with the divine teaching, hail the arbitrary inventions of men as the precepts of God, and misuse the authority of Scripture. Who, I ask, can fail to see that this is the main reason why the sectaries teach so many contradictory opinions as articles of faith, and can confirm them with so many scriptural illustrations? Or that this is why "No heretic without a text" has long since become proverbial among the Dutch? The fact is that the sacred books were not written by one man only, or for the common people of a single age, but by many men of different temperaments and periods; so that if we calculate the time covered by them all we shall find that it amounts to nearly two thousand years and perhaps much longer. . . .

Let us proceed methodically by recalling at the outset the chief object of Scripture as a whole; . . . the object of Scripture was simply to inculcate obedience. Now this no one can deny; for who can fail to see that both Testaments are simply a training in obedience, and that the sole object of both is to inspire men to sincere devotion? . . . Moses, for instance, did not seek to convince the children of Israel by reason, but to bind them by a covenant, by oaths, and by gratitude for services; besides, he threatened the people with penalties for disobeying his laws, and held out rewards to encourage it to observe them. All these devices are means of inculcating obedience only, and not knowledge. . . .

(Chapter XIV)

. . . It was democracy in particular that I wished to discuss, because it seemed to be the most natural form of state, and to come nearest to preserving the freedom which nature allows the individual. For in it no one transfers his natural right to another so completely that he is never consulted again, but each transfers it to a majority of the whole community of which he is a member. In this way all remain equal, as they were before in the condition of nature. . . .

(Chapter XVI)

. . . It is impossible for thought to be completely subject to another's control, because no one can give up to another his natural right to reason freely and form his own judgment about everything, nor can he be compelled to do so. This is why a government is regarded as oppressive if it tries to control men's minds, and why a sovereign is thought to wrong its subjects, and to usurp their right, if it seeks to tell them what they should embrace as true and reject as false, and to prescribe the beliefs which should inspire their minds with devotion to God; for in such matters an individual cannot alienate his right even if he wishes. . . .

If no man, then, can surrender his freedom to judge and think as he pleases, and everyone is master of his own thoughts by perfect natural right, the attempt to make men speak only as the sovereign prescribes, no matter how different and opposed their ideas may be, must always meet with very little success in a state; for even men of great experience cannot hold their tongues, far less the mass of the people. . . .

It is abundantly clear from my previous account of the basis of the state that its ultimate purpose is not to subject men to tyranny, or to restrain and enslave them through fear, but rather to free everyone from fear so that he may live in all possible security, i.e. may preserve his natural right to exist and act in the best possible way, without harm to himself or his neighbor. It is not, I say, the purpose of the state to change men from rational beings into brutes or puppets, but rather to enable them to exercise their mental and physical powers in safety and use their reason freely, and to prevent them from fighting and quarreling through hatred, anger, bad faith, and mutual malice. . . .

If honesty, then, is to be valued above servility, and sovereigns are to retain full control, without being forced to yield to agitators, it is necessary to allow freedom of judgment and so to govern men that they can express different and conflicting opinions without ceasing to live in harmony. This method of government is undoubtedly best, and least subject to inconveniences; for it is best suited to human nature. I have shown that in a democracy (which comes nearest to the natural condition) all make a covenant to act, but not to judge and think, in accordance with the common decision; that is, because all men cannot think alike, they agree that the proposal which gets the most votes shall have the force of a decree, but meanwhile retain the authority to revoke such decrees when they discover better. Thus the less freedom of judgment men are allowed, the greater is the departure from the most natural condition, and, in consequence, the more oppressive is the government.

(Chapter XX)

PART ONE
KINDRED SPIRITS

Theodor Herzl (1860-1904)

Introduction

Theodor Herzl, the foremost proponent of establishing a Jewish state in Palestine and the founder of the World Zionist Organization, is regarded as the founder of the State of Israel. His advocacy of the formation of a Jewish state stemmed from his conviction that it was the only solution to the disease of antisemitism.

Herzl was born in Budapest, Hungary, in 1860, at a time when German culture was dominant. His father was a rich merchant, and his mother encouraged him to aspire to greatness. He received a secular education, and when his family moved to Vienna, studied law at the university there, receiving his doctorate in 1884. Within a year, however, he decided to devote himself entirely to writing, since a literary career was what he had dreamed of. He became a well-known essayist and writer of fashionable plays. In 1892 he joined the staff of the *Neue Freie Presse,* the most important Viennese newspaper, and was shortly thereafter sent to Paris as its French correspondent. For several years, Herzl lived the life of a successful assimilated writer and journalist, sharing the view of westernized Jewish intellectuals that progress required their total assimilation.

It was the Dreyfus affair, which Herzl covered for his newspaper, that turned him into a Zionist. While Herzl had personally encountered antisemitism in his student days and was familiar with the writings of antisemitic propagandists, he had long believed in the possibility of accommodation between Christian and Jew in the future. The Dreyfus affair convinced him that the emancipation of the Jews in the nineteenth century had not solved the Jewish question but instead had exacerbated it by making it possible for so many Jews to enter the middle class and the professions, fueling antisemitic sentiment. He began to formulate his ideas about a political solution for the Jewish problem in the modern world. In 1895, he wrote *The Jewish State*. Its major thesis was that the Jews constituted a nation more than a religious group and that neither emancipation nor cultural assimilation would be a viable solution for the problem of Jewish identity. Only the establishment of a Jewish national state would solve the problem.

In 1897 he convened the first Zionist Congress, which established the World Zionist Organization with Herzl as its president. He then undertook a campaign to promote the Zionist movement and to gain political and diplomatic support for a Jewish state. His efforts to persuade the sultan of Turkey to permit Jewish settlement and autonomy in Palestine failed. The British government offered the possibility of a tract of land in Uganda for a Jewish self-governing settlement, but Herzl encountered furious opposition to the proposal from the Russian Zionists and the idea was dropped.

The continual activity on behalf of Zionism and the struggles within the movement wore Herzl out, as he suffered from a weak heart. He died in 1904 near Vienna. In 1949 he was reburied in the new state of Israel.

Herzl had, at first, little knowledge of Jewish religion and culture, particularly that of East European Jewry, the majority force within the Zionist movement. His political and non-spiritual Zionism was strongly opposed by critics such as Ahad Ha'am and the young Chaim Weizmann. But Herzl was clear on his expectations for the character of the future Jewish state. He warned against theocratic tendencies and demanded that the rabbis be kept "in their synagogues." He expected that the Jewish state would be tolerant, liberal, and based on the Jewish tradition of social justice. It must grant full equality and rights to non-Jewish faiths and people. The rabbis, in turn, became his staunch opponents, with few exceptions. The great majority of rabbis continued to oppose Zionism for several decades.

THE JEWISH STATE

The idea which I have developed in this pamphlet is a very old one: it is the restoration of the Jewish State.

The world resounds with outcries against the Jews, and these outcries have awakened the slumbering idea. . . If, therefore, this attempt to solve the Jewish Question is to be designated by a single word, let it be said to be the result of an inescapable conclusion rather than that of a flighty imagination. . . .

(Preface)

The Jewish question still exists. It would be foolish to deny it. It is a remnant of the Middle Ages, which civilized nations do not even yet seem able to shake off, try as they will. They certainly showed a generous desire to do so when they emancipated us. The Jewish question exists wherever Jews live in perceptible numbers. Where it does not exist, it is carried by Jews in the course of their migrations. We naturally move to those places where we are not persecuted, and there our presence produces persecution. This is the case in every country, and will remain so, even in those highly civilized—for instance, France—until the Jewish question finds a solution on a political basis. The unfortunate Jews are now carrying the seeds of Anti-Semitism into England; they have already introduced it into America.

I believe that I understand Anti-Semitism, which is really a highly complex movement. I consider it from a Jewish standpoint, yet without fear or hatred. I believe that I can see what elements there are in it of vulgar sport, of common trade jealousy, of inherited prejudice, of religious intolerance, and also of pretended self-defense. I think the Jewish question is no more a social than a religious one, notwithstanding that it sometimes takes these and other forms. It is a national question, which can only be solved by making it a political world-question to be discussed and settled by the civilized nations of the world in council.

We are a people—one people.

We have honestly endeavored everywhere to merge ourselves in the social life of surrounding communities and to preserve the faith of our fathers. We are not permitted to do so. In vain are we loyal patriots, our loyalty in some places running to extremes; in vain do we make the same sacrifices of life and property as our fellow-citizens; in vain do we strive to increase the fame of our native land in science and art, or her wealth by trade and commerce. In countries where we have lived for centuries we are still cried down as strangers, and often by those whose ancestors were not yet domiciled in the land where Jews had already had experience of suffering. The majority may decide which are the strangers; for this, as indeed every point which arises in the relations between nations, is a question of might. I do not here surrender any portion of our prescriptive right, when I make this statement merely in my own name as an individual. In the world as it now is and for an indefinite period will probably remain, might precedes right. It is useless, therefore, for us to be loyal patriots, as were the Huguenots who were forced to emigrate. If we could only be left in peace.. . .

But I think we shall not be left in peace.

(Chapter 1)

. . . Modern Anti-Semitism is not to be confounded with the religious persecution of the Jews of former times. It does occasionally take a religious bias in some countries, but the main current of the aggressive movement has now changed. In the principal countries where Anti-Semitism prevails, it does so as a result of the emancipation of the Jews. When civilized nations awoke to the inhumanity of discriminatory legislation and enfranchised us, our enfranchisement came too late. It was no longer possible to remove our disabilities in our old homes. For we had, curiously enough, developed while in the Ghetto into a bourgeois people, and we stepped out of it only to enter into fierce competition with the middle classes. Hence, our emancipation set us suddenly within this middle-class circle, where we have a double pressure to sustain, from within and from without. The Christian bourgeoisie would not be unwilling to cast us as a sacrifice to Socialism, though that would not greatly improve matters. . . .

. . . For a little period they manage to tolerate us, and then their hostility breaks out again and again. The world is provoked somehow by our prosperity, because it has for many centuries been accustomed to consider us as the most contemptible among the poverty-stricken. In its ignorance and narrowness of heart, it fails to observe that prosperity weakens our Judaism and extinguishes our peculiarities. It is only pressure that forces us back to the parent stem; it is only hatred encompassing us that makes us strangers once more.

Thus, whether we like it or not, we are now, and shall henceforth remain, a historic group with unmistakable characteristics common to us all.

We are one people—our enemies have made us one without our consent, as repeatedly happens in history. Distress binds us together, and, thus united, we suddenly discover our strength. Yes, we are strong enough to form a State, and, indeed, a model State. We possess all human and material resources necessary for the purpose.

The Plan

The whole plan is in its essence perfectly simple, as it must necessarily be if it is to come within the comprehension of all.

Let the sovereignty be granted us over a portion of the globe large enough to satisfy the rightful requirements of a nation; the rest we shall manage for ourselves.

The creation of a new State is neither ridiculous nor impossible. We have in our day witnessed the process in connection with nations which were not largely members of the middle class, but poorer, less educated, and consequently weaker than ourselves. The Governments of all countries scourged by Anti-Semitism will be keenly interested in assisting us to obtain the sovereignty we want.

(Chapter 2)

Shall we end by having a theocracy? No, indeed. Faith unites us, knowledge gives us freedom. We shall therefore prevent any theocratic tendencies from coming to the fore on the part of our priesthood. We shall keep our priests within the confines of their temples in the same way as we shall keep our professional army within the confines of their barracks. Army and priesthood shall receive honors high as their valuable functions deserve. But they must not interfere in the administration of the State which confers distinction upon them, else they will conjure up difficulties without and within.

Every man will be as free and undisturbed in his faith or his disbelief as he is in his nationality. And if it should occur that men of other creeds and different nationalities come to live amongst us, we should accord them honorable protection and equality before the law. We have learnt toleration in Europe. This is not sarcastically said; for the Anti-Semitism of today could only in a very few places be taken for old religious intolerance. It is for the most part a movement among civilized nations by which they try to chase away the spectres of their own past.

(Chapter 5)

Aaron David Gordon (1856–1923)

Introduction

Aaron David Gordon arrived in Palestine as a pioneer in 1904, when he was almost fifty years old. Although much older than the young idealists who made up the majority of the Zionist pioneers, he worked alongside them on the land, and quickly became their "grandfather," a highly esteemed and revered figure. In his essays, Gordon expressed a love of the soul and physical labor, leading to the designation of his pantheistic Zionism as the "religion of labor." He was also a socialist, a pacifist, and a humanist.

Gordon brought with him from his native Ukraine, where he was born in 1856 and had worked as an official for many years, ideas derived from Jewish sources as well as from Tolstoy, Dostoyevsky, and the Russian populists. Despite the fact that he had never worked with his hands, he became a day laborer in the vineyards and wineries of Petah Tikvah and later in the kibbutz at Degania, the oldest Jewish agricultural settlement in Palestine. Even after he fell ill, he insisted on doing physical labor until he died in 1923.

Gordon's essays idealized physical labor on the soil. For him, Zionism required a fundamental change in the soul of the Jew, as well as a new way of life and a transformation in values. Jews needed to leave their parasitic, nonproductive way of life in the cities of the alien world and return to what their ancestors had been: a people of the earth, farmers toiling on their own soil. He rejected what he termed the dehumanization of urban life and mass industrial society, and envisioned that life in small agricultural communities in Palestine would lead to the regeneration of Jews as individuals and as a people.

Even though he was surrounded in Palestine by ardent socialists and atheists, Gordon developed his own ideas about Jewish tradition and religion. For him, religion expressed a mystical union between the individual and nature. Rejecting the practice of traditional Judaism, Gordon saw in religion the way for individuals to experience cosmic unity and to intuit universal purpose. Nations, like individuals, also need to bond to purposeful existence. For Jews, the return to their original homeland and the reappropriation of life on the land constituted the way toward moral rebirth and a "religion of nature."

The Nation

. . . We, who belong to a people that has suffered more than any other, that has been torn up from its soil, alienated from nature, yet continues vigorous; we, a nation which has not been destroyed by two thousand years of misfortune, we consider that in our aim for a complete regeneration there can be no other possibility for attaining the life we seek except to base it wholly upon its natural foundation. We must return fully to nature, to creative work, to a sense of order, and to a spiritual life, in short, to family-nationhood. More than others we must be concerned, indeed, we are charged with the task of the regeneration of the nation. We must direct it toward the development of the human spirit, toward the search for truth and righteousness in its relation with other peoples and with all mankind. We must reinstate the nation to its former strength. Our national renaissance is not mere national freedom or rejuvenation: our national revival is like a resurrection of the dead, an event that has no parallel. For such an achievement in general, and for our nation in particular, one rule must govern: either there is complete achievement or none at all. The full power of the creativeness of the human spirit has not yet been realized. The human spirit must grow in proportion to the growth of human consciousness. This cannot take place without a thorough regeneration of the nation. The nation may be likened to a funnel: at its wide receiving end endless existence is poured in, while through its concentrated, restricted end the funnel empties its contents into the soul of man. The nation, therefore, is the force which creates the sprit of man. It is the link which unites the life of the individual to the life of mankind and to the world at large.

There are no gaps in nature. The cosmic order of the expansion of life starts with the individual, proceeds to the family, then to the nation and from the nation to the race, and throughout to the whole of humanity.

This is the basis of our idea, the idea of our revival and redemption; it is founded on this dual concept; human-nation, nation-man. Where there is no "nation-man" relation, there is no "man," no individual man. Who should be more aware of this than we Jews? At the cost of untold suffering we have acquired the privilege of being the first to sponsor this creative principle. Out of the misfortunes and the purgatory which we have suffered, we generated a secret light. This light we shall direct into the open.

In truth, this is an idea for the future, possibly for a very remote future but from the very beginning of our efforts for national revival and redemption we must hold to this idea as to a guiding star, a star for lighting our path.

Some may consider that the essence of the idea belongs to the realm of the imagination. Possibly. I shall not argue the point. Who knows whether the human spirit is on the ascendant or on the decline! I do not question the basic principle in the idea, but I doubt whether there will be an upward swing of the human spirit. Yet this much is clear to me: there is no other way for the renewing of life, for the regeneration of man. No, there is no other way.

Our renaissance demands an exalted spirit, a vigorous idea that will overwhelm and pervade the whole of man with the strength of a religious conviction; its force must be powerful enough to revolutionize his world and to regenerate the spirit of man.

The Immortality of the Soul

. . . The man who comprehends eternity, that is the infinity that exists in all the life of the world, both in space and in time, who sees that the very secret of existence is eternity—such a man is naturally, logically, vitally compelled to acknowledge that he who comprehends all this, who consciously expresses all this, is also a part of the same eternity; from every point of view, he himself is eternal. If, however, the individual asking this question were free of any personal interest and inspired only to comprehend the truth and the eternity in himself and in existence, he would ask the question differently, in a more fundamental form: did his individual soul live before his birth, before his appearance into this world, in an individual form? He would then see clearly that eternity does not begin in time, for the eternity he seeks is the same eternity that was in life and in existence before his birth and will continue in the life and in existence after his death. He will realize that he, in his individual form, is only one of the waves of which eternity is composed. He would then seek eternity not after death but in his very life. He would seek the secret of eternity in the fleeting second. Human life would perhaps then take on a different content and a different form. Maybe it would then be worthwhile to live—perhaps even to die.

One of the forms of the secret yearning of man for eternity is the aspiration of the majority of mankind—especially of those who to a certain extent, have made some imprint on life—to leave their name as a memorial in life after their death. One wishes to preserve his memory in books which he has written; another, in artistic creations; a third, in scientific discoveries, a fourth, in ideas, thoughts and opinions which he has uttered; a fifth, in deeds and accomplishments which he has performed or undertaken. The important point is that all this be sufficiently noted, emphasized, and always that it bear the name of its author. Men in all generations and for all time should know that at such a place and in such a time there lived this man who composed, created, discovered, meditated, performed, undertook a certain thing.

How petty is all this! How superficial! How long can an individual, be he ever so great, remain in the memory of generations to come, as a definite, recognized, outstanding individual? At most, a few generations, possibly a few hundred years. Beyond that, only the name remains; it makes no difference to anyone whom it designates, for, properly speaking, it has become an abstract name for an abstract personality. In the end, after thousands of years, the name becomes blurred. Doubt arises whether there ever lived such a man; perhaps his creation represents a popular, a collective expression. What man knows who Homer was, or Buddha, or Moses, and so on? Who can picture them to us in their real, living individual, and not in their abstract form? Does not doubt arise as to their very existence? Even within the period since scientific history has been written, who can predict for us what will happen along this line when tens of thousands of years and more shall have passed? When hundreds of thousand of years, millions of years, have passed, who will mention the names of Copernicus, Spinoza, Kant, Tolstoy, and so on? What is such a number of years compared to eternity? Less than a drop in the ocean.

Here again is revealed the same fundamental viewpoint that is present in the yearning for eternity discussed above. The individual personality is a passing wave in the eternal sea of life and of existence. What is eternal in the individual personality is the hidden, vital impression that it leaves in life, that is eternal to the degree that it aids in strengthening the regenerative, the creative spirit of life. That which the individual personality leaves behind after death will influence life only to the extent that it failed in its aim during life. Further, what the individual personality leaves will affect life to the extent that it had not reached into or been accepted by the hearts and minds of its contemporaries, or to the extent that this "something" had failed to emerge from its hidden cell. One may compare this to a man who died leaving a pregnant wife that bears him a posthumous child; in a wider sense, this may be likened to those distant stars whose light reaches the earth after they are extinguished and are no longer what they were. Yet their light, too, will finally perish and die. . . .

Labor

A people that was completely divorced from nature, that during 2000 years was imprisoned within walls, that became inured to all forms of life except to a life of labor, cannot become once again a living, natural, working people without bending all its will-power toward that end. We lack the fundamental element; we lack labor, but labor by which a people becomes rooted in its soil and in its culture. To be sure, not every individual among other peoples exists by labor. Many among such peoples despise labor and search for a way of life that can maintain itself on the labor of others. But the majority of a living people works in normal fashion; work is ingrained in their lives, and so it is carried on as an organic function.

A living people always possesses a great majority to whom labor is its second nature. Not so among us. We despise labor. Even among our workers there are those who work because of necessity and with the continual hope of some day escaping from it and leading "the good life." We must not deceive ourselves. We must realize how abnormal we are in this respect, how alien labor has become to our spirit, and not alone to the individual life, but also to the life of the nation. . . .

To me the thing is clear and simple. All this should teach us that from now on our chief ideal must be labor. We were defeated through lack of labor—I do not say that we sinned—for we ourselves were not responsible for the situation. Work will heal us. In the centre of all our hopes we must place work; our entire structure must be founded on labor. If only we set up work itself as the ideal—rather, if only we bring into the open the ideal of labor, shall we be cured of the disease which attacked us. We shall then sew together the rents by which we were torn from nature. Labor is a lofty human ideal, an ideal of the future. A great ideal in this sense is like the healing sun. Even if it be true that history is not concerned with pointing a moral nor with disseminating knowledge, yet everyone with vision can and should learn from history. Our condition in the past, our situation in the present can teach us that we must take the lead in this—we must all work

David Ben-Gurion (1886–1975)

Introduction

David Ben-Gurion was a great Zionist, statesman, and socialist labor leader. It was Ben-Gurion who proclaimed Israel's independence on May 14, 1948, and then served as its first prime minister and minister of defense. Although he was a nonobservant Jew throughout the years of his active political life, he was a student of the Bible (with particular interest in the Book of Joshua) and of religions (with special interest in Buddhism). When he retired from politics toward the end of his life and went to live in a settlement in the Negev desert, he gave expression to his inner beliefs. He spoke at that time about his belief in "God," but it was not the traditional God of Jewish orthodoxy but rather the "God of Spinoza," a rational force that was revealed or hidden within the universe.

Ben-Gurion was born in Plonsk, Russian Poland, in 1886 to an enlightened Zionist family. He became active in Socialist Zionist groups early in his life and was one of the founders of Poale Zion, (Workers of Zion). In 1906 he went to Palestine and worked for some time as an agricultural laborer. He soon became involved, however, in organizational and political work and was active in founding Poale Zion in Palestine in 1907. Having had some experience in Jewish self-defense organized in response to pogroms in Russia, he was one of the founders of the Hashomer Jewish defense organization in Palestine. During World War I, as one of the many Zionist settlers expelled from Palestine by its Turkish rulers, he went to the United States. During the three years of his stay there, he helped organize an American wing of Labor Zionism. He volunteered for the Jewish Legion of Russian Jews residing in the

United States who went to fight in the British army in Palestine against the Turks in 1918.

After the war, in 1920, he was among the founders of the Histadrut, the congress of labor unions in Palestine, and served as its secretary-general from 1921 to 1935. He also was a founder of Mapai, the Jewish Labor Party, in 1930, and in 1935 was named the chairman of the Jewish Agency for Palestine, a post he held until the founding of the state of Israel. During this period he was recognized as the leader of the Yishuv (the Jewish settlement in Palestine) and of the Zionist movement. When World War II ended, he was at the forefront of the struggle to declare a Jewish state in Palestine, and when, in May, 1948, he read the Declaration of Independence of Israel, he came to be recognized as its Founding Father.

Ben-Gurion was a political Zionist and presented the "in-gathering of the exiles" as the sole definition of Zionism. At the same time, however, he believed that establishment of the state was not the final goal. Rather, he envisioned that Israel would be dedicated to achieving "spiritual supremacy" as a society of justice and of spiritual excellence. In that sense the Jews can be a "chosen people" that will serve as a light to the nations. For Ben-Gurion, following the vision of the ancient prophets, the return to the biblical homeland would not only bring about the redemption of the Jews; it was inextricably bound up with universal redemption.

The Imperatives of the Jewish Revolution

. . . What, therefore, is the meaning of our contemporary Jewish revolution—this revolt against destiny which the vanguard of the Jewish national renaissance has been cultivating in this small country for the last three generations? Our entire history in the Galut [exile] has represented a resistance of fate—what, therefore, is new in the content of our contemporary revolution? There is one fundamental difference: In the Galut the Jewish people knew the courage of *non-surrender*, even in the face of the noose and the *auto-da-fé*, even, as in our day, in the face of being buried alive by the tens of thousands. But the makers of the contemporary Jewish revolution have asserted: Resisting fate is not enough. *We must master our fate; we must take our destiny into our own hands!* This is the doctrine of the Jewish revolution-not non-surrender to the Galut but making an end of it. . . .

The meaning of the Jewish revolution is contained in one word-independence! Independence for the Jewish people in its homeland! Dependence is not merely political or economic; it is also moral, cultural, and intellectual, and it affects every limb and nerve of the body, every conscious and subconscious act. Independence, too, means more than political and economic freedom; it involves also the spiritual, moral, and intellectual realms, and, in essence, it is *independence in the heart,* in sentiment, and in will. From this inner sense of freedom outer forms of independence will develop in our way of life, social organization, relations with other people, and economic structure. Our independence will be shaped further by the conquest of labor and the land, by broadening the range of our language and its culture, by perfecting the methods of self-government and self-defense, by creating the framework and conditions for national independence and creativity, and finally—by attaining political independence. This is the essence of the Jewish revolution.

What makes this revolution so different is that it bears no relation to an existing order. The tragedy of the Jews is that we are not part of any order. A revolution directed against a well-defined social structure is a one-time affair; it can succeed by seizing control of the government and wielding the newly seized power to change the existing social and economic order. The Jewish revolution against our historic destiny must be a prolonged and continuing struggle, an enlistment of our own generation and even of those to come, and its road to success is not through seizure of power but only by the gradual shaping of the forces, mentioned above, that lead to independence, by girding ourselves with unyielding tenacity for changing our national destiny. There are only two means to this end: the ingathering of the exiles and independence in the homeland. . . .

The second indispensable imperative of the Jewish revolution is *the unity of its protagonists.* This sharing together in a fate, a creative process, and a struggle is what unites this vanguard—the pioneers, the builders of the homeland, the workers of the land of Israel, who are inspired by the vision of a Jewish renaissance on humanistic, Zionist, and socialist foundations. The conquest of labor and the land, self-defense, the development of the Hebrew language and culture, freedom for the individual and the nation, co-operation and social responsibility, preparation for further immigration, and the welding of the arrivals from the various Diasporas into a nation—these fundamental purposes are held in common, both in theory and in practice, by all those who are faithful to our revolution. These values make it possible, and indeed mandatory, that they be united. The Jewish revolution is incomparably difficult, and, unless there is unity and co-operation, it will fail. Without such inner unity we cannot hope for full realization of our creative potential; only such unity can give us the strength to withstand obstacles and reverses and make it possible for both the individual and the community to rise to their task.

The ingathering of the exiles into a socialist Jewish state is in fact only a precondition for the fulfillment of the real mission of our people. We must first break the constricting chains of national and class oppression and become free men, enjoying complete individual and national independence on the soil of a redeemed homeland. After that we can address ourselves to the great mission of man on this earth—to master the forces of nature and to develop his unique creative genius to the highest degree. . . .

Martin Buber (1878–1965)

Introduction

Martin Buber was one of the most renowned twentieth-century religious philosophers. His most original contribution was to project a new image for modern humanity, whose existence he described as isolated, alienated, and fragmented. He proposed that people must be turned toward each other, integrated and involved in genuine dialogical relationships with each other and with God, establishing an I-Thou connection.

Martin Buber was born in Vienna in 1878, and raised in the home of his grandfather, Solomon Buber, who was a talmudic scholar. Shortly after celebrating his bar mitzvah, however, the young Buber ceased the religious practices he had been observing, and he left his grandfather's home a year later to live with his father in Poland. After graduating from a Polish gymnasium, he went on to study at the universities of Vienna, Leipzig, Zurich, and Berlin, receiving his doctorate from the University of Vienna in 1904. He was, at this time, strongly influenced by some existentialist writings.

For the next two decades Buber was engaged in journalism and publishing work. He became a Zionist and served briefly as editor of the journal of the Zionist movement. He was drawn to the minority faction which advocated that Zionism be based on a great

Jewish cultural renaissance and direct its energies to achieving a larger measure of spiritual health and integrity among Jews. In 1916 he founded a German-Jewish monthly, *Der Jude,* writing articles which marked him as an original Zionist thinker.

In 1923 Buber published his most famous work, *I and Thou.* That same year he was appointed to a newly established chair of Jewish religious thought at the University of Frankfurt. He befriended Franz Rosenzweig and the two men jointly published a new German translation of the Bible and co-founded the famous Jewish Lehrhaus (House of Study). Buber was dismissed from his university position by the Nazis in 1933, and after spending the next few years doing Jewish educational work in Germany, he left for Palestine in 1939.

He was appointed professor of social philosophy at the Hebrew University of Jerusalem and taught there until his retirement. He joined Judah Magnes, the president of the university, Henrietta Szold, and others in Ihud, a group which advocated greater cooperation between the Jewish and Arab communities and the establishment of a binational state. He and his associates were often derided and attacked for their position, but his deep sincerity and moral passion were respected by many. After he retired he continued to write and lecture until his death.

Buber had been drawn to the Hasidic movement while in Poland and had studied Hasidism extensively, but he could not become a practitioner himself because he was unable to accept the authority of traditional Jewish religion as divinely revealed in its entirety. Buber was a critic of all established religion, but developed a unique vision of God as the eternal Thou, the being that appears in a true dialogic relationship with oneself. Since this God can only be reached through personal experience, it cannot be worshipped in the traditional religious manner.

I AND THOU

I consider a tree.

I can look on it as a picture: stiff column in a shock of light, or splash of green shot with the delicate blue and silver of the background.

I can perceive it as movement: flowing veins on clinging, pressing pith, suck of the roots, breathing of the leaves, ceaseless commerce with earth and air—and the obscure growth itself.

I can classify it in a species and study it as a type in its structure and mode of life.

I can subdue its actual presence and form so sternly that I recognize it only as an expression of law—of the laws in accordance with which a constant opposition of forces is continually adjusted, or of those in accordance with which the component substances mingle and separate.

I can dissipate it and perpetuate it in number, in pure numerical relation.

In all this the tree remains my object, occupies space and time, and has its nature and constitution.

It can, however, also come about, if I have both will and grace, that in considering the tree I become bound up in relation to it. The tree is now no longer *It*. I have been seized by the power of exclusiveness.

To effect this it is not necessary for me to give up any of the ways in which I consider the tree. There is nothing from which I would have to turn my eyes away in order to see, and no knowledge that I would have to forget. Rather is everything, picture and movement, species and type, law and number, indivisibly united in this event.

Everything belonging to the tree is in this: its form and structure, its colours and chemical composition, its intercourse with the elements and with the stars, are all present in a single whole.

The tree is no impression, no play of my imagination, no value depending on my mood; but it is bodied over against me and has to do with me, as I with it—only in a different way.

Let no attempt be made to sap the strength from the meaning of the relation: relation is mutual.

The tree will have a consciousness, then, similar to our own? Of that I have no experience. But do you wish, through seeming to succeed in it with yourself, once again to disintegrate that which cannot be disintegrated? I encounter no soul or dryad of the tree, but the tree itself.

If I face a human being as my *Thou,* and say the primary word *I-Thou* to him, he is not a thing among things, and does not consist of things.

Thus human being is not *He* or *She,* bounded from every other *He* and *She,* a specific point in space and time within the net of the world; nor is he a nature able to be experienced and described, a loose bundle of named qualities. But with no neighbour, and whole in himself, he is *Thou* and fills the heavens. This does not mean that nothing exists except himself. But all else lives in *his* light.

Just as the melody is not made up of notes nor the verse of words nor the statue of lines, but they must be tugged and dragged till their unity has been scattered into these many pieces, so with the man to whom I say *Thou.* I can take out from him the colour of his hair, or of his speech, or of his goodness. I must continually do this. But each time I do it he ceases to be *Thou.*

And just as prayer is not in time but time in prayer, sacrifice not in space but space in sacrifice, and to reverse the relation is to abolish the reality, so with the man to whom I say *Thou.* I do not meet with him at some time and place or other. I can set him in a particular time and place; I must continually do it: but I set only a *He* or a *She,* that is an *It,* no longer my *Thou.*

So long as the heaven of *Thou* is spread out over me the winds of causality cower at my heels, and the whirlpool of fate stays its course.

I do not experience the man to whom I say *Thou.* But I take my stand in relation to him, in the sanctity of the primary word. Only when I step out of it do I experience him once more. In the act of experience *Thou* is far away.

Even if the man to whom I say *Thou* is not aware of it in the midst of his experience, yet relation may exist. For *Thou* is more than *It* realizes. No deception penetrates here; here is the cradle of the Real Life.

(Part I)

Mordecai Kaplan (1881–1982)

Introduction

Mordecai Kaplan proposed a reformulation of Judaism that combined a modern scientific worldview with a democratic and rational reformulation of Jewish identity. His new movement, called Reconstructionism, drew upon social psychology, cultural Zionism, and philosophical pragmatism but has found adherents only among a small number of American Jews.

Kaplan was born in Lithuania in 1881 and came to the United States as a small child. While he began with a traditional religious education, he received a secular education at the College of the City of New York and Columbia University. He was ordained by the Jewish Theological Seminary and served as the rabbi of an Orthodox synagogue in New York for several years. Then he was appointed dean of the Teachers Institute of the Seminary, where he also served as professor of Talmud and religious philosophy for several decades. He remained active as a rabbi and community leader, however, and pioneered the idea of the synagogue as a community center when he organized the Jewish Center in Manhattan in 1917. When his religious ideas became too liberal for his congregation, he left to organize the Society for the Advancement of Judaism in 1922. This new synagogue and community center was based on Kaplan's belief that worship was only one of the functions a synagogue should provide for.

In 1934 Kaplan's *Judaism as a Civilization* spelled out his philosophy of Judaism; the following year he began publishing a journal, *The Reconstructionist*. In the 1940s the Reconstructionist Foundation began publishing new prayer books with deletions from the traditional text and a revised Passover Haggadah. Kaplan continued to publish books in which he expounded his innovative views, including *The Future of the American Jew*. The Reconstructionist movement opened its own rabbinic college in Philadelphia in 1968. Kaplan, an ardent Zionist, went to live in Jerusalem in his old age but returned to the United States before his death.

Kaplan followed Ahad Ha'am and Simon Dubnow in describing Judaism as a civilization, a body of culture, and not merely a religion. From Ahad Ha'am he adopted the view that the land of Israel must be the spiritual center of modern Jewish culture, but from Dubnow he embraced the idea of the continuation of autonomous, global Jewish communities in the Diaspora. These organic Jewish communities would ensure the continuity of Jewish identity and be devoted to the maintenance and advancement of the secular as well as the religious component of Jewish culture. Judaism, said Kaplan, would survive only if it met the real needs of people. He believed in cultural as well as religious pluralism and insisted that diversity in modern Jewish life must be upheld.

Despite his affinity to Dubnow and Ahad Ha'am, Kaplan was not a secularist in the full sense. He could not free himself from the belief that religion was an integral part of a civilization and a necessary element of Jewish identity. He was wedded to the significance of "sancta," spiritual symbols which lead to feelings of reverence, undergirding a people's collective and communal experiences. While he was a humanist in much of his philosophy, he could never give up the need to pray, although he redefined God as "the sum of the animating, organizing forces and relationships which are forever making a cosmos out of chaos." Kaplan's development of Reconstructionism, however, was another step toward a new Humanistic Judaism.

JUDAISM AS A CIVILIZATION

The differences between the world from which the Jew has emerged and that in which he now lives are so sharp and manifold that they almost baffle description. The Jew shared with the rest of the ancient world the universal belief that salvation meant the attainment of bliss in the hereafter as a result of having lived according to the will of God in this life. Consequently he was free from all self-questioning and doubt. He was sure of his privileged position in the scheme of divine redemption. But all such conceptions together with the reasoning upon which they are based are alien to the modern world. In the short time that the Jew has lived in the modern world, these conceptions have become almost unintelligible to him. He thus finds himself deprived of what had been the principal justification for his loyalty to Judaism.

The only adequate substitute for other-worldly salvation which formerly motivated the loyalty of the Jew to his social heritage is a creative Judaism. This means that Judaism must be so reconstructed as to elicit from him the best that is in him. It must be so conditioned as to enlarge his mental horizon, deepen his sympathies, imbue him with hope and enable him to leave the world better for his having lived in it.

The Jews who are likely to assume the task of thus conditioning Judaism are they who cannot do without it, and yet cannot do with it as it is. As a rule, they are those with whom Judaism is a habit. Coming from intensely Jewish homes, they have had Judaism bred into their very bones. Jewish modes of self-expression and association with fellow-Jews are as indispensable to them as the very air they breathe. They would like to observe Jewish rites, but so many of those rites appear to them ill-adapted to the conditions and needs of our day. They are affiliated with congregations, but they are bored by the services. They take an active part in Jewish organizations, but are revolted by the futility, waste and lack of sincerity. They cannot help feeling that many an opportunity for reaching into the soul of the Jew, improving his character and eliciting his powers for good is thoughtlessly neglected. Anachronisms abound where cogency and relevance could prevail. Much that might be rendered beautiful and appealing is allowed to remain stale and flat. The teachers and scholars, instead of following the example of Moses, the teacher of all teachers, who went down to the people, ensconce themselves in the ivory tower of abstract learning.

Others, again, cannot do without Judaism because it is a nostalgia with them. It haunts them and gives them no rest. But as it is constituted at present, it offers no field for the expression of their innermost selves. Such Jews may never have seen anything Jewish in their homes, but some atavistic yearning or childhood memory has awakened within them. Now they want to become reunited with their people. If they are of a romantic temperament they may idealize their people's failings. Otherwise they may be repelled by the petrifaction of many of its lauded traditions and institutions and the aimlessness of most of its collective activities.

What must these Jews do to render Judaism creative?

1. In the first place they must rediscover Judaism; they must learn to know its true scope and character. The rediscovery of Judaism implies the lifting of the fog of pious sentimentalities and the mists of wish-thoughts which have enveloped it since the days of the emancipation. For fear lest Jews be charged with hyphenating their loyalties to the countries in which they are citizens, timid leaders and teachers have made it appear that Judaism is nothing more than a religion, or a cult. The Neo-Orthodox have taught that it is a revealed religion which so transcends all laws of social life as to be in no way affected or determined by them. As a revealed religion, Judaism is final and authoritative, destined to transform the environment but not to be transformed by it. The Reformists have interpreted Judaism as a historically evolved religion. According to them, the only bond which united Jews is the mission to promulgate the truth about the unity of God and the brotherhood of mankind. These conceptions of Judaism have so emptied it of content that it has come to mean to most Jews nothing more than a medley

of antiquated ideas and archaic practices which persist as an irrational hangover from the past.

A number of Jews who could not reconcile themselves to the vacuity of Reformism, or the intransigence of the Neo-Orthodoxy, are advocating the elimination of religion from Jewish collective life, and are staking the future of the Jewish people upon the spirit of nationalism. They point to nationalism as the most potent social energy in the modern world, and therefore conclude that it should be fostered as a means of solidifying and fructifying the life of the Jewish people. They forget, however, that, if nationalism is to unite the Jews, it must be rooted in the history and spirit of the Jewish people, otherwise the Jews would be merely playing at the kind of nationhood which has balkanized the world. Thus have the Secularists added to the general confusion of ideas which has obscured the true character of Judaism.

There must be an end to all these misconceptions and misunderstandings. The quality and quantity of life that spell Judaism must be rediscovered and reemphasized. It must be recognized as nothing less than a civilization. It must figure in the consciousness of the Jew as the *tout ensemble* of all that is included in a civilization, the social framework of national unity centering in a particular land, a continuing history, a living language and literature, religious folkways, mores, laws and art.

As a civilization, Judaism is that dynamic pattern of life which enables the Jewish people to be a means of salvation to the individual Jew. In the past when salvation meant attainment of bliss in the hereafter, the Jewish civilization was other-worldly in its entire outlook, content and motivation. Now when salvation depends on making the most of the opportunities presented by this world, the form of social organization, the language, literature, religion, laws, folkways and art must so function that through them the Jewish people will help to make the life of the Jew creative and capable of self-fulfillment. Jewish life must not depend upon syllogistic rationalization. It must have body and substance. It must function through vital institutions and articulate itself in a plastic and creative ideology.

The only way in which Jews will ever be able to coordinate their own mode of life satisfactorily with the life which they must share with their neighbors will be by rethinking their beliefs, reorganizing their institutions and developing new means of self-expression as Jews. To that end it will be necessary for them to operate with Judaism not merely as a religion but as a civilization. . . .

For Judaism to become creative once again, it must assimilate the best in contemporary civilizations. In the past this process of assimilating cultural elements from the environment was carried on unconsciously. Henceforth that process will have to be carried on in deliberate and planned fashion. Therein Judaism will, no doubt, have to depart from its own tradition. But conscious and purposeful planning is coming to be part of the very life process of society. No civilization, culture, economy or religion that is content to drift aimlessly has the slightest chance of surviving. It is in the spirit, therefore, of adopting the best in other civilizations and cooperating with them, and not in the spirit of yielding to their superior force or prestige, that Judaism should enter upon what will constitute a fourth stage in its development.

This development in Judaism necessarily presupposes many changes in its ideology, sanctions, practices and social organization. The criterion which is to determine whether a suggested change is beneficial or detrimental to Judaism is the extent to which it helps Judaism to retain its *continuity*, its *individuality* and its *organic character.*

The continuity of Judaism is maintained so long as the knowledge of Israel's past functions as an integral part of the Jew's personal memory, and is accompanied by some visible form or action symbolic of that fact. . . .

The individuality of Judaism is maintained so long as the newly instituted custom, sanction, idea or ideal helps to keep alive the element of otherness in the Jewish civilization. Not separatism must henceforth be the principle of living as a Jew, but otherness. Separatism is the antithesis of cooperation, and results in an ingrown and clannish remoteness which leads to cultural and spiritual stagnation. Otherness thrives best when accompanied by active cooperation and interaction with neighboring cultures and civilizations, and achieves an individuality which is of universal significance.

The organic character is maintained so long as all the elements that constitute the civilization play a role in the life of the Jew. Any attempt to live or transmit only certain elements in Judaism to the neglect of others is bound to end in failure, since in Judaism as a civilization the normal functioning of each element is bound up with and conditioned by the normal functioning of every other. . . .

2. To render Judaism creative it is essential to redefine the national status and reorganize the communal life of the Jews. Fundamental to the reconstitution of the Jewish people is national unity. That unity is not determined by geographic boundaries; it is cultural rather than political. The Jews are an international people, functioning as such by virtue of their consciousness of a common past, their aspiration toward a common future and the will-to-cooperate in the achievement of common ends.

The State of Israel should serve as the symbol of the Jewish renascence and the homeland of Jewish civilization. Without such a center upon which Jews throughout the world might focus their interest, it is impossible for Jews to be conscious of their unity as a people. Without the spiritual aid and example of the adjustment of Judaism to modern life in the new Jewish environment possible only in the State of Israel, the efforts at similar adjustment by other Jewries of the world would be without impelling stimulus. Judaism cannot maintain its character as a civilization without a homeland. There essential Jewish creativeness will express itself in Hebraic forms not so easily developed in other lands. There Jews will attain sufficient autonomy to express their ideas and social will in all forms of organized life and thought. . . .

As a result of a peculiar conjuncture of historic forces, the citizen of a modern state is not only permitted but encouraged to give allegiance to two civilizations: one, the secular civilization of the country in which he lives, and the other, the Christian civilization which he has inherited from the past. He turns to the civilization of his country for his literary and esthetic values. From his national life arise those duties of civic allegiance which are the substance of patriotism. He turns to the Christian civilization for his moral and spiritual sanctions. The separation of church from state has put into the class of hyphenates all who adhere to both organizations. The necessity which justifies the Christian in hyphenating his Christianity with Americanism, justifies also the Jew in hyphenating his Jewishness with Americanism. . . .

3. To render Judaism creative, its tradition must be revitalized. The main reason Jews display such a negative attitude to their tradition is no doubt the fact that they labor under the assumption that it is inextricably bound up with a theology which has ceased to have any vital meaning for them. They conceive tradition as a series of fixed and static ideas which either have to be accepted in

the form in which they have come down, or be ignored entirely. This erroneous idea must be offset by the realization that the only way tradition will ever come into its own as an active factor in the Jewish consciousness is to disengage from it the element of past interpretation, and to identify the way it functioned socially and spiritually.

The future of Judaism is contingent upon the formulation of a Jewish ideology which will make it possible for Jews, despite their unlike-mindedness, to accept the intrinsic value of Jewish life. Only through a participation in Jewish interests and aspirations which elicits the best that is in him will the individual Jew find salvation through his people. But if such participation is to have a truly redeeming or saving influence, it must be accompanied by a clear perspective on the whole of Jewish life.

The crux of the problem of how to foster a constructive and unifying Jewish ideology at the present time is to disabuse the average person of the deeply rooted preconception that for a people or community to function as an instrument of salvation, all who compose it must think alike and behave alike. Out of this preconception stems the intolerance which is by no means confined to the historic churches. Modern nations are no less adept in intolerance. An inference which some wrongly draw from this hitherto unquestioned assumption is that, since it is impossible to get people to think and behave alike, there can be no such thing as a group acting as an instrument of salvation. Salvation, they maintain, is purely an individual achievement. Such a conclusion is tantamount to nihilism, yet it is the inevitable one to which any sincere and conscientious person is driven, so long as the churches and nations continue in their refusal or inability to reconcile the salvation they proffer with tolerance of credal differences. It is doubtful whether they will change their attitude. With the Jewish people, however, this synthesis is a matter of life and death. Its very existence depends upon its making a virtue of the necessity of giving its individual men and women wide scope in views, and at the same time extending salvation to all of them alike.

A people does not offer itself to the individual as an instrument of salvation, in the same way as a system of philosophy usually does, by appealing to his reason to accept certain general principles or abstract truths. It always comes to him with a story about itself which he is made to feel is in a deeper and truer sense his story than the experiences that are confined to his person. In the course of that story there figure certain events, persons, places, objects, or, in brief, *sancta,* which come to possess a vital interest for him, since they belong to a history that he comes to look upon as his own. These *sancta* the people interprets, and these interpretations form the ideology and rationale of its existence and strivings. In the past, when everybody thought alike, one type of interpretation or ideology was enough to enable the *sancta* to help the individual orient himself to the world about him. One ideology, uniform and unchangeable, thus came to be regarded as indispensable to salvation.

Now that such uniformity is no longer possible, there is the alternative of permitting different ideologies to be developed whereby the *sancta,* which have played an important part in the history of the people or church, may retain their place as sources of and occasions for ethical motivation and spiritual exaltation for individuals with different philosophies of life. The sense of unity and even of like-mindedness is not contingent upon the sameness of interpretation, but upon the sameness of the constellation of realities interpreted. . . .

(Chapter 32)

Albert Einstein (1879–1955)

Introduction

Albert Einstein, one of the most eminent scientists in human history, was also a great humanitarian, a Jew, a humanist, and a self-proclaimed Zionist. He was born in Ulm, Germany, in 1879, and studied in Switzerland. He wrote his first important scientific papers early in the twentieth century and served as a professor at the universities of Zurich, Prague, and finally Berlin. He was the principal founder of twentieth-century theoretical physics, and was awarded the Nobel Prize in Physics in 1921.

Einstein had no special Jewish education, but became attuned to his Jewishness while in Prague, where he also came to know about East European Jewry. He disliked the assimilated and denationalized among the German Jews. While he was opposed to narrow nationalism, he appreciated the unique position of the Jewish people and realized the dangers they faced. Einstein became an active Zionist, especially of the Ahad Ha'am school. He developed a friendship with Chaim Weizmann, another scientist, who was a leader of the Zionist movement, and went with him to the United States to collect funds for Jewish settlements in Palestine and for the Hebrew University of Jerusalem. Einstein was named a governor of the university and bequeathed his original writings on the theory of relativity to it. Following the rise of the Nazis to power in

Germany, Einstein left and accepted a teaching position at Princeton University in the United States.

Although Einstein played a role in the development of the atomic bomb, he became active in the movement to abolish such weapons after World War II. He was concerned with the social consequences of science and took a leading part in attempts to seek international agreement for the control of nuclear energy.

After the death of Weizmann, who served as Israel's first president, Ben-Gurion offered to nominate Einstein, but he declined gratefully. He died in 1955.

Einstein was a humanist in the best sense of the word. He had great respect for the achievements of science but had a love for simplicity and the search for truth. He played the violin, was a lover of music, and had a great sense of humor.

Einstein attests in his writings to his belief in God. But his was the God of Spinoza, the conviction that in a somewhat incomprehensible universe there must be some superior reasoning intelligence. This God, however, was not a personal one, not a being concerned with the fate of human individuals. For Einstein, Judaism was not essentially a concern with rituals and taboos. A Jew was not defined by religion but was the possessor of a set of moral beliefs and attitudes, particularly the notion of social justice.

Just What Is a Jew?

The formation of groups has an invigorating effect in all spheres of human striving, perhaps mostly due to the struggle between the convictions and aims represented by the different groups. The Jews too form such a group with a definite character of its own, and anti-Semitism is nothing else but the antagonistic, hostile attitude produced in the non-Jews by the Jewish group. This is a normal social reaction. But for the political abuse resulting from it, it might never have been designated by a special name.

What are the characteristics of the Jewish group? What, in the first place, is a Jew? There are no quick answers to this question.

The most obvious answer would be the following: a Jew is a man professing the Jewish faith. The superficial character of this answer is easily recognized through a simple parallel. Let us ask the question: what is a snail? An answer similar in kind to the one given above might be: a snail is an animal inhabiting a snail shell. This answer is not altogether incorrect, nor, to be sure, is it exhaustive; for the snail shell happens to be one of the material products of the snail. Similarly, the Jewish faith is but one of the characteristic products of the Jewish community. It is, furthermore, known that a snail can shed its shell without thereby ceasing to be a snail. The Jew who abandons his faith (in the formal sense of the word) is in a similar position. He remains a Jew. Difficulties of this kind appear whenever one seeks to explain the essential character of a group.

The bond that has united the Jews for thousands of years, and unites them today is, above all, the democratic ideal of social justice, coupled with the ideal of mutual aid and tolerance among all men. Even the most ancient religious scriptures of the Jews are steeped in these social ideals, which have powerfully affected Christianity and Mohammedanism and have a benign influence upon the social structure of a great part of mankind. The introduction of a weekly day of rest should be remembered here—a profound blessing to all mankind. Personalities such as Moses, Spinoza, Karl Marx, dissimilar as they may be, all lived and sacrificed themselves for the idea of social justice; and it was the tradition of their forefathers that led them on this thorny path. The unique accomplishments of the Jews in the field of philanthropy spring from the same source.

The second characteristic trait of Jewish tradition is the high regard in which it holds every form of intellectual aspiration and spiritual effort. I am convinced that this great respect for intellectual striving is solely responsible for the contributions that the Jews have made toward the progress of knowledge, in the broadest sense of the term. In view of their relatively small number and the considerable external obstacles placed in their way on all sides, the extent of those contributions deserves the admiration of all sincere men. I am convinced that this is not due to any special wealth of endowment, but to the fact that the esteem in which intellectual accomplishment is held among the Jews creates an atmosphere particularly favorable to the development of any talents that may exist. At the same time a strong critical spirit prevents blind obedience to any mortal authority.

I have confined myself here to these two traditional traits, which seem to me the most basic. These standards and ideals find expression in small things as in large. They are transmitted from parents to children; they color conversation and judgment among friends; they fill the religious scriptures; and they give to the community life of the group its characteristic stamp. It is in these distinctive ideals that I see the essence of Jewish nature. That these ideals are but imperfectly realized in the group—in its actual everyday life—it is only natural. However, if one seeks to give brief expression to the essential character of a group, the approach must always be by the way of the ideal.

Perhaps even more than on its own tradition, the Jewish group has thrived on oppression and on the antagonism it has forever met in the world. Here undoubtedly lies one of the main reasons for its continued existence through so many thousands of years.

. . . Their significance as a political factor is negligible. They are scattered over almost the entire earth and are in no way organized as a whole—which means that they are incapable of concerted action of any kind.

Were anyone to form a picture of the Jews solely from the utterances of their enemies, he would have to reach the conclusion that they represent a world power. At first sight that seems downright absurd; and yet, in my view, there is a certain meaning behind it. The Jews as a group may be powerless, but the sum of the achievements of their individual members is everywhere considerable and telling, even though these achievements were made in the face of obstacles. The forces dormant in the individual are mobilized, and the individual himself is stimulated to self-sacrificing effort, by the spirit that is alive in the group.

Hence the hatred of the Jews by those who have reason to shun popular enlightenment. More than anything else in the world, they fear the influences of men of intellectual independence. I see in this the essential cause for the savage hatred of Jews raging in present-day Germany. To the Nazi group the Jews are not merely a means for turning the resentment of the people away from themselves, the oppressors; they see the Jews as a nonassimilable element that cannot be driven into uncritical acceptance of dogma, and that, therefore—as long as it exists at all—threatens their authority because of its insistence on popular enlightenment of the masses.

Proof that this conception goes to the heart of the matter is convincingly furnished by the solemn ceremony of the burning of the books staged by the Nazi regime shortly after its seizure of power. This act, senseless from a political point of view, can only be understood as a spontaneous emotional outburst. For that reason it seems more revealing than many acts of greater purpose and practical importance.

In the field of politics and social science there has grown up a justified distrust of generalizations pushed too far. When thought is too greatly dominated by such generalizations, misinterpretations of specific sequences of cause and effect readily occur, doing injustice to the actual multiplicity of events. Abandonment of generalizations, on the other hand, means to relinquish understanding altogether. For that reason I believe one may and must risk generalizations, as long as one remains aware of its uncertainty. It is in this spirit that I wish to present in all modesty my conception of anti-Semitism, considered from a general point of view.

In political life I see two opposed tendencies at work, locked in constant struggle with each other. The first, optimistic, trend proceeds from the belief that the free unfolding of the productive forces of individuals and groups essentially leads to a satisfactory state of society. It recognizes the need for a central power, placed above groups and individuals, but concedes to such power only organizational and regulatory functions. The second, pessimistic, trend assumes that free interplay of individuals and groups leads to the destruction of society; it thus seeks to base society exclusively upon authority, blind obedience and coercion. Actually this trend is pessimistic only to a limited extent: for it is optimistic in regard to those who are and desire to be, the bearers of power and authority. The adherents of this second trend are the enemies of the free groups and of education for independent thought. They are, moreover, the carriers of political anti-Semitism.

Jewish Ideals

There is, in my opinion, no Jewish view of life in the philosophic sense. Judaism appears to me to be almost exclusively concerned with the moral attitude in and toward life.

Judaism I believe to be rather the content of the life approach of the Jewish people than the contents of the laws laid down in the Torah and interpreted in the Talmud. Torah and Talmud are for me only the most weighty evidence of the governing concepts of Jewish life in earlier times.

The essence of the Jewish concept of life seems to me to be the affirmation of life for all creatures. For the life of the individual has meaning only in the service of enhancing and ennobling the life of every living thing. Life is holy; i.e. it is the highest worth on which all other values depend. The sanctification of the life which transcends the individual brings with it reverence for the spiritual, a peculiarly characteristic trait of Jewish tradition.

Judaism is not a faith. The Jewish God is but a negation of superstition and an imaginative result of its elimination. It also represents an attempt to ground morality in fear—a deplorable discreditable attempt. Yet it seems to me that the powerful moral tradition in the Jewish people has, in great measure, released itself from this fear. Moreover, it is clear that "to serve God" is an equivalent to serving "every living thing." It is for this that the best among the Jewish people, especially the prophets including Jesus, ceaselessly battle. Thus Judaism is not a transcendental religion. It is concerned only with the tangible experience of life, and with nothing else. Therefore, it seems to me to be questionable whether it may be termed a "religion" in the customary sense of the word, especially since no "creed" is demanded of Jews, but only the sanctification of life in its all-inclusive sense.

There remains, however, something more in the Jewish tradition, so gloriously revealed in certain of the psalms; namely, a kind of drunken joy and surprise at the beauty and incomprehensible sublimity of this world, of which man can attain but a faint intimation. It is the feeling from which genuine research draws its intellectual strength, but which also seems to manifest itself in the song of birds. This appears to me to be the loftiest content of the God-idea.

Is this, then, characteristic of Judaism? And does it exist elsewhere under other names? In pure form it exists nowhere, not even in Judaism where too much literalism obscures the pure doctrine. But, nevertheless, I see in Judaism one of its most vital and pure realizations. This is especially true of the fundamental principle of the sanctification of life.

It is noteworthy that in the commandment to keep the Sabbath holy the animals were also expressly included—so strongly was felt as an ideal the demand for the solidarity of all living things. Far more strongly yet is expressed the demand for the solidarity of all humankind; and it is no accident that the socialistic demands for the most part emanated from Jews.

To how great an extent the consciousness of the sanctity of life is alive in the Jewish people is beautifully illustrated by a remark once made to me by Walther Rathenau: "When a Jew says he takes pleasure in the hunt, he lies." It is impossible to express more simply the consciousness of the sanctity and the unity of all life as it exists in the Jewish people.

Science and Ethics

. . . For the scientist, there is only "being," but no wishing, no valuing, no good, no evil; no goal. As long as we remain within the realm of science proper, we can never meet with a sentence of the type: "Thou shalt not lie." There is something like a Puritan's restraint in the scientist who seeks truth: he keeps away from everything voluntaristic or emotional. Incidentally, this trait is the result of a slow development, peculiar to modern Western thought.

From this it might seem as if logical thinking were irrelevant for ethics. Scientific statement of facts and relations, indeed cannot produce ethical directives. However, ethical directives can be made rational and coherent by logical thinking and empirical knowledge. If we can agree on some fundamental ethical propositions, then other ethical propositions can be derived from them, provided that the original premises are stated with sufficient precision. Such ethical premises play a similar role in ethics, to that played by axioms in mathematics.

This is why we do not feel at all that it is meaningless to ask such questions as: "Why should we not lie?" We feel that such questions are meaningful because in all discussions of this kind some ethical premises are tacitly taken for granted. We then feel satisfied when we succeed in tracing back the ethical directive in question to these basic premises. In the case of lying this might perhaps be done in some way such as this: Lying destroys confidence in the statements of other people. Without such confidence, social co-operation is made impossible or at least difficult. Such co-operation, however, is essential to make human life possible and tolerable. This means that the rule "Thou shalt not lie" has been traced back to the demands: "Human life shall be preserved" and "Pain and sorrow shall be lessened as much as possible."

But what is the origin of such ethical axioms? Are they arbitrary? Are they based on mere authority? Do they stem from experience of men and are they conditioned indirectly by such experiences?

For pure logic all axioms are arbitrary, including the axioms of ethics. But they are by no means arbitrary from a psychological and genetic point of view. They are derived from our inborn tendencies to avoid pain and annihilation, and from the accumulated emotional reaction of individuals to the behavior of their neighbours.

It is the privilege of man's moral genius, impersonated by inspired individuals, to advance ethical axioms which are so comprehensive and so well founded that men will accept them as grounded in the vast mass of their individual emotional experiences. Ethical axioms are found and tested not very differently from the axioms of science. Truth is what stands the test of experience. . . .

Louis Brandeis
(1856–1941)

Introduction

Louis Brandeis was one of the most distinguished justices who ever sat on the United States Supreme Court. He was also a scholar, humanist, and Zionist. He transformed Zionism in America from the concern of a small group of Jews into a vibrant and powerful force. Brandeis advocated cultural pluralism in American life, believing that rather than a melting pot, America was an "inclusive brotherhood."

Brandeis was born in Louisville, Kentucky, in 1856, studied at Harvard University, and graduated from its law school in 1877. He began his practice of law in Boston, but while working as a corporate lawyer, he embarked on activities in defense of consumers and working people. Having been raised with no religious training, it was not until 1910, when he was called in to arbitrate a garment workers' strike in New York, that he had his first real contact with Jews, who were the majority of the strikers. He was so impressed by the moral fiber of the Jewish working class that he began to feel a sense of solidarity with other Jews. A few years later, he was introduced to Zionism, which was then a small minority movement among American Jews. He quickly rose to leadership of the American Zionist movement, drew new talent into the organization, and made it a potent force in American Jewish life.

Brandeis was careful to emphasize that his loyalty as a Zionist was not at odds with his American patriotism. For Brandeis, ethnic loyalty was not a barrier to humanism or cultural democracy. True liberalism (humanism), he stated, does not mean abandoning one's national culture and heritage in order to create a universal, non-rooted culture. True liberalism means upholding traditions and ethnic cultural patterns. He explained in a speech in 1914 that American ideals had been the ideals of Jews throughout their history. Jews, he said, "have inherited these ideals of democracy and of social justice. . . . We have inherited also that fundamental longing for truth on which all science . . . rests."

President Woodrow Wilson appointed Brandeis to the Supreme Court in 1916, and along with Oliver Wendell Holmes, Brandeis was the author of many dissenting progressive opinions that differed radically from the majority in matters of social and economic policy. He served on the court with great distinction for twenty-two years.

Brandeis was also the moving spirit behind the movement for the creation of a democratically elected American Jewish Congress that would represent American Jewry on questions concerning the future status of the Jews of Eastern Europe and Palestinian settlement after World War I. He remained active in the Zionist cause and in support of the settlement of Jews in Palestine for the remainder of his life.

Concurring Opinion in Whitney v. California

. . . Those who won our independence believed that the final end of the State was to make men free to develop their faculties, and that in its government the deliberative forces should prevail over the arbitrary. They valued liberty both as an end and as a means. They believed liberty to be the secret of happiness and courage to be the secret of liberty. They believed that freedom to think as you will and to speak as you think are means indispensable to the discovery and spread of political truth; that without free speech and assembly discussion would be futile; that with them, discussion affords ordinarily adequate protection against the dissemination of noxious doctrine; that the greatest menace to freedom is an inert people; that public discussion is a political duty; and that this should be a fundamental principle of the American Government. They recognized the risks to which all human institutions are subject. But they knew that order cannot be secured merely through fear of punishment for its infraction; that it is hazardous to discourage thought, hope, and imagination; that fear breeds repression; that repression breeds hate; that hate menaces stable government; that the path of safety lies in the opportunity to discuss freely supposed grievances and proposed remedies; and that the fitting remedy for evil counsels is good ones. Believing in the power of reason as applied through public discussion, they eschewed silence coerced by law—the argument of force in its worst form. Recognizing the occasional tyrannies of governing majorities, they amended the Constitution so that free speech and assembly should be guaranteed.

Fear of serious injury cannot alone justify suppression of free speech and assembly. Men feared witches and burnt women. It is the function of speech to free men from the bondage of irrational fears. To justify suppression of free speech there must be reasonable ground to fear that the serious evil will result if free speech is practiced. There must be reasonable ground to believe that the danger apprehended is imminent. There must be reasonable ground to believe that the evil to be prevented is a serious one. Every denunciation of existing law tends in some measure to increase the probability that there will be violation of it. Condonation of a breach enhances the probability. Expressions of approval add to the probability. Propagation of the criminal state of mind by teaching syndicalism increases it. Advocacy of law-breaking heightens it still further. But even advocacy of violation, however reprehensible morally, is not a justification for denying free speech where the advocacy falls short of incitement and there is nothing to indicate that the advocacy would be immediately acted on. The wide difference between advocacy and incitement, between preparation and attempt, between assembling and conspiracy, must be borne in mind. In order to support a finding of clear and present danger it must be shown either that immediate serious violence was to be expected or was advocated, or that the past conduct furnished reason to believe that such advocacy was then contemplated.

Those who won our independence by revolution were not cowards. They did not fear political change. They did not exalt order at the cost of liberty. To courageous, self-reliant men, with confidence in the power of free and fearless reasoning applied through the processes of popular government, no danger flowing from speech can be deemed clear and present, unless the incidence of the evil apprehended is so imminent that it may befall before there is opportunity for full discussion. If there be time to expose through discussion the falsehood and fallacies, to avert the evil by the processes of education, the remedy to be applied is more speech, not enforced silence. Only an emergency can justify repression. Such must be the rule if authority is to be reconciled with freedom. Such, in my opinion, is the command of the Constitution. It is therefore always open to Americans to challenge a law abridging free speech and assembly by showing that there was no emergency justifying it. . . .

Mendele Mocher Sforim (1835–1917)

Introduction

Mendele Mocher Sforim was regarded by Sholem Aleichem as "the grandfather of Yiddish literature." Mendele was a novelist in both Hebrew and Yiddish, a writer of short stories, plays, and critical essays. His self-deprecating wit and detailed realistic descriptions are considered to be a totally honest representation of Jewish life in the Pale of Settlement at the end of the nineteenth century.

Mendele was born in Byelorussia in 1835 and spent his youth in several yeshivas in Lithuania. He was influenced by the Jewish Enlightenment (Haskalah) which was impacting Russian Jews at that time. He launched his literary career by trying to breathe new life into Hebrew literary criticism. Then, motivated by the belief that he could effect real change in Jewish society by exposing many of its follies, he began to write stories in Yiddish, selecting this language so that "ordinary Jews" would be able to read them. Much of his early writing was steeped in realism and was critical of shtetl life, since he believed that if Russian Jews were able to gain an understanding of their weaknesses and ailments they would be able to correct them and then be accepted by non-Jewish society.

After suffering a personal crisis, Mendele moved to Odessa, where he spent the rest of his life. He created a modern Yiddish prose style, and in 1888 revised and published his finest Yiddish work, *Fishke der krumer.*

Mendele became a supporter of Hibbat Zion (Lovers of Zion) after the pogroms of 1881–82 and later took a full-fledged Zionist position. He continued writing his ironical and satirical stories in Yiddish and then translated them into Hebrew. He described himself as split between the pious Jew of the synagogue and the skeptic of the Enlightenment. In a particularly bitter joke he said that only God above hated the Jews as much as those below. He is considered to have been a great writer, one with a mission to move his people out from under the yoke of a stultifying orthodoxy.

Shlomo Reb-Khayim's

. . . What is there to tell about the way we lived in my day? Did we astound the world with great and wonderful inventions? We did not. Did we have noblemen or princes or generals? We did not. Did we have love affairs with beautiful ladies of the court? No. Did we fight duels-to-the-death with swords or pistols over these ladies? No. Did we even know how to dance the quadrille with pretty young women at fancy dress balls? Ridiculous! Did we go out into the woods and fields to hunt bear? Did we sail our ships across the seven seas to discover new islands? Of course not. In short, all these juicy tidbits that add spice to the story—of those we had none at all.

What we did have was a *melamed* [teacher] in a *kheder* [Hebrew school], and a *ba-helfer* to assist the *melamed*. We had matchmakers, child bridegrooms, wives with many children. We had widows and orphans, deserted wives who were not allowed to marry again and young widows who were. We had families burned out of their homes, we had people down on their luck. We had suddenly impoverished families. We had all varieties of poor people going from house to house *erev shabbes* [Sabbath eve], *erev yontef* [holiday eve], and even on an ordinary Monday or Thursday. We had able-bodied men who did nothing but sit and study day and night. We had charity boxes, we had all kinds of afflictions, we had a large assortment of paupers and all sorts of bizarre ways of earning one's living. In short, that was our life.

Is there another people in the world where the whole way of life of each individual person stretches from birth to death in the selfsame "style," as it does with us? Learning, studying, reading, praying—the melody to every prayer, every liturgical poem, every passage of Talmud—has its own prescribed style. Even our meals have a prescribed style.

Was such a thing ever heard of before—that at a prescribed time—Friday evening, for example—a whole people should sit down to eat the same thing—fish, noodles and *tsimmis*? And then the next morning—*Shabbes*—radishes and jellied-calves-feet, chopped liver with onions and eggs, boiled kasha with a big marrow bone in it? Or that on such and such a day you must eat *kreplekh*, or *homentashn*, or a yellow *khallah* with safran?

That is our life. . . .

Isaac Leib Peretz (1852–1915)

Introduction

Together with Mendele Mocher Sforim, and Sholem Aleichem, Isaac Leib Peretz was a founder of modern Yiddish literature. He was also a writer in Hebrew, a humanist, and a trailblazer of a secular national Jewish identity.

Peretz was born in Zamosc, Poland, in 1852. He received a traditional Jewish education but went on to study law. For several years he practiced law in his hometown, but due to his sympathy with workers' causes, he was forced to abandon his law practice. In 1890 he moved to Warsaw, which was then developing as a major Jewish cultural center, and took a routine job with the Jewish Communal Bureau. In the spare time this left him, he embarked upon a prolific career as a writer in Yiddish. One of his major undertakings was the Yiddish Bibliotek (Jewish Library). Peretz's home became a meeting place for young Jewish writers and intellectuals, thus enhancing the reputation of Warsaw as a center of Jewish creativity. In 1894 he began writing his *Hasidic Tales*, and from 1902 to 1904 he wrote his *Popular Tales*. In the period from 1906 to 1908 he was active as a dramatist. When he died in 1915, one hundred thousand mourners came to his funeral.

Peretz's views were often changeable and contradictory, reflecting the dilemmas and contradictions inherent in the Jewish problems of the time. At first he regarded Yiddish with disdain, as jargon. He changed his mind after the pogroms in 1881–82. Then he decided that writing in Yiddish would enable him to reach the Jewish masses and to reflect their lives in his work. However, he opposed the designation of Yiddish rather than Hebrew as the national language of the Jewish people when a resolution to this effect was put before the Czernowitz Conference in 1908, preferring both to be designated as Jewish languages. He was a Jewish nationalist, but not a Zionist, a labor sympathizer but not an outright socialist.

In his attitude toward the Jewish religion of his time, Peretz was a typical Eastern European *maskil* (follower of the Enlightenment). He consistently called for breaking free from Orthodox isolation and monopoly, advocating secular education and openness to "general culture." He was a severe and effective critic of the tyranny of the fundamentalist ultra-Orthodox establishment in the Jewish shtetl. Yet he also wrote romantic stories about the humanitarian aspects of the Hasidic movement.

Peretz tried to reinterpret the Jewish religious tradition in a contemporary non-Orthodox way in his famous story "Yontev Bletlech" (Holiday Leaflets). In articles like "What Is Jewishness?" he pioneered such ideas as religious pluralism, and the ongoing adaptation of religion to changing times and needs. It was, however, his passionate and critical writing, permeated with empathy and compassion for the poor and oppressed, that made a major impact on his readers.

The Pious Cat

One after the other three canaries had been brought into the house, and one after the other the cat had taken care of them.

Now this cat, it must be kept in mind, is no common alley serenader but a truly devout soul. A model of piety. One who wears his white garment at all times, not only on holidays. One whose eyes reflect the compassion of Heaven itself. . . .

Such piety! Only the most devout, anxious as they for are any excuse to pronounce a blessing would—as he does—wash themselves ten times a day! And such refinement! He eats his meals quietly and unobtrusively, in some out of the way corner. . . .

Pious soul that he is, his regimen is limited to dairy dishes during the day; only toward nightfall does he permit himself meat—kosher mouse meat. . . .

Nor does he set to and, as would an uncouth creature, devour the evening meal like a glutton. No; he proceeds daintily, gently—let the mouse live another moment, and another . . . let it dance about a little, tremble a little, confess its sins . . . a pious cat does not rush things. . . .

When the first canary was brought into the house the cat's pity was aroused immediately; his heart was touched to the very depths.

"Alas," sighed he, "to think that such a gorgeous little bird, such a delightful little creature, should have no share in the next world!"

That the bird could not possible have a share in the next world, of that the cat was certain. In the first place its manner of washing was that of a non-conformist—its whole body in a bowl of water! In the second place, since it must be kept in a cage, that in itself is proof that it is a wild animal, a soulless creature even though it is a young, pretty, refined songster—it obviously must lay more store by violence than by the Book of Regulations!

And when one takes into consideration the singing itself—the wanton manner, the warbling and whistling and looking straight up at the sky without the least sign of humility and respect; the fluttering at the bars of the cage seeking an opening to the sinful world, to the open window. . . .

Was then a cat ever confined in a cage? Or was there ever a cat that whistled so boisterously, so brazenly?

—A shame! —The pious cat's generous heart bled for the poor bird. —In spite of everything it is still a living creature, a precious thing, a spark from On High!—

Tears sprang into the cat's eyes.

—And the whole tragedy is that the sinful body is so lovely, the material world thereby so pleasing, the *Yetzer hora* [temptation] so powerful. . . .

—How can so sweet and tiny and frail a bird stand up against so mighty a *Yetzer hora*?

—And the longer it lives, the more it sins, the greater will be its punishment. . . .

—Ha!—

And a holy fire was kindled in the pious cat's soul—the fire of Pinkhas ben Eliezer, the priest who destroyed the golden calf. He sprang onto the table where the cage stood. . . .

Feathers flew in the house.

* * *

The cat was soundly thrashed.

He accepted the beating meekly, groaned piously, and meowed out a caterwauling atonement. . . .

No more, vowed he, would he sin . . . .

No fool, the cat understood full well why the beating, and vowed never again to incur such wrath. He was spanked, the cat realized, because he had scattered feathers over the house, because he had sprinkled the embroidered white tablecloth with blood. . . .

Such sentences must be executed quietly, carefully and devoutly, without a single feather misplaced, without a drop of blood spilled. . . .

When the second songbird was brought into the house he carefully and quietly strangled it and ate it feathers and all. . . .

* * *

The cat was given a severe whipping.

Now the cat realized that the fault lay, not with flying feathers, not with blood spilled on the tablecloth; the secret was—we must not kill! We must love, we must forgive . . . not with death sentences will we improve this sinful world . . . we must win sinners over with compassion, with the power of persuasion; we must show the wayward the true path to glory. A repentant canary can attain heights to which even the most devout cat cannot aspire!

The cat felt his heart swelling within him for joy—away with the old times, the harsh, nasty times! Have done with bloodshed!

Mercy, mercy—only mercy. . . .

* * *

His soul overflowing with tenderness, the cat approached the third canary.

"Don't be frightened," he purred in the gentlest voice ever to issue from a feline throat, "though you are black with sin I shall do you no harm for I am filled with compassion for you.

"I shall not open your cage; I shall not even touch you with my paw!

"You are silent? Excellent! Rather than singing brazen songs it is better that you be silent!

"You quiver? Better still! Tremble, tremble my child! But not because of me—tremble before the Creator of the Universe, tremble for His Sacred Name!

"May you remain ever thus—silent, pure and quivering. . . .

"I shall help you quiver! I shall, from the bottom of my pious soul, breathe upon you with sweetness, silence and piety . . . with my breath may there enter faith into your body, fear of God into your bones, repentance and remorse into your heart . . ."

Now for the very first time the cat felt the truly benign delight that comes with forgiveness, that comes with winning an errant soul to ways of piety and truth. . . .

The most compassionate heart in the most pious white cat swelled with pride and joy. . . .

But the canary could not live in the feline atmosphere; he could not draw breath. . . .

That air suffocated him.

A Woman's Wrath

The small room is dingy as the poverty that clings to its walls. There is a hook fastened to the crumbling ceiling, relic of a departed hanging lamp. The old, peeling stove is girded about with a coarse sack, and leans sideways toward its gloomy neighbor, the black empty fireplace, in which stands an inverted cooking pot with a chipped rim. Beside it lies a broken spoon, which met its fate in unequal contest with the scrapings of cold, stale porridge.

The room is choked with furniture; there is a fourpost bed with torn curtains. The pillows visible through their holes have no covers.

There is a cradle, with the large, yellow head of a sleeping child; a chest with metal fittings and an open padlock—nothing very precious left in there, evidently; further, a table and three chairs (originally painted red), a cupboard, now somewhat damaged. Add to these a pail of clean water and one of dirty water, an oven rake with a shovel, and you will understand that a pin could hardly drop onto the floor.

And yet the room contains *him* and *her* beside.

She, a middle-aged Jewess, sits on the chest that fills the space between the bed and the cradle.

To her right is the one grimy little window, to her left, the table. She is knitting a sock, rocking the cradle with her foot, and listens to *him* reading the Talmud at the table, with a tearful, Wallachian, singing intonation, and swaying to and fro with a series of nervous jerks. Some of the words he swallows, others he draws out; now he snaps at a word, and now he skips it; some he accentuates and dwells on lovingly, others he rattles out with indifference, like dried peas out of a bag. And never quiet for a moment. First he draws from his pocket a once red and whole handkerchief, and wipes his nose and brow, then he lets it fall into his lap, and begins twisting his earlocks or pulling at his thin, pointed, faintly grizzled beard. Again, he lays a pulled-out hair from the same between the leaves of his book, and slaps his knee. His fingers coming into contact with the handkerchief, they seize it, and throw a corner in between his teeth; he bites it, lays one foot across the other, and continually shuffles with both feet.

All the while his pale forehead wrinkles, now in a perpendicular, now in a horizontal, direction, when the long eyebrows are nearly lost below the folds of skin. At times, apparently, he has a sting in the chest, for he beats his left side as though he were saying the Al-Chets. Suddenly he leans his head to the left, presses a finger against his left nostril, and emits an artificial sneeze, leans his head to the right, and the proceeding is repeated. In between he takes a pinch of snuff, pulls himself together, his voice rings louder, the chair creaks, the table wobbles.

The child does not wake; the sounds are too familiar to disturb it.

And she, the wife, shriveled and shrunk before her time, sits and drinks in delight. She never takes her eye off her husband, her ear lets no inflection of his voice escape. Now and then, it is true, she sighs. Were he as fit for *this* world as he is for the *other* world, she would have a good time of it here, too—here, too—.

"Ma!" she consoles herself, "who talks of honor? Not every one is worthy of both tables!"

She listens. Her shriveled face alters from minute to minute; she is nervous, too. A moment ago it was eloquent of delight. Now she remembers it is Thursday, there isn't a dreier to spend in preparation for Sabbath. The light in her face goes out by degrees, the smile fades, then she takes a look through the grimy window, glances at the sun. It must be getting late, and there isn't a spoonful of hot water in the house. The needles pause in her hand, a shadow has overspread her face. She looks at the child, it is sleeping less quietly, and will soon wake. The child is poorly, and there is not a drop of milk for it. The shadow on her face deepens into gloom, the needles tremble and move convulsively .

And when she remembers that it is near Passover, that her earrings and the festal candlesticks are at the pawnshop, the chest empty, the lamp sold, then the needles perform murderous antics in her fingers. The gloom on her brow is that of a gathering thunder-storm, lightning plays in her small, grey, sunken eyes.

He sits and "learns," unconscious of the charged atmosphere; does not see her let the sock fall and begin wringing her finger-joints; does not see that her forehead is puckered with misery, one eye closed, and the other fixed on him, her learned husband, with a look fit to send a chill through his every limb; does not see her dry lips tremble and her jaw quiver. She controls herself with all her might, but the storm is gathering fury within her. The least thing, and it will explode.

That least thing has happened.

He was just translating a Talmudic phrase with quiet delight, "And thence we derive that—" He was going on with "three,—" but the word "derive" was enough, it was the lighted spark, and her heart was the gunpowder. It was ablaze in an instant. Her determination gave way, the unlucky word opened the floodgates, and the waters poured through, carrying all before them,

"Derived, you say, derived? O, derived may you be, Lord of the World," she exclaimed, hoarse with anger, "derived may you be! Yes! You!" she hissed like a snake. "Passover coming—Thursday—and the child ill—and not a drop of milk is there. Ha?"

Her breath gives out, her sunken breast heaves, her eyes flash.

He sits like one turned to stone. Then, pale and breathless, too, from fright, he gets up and edges toward the door.

At the door he turns and faces her, and sees that hand and tongue are equally helpless from passion; his eyes grow smaller; he catches a bit of handkerchief between his teeth, retreats a little further, takes a deeper breath, and mutters:

"Listen, woman, do you know what Bittul-Torah means? And not letting a husband study in peace, to be always worrying about livelihood, ha? And who feeds the little birds, tell me? Always this want of faith in God, this giving way to temptation, and taking thought for *this* world . . . foolish, ill-natured woman! Not to let a husband study! If you don't take care, you will go to Gehenna."

Receiving no answer, he grows bolder. Her face gets paler and paler, she trembles more and more violently, and the paler she becomes, and the more she trembles, the steadier his voice as he goes on:

"Gehenna! Fire! Hanging by the tongue! Four death penalties inflicted by the court!"

She is silent, her face is white as chalk.

He feels that he is doing wrong, that he has no call to be cruel, that he is taking a mean advantage, but he has risen, as it were, to the top, and is boiling over. He cannot help himself.

"Do you know," he threatens her, " what Skiloh means? It means stoning, to throw into a ditch and cover up with stones! Srefoh—burning, that is, pouring a spoonful of boiling lead into the inside! Hereg—beheading, that means they cut off your head with a sword! Like this " (and he passes a hand across his neck). "Then Cheneck—strangling! Do you hear? To strangle! Do you understand? And all four for making light of the Torah! For Bittul-Torah!"

His heart is already sore for his victim, but he is feeling his power over her for the first time, and it has gone to his head. Silly woman! He had never known how easy it was to frighten her.

"That comes of making light of the Torah!" he shouts, and breaks off. After all, she might come to her senses at any moment, and take up the broom! He springs back to the table, closes the Gemoreh, and hurries out of the room.

"I am going to the house-of-study!" he calls out over his shoulder in a milder tone, and shuts the door after him.

The loud voice and the noise of the closing door have waked the sick child. The heavy-lidded eyes open, the waxen face puckers, and there is a peevish wail. But she, beside herself, stands rooted to the spot, and does not hear.

"Ha!" comes hoarsely at last out of her narrow chest. "So that's it, is it? Neither this world nor the other. Hanging, he says, stoning, burning, beheading, strangling, hanging by the tongue, boiling lead poured into the inside, he says—for making light of the Torah—Hanging, ha, ha, ha!" (in desperation). "Yes, I'll hang, *but here, here!* And soon! What is there to wait for?"

The child begins to cry louder; still she does not hear. "A rope! a rope!" she screams, and stares wildly into every corner.

"Where is there a rope? I wish he mayn't find a bone of me left! Let me be rid of *one* Gehenna at any rate! Let him try it, let him be a mother for once, see how he likes it! I've had enough of it! Let it be an atonement! An end, an end! A rope, a rope!"

Her last exclamation is like a cry for help from out of a conflagration.

She remembers that they *have* a rope somewhere. Yes, under the stove—the stove was to have been tied round against the winter. The rope must be there still.

She runs and finds the rope, the treasure, looks up at the ceiling—the hook that held up the lamp—she need only cling onto the table.

She climbs—

But she sees from the table that the startled child, weak as it is, has sat up in the cradle, and is reaching over the side—it is trying to get out—

"Mame, M-mame," it sobs feebly.

A fresh paroxysm of anger seizes her.

She flings away the rope, jumps off the table, runs to the child, and forces its head back into the pillow, exclaiming:

"Bother the child! It won't even let me hang myself! I can't even hang myself in peace! It wants to suck. What is the good? You will suck nothing but poison, poison, out of me, I tell you!"

"There, then, greedy!" she cries in the same breath, and stuffs her dried-up breast into his mouth.

"There, then, suck away—bite!

But a Person Has to Davn

Berl the Tailor could hardly wait for his son the doctor to come home. Here he would have plenty of patients. People could get sick whenever they felt like it!

The doctor came home on a Friday. Saturday morning his father wanted to take him along to shul.

"I'm not going, *Tatte,*" said the doctor.

"Why not? You're ashamed to be seen with me?"

"God forbid, *Tatte,* what an idea!"

"Now that you're a doctor you think you don't have to go and pray to God, to praise Him, is that it?"

No, *Tatte.*"

"What, then? Tell me. Are you too tired? Or maybe you're sick. God forbid?"

"No, it's not that. I just don't want to go."

"I'm curious to know why."

"Well, of course, if you want to know. Sit down and I'll tell you."

The old man put his *tallis* back on the table and sat down. "So, tell me, son, let me understand it, too."

"Good. Imagine, *Tatte,* that you are a rich man, so rich that a few rubles more or a few rubles less don't make any difference to you."

His father sighed. To make a doctor out of his son he'd had to go into hock. He used to own a little house. But no more. Now he lived in a rented one. He had even sold his sewing machines.

"Well," he said, and sighed again.

"So, *Tatte,* You're a wealthy man. And across the street from you lives a widow, a sick widow. Let's say she has children. They need help. What would you do?"

"I'd help them, of course!"

"I'm sure you would. But would you wait until the widow came and begged you for help? Cried her heart out to you? Fainted for you?"

"God forbid! If I knew, why would I wait?"

"And God—is He better than you or worse than you?"

"What are you saying? What kind of question is that?"

"Well," said the doctor triumphantly. "If God is better than you, then He already knows what poor, weak, sickly people need, and He doesn't wait for them to come and beg Him. . . ."

"But—"

"You mean about praising Him?"

"That too . . ."

"Well, *Tatte,* how would you like it if someone came and stood before you and praised you right to your face: What a good tailor, what a fine tailor, what an honest tailor, what a terrific tailor! A real tailor! The one-and-only tailor in the world—"

"Stop, already," interrupted the old man. "I'm getting nauseous just from—"

"Sure. And you know why? Because you're not a fool who enjoys having someone praise you in this ridiculous way. But you're also a human being, a weak human being whom insults can hurt and praise can help."

"But—"

"No buts, *Tatte,* no buts! God is wiser and cleverer than we are. Do you think He needs our praises? You think He needs us to stand before Him three times a day and say: A good tailor! A fine tailor!"

"What are you saying?"

"Well, all right—a good God, a fine God, a God who created heaven and earth. You think He doesn't know better?"

The old man thought about this for a moment and then suddenly bounced up out of his chair.

"Everything you say is correct, son. But a person still has to *davn,* doesn't he?"

Sholem Aleichem (1859–1916)

Introduction

Sholem Aleichem, the third of the classic masters of Yiddish prose, was born Solomon Rabinowitz in the Ukraine in 1859 to an impoverished family. In addition to the Hebrew he acquired at cheder, he learned Russian at a district school; when he left home at age seventeen he was able to support himself by tutoring in Russian.

He began his writing career in Hebrew, but when he married in 1883, he wrote a love story in Yiddish. He adopted his pseudonym to hide his identity from the Jewish intelligentsia, including his father, who held Yiddish literature in contempt. He moved a few years later to Kiev, where he wrote many novels, critical essays, and poems in Yiddish, and in 1888 he founded a literary annual in Yiddish whose first two volumes represented an historic turning point for Yiddish literature.

Sholem Aleichem, as prolific a writer as he was, could not escape poverty, and after the terrible 1905 pogroms he moved his family out of Russia. He left them in Switzerland while he went on lecture tours to earn money. At the outbreak of World War I, he moved his family to New York, where promised financial help unfortunately never materialized and his new plays failed. He was the most successful (although not materially) of the Yiddish writers, and his fiction received almost instantaneous recognition and popularity. When he died in 1916, hundreds of thousands attended his funeral.

Sholem Aleichem's literary output in Yiddish fills forty volumes of short stories, novels, and plays, of which only twelve volumes were printed during his lifetime. He had no peer among Yiddish writers in his ability to capture the linguistic resources of the language, with its wonderful raciness and its picturesque idioms that vibrate with life. He undertook a crusade to raise the dignity of the language and railed against writers who catered only to the uneducated. Sholem Aleichem's humor, his most salient characteristic, often took the form of pathos, exhibiting a basic optimism and faith in human beings no matter how humble their circumstances. While the hundreds of individual characters he created in his works believe in God, many of them are skeptics who freely question God's handling of the universe. The fictional Kasrilevke created by Sholem Aleichem is populated with people who are poor but resourceful, both materially and spiritually. Sholem Aleichem's rich humor and his faith in the innate nobility of the men and women who peopled his tales rank him as an outstanding humanist among the world's literary masters.

A Yom Kippur Scandal

That's nothing!" called out the man with round eyes, like an ox, who had been sitting all this time in a corner by the window, smoking and listening to our stories of thefts, robberies and expropriations. "I'll tell you a story of a theft that took place in our town, in the synagogue itself, and on *Yom Kippur* at that! It is worth listening to.

"Our town, Kasrilevka—that's where I'm from, you know—is a small town, and a poor one. There is no thievery there. No one steals anything for the simple reason that there is nobody to steal from and nothing worth stealing. And besides, a Jew is not a thief by nature. That is, he may be a thief, but not the sort who will climb through a window or attack you with a knife. He will divert, pervert, subvert, and contravert as a matter of course; but he won't pull anything out of your pocket. He won't be caught like a common thief and led through the streets with a yellow placard on his back. Imagine, then, a theft taking place in Kasrelevka, and such a theft at that. Eighteen hundred *rubles* at one crack.

"Here is how it happened. One *Yom Kippur* eve, just before the evening services, a stranger arrived in our town, a salesman of some sort from Lithuania. He left his bag at an inn, and went forth immediately to look for a place of worship, and he came upon the old synagogue. Coming in just before the service began, he found the trustees around the collection plates. '*Sholom aleichem,*' said he. '*Aleichem sholom,*' they answered. 'Where does our guest hail from?' 'From Lithuania.' 'And your name?' 'Even your grandmother wouldn't know if I told her.' 'But you have come to our synagogue!' 'Where else should I go?' 'Then you want to pray here?' 'Can I help myself? What else can I do?' 'Then put something into the plate.' 'What did you think? That I was not going to pay?'

"To make a long story short, our guest took out three silver *rubles* and put them in the plate. Then he put a *ruble* into the cantor's plate, one into the rabbi's, gave one for the *cheder,* threw a half into the charity box, and then began to divide money among the poor who flocked to the door. And in our town we have so many poor people that if you really wanted to start giving, you could divide Rothschild's fortune among them.

"Impressed by his generosity, the men quickly found a place for him along the east wall. Where did they find room for him when all the places along the wall are occupied? Don't ask. Have you ever been at a celebration—a wedding or circumcision—when all the guests are already seated at the table, and suddenly there is a commotion outside—the rich uncle has arrived? What do you do? You push and shove and squeeze until a place is made for the rich relative. Squeezing is a Jewish custom. If no one squeezes us, we squeeze each other."

The man with the eyes that bulged like an ox's paused, looked at the crowd to see what effect his wit had on us, and went on.

"So our guest went up to his place of honor and called to the *shammes* to bring him a praying stand. He put on his *tallis* and started to pray. He prayed and he prayed, standing on his feet all the time. He never sat down or left his place all evening long or all the next day. To fast all day standing on one's feet, without ever sitting down—that only a Litvak can do!

"But when it was all over, when the final blast of the *shofar* had died down, the Day of Atonement had ended, and Chaim the *melamed,* who had led the evening prayers after *Yom Kippur* from time immemorial, had cleared his throat, and in his tremulous voice had already begun—'*Ma-a-riv a-ro-vim . . .*' suddenly screams were heard. 'Help! Help! Help!' We looked around: the stranger was stretched out on the floor in a dead faint. What was the trouble? Plenty! This Litvak tells us that he had brought with him to Kasrilevka eighteen hundred *rubles.* To leave that much at the inn—think of it, eighteen hundred *rubles*—he had been afraid. Whom could he trust with such a sum of money in a strange town? And yet, to keep it in his pocket on *Yom Kippur* was not exactly proper either. So at last this plan had occurred to him: he had taken the money to the synagogue and slipped it into the praying stand. Only a Litvak could do a thing like that! . . . Now do you see why he had not stepped away from the praying stand for a single minute? And yet during one of the many prayers when we all turn our face to the wall, someone must have stolen the money. . . .

"Well, the poor man wept, tore his hair, wrung his hands. What would he do with the money gone? It was not his own money, he said. He was only a clerk. The money was his employer's. He himself was a poor man, with a house full of children. There was nothing for him to do now but go out and drown himself, or hang himself right here in front of everybody.

"Hearing these words, the crowd stood petrified, forgetting that they had been fasting since the night before and it was time to go home and eat. It was a disgrace before a stranger a shame and a scandal in our own eyes. A theft like that—eighteen hundred *rubles!* And where? In the Holy of Holies, in the old synagogue of Kasrilevka. And on what day? On the holiest day of the year, on *Yom Kippur!* Such a thing had never been heard of before.

"*Shammes,* lock the door!" ordered our Rabbi. We have our own Rabbi in Kasrilevka, Reb Yozifel, a true man of God, a holy man. Not too sharp witted, perhaps, but a good man, a man with no bitterness in him. Sometimes he gets ideas that you would not hit upon if you had eighteen heads on your shoulders . . . When the door was locked, Reb Yozifel turned to the congregation, his face pale as death and his hands trembling, his eyes burning with a strange fire.

"He said, 'Listen to me, my friends, this is an ugly thing, a thing unheard of since the world was created—that here in Kasrilevka there should be a sinner, a renegade to his people, who would have the audacity to take from a stranger, a poor man with a family, a fortune like this. And on what day? On the holiest day of the year, on *Yom Kippur*, and perhaps at the last, most solemn moment—just before the *shofar* was blown! Such a thing has never happened anywhere. I cannot believe it is possible. It simply cannot be. But perhaps—who knows? Man is greedy, and the temptation—especially with a sum like this, eighteen hundred *rubles*, God forbid—is great enough. So if one of us was tempted, if he were fated to commit this evil on a day like this, we must probe the matter thoroughly, strike at the root of this whole affair. Heaven and earth have sworn that the truth must always rise as oil upon the waters. Therefore, my friends, let us search each other now, go through each other's garments, shake out our pockets—all of us from the oldest householder to the *shammes*, not leaving anyone out. Start with me. Search my pockets first.'

"Thus spoke Reb Yozifel, and he was the first to unbind his gabardine and turn his pockets inside out. And following his example all the men loosened their girdles and showed the linings of their pockets, too. They searched each other, they felt and shook one another, until they came to Lazer Yossel, who turned all colors and began to argue that, in the first place, the stranger was a swindler; that his story was the pure fabrication of a Litvak. No one had stolen any money from him. Couldn't they see that it was all a falsehood and a lie?

"The congregation began to clamor and shout. What did he mean by this? All the important men had allowed themselves to be searched, so why should Lazer Yossel escape? There are no privileged characters here. 'Search him! Search Him!' the crowd roared.

"Lazer Yossel saw that it was hopeless, and began to plead for mercy with tears in his eyes. He swore by all that was holy that he was as innocent in this as he would want to be of any wrongdoing as long as he lived. Then why didn't he want to be searched? It was a disgrace to him, he said. He begged them to have pity on his youth, not to bring this disgrace down on him. 'Do anything you wish with me', he said, 'but don't touch my pockets.' How do you like that? Do you suppose we listened to him?

"But wait . . . I forgot to tell you who this Lazer Yossel was. He was not a Kasrilevkite himself. He came from the Devil knows where, at the time of his marriage, to live with his wife's parents. The rich man of our town had dug him up somewhere for his daughter, boasted that he had found a rare nugget, a fitting match for a daughter like his. He knew a thousand pages of *Talmud* by heart, and all of the Bible. He was a master of Hebrew, arithmetic, bookkeeping, algebra, penmanship—in short, everything you could think of. When he arrived in Kasrilevka—this jewel of a young man—everyone came out to gaze at him. What sort of bargain had the rich man picked out? Well, to look at him you could tell nothing. He was a young man, something in trousers. Not bad looking, but with a nose a trifle too long, eyes that burned like two coals, and a sharp tongue. Our leading citizens began to work on him: tried him out on a page of *Gamorah,* a chapter from the Scriptures, a bit of *Rambam,* this, that and the other. He was perfect in everything, the dog! Whenever you went after him, he was at home. Reb Yozifel himself said he could have been a rabbi in any Jewish congregation. As for world affairs, there is nothing to talk about. We have an authority on such things in our town, Zaidel Reb Shaye's, but he could not hold a candle to Lazer Yossel. And when it came to chess—there was no one like him in all the world! Talk about versatile people . . . Naturally the whole town envied the rich man his find, but some of them felt he was a little too good to be true. He was too clever (and too much of anything is bad!). For a man of his station he was too free and easy, a hail-fellow-well-met , too familiar with all the young folk—boys, girls, and maybe even loose women. There were rumors . . . At the same time he went around alone too much, deep in thought. At the synagogue he came in last, put on his *tallis,* and with his skullcap on askew, thumbed aimlessly through his prayerbook without ever following the services. No one ever saw him doing anything exactly wrong, and yet people murmured that he was not a God-fearing man. Apparently a man cannot be perfect . . .

"And so, when his turn came to be searched and he refused to let them do it, that was all the proof most of the men needed that he was the one who had taken the money. He begged them to let him swear any oath they wished, begged them to chop him, roast him, cut him up—do anything but shake his pockets out. At this point even our Rabbi, Reb Yozifel, although he was a man we had never seen angry, lost his temper and started to shout.

" 'You!' he cried. 'You thus and thus! Do you know what you deserve? You see what all these men have endured. They were able to forget the disgrace and allowed themselves to be searched; but you want to be the only exception! God in heaven! Either confess and hand over the money, or let us see for ourselves what is in your pockets. You are trifling now with the entire Jewish community. Do you know what they can do to you?'

"To make a long story short, the men took hold of this young upstart, threw him down on the floor with force, and began to search him all over, shake out every one of his pockets. And finally they shook out . . . Well, guess what! A couple of well-gnawed chicken bones and a few dozen plum pits still moist from chewing. You can imagine what an impression this made—to discover food in the pockets of our prodigy on this holiest of fast days. Can you imagine the look on the young man's face, and on his father-in-law's? And on that of our poor Rabbi?

"Poor Reb Yozifel! He turned away in shame. He could look no one in the face. On *Yom Kippur*, and in his synagogue . . . As for the rest of us, hungry as we were, we could not stop talking about it all the way home. We rolled with laughter in the streets. Only Reb Yozifel walked home alone, his head bowed, full of grief, unable to look anyone in the eyes, as though the bones had been shaken out of his own pockets."

The story was apparently over. Unconcerned, the man with the round eyes on an ox turned back to the window and resumed smoking.

"Well," we all asked in one voice, "and what about the money?"

"What money?" asked the man innocently, watching the smoke he had exhaled.

"What do you mean—what money? The eighteen hundred *rubles*!"

"Oh, he drawled. "The eighteen hundred. They were gone."

"Gone?"

"Gone forever."

Haim Nahman Bialik (1873–1934)

Introduction

Haim Nahman Bialik is generally recognized as the greatest Hebrew poet of modern times. He engineered the renaissance of Hebrew poetry and revitalized the language in its poetic possibilities. He was essentially a lyric poet, but his poetry possesses great power.

Bialik was born to poor parents in a village in the Ukraine in 1873 and lost his father when he was seven. He went to study at the yeshiva at age fifteen but remained there only a few years. He moved to Odessa, which was then the intellectual center of Russian Jewry, in 1891, and began to move about in literary circles. Deeply influenced by articles written by Ahad Ha'am, he was attracted to Haskalah and the movement to revive Hebrew as a national language. Encouraged by Ahad Ha'am, who arranged for his first poem to be published, Bialik began to write. He did not yet think of himself as a writer, however, and had to leave Odessa in order to earn a living. He taught school for several years and then returned to Odessa in 1900, working as a teacher, poet, and literary editor of a weekly Hebrew journal. In 1903 he was sent to Kishinev by the Odessa relief committee to investigate the terrible pogrom that had taken place there. His encounter with the victims of the pogrom led to one of his most famous and influential poems, "The

City of Slaughter." In 1921, thanks to the intercession of Maxim Gorky, the Soviet government permitted him to leave and he went to Berlin, where he founded a publishing house. In 1924 he moved to Tel Aviv, where he devoted himself to cultural activities and public affairs.

Bialik, following Ahad Ha'am, was interested in a Jewish cultural revival, creating a modern culture that was secular, but recognized the value of the religious heritage. One of his major works, for example, was an anthology of Aggadah, rabbinic legends and folklore culled from the religious literature. He wanted to provide secular Jews who had no knowledge of this literature with an insight into the Jewish heritage and an appreciation of its humanistic content.

Bialik's national poetry laments the degeneration of the Jewish nation in the Diaspora and the decline of its ancient culture. He hoped to anger his readers enough to motivate them to carve out a new destiny. The poetry is critical of the egoism and pettiness that in his view pervaded Jewish society. He lamented the absence of Jewish pride and dignity at the time of the pogroms; his "City of Slaughter" was an outcry not only against God but also against Jewish passivity.

ON THE SLAUGHTER

Ah, Heavens, intercede for me!
If a god in you there be, and he hold concourse among you—
(He has eluded me)
Then you must pray for me!
Myself—my heart is numb and no more prayer to my lips may come,
Just helplessness and hopelessness remain—
How much longer, again and again?

Executioner! Take me by the throat and cut!

Behead me like a mutt, yours the forearm and the axe—
And all the earth for me—a rack—
And we—we are the few!
My blood is a free-for-all—now hew the skull and let the death-blood spurt,
The blood of infant and sage upon your shirt—
That it may not ever, ever be washed clean.

And if there be Justice—Let it enter now!
But if after I'm obliterated from under the heavens
Justice make its bow
May its throne be deposed forever!
And in eternal corruption may the firmament rot;
You too, villains, go, in your wickedness,
And live and suckle in your blood.

Ana cursed he who says, Avenge!
Such a vengeance, of a small child's blood,
Even Satan has not fashioned yet—
May that blood pierce the abyss!
Pierce the very depths of the abyss,
And feed in darkness and undermine
All the rotted pillars of this earth.

PART TWO
PATHBREAKERS

Simon Dubnow (1860–1941)

Introduction

Simon Dubnow, historian and theoretician, was one of the founding fathers of modern Jewish secularism and nationalism. He contributed decisively to the development of a Jewish history which was "sociological," i.e., not focusing primarily and almost exclusively on the Jews as a religious group. He conceived of the Jews as a living world people with a specific communal organization. He formulated a theory of the Jewish people as a "spiritual nation," maintaining that Jewish survival was the result of a specific capability to build successive "centers."

Dubnow was born in Byelorussia in 1860 into a family of rabbis and received a strict Orthodox education. Refusing to continue the study of Talmud after his bar mitzvah, he turned to secular studies on his own and was profoundly impressed by the writings of the Russian positivists and the English utilitarians (especially J. S. Mill). Subsequently he became an agnostic. At first, in the atmosphere of "liberalism" that prevailed during the reign of Tsar Alexander II, he assumed an assimilationist attitude, believing it possible for Jews to be absorbed into Russian society. The pogroms of the early 1880s, following the assassination of the tsar, changed his views radically. He became deeply involved in the study of Jewish history, and this gave him a foundation for Jewish pride and for a nonreligious yet strong Jewish identity. Convinced that the study of Jewish history could do for other Jews what it had done for him, Dubnow devoted his life to historical study and writing. His first published work was the *History of the Jews in Russia and Poland*. In 1922, after the Bolshevik Revolution, he moved to Berlin. It was there that he published his great multivolume *World History of the Jewish People*. After the rise of the Nazis he left Berlin for Riga. He lived there until 1941, when he was murdered by the Nazis at the age of eighty-one.

Dubnow regarded himself as a "religious agnostic" and declared that the writing of Jewish history must follow national and social rather than religious criteria. He defined the Jews as a nation rather than a religious group. To him, a nation was a collective composed of common memories, a sense of kinship, and the desire to affirm a single destiny. Jews were the archetype of a nation because they had passed through all the stages of national evolution: from primitive tribe to territorial-political entity, to creative forms of self-governance and the adaptation of its cultural forms to a wide range of differing conditions in the Diaspora. As a proponent of Diaspora nationalism, Dubnow believed that Jewish survival was not dependent on the establishment of a homeland; Jewish cultural activity would continue to flourish in the Diaspora as a minority but autonomous culture. This ideology, called "autonomism," was at first perceived as opposed to Zionism, but actually, what Dubnow objected to was the tendency he saw in Zionism to negate the Diaspora.

Dubnow was determined to have secular, agnostic Jews accepted as full members of the Jewish nation. Since he regarded Jewishness as synonymous with Jewish culture, of which religion was just one aspect, Jewish nationalism of necessity included all Jews, secular as well as religious.

NATIONALISM AND HISTORY

. . . Since religion completely dominated all spheres of Jewish life for two thousand years, the mass of orthodox Jews accepted the idea that Judaism is not a nationality in the accepted sense but a religious community living according to sacred traditions, laws and commandments that encompass the life of the individual and the community. The mass of the people who do not understand the interdependence of historic events failed to see that all the ancient national values of the Jewish nation—the historical festivals, customs and usages, laws, social institutions, the whole system of self-administration retained in the Diaspora—all had been incorporated gradually and artificially into the sphere of religion. The national body became wrapped in the garb of religion so that . . . its true form was unrecognizable.

In essence the views of the orthodox may be formulated as follows: "Judaism is a religious nation, its members are held together by religious ordinances and practical commandments; whoever violates this religion removes himself from the national community." This view is not opposed to the concept of a spiritual or cultural nation. It is mistaken only in the sense that it confuses the concepts of "spiritual" and "cultural" with "religious." It is the result of a limited perspective characteristic of men who do not distinguish between fossilized tradition and living, creative development. Let the mass of the orthodox consider nationality and religion as one, for the time being; . . . let them be satisfied with this partial understanding as long as they cannot arrive at a full and complete understanding based on theoretical analysis and research. In the end they too will see the light. The observing and believing Jew will realize that there are many Jewish freethinkers who, while disregarding the religious laws and commandments, are nevertheless true and dedicated members of their people and that they not only remain within the fold of Judaism but strive with all their power to strengthen and exalt it. From this realization it is but one step to theoretical analysis and research. These Jews will then come to differentiate religion from nationality, and the scientific study of history will reveal to them how these concepts came to be confused. When that happens the movement of the secularization of the national idea, which has already begun among an important segment of the community in modern times, will gain ground among the broad strata of the people.

While the mass of old-type orthodox Jews sees itself in practice as a religious nation and resists assimilation in the surrounding nations by the force of its faith, the assimilationist intelligentsia, on the other hand (mostly freethinkers or the neo-orthodox of the West), sees in Judaism only a religious community, a union of synagogues which imposes no national duties or discipline whatsoever on its members. According to this view, the Jew can become a member of another nation and remain a member of the Mosaic faith. He is a German Jew, for example, in the same way that there are German Protestants or German Catholics. It follows logically from this premise that a freethinking or non-religious Jew must be excluded from the community of Jews of the Mosaic faith. This corollary is usually glossed over so that whatever remains of Jewish "unity" may not be disturbed. I shall discuss this doctrine, which was in vogue only a short time ago but has recently lost ground among its adherents, in greater detail in the following Letters. Here I only wish to point out that it contradicts both the traditional view of many past generations that the "religious nation" must be kept pure, and the scientific view of the non-assimilabilitly of the spiritual or cultural nation. This kind of doctrine comes neither from religion nor from science. It is the invention of naive ideologues, or calculating opportunists, who seek to justify by means of this artificial doctrine their desire to assimilate into the foreign environment in order to benefit themselves and their children. This is but a repetition of the process of natural selection and of the weeding out of those weak elements of the nation which are unable to bear the pressure of the alien environment.

The natural tendency to strip the Jewish national idea of its religious cloak is liable to lead to still another extreme position. While the orthodox say: "The Jewish religion is the sole foundation of our nationality," the freethinkers can claim: "The Jewish religion is not at all a necessary condition of nationality; it can exist without it by virtue of the law of psychic heredity and cultural-historical factors." In practice this theory would make it possible to justify religious apostasy. A Jew could give up Judaism, embrace another religion, and still remain a Jew by nationality. Those who hold this view are guilty of a grave and dangerous error. By aspiring to secularism, by separating the national idea from religion, we aim only to negate the supremacy of religion, but not to eliminate it from the storehouse of national cultural treasures. If we wish to preserve Judaism as a cultural-historical type of nation, we must realize that the religion of Judaism is one of the integral foundations of national culture and that anyone who seeks to destroy it undermines the very basis of national existence. Between us and the orthodox Jews there is only this difference: they recognize a traditional Judaism the forms of which were set from the beginning for all eternity, while we believe in an evolutionary Judaism in which new and old forms are always being assumed or discarded and which adjusts itself unceasingly to new cultural conditions. Their main concern is holiness, ours is creative freedom. Here I may be asked: "And what of those who do not accept religion in general and the Jewish religion in particular?" This is a most important question and demands special attention.

Historical Judaism is not merely a religion, like Christianity or Islam. Judaism is a body of culture. Unique historical conditions which brought the life of the Jewish nation under the dominance of religion converted Judaism into an all-embracing world view which encompasses religious, ethical, social, messianic, political and philosophical elements. In each of these areas history has piled up layer upon layer. The Bible, the Talmud, Rabbinic Judaism, rationalist Jewish theology, Jewish mysticism are not merely chapters in Jewish religious teaching but also stages in the development of Judaism. Judaism is broad enough and variegated enough so that any man in Israel can draw from its source according to his spirit and outlook. . . .

. . . The call "Back to the Ghetto" is not a new one. We have heard it several times during the past decades. Insofar as this means "Back to the Jewish culture," or to "Judaism in the modern sense," it is part of the program of the national movement. But progressive Jews will never return to the *medieval* ghetto and its Judaism. The call "Back to God, to our Traditional Orthodoxy" will have as much success as similar calls issued by Christian Churches to their peoples. The religious masses will remain true to their faith, but the progressives will not be dragged back into the synagogue or the church.

A hundred years ago Samson Raphael Hirsch, the founder of neo-orthodoxy, proclaimed in his *Nineteen Letters* the following severe demand: "It is not the Torah that has to adapt itself to life, but life must adapt itself to the Torah." Yet recent generations have demonstrated that the pure core of Judaism can be preserved only by making adjustments to modern life. We now have a religious Judaism and a national Judaism, or a combination of the two. Let each party go its way. But no one has the right to claim a monopoly of all of Judaism for himself. Our divisions of opinion were created by the great historical processes which every living people experiences. The free competition of ideas must continue and the instinct of national survival will direct the oldest historical nation to the right path for its continued existence. . . .

The Sociological View of Jewish History

Only recently have we arrived at a more comprehensive and more strictly scientific conception of Jewish history that may be termed "sociological." Basic to this conception is the idea derived from the totality of our history, that the Jewish people has at all times and in all countries, always and everywhere, been the subject, the creator of its own history, not only in the intellectual sphere but also in the general sphere of social life. During the period of its political independence as well as in its stateless period, the Jews appear among the other nations, not merely as a religious community, but with the distinctive characteristics of a nation. This nation, endowed with perennial vitality, fought always and everywhere for its autonomous existence in the sphere of social life as well as in all other fields of cultural activity. Even at the time of the existence of the Judean state, the Diaspora had already attained high development and had its autonomous communities everywhere. Later on, it also had central organs of self-administration, its own legislative institutions (corresponding to the Sanhedrin, the academies and patriarchs in Roman-Byzantine Palestine; Exilarchs, Geonim, and legislative academies in Babylonia; the *aljamas* and congresses of communal delegates in Spain; *kahals* and *vaads*, or congresses of *kahals*, in Poland and Lithuania, etc.). The latest national movement among the Jews, linked as it is with this historical process and combining the older heritage of autonomism with the modern principle of national minority rights, testifies to the immortality of this eternal driving force of Jewish history. Even during the epoch of assimilation and of revolutionary change in the life of the people, it has been able to assert itself.

The causes of the one-sided conception of Jewish history, which was still widespread in the recent past, are obvious. Scientific Jewish historiography originated in western Europe in the middle of the nineteenth century, when the dogma of assimilation held complete sway there. This dogma asserted that Jewry is not a nation, but a religious community. Jewish historiography was also carried away by the general current and therefore concerned itself more with the religion of Judaism than with its living creator, the Jewish people. Even an opponent of this universally accepted dogma, like Graetz, was not able to go counter to this current. The profound evolution of national consciousness which characterizes our age inevitably wrought a transformation in our conception of the historical process. The secularization of the Jewish national idea was bound to effect the secularization of historical writing, liberating it from the shackles of theology and, subsequently, of spiritualism or scholasticism. A new conception of Jewish history came into being, a conception much more appropriate to the content as well as the scope of this history. Slowly the awareness grew that the Jewish people had not been entirely absorbed all these centuries by its "thought and suffering," but that it had concerned itself with constructing its life as a separate social unit, under the most varied conditions of existence, and that, therefore, it was the foremost task of historiography to try to understand this process of building the life of the Jewish people. . . .

The Significance of Jewish History

. . . We turn now to the question of the significance to be attached to Jewish history. In view of its peculiar qualities, what has it to offer to the present generation and to future generations as a subject of study and research?

The significance of Jewish history is twofold. It is at once national and universal. At present the fulcrum of Jewish national being lies in the historical consciousness. In the days of antiquity, the Jews were welded into a single united nation by the triple agencies of state, race, and religion, the complete array of material and spiritual forces directed to one point. Later, in the period of homelessness and dispersion, it was chiefly religious consciousness that cemented Jewry into a whole, and replaced the severed political bonds as well as the dulled racial instinct, which is bound to go on losing in keenness in proportion to the degree of removal from primitive conditions and native soil. In our days, when the liberal movements leavening the whole of mankind, if they have not completely shattered the religious consciousness, have at least, in an important section of Jewry, effected a change in its form; when abrupt differences of opinion with regard to questions of faith and cult are asserting their presence; and traditional Judaism developed in historical sequence is proving powerless to hold together the diverse factors of the national organism,—in these days the keystone of national unity seems to be the historical consciousness. Composed alike of physical, intellectual, and moral elements, of habits and views, of emotions and impressions nursed into being and perfection by the hereditary instinct active for thousand of years, this historical consciousness is a remarkably puzzling and complex psychic phenomenon. By our common memory of a great, stirring past and heroic deeds on the battle-fields of the spirit, by the exalted historical mission allotted to us, by our thorn-strewn pilgrim's path, our martyrdom assumed for the sake of our principles, by such moral ties, we Jews, whether consciously or unconsciously, are bound fast to one another. As Renan well says: "Common sorrow unites men more closely than common joy." A long chain of historical traditions is cast about us all like a strong ring. Our wonderful, unparalleled past attracts us with magnetic power. In the course of centuries, as generation followed generation, similarity of historical fortunes produces a mass of similar impressions which have crystallized, and have thrown off the deposit that may be called "the Jewish national soul." This is the soil in which, deep down, lies imbedded, as an unconscious element, the Jewish national *feeling* and as a conscious element, the Jewish national *idea*.

It follows that the Jewish national idea and the national feeling connected with it have their origin primarily in the historical consciousness, in a certain complex of ideas and psychic predispositions. These ideas and predispositions, the deposit left by the aggregate of historical impressions, are of necessity the common property of the whole nation, and they can be developed and quickened to a considerable degree by renewal of the impressions through the study of history. Upon the knowledge of history, then, depends the strength of the national consciousness.

The Teachings of Jewish History

Above all, Jewish history possesses the student with the conviction that Jewry at all times, even in the period of political independence, was pre-eminently a spiritual nation, and a spiritual nation it continues to be in our own days too. Furthermore, it inspires him with the belief that Jewry, being a spiritual entity, cannot suffer annihilation: the body, the mold, may be destroyed, the spirit is immortal. Bereft of country and dispersed as it is, the Jewish nation lives, and will go on living, because a creative principle permeates it, a principle that is the root of its being and an indigenous product of its history. This principle consists first in a sum of definite religious, moral, or philosophic ideals, whose exponent at all times was the Jewish people, either in its totality, or in the person of its most prominent representatives. Next, this principle consists in a sum of historical memories, recollections of what in the course of many centuries the Jewish people experienced, thought, and felt, in the depths of its being. Finally, it consists in the consciousness that true Judaism, which has accomplished great things for humanity in the past, has not yet played out its part, and, therefore, may not perish. In short the Jewish people lives because it contains a living soul which refuses to separate from its integument, and cannot be forced out of it by heavy trials and misfortunes, such as would unfailingly inflict mortal injury upon less sturdy organisms. . . .

. . . "The privilege of belonging to a people to whom the honorable title of the 'veteran of history' has been conceded, puts serious responsibilities on your shoulders. You must demonstrate that you are worthy of your heroic past. The descendants of teachers of religion and martyrs of the faith dare not be insignificant, not to say wicked. If the long centuries of wandering and misery have inoculated you with faults, extirpate them in the name of the exalted moral ideals whose bearers you were commissioned to be. If, in the course of time, elements out of harmony with your essential being have fastened upon your mind, cast them out, purify yourselves. In all places and at all times, in joy and in sorrow, you must aim to live for the higher, the spiritual interests. But never may you deem yourself perfect. If you become faithless to these sacred principles, you sever the bonds that unite you with the most vital elements of your past, with the first cause of your national existence."

The final lesson to be learned is that in the sunny days of mankind's history, in which reason, justice, and philanthropic instinct had the upper hand, the Jews steadfastly made common cause with the other nations. Hand in hand with them, they trod the path leading to perfection. But in the dark days, during the reign of rude force, prejudice, and passion, of which they were the first victims, the Jews retired from the world, withdrew into their shell, to await better days. Union with mankind at large, on the basis of the spiritual and the intellectual, the goal set up by the Jewish Prophets in their sublime vision of the future (Isaiah, ch. ii, and Micah, ch. iv), is the ultimate ideal of Judaism's noblest votaries. Will their radiant hope ever attain to realization?

If ever it should be realized,—and it is incumbent upon us to believe that it will,—not a slight part of the merits involved will be due to Jewish history. We have adverted to the lofty moral and humanitarian significance of Jewish history, in its role as conciliator. With regard to one-half of Jewish history, this conciliatory power is even now a well-established fact. The first part of Jewish history, the Biblical part, is a source from which for many centuries, millions of human beings belonging to the most diverse denominations have derived instruction, solace, and inspiration. It is read with devotion by Christians in both hemispheres, in their houses and their temples. Its heroes have long ago become types, incarnations of great ideas. The events it relates serve as living ethical formulas. But a time will come—perhaps it is not very far off—when the second half of Jewish history, the record of the two thousand years of the Jewish people's life after the Biblical period, will be accorded the same treatment. This latter part of Jewish history is not yet known, and many, in the thrall of prejudice, do not wish to know it. But ere long it will be known and appreciated. For the thinking portion of mankind it will be a source of uplifting moral and philosophical teaching. The thousand years' martyrdom of the Jewish people, its unbroken pilgrimage, its tragic fate, its teachers of religion, its martyrs, philosophers, champions, this whole epic will in the days to come sink deep into the memory of men. It will speak to the heart and the conscience of men, not merely to their curious mind. It will secure respect for the silvery hair of the Jewish people, a people of thinkers and sufferers. It will dispense consolation to the afflicted, and by its examples of spiritual steadfastness and self-denial encourage martyrs in their devotion. It is our firm conviction that the time is approaching in which the second half of Jewish history will be to the noblest part of *thinking* humanity what its first half has long been to *believing* humanity, a source of sublime moral truths. In this sense, Jewish history in its entirety is the pledge of the spiritual union between the Jews and the rest of the nations.

Haim Zhitlovsky (1865–1943)

Introduction

Haim Zhitlovsky has been called an architect of American Jewish secularism. Clearly he was one of the most visionary and dedicated philosophers of Jewish secularism as well as a teacher and political activist.

Zhitlovsky, born in 1865 in Byelorussia, received a traditional Jewish education. In his early teens, however, he turned to general studies and became an advocate of Jewish assimilation into Russian society. Shortly thereafter he became active in the Russian revolutionary movement; but the pogroms of the early 1880s made him return to Jewish interests. In 1885 he organized a Jewish socialist revolutionary group which was anti-Zionist and promoted the idea of progressive Jewish nationalism built on socialist foundations.

In 1888 he had to leave Russia "for political reasons," moving to Berlin and later to Switzerland. There he studied at the universities of Zurich and Bern and received a doctorate in 1892. At about that same time he was one of the founders of the Russian Socialist Revolutionary Party.

Returning to Russia in 1905, Zhitlovsky participated actively in politics, but his election to the Duma was invalidated by the tsarist government. He left Russia in 1907 and came to the United States, where he began a campaign on behalf of socialist Jewish nationalism. The next year he helped organize the Czernowitz Conference, an international gathering that proclaimed Yiddish the national language of the Jews.

In the United States Zhitlovsky worked as an editor, public speaker, and Jewish socialist leader. He founded a periodical, *Neilebn,* for which he wrote a continuing series of essays on Jewish and general philosophical problems. In 1910 he published a systematic history of philosophy in Yiddish. He remained an active member of the progressive Jewish community until his death in 1943.

Zhitlovsky was a staunch critic of assimilation and an advocate of secular Jewish nationalism based on Yiddish, humanist, and socialist ideals. Among the first to argue for the establishment of Jewish secular schools, he believed that Jews were a nationality with a historic culture whose central characteristic was the Yiddish language. The Jewish religion, he felt, had the power to thwart the free advancement of the individual. Yiddish would unite all segments of the Jewish people and give individuals the freedom to accept or reject religious belief.

Death and Rebirth of Gods and Religion

Religions and gods are born in holiness, grow old in decay, die alone behind a fence somewhere, rejected and forgotten, and then are resurrected to everlasting life in the Paradise of human poetry.

The Jewish religion too experienced an internal period of decay in the hearts of those who once fervently believed in it. But when the *apikoyres* [non-believer] stopped believing in the truths of his religion it did not become a totally alien thing for him, something that he could forget about. On the contrary, sooner or later it became a sort of hostile force which it was a *mitzva* [commandment] for him to combat. Its commandments and its sins were not abolished for him; he observed practically all of them—but in reverse.

Whereas previously he had sought to find favor in the eyes of a God in whom he believed, he now tried hard to defy the God in whom he did not believe. More accurately, to become a thorn in the eyes of people who still stuck to their old beliefs. If formerly it was forbidden to smoke on shabbos, to eat on Yom Kippur, to live with a woman without benefit of *khupah and kedusshin* [marriage ceremony], it now became a kind of *mitzva* to smoke on shabbos, to organize Yom Kippur parties, and not to have his love sanctified by a rabbi or by a ceremony of any kind. The decay was thus intensified into something unwholesome that had to be avoided at all costs. (The Hebrew word for this "impurity" is *tumah,* also pronounced *timah.*)

But gradually the "tumah" recedes, the anger fades, and the urge to fight an opponent who doesn't even exist grows weaker and weaker. The *apikoyres* sees Jews running to shul on *Succos* with lulavs in their hands, he sees *shabbos* candles twinkling on a table, but all this leaves him cold. It arouses neither love nor hate in him—it has nothing to do with him at all!

But gods are born to eternal life. For the Jewish religion a period of resurrection began in the paradise of human poetry. Yizhok Leyb Peretz was the first Yiddish writer to revivify, to poeticize, the religious world of Hasidism which at one time had evoked among enlightened Jews the bitterest feelings of *tumah.* The hasid's deeply religious soul, his exaltation, his mystical faith—today they are no longer foreign to us, nor do we consider them repulsive indignities. They are surrounded by a glow of supernatural poetry. They are a slice of human nature in a poetic-religious gestalt.

The same is true of other religious customs and emotions. They are no longer strange even to the most rational or the militant atheist. When we sit at a meeting and we all stand up together to honor a fallen hero, is this not really a kind of religious ceremony into which we pour our unspoken feelings of reverence? The same psychological transference takes place in the modern non-believer with regard to ceremonies that are part of the ancient Jewish religion. When he listens to the lament of the cantor on Tisha b'av, when his eyes follow the graceful undulations of the slender willow-branches on Succos, when he watches his mother bless the Sabbath candles, for him at that moment these ceremonies are not supernatural commandments but the poetic embodiment of thoughts and feelings that he considers humanly sanctified.

It would be a mistake to think that the four stages of this biography of the gods follow each other in strict sequence, like the stages of a living organism. Sometimes a stage is skipped. Sometimes all the stages live among a people at one and the same time. When this occurs in one and the same household, it can sometimes lead to tragedy.

Like poetry and philosophy, religion is an everlasting branch on the tree of human culture. Its leaves may wither and fall, but others sprout in their place. The source of religion is an eternal wellspring—the yearning of the human soul for a better and more beautiful world. As Ludwig Feuerbach put it: "God is a tear that human beings weep over their own destiny." And the wellsprings of such tears will never dry up.

The National Poetic Rebirth of the Jewish People

Since I wrote down the ideas in my first essay, a lot of water has flowed under the bridge, but the process of poetic rebirth which the Jewish religion is now going through has grown stronger rather than weaker. In Russia and Galicia, and even in America—where the growth of Jewish consciousness is so distorted by the bizarre national situation there—the process of rebirth is visible. Much of this is due to the *national* revival of the Jewish people now taking place all over the Diaspora.

Now, every religious yearning—for God, for holiness, for "something outside ourselves," for something transcendent—is a kind of poetry. *But this is not the kind of rebirth of the Jewish religion that I have in mind.* I am talking about conscious poetic expression, where religious images, myths and ceremonies become precious to us not because we believe in their divine origin, but because our spirit is moved by their human beauty. They evoke in us such poetic feelings and thoughts that we consider them humanistic sanctities. Only this kind of rebirth can remain free of any metaphysical and theological traces.

With the appearance of modern Jewish nationalism and its acceptance by the masses of our people, the possibility of a world-view is created that neither rejects its own people nor spits in the face of its religious parents. One should not imagine, however, that this rebirth is a sort of program with a ready-made *shulkhan-arukh* [Jewish code of law] or even with a clearly formulated statement of principles. It is rather a mood, an approach.

This process is taking place among other peoples too, but with us the matter is more complicated. The problems of cultural evolution among most peoples of the world are simpler because the physical existence of most European peoples is not in danger. Most of them at least live in their own land, which in itself is a strong safeguard against national extinction. Significant as it is, religion is not the only cultural form in which their national uniqueness is expressed.

So we who believe in the rational interpretation of human development need to pose the problem even more sharply: What can we do, so that the national and progressive factors in our culture can better compete with the religious traditions? Can we pour into the old religious forms themselves a content that will be in complete accord with our views? Or is there in the old forms themselves a content that can be cleansed of all the supernatural accretions and still retain enough attraction for the people? In my opinion, the answer to both these questions is Yes.

We believe that no matter how divine a god or a religious concept may appear, it has grown out of human needs and human ideals. The movement for a national poetic rebirth of the Jewish religion therefore has to examine all the old sanctities critically. It will reject those in which the human essence has been entirely eroded. It will preserve those that still retain their human essence. Already a large section of our generation is working at this task.

It goes without saying that we must put aside any discussion of the universal Jewish God, even the rarefied Holy Being of Jewish religious philosophy, which reached its highest stage in Spinoza's pantheism. This concept belongs to the supernatural world and for the modern religious believer it remains a living, eternal God in the simplest sense of the term, a divine power that cannot be transformed into a poetic symbol. Secularists must leave God alone—let Jewish theology concern itself with Him. . . .

[Zhitlovsky concludes his essay by replying to a critic who charged him with trying to create a new Reform movement. In his response Zhitlovsky says that one of the mistakes of the Reform movement was that it cut out the soul upon which the entire vital strength of the Jewish people rests, namely, the belief in its future national rebirth.] Should anyone challenge me, what is the soul of *your* "national poetic rebirth"?, I would reply:

"The common hope for the national rebirth of the Jewish people and the common belief in *Moshiakh's tseit*—a better world in the future—when the ideals of our prophets will be realized and all the people of the earth will live peacefully together in one common humanity—in this belief and in the work to bring that time closer lies the soul of the national poetic rebirth of the Jewish people."

Micah Joseph Berdichevsky (1865–1921)

Introduction

Micah Joseph Berdichevsky, Hebrew author and indefatigable collector of Jewish folklore, has been called the *enfant terrible* of modern Hebrew letters. He sharply rejected the synthesis between traditional Judaism and modernity proposed by Ahad Ha'am and insisted that as individuals we have to throw over the weight of the past in order to find our authentic self and our own creative impulses. Echoing Nietzsche, Berdichevsky called on the Jewish people to undergo a "transvaluation of its values" if they were going to survive.

Berdichevsky's origins made him an unlikely rebel. He was born in the Ukraine, heir to a long chain of Hasidic rabbis, and was a gifted talmudic scholar. His great intellectual curiosity, however, led him to read nonreligious and secular books; caught in this crime by his pious father-in-law, his marriage was dissolved and he was thrown into the streets to live the life of a poor student. After 1890 he lived in Switzerland and then Germany; he spent the rest of his life studying philosophy, writing novels, essays, and stories in Hebrew, as well as in Yiddish and German. He published collections of folk legends from the Talmud, and from the post-talmudic and Hasidic periods, lending them his individual style and interpretation.

In his Hebrew writings, which fill twenty volumes, Berdichevsky expounded his major ideas about Judaism. He vehemently rejected Orthodox Judaism, believing it made Jews passive and parochial. He championed the rights of the individual against what he termed the stifling and oppressive dogmas of traditional Judaism. The heroes of the Jewish past were the dissenters, the heretics, and the false prophets. Rejecting Ahad Ha'am's resolution of the conflict between tradition and the present through a stress on a spiritual, cultural revival, Berdichevsky called for Jewish participation in the realities of the modern age. His thesis that the religion of the early Israelites, nature-loving farmer-warriors, had been transformed into one suited to nature-rejecting, weak, shtetl-ghetto recluses, had a considerable impact on young Jews. Berdichevsky believed that Jewish regeneration was possible only thorough a revitalization of the individual Jew, living a humanistic, secular Jewish existence.

Wrecking and Building

This time in which we live is not like yesterday or the day before—it has no counterpart, for all the bases and conditions of our previous existence are now undermined and changed. The "long, dark night" is gone, and new days, with new circumstances, have replaced it. There is reason for the fear in our hearts—it is true that we are no longer standing on a clear road; we have come to a time of two worlds in conflict: To be or not to be! To be the last Jews or the first Hebrews.

Our people has come to its crisis, its inner and outer slavery has passed all bounds, and it now stands one step from spiritual and material annihilation. Is it any wonder that all who know in their hearts the burden, the implications, and the "dread" of such an hour should pit their whole souls on the side of life against annihilation? And this, too, such men must feel: that a new life must arise, broader in scope and different in condition from what has been. In devoting ourselves to the essential task, the resurrection of the people, we cannot even be indulgent to its tradition.

It is true that our past is that which gives us an historic claim and title to live on in the future; and as we go forward in our struggle for existence we look back to the day of Judah's bannered camp, to our heroes and ancient men of war, to our sages, the beacons of our spirit. Yet we cannot hide from ourselves that our ancestral heritage is not entirely an asset; it has also caused us great loss.

After the destruction of the Temple our political status declined and our independence came to an end. We ceased to be a people actively adding to its spiritual and material store and living in unbroken continuity with its earlier days. As our creativity diminished, the past—whatever had once been done and said among us, our legacy of thoughts and deeds—became the center of our existence, the main support of our life. The Jews became secondary to Judaism.

All sentiments of survival, all vital desires that had swelled the hearts of Jacob's children in former times, sought an outlet through these channels. Many thought that they could satisfy the national conscience that lived in their hearts by preserving what had been handed down from their ancestors.

Apart from turning us into spiritual slaves, men whose natural forces had dried up and whose relation to life and to the world was no longer normal, this brought about the great interruption in our social and political development, an interruption that has almost led us to total decay.

Our young people were made to believe that spiritual attachment to the Jewish people necessarily meant faith in a fixed and parochial outlook, so they turned away and left us, for their souls sought another way.

We are torn to shreds: at one extreme, some leave the House of Israel to venture among foreign peoples, devoting to them the service of their hearts and spirits and offering their strength to strangers; while at the other extreme, the pious sit in their gloomy caverns, obeying and preserving what God had commanded them. And the enlightened, standing between, are men of two faces: half Western—in their daily life and thoughts; and half Jews—in their synagogues. Our vital forces disperse while the nation crumbles.

For all the yearning for a revival which has begun to awaken in the hearts of the remaining few, we feel that such a revival must encompass both the inner and the outer life. It cannot arise other than by a total overturn, that is, by a transvaluation of the values which have been the guide lines of our lives in the past.

Our hearts, ardent for life, sense that the resurrection of Israel depends on a revolution—the Jews must come first, before Judaism—the living man, before the legacy of his ancestors.

We must cease to be Jews by virtue of an abstract Judaism and become Jews in our own right, as a living and developing nationality. The traditional "credo" is no longer enough for us.

We desire to elevate our power of thought, to enrich our spirit, and to enlarge our capacity for action; but let us never force our spirits into set forms which prescribe for us what we may think and feel.

It is not reforms but transvaluations that we need—fundamental transvaluations in the whole course of our life, in our thoughts, in our very souls.

Jewish scholarship and religion are not the basic values—every man may be as much or as little devoted to them as he wills. But the people of Israel come before them—"Israel precedes the Torah."

The world about us, life in all its aspects, the many desires, resolves, and dispositions in our hearts—all these concern us as they would any man and affect the integrity of our soul. We can no longer solve the riddles of life in the old ways, or live and act as our ancestors did. We are the sons, and sons of sons, of older generations, but not their living monuments. . . .

We must cease to be tablets on which books are transcribed and thoughts handed down to us—always handed down.

Through a basic revision of the very foundations of Israel's inner and outer life, our whole consciousness, our predispositions, thoughts, feelings, desires, and will and aim will be transformed: and we shall live and stand fast.

Such a fundamental revision in the people's condition, the basic drive toward freedom, and the boundless urge to new life will revive our souls. Transvaluation is like a flowing spring. It revives whatever is in us, in the secret places of the soul. Our powers are filled with a new, life-giving content.

Such a choice promises us a noble future; the alternative is to remain a straying people following its erring shepherds. A great responsibility rests upon us, for everything lies in our hands. We are the last Jews—or we are the first of a new nation.

Max Nordau (1849–1923)

Introduction

Max Nordau, although distinguished in his lifetime as a writer and literary critic of society, is remembered today only as Herzl's most important collaborator and disciple. Yet at the time of the founding of the World Zionist Organization, Nordau was the better known of the two men.

Nordau was born in Budapest, the birthplace also of Herzl, in 1849. Because his father was a rabbi and Hebrew teacher, Nordau received a traditional Jewish education but he ceased to be an observant Jew in his late teens. He studied medicine at the University of Budapest but was already pursuing a career in journalism at the same time. A few years after receiving his M.D. degree, he moved to Paris, where he served as correspondent for several German-language newspapers while also practicing medicine. In 1883 his *Conventional Lies of Our Civilization* was published. The first of his books to be viewed as scandalous, it became an international best seller. In it, using scientific analysis and positivist philosophy, he harshly criticized the cultural conventions of society and was particularly brutal in attacking religion. He proposed, as an alternative, a new philosophy of human solidarity. He followed this attack with two other volumes, *Paradoxes* and *Degeneration,* in which he named specific writers as hypocrites and degenerates. In later books he proposed an evolutionary ethics to replace religion. He also wrote plays and short stories.

During the Dreyfus affair, Nordau was profoundly affected by the antisemitism he witnessed, and so, when his friend Herzl came to discuss his Zionist ideas with him in 1896, Nordau was ready to be totally supportive. In his speech to the first Zionist Congress in 1897, Nordau gave a shattering analysis of the crisis of the Jewish people, particularly those Western Jews just coming out of the ghettos. At each of the subsequent congresses for many years he provided such excellent surveys of the conditions affecting world Jewry that they became famous among the Zionists.

A few years after Herzl's death, Nordau found himself becoming alienated from the new leadership of the Zionist movement. He was implacably opposed to the spiritual, cultural Zionism of Ahad Ha'am. Nordau believed that political Zionism, the founding of a Jewish state in Palestine, was essential in order to avert a major crisis for European Jewry. Later he opposed the pragmatic settlement policies of Chaim Weizmann for the same reason.

Declaring himself to be a pacifist, he was forced to leave France during World War I and moved to Madrid, where he spent his time writing. He was permitted to return to Paris in 1920 and died there in 1923. He was later reburied in Tel Aviv.

THE CONVENTIONAL LIES OF OUR CIVILIZATION

. . . Historical investigations have revealed to us the origin and growth of the Bible; we know that by this name we designate a collection of writings, as radically unlike in origin, character and contents, as if the Nibelungen Lied, Mirabeau's speeches, Heine's love poems and a manual of zoology, had been printed and mixed up promiscuously, and then bound into one volume. We find collected in this book the superstitious beliefs of the ancient inhabitants of Palestine, with indistinct echoes of Indian and Persian fables, mistaken imitations of Egyptian theories and customs, historical chronicles as dry as they are unreliable, and miscellaneous poems, amatory, human and Jewish-national, which are rarely distinguished by beauties of the highest order, but frequently by superfluity of expression, coarseness, bad taste and genuine Oriental sensuality. As a literary monument the Bible is of much later origin than the Vedas; as a work of literary value it is surpassed by everything written in the last two thousand years by authors even of the second rank, and to compare it seriously with the productions of Homer, Sophocles, Dante, Shakespeare or Goethe, would require a fanaticized mind that had entirely lost its power of judgment; its conception of the universe is childish, and its morality revolting, as revealed in the malicious vengeance attributed to God in the Old Testament and in the New, the parable of the laborers of the eleventh hour and the episodes of Mary Magdalen and the woman taken in adultery. And yet men, cultivated and capable of forming a just estimate, pretend to reverence this ancient work, they refuse to allow it to be discussed and criticized like any other production of the human intellect, they found societies and place enormous sums at their disposal to print millions of copies of it, which they distribute all over the world, and they pretend to be edified and inspired when they read in it.

The formulas used in public worship by all established religions are founded upon ideas and customs which originated in the most ancient barbaric periods, in Asia and northern Africa. We can see the traces of the worship of the sun by the Aryans, of the mysticism of the Buddhists and of the worship of Isis and Osiris by the Egyptians, in the observances and prayers of public worship and in the festivals and offerings of Jews and Christians of the present day. And the people of the Nineteenth Century assume a reverent and solemn expression as they repeat the kneelings, gestures, ceremonies and prayers invented thousands of years ago, on the banks of the Nile or the Ganges, by the miserable, undeveloped human beings of the stone or bronze ages, to manifest in some material way their conceptions of the universe, its origin and its laws—all, conceptions of the rankest heathenism.

As we study this disgraceful comedy, the more we expose to view the grotesque contrast between the modern tone of mind and the established religions, the more difficult does it become to speak calmly and dispassionately on this subject. The inconsistency is so superhumanly nonsensical, so gigantic, that the arguments set forth in detail against it, appear as inadequate and inefficient as a broom to sweep out the sands of Sahara; only the satire of a Rabelais or the inkstand of a Luther thrown against it, could do it justice. . . .

. . . Every separate act of a religious ceremony becomes a fraud and a criminal satire when performed by a cultivated man of this Nineteenth Century.

He sprinkles himself with holy water, and expresses by the act his conviction that the priest who said certain words over it, accompanied by certain gestures, had conferred some mysterious virtues upon it, changing its nature in some way, although a chemical analysis of it would show that it differs in no respect from any other water, except in being a little more dirty. He repeats prayers, kneels, goes to church services with all their ceremonies, and thus asserts his conviction that there is a God, who enjoys prayers, gestures, incense and anthems, if the prayers are in certain stereotyped words, the gestures in certain prescribed forms, and the ceremonies presided over by persons in odd clothing, with robes and capes of such peculiar colors and shapes as no sensible man would ever dream of wearing. The fact that a liturgy or form of public worship once established, is observed with painful minuteness, can only be explained to a rational mind somewhat in this way: the priests learned from some good source, and acted upon this knowledge, that God not only had the vanity to insist upon praises, compliments and flattery being offered to Him as well as glorification of His goodness, His wisdom and His greatness, but combined with this vanity was the whim that He would only accept these praises and glorifications when they were offered according to a certain formula, never to be deviated from. And the men of our age of natural science pretend to reverence these liturgies, and will not allow any one to speak of them with the contempt they deserve.

More revolting and insufferable even than the lie of Religion as acted by the individual, is the same lie of Religion as acted by the community. The individual citizen although he belongs ostensibly to some established religion, and takes part in its ceremonies, often makes no secret of his disbelief in its superstitions, and refuses to be convinced that a certain form of words, repeated in concert by the congregation will suspend or alter the laws of nature, that the devil is driven out from an infant when sprinkled with holy water, or that the chanting and speech of a man in a black or white robe beside a corpse, will open the gates of Paradise to the soul of the dead man. But as a member of the community and of the body politic, this same citizen does not hesitate to declare necessary all the points claimed by the established religions, and he offers up to them all the substantial and spiritual sacrifices which the salaried minister of this superstition, recognized and supported by the State, may demand. The same Government that builds universities, schools and libraries, builds churches too; the same Government that pays salaries to professors, supports the ministers also; the same code of laws that compels children to go to school, forbids blasphemy and any expression of scorn or defiance of established religions. What do these incongruities mean? This is their meaning: we say that the earth stands still and the sun revolves around it, although science has proved the contrary beyond a doubt; that the earth is only about five thousand years old, and no monuments from Egypt or anywhere else, known to be thousands of years older, will be accepted as contradicting this fact. We are not imprisoned in lunatic asylums for asserting these incongruities to be reconcilable truths; we are not declared incapable of filling office and carrying on our business, although we have certainly given the most striking proofs of mental imbecility, and that we do not possess the intellectual qualifications for looking after our own affairs, much less the destinies of the country entrusted to us. As private citizens we assert that we do not believe in the existence of God, that the God of the established religions is the outgrowth of childish and undeveloped minds; but as members of the body politic, we declare any one holding such views to be guilty of blasphemy before the law and incapable of holding office. And this, notwithstanding the fact that no scientific or rational proof has ever been offered in evidence of the reality of God, that even the most enthusiastic theologian can produce no testimony to prove the existence of God, that approaches in clearness and convincing force, that offered by the archaeologian and geologist to prove the antiquity of the earth and its inhabitants, or by the astronomer to convince us of the revolution of the earth around the sun; notwithstanding the fact that a man is excused, even from a theological standpoint, much more readily when he doubts the existence of God, than when he questions the results of scientific investigations, which are capable of such overwhelming demonstration. . . .

Ahad Ha'am (1856–1927)

Introduction

Ahad Ha'am, the foremost exponent of "Spiritual Zionism," and one of the most revered intellectuals of the Zionist movement, was born as Asher Zvi Ginsburg in the Ukraine in 1856. His family were wealthy Hasidim and his early education was totally pious. Although he was a Talmud scholar, he found his way to "forbidden" learning as a teenager, and after exposure to the works of the Hebrew enlightenment and then to secular literature and philosophy, he lost his religious faith.

As a result of new tsarist regulations that Jews could not lease land, in 1886 his family had to leave the country estate where Ginsburg had grown up and move to Odessa. At that time Odessa was the intellectual center of Russian Jewry, and in 1889 Ginsburg published his first article, signing it Ahad Ha'am, "one of the people," since he did not believe himself to be a writer. That became his pen name for the remainder of his life. In 1896, in order to support his wife and children, he took on the job of editing *Ha-Shiloah,* the Hebrew monthly, seeing it as a platform to discuss contemporary Jewish problems. But in 1903, feeling burdened by the position, he took a job as an official of a tea company, traveling in its behalf and moving to its branch office in London in 1907. He remained in London until 1921, when he moved to Tel Aviv where he died in 1927.

Beginning with his first essay, Ahad Ha'am took a position distinct from other Zionist writers. He called for a cultural renaissance to take place in the Diaspora before Jews emigrated to Palestine. Judaism, he insisted, needed to undergo a cultural revival and modernization. Influenced by positivism as a philosophy, he saw traditional Orthodox Judaism as archaic but wanted secular modern Jewish culture to be built on the underlying foundations of the historical heritage of the Jewish tradition. The Jewish people, he believed, possessed a special genius in the field of religion and morals, and its quest for social justice served as the mainspring of the Jewish spirit. The Jewish creative spirit, however, as a result of emancipation, secularization, modernization, and assimilation, had fallen on hard times. Zionism was necessary to "save Judaism," to provide a place where the Jewish creative spirit could flourish again. He was opposed to the political, materialistic Zionism proposed by Herzl, which, Ahad Ha'am felt, could not solve the Jewish problem simply by giving poor and persecuted Jews a homeland. He denied that the Jewish spirit could develop fully in the Diaspora, as Dubnow proposed, because it would always remain a minority culture, caught in the shadow of some dominant national culture. The goal of Zionism, according to Ahad Ha'am, should be to create a national spiritual center in Palestine. A new Hebrew culture would be developed there which would form a new Judaism that would emanate out to the Diaspora. He believed, somewhat mystically, that the return of the Jews to their homeland would necessarily bring about a return of the Jewish people to its ancient role as a spiritual-moral creative force. Jewish survival would thus be assured as the new Judaism, secular but spiritually based on the religious tradition, would flourish in the national center in Palestine.

Ahad Ha'am also emphasized that the Jews who went to Palestine had to recognize the existence of the sizable Arab population there and avoid enraging it by thoughtless acts and supremacist policies and attitudes.

Ahad Ha'am's designation by critics as an "agnostic rabbi" recognizes that although he was an agnostic and a secularist, he held a positive attitude toward the Jewish religious heritage. He severely criticized the new generation of rejectionist secularists who advocated the creation of a new, totally secular Zionist-Jewish culture, devoid of the traditional past.

Jewish and Christian Ethics

. . . Judaism conceives its aim not as the salvation of the individual, but as the well-being and perfection of a group, of the Jewish people, and ultimately of the whole human race. That is to say, the aim is always defined in terms of a collectivity which has no defined and concrete form. In its most fruitful period, that of the Prophets and the divine revelation, Judaism had as yet no clear ideal of personal immortality or of reward and punishment after death. The religious and moral inspiration of the Prophets and their disciples was derived not from any belief of that kind, but from the conviction of their belonging to "the chosen people," which had according to their belief, a divine call to make its national life the embodiment of the highest form of religion and morality. Even in later times, when the Babylonian exile had put an end to the free national life of the Jews, and as a result the desire for individual salvation had come to play a part in the Jewish religious consciousness, the highest aim of Judaism still remained a collective aim. For proof of the truth of this statement there is no need to look further than the prayers in the daily and festival prayer-books, of which only a minority turn on the personal needs of the individual worshipper, while the majority deal with the concerns of the nation and of the whole human race.

Which of these two aims is the higher? This question has been endlessly debated; but the truth is that in this matter we cannot establish any scale of values. A man may attain to the highest level in his religious and moral life whether he is inspired by the one aim or by the other. But individual salvation certainly makes a stronger appeal to most men, and is more likely to kindle their imagination and to inspire them to strive after moral and religious perfection. If Judaism, unlike the other religions, prefers the collective aim, this is yet another instance of the characteristically Jewish tendency to abstractness and to the repudiation of the concrete form. So long as this tendency persists—so long, that is, as the Jewish people does not lose its essential character—no true Jew can be attracted by the doctrine of the Gospels, which rests wholly and solely on the pursuit of individual salvation.

The same tendency shows itself in yet another direction, and this perhaps the most important of all: I mean in regard to the basis of morality. That Jewish morality is based on justice, and the morality of the Gospels on love, has become a platitude; but it seems to me that not all those who draw this distinction fully appreciate its significance. It is usual to treat the difference as merely one of degree, the moral scale and its basis being the same in either case. Both doctrines, it is supposed, are directed against egoism; but the Christians claim that their religion has reached a higher point on the scale, and the Jews refused to admit this claim. Thus Christian commentators point proudly to the positive principle of the Gospels: "Whatsoever ye would that men should do unto you, do ye even so to them," and throw it in the teeth of Judaism, which has only the negative principle of Hillel: "Do not unto your neighbour what you would not have him do unto you."

But if we look deeper, we shall find that the difference between Judaism and Christianity on this point is not one of less or more, but is a fundamental difference of view as to what is the basis of moral conduct. It was not by accident that Hillel put his principle in the negative form; it was because the positive formulation is repugnant to the Jewish conception of the basis of morality. We should have no cause for satisfaction if we found the doctrine in its positive form attributed to Hillel in some text or other; we should question the authenticity of a text which put into Hillel's mouth a pronouncement so out of harmony with the spirit of Judaism.

The root of the distinction lies here also, as I have said, in the preference of Judaism for abstract principles. The moral law of the Gospels asks the "natural man" to reverse his natural attitude towards himself and others, and to put the "other" in the place of the "self"—that is, to replace straight-forward egoism by inverted egoism. For the altruism of the Gospels is neither more nor less than inverted egoism. Altruism and egoism alike deny the individual as such all objective moral value, and make him merely a means to a subjective end; but whereas egoism makes the "other" a means to the advantage of the "self," altruism does just the reverse. Judaism, however, gets rid of this subjective attitude entirely. Its morality is based on something abstract and objective, on *absolute justice*, which attaches moral value to the individual as such, without any distinction between the "self" and the "other." On this theory a man's sense of justice is the supreme judge both of his own actions and those of other men. This sense of justice must be made independent of individual relations, as though it were a separate entity; and before it all men, including the self, must be equal. All men, including the self, are under obligation to develop their lives and their faculties to the limit of their capacity, and at the same time each is under obligation to assist his neighbour's self-development, so far as he can. But just as I have no right to ruin another man's life for the sake of my own, so I have no right to ruin my own life for the sake of another's. Both of us are men, and both our lives have the same value before the throne of justice.

I know no better illustration of this point of view than the following well-known *B'raita* [rabbinic saying]: "Suppose two men journeying through the desert, only one of whom has a bottle of water. If both of them drink, they will both die; if one of them only drinks, he will reach safety. Ben P'tura held that it was better that both should drink and die, than that one should witness the death of his comrade. But Akiba refuted this view by citing the scriptural verse: 'and thy brother shall live with thee.' *With thee*—that is to say, thine own life comes before thy neighbour's" (*Baba M'zia*, 62a).

We do not know who Ben P'tura was; but we do know Akiba, and we may be sure that his is the authentic voice of Judaism. Ben P'tura, the altruist, does not value human life for its own sake; for him it is better that two lives should perish, where death demands no more than one, so long as the altruistic sentiment prevails. But Jewish morality looks at the question objectively. Every action that leads to loss of life is evil, even if it springs from the purest sentiments of love and compassion, and even if the victim is himself the agent. In the case before us, where it is possible to save one of the two lives, it is a moral duty to overcome the feeling of compassion, and to save what can be saved. But to save whom? Justice answers: let him who has the power save himself. Every man's life is entrusted to his keeping, and to preserve your own charge is a nearer duty than to preserve your neighbour's.

But when a man came to Raba, and asked him what he should do when one in authority threatened to kill him unless he would kill another man, Raba answered him: "Be killed and kill not. What hath told thee that thy blood is redder than his? Perhaps his blood is redder" (*Pesahim*, 25b). And Rashi, who generally gets to the root of the matter with his instinctive understanding of Judaism, correctly explains thus: "The question arises only because you know that no religious law is binding in the face of danger to life, and think that in this case also the prohibition of murder ceases to be binding because your own life is in danger. But this transgression is not like others. For do what you will, there must be a life lost. . . . How do you know that your life is more precious than his in the sight of God? Perhaps his life is more precious."

If a question like this were put to a Christian priest, we may be sure that he would begin to expatiate in glowing terms on a man's duty to sacrifice his life for another to "bear his cross" in the footsteps of his Messiah, so that he might win the kingdom of heaven—and so forth. But the Jewish teacher weighs the question in the scales of objective justice. As a life must be lost in any case, and nobody can say which of the two lives is more precious in God's sight, the plea that the law may be broken in order to save life does not entitle you to break the sixth commandment. You must therefore be killed, and not kill. But suppose the case reversed: suppose the question to be whether I can save another from death by giving my life instead of his. Raba would reply: "Let the other be killed, and do not destroy yourself. For do what you will there must be a life lost; and how do you know that his blood is redder than yours? Perhaps yours is redder." From the standpoint of Judaism every man's blood is as red as any other's; every soul is "precious in the sight of God," be it mine or another's. Consequently no man is at liberty to treat his life as his own property; no man may say: "I am endangering myself; what right have others to complain of that?" (Maimonides' Code, *Laws of Murder* XI.5). Jewish history of course records many cases of martyrdom, which will remain precious and sacred memories for all time. But these are not cases of one life given for the preservation of another similar life; they are sacrifices of human life for "the sanctification of the Name" (the religious and moral ideal) or for "the good of the community" (the religious and moral aim).

And justice demands that we rise above sentiment not only in deciding between the self and another, but also in deciding between two other persons. Forty years ago Abraham Geiger drew attention to the unique character of the Biblical injunction "Neither shalt thou countenance a poor man in his cause." All other moral codes warn us only against favouring the rich and powerful; the Gospels themselves favour the poor, and exaggerate their merits and the greatness that awaits them in the Kingdom of Heaven. All this is very well from the point of view of sentiment; but a morality based on justice rises above sentiment, and teaches us that, while charity is a virtue, and it is our duty to help the poor if we are able, we must not let compassion induce us to sin against justice by favouring the poor man in his suit.

According to Herbert Spencer, the pinnacle of moral development will be reached when the altruistic sentiment becomes a natural instinct, and human beings can find no greater pleasure than in working for the good of others. Similarly Judaism, in conformity with its own principles, looks forward to the development of morality to a point at which Justice will become an instinct with good men, so that in any given situation they will be able to apply the standard of absolute justice without any long process of reflection. They will feel even the slightest deviation from justice instantaneously, and with the certainty of intuition. Personal and social considerations will not affect them in the slightest degree; their instinct will judge every action with absolute impartiality, ignoring all human relations, and making no difference between X and Y, between the self and the other, between rich and poor. Such is the moral ideal of Judaism; and because Judaism links the fulfillment of its moral aspirations with the advent of the Messiah, it endows the Messiah with this faculty of intuitive justice. The Talmud (*Sanhedrin*, 93b) says of the Messiah that "he will smell and judge," on the basis of the scriptural verse (Isaiah xi.3): "And shall make him quick of understanding (Heb. 'smell') in the fear of the Lord; and he shall not judge after the sight of his eyes,"; and Kimhi comments on this verse as follows: "Because the sense of smell is a very delicate sense, he gives the name of smell to the most delicate perception—that is to say, the Messiah with little scrutiny will feel which men are good, and which evil."

But this development lies hidden in the bosom of a distant future. For the present the human race still lacks the instinctive sense of justice, and even the best men are apt to be so blinded by self-love or prejudice as to be unable to distinguish between good and evil. For the present, therefore, we all need some touchstone, some fundamental principle, to help us to avoid us weighting the scales of justice to suit our personal ends or inclinations. Hillel has given us such a principle: "Do not unto your neighbour what you would not have him to do unto you." Altruism would substitute: "Do unto your neighbor what you would like him to do unto you." In other words, take the circle of egoism, and put the "other" at its centre instead of the "self"; then you will know your whole duty. But Judaism cannot accept the altruistic principle; it cannot put the "other" in the centre of the circle, because that place belongs to justice, which knows no distinction between "self" and "other." But in the circle of egoism there is no place for justice except in a negative form. It will certainly be just not to do as egoism would not be done by; but to do as egoism would be done by—that is something without any limit, and to make it obligatory is to tilt the scales of justice to the side of the "other" and against the "self."

Even that "great principle of the Torah" (as Akiba called it) 'thou shalt love thy neighbour as thyself' (Leviticus xix.18), though in form it appears to be positive, is in reality, if rightly understood, negative. If the Torah had meant that a man must love his neighbour to the extent of sacrificing his life for him, it would have said: "Thou shalt love thy neighbour more than thyself." But when you love your neighbour *as* yourself, neither more nor less, your feelings are in a state of equilibrium, with no leaning either to your own side or to your neighbour's. The true meaning of the verse is "Self-love must not be allowed to incline the scale on the side of your own advantage; love your neighbour as yourself, and then justice will necessarily decide, and you will do nothing to your neighbour that you would consider a wrong if it were done to yourself." For proof that this is the real meaning we have only to look further in the same passage of Leviticus, where we find (*ib.* 33–34): "And if a stranger sojourn with thee in your land, ye shall not do him wrong. The stranger that sojourneth with you shall be unto you as the homeborn among you, and thou shalt love him as thyself." Here it is evident that to love the stranger "as thyself" means to carry out the negative precept "ye shall not do him wrong"; and if the stranger is expressly placed on the same footing as the native, this shows that in relation to the native also the intention is only that self-love must not prove a stronger motive than justice.

But in the Gospels "Thou shalt love thy neighbour as thyself" is interpreted in an altruistic sense: it means that your own life is less important than your neighbour's. Hence there is some excuse for the Christian habit of attributing this verse to the Gospels, as though it had originally appeared in the New and not in the Old Testament. It is true that the meaning which they put on the verse belongs not to the Mosaic Law, but to the Gospels.

But it must be remembered that in addition to the relation of individual to individual there is another and more important moral relation—that of nation to nation. Here, also, some great principle is needed to keep without bounds that national egoism which is fraught perhaps with even greater danger to the collective progress of humanity than individual egoism. If we look at the difference between Jewish and Christian ethical teaching with this requirement in mind, we shall see at once that the altruism of the Gospels provides no sort of basis for international relations. A nation can never believe that its moral duty lies in self-abasement or in the renunciation of its rights for the benefit of other nations. On the contrary, every nation feels and knows that its moral duty is to maintain its position and to use its opportunities to create conditions in which it can develop its potentialities to the full. But the Jewish law of justice is not confined within the narrow sphere of individual relations. In its Jewish sense the precept "Thou shalt love thy neighbour as thyself" can be carried out by a whole nation in its dealings with other nations. For this precept does not oblige a nation to sacrifice its life or its position for the benefit of others nations. It is, on the contrary, the duty of every nation, as of every individual human being, to live and to develop to the utmost limit of its powers; but at the same time it must recognize the right of other nations to fulfill the like duty without let or hindrance. Patriotism—that is, national egoism—must not induce it to disregard justice, and to seek self-fulfillment through the destruction of other nations. Hence Judaism was able thousands of years ago to enunciate the lofty ideal "Nation shall not lift up sword against nation" (Isaiah ii.4) because that ideal is no more than the logical consequence of the idea of absolute justice, which lies at the foundation of Judaism.

The People of the Book

The relation between a normal people and its literature is one of parallel development and mutual interaction. Literature responds to the demands of life, and life reacts to the guidance of literature. The function of literature is to plant the seed of new ideas and new desires; the seed once planted, life does the rest. The tender shoot is nurtured and brought to maturity by the spontaneous action of men's minds, and its growth is shaped by their needs. In time the new idea or desire becomes an organic part of consciousness, an independent dynamic force, no more related to its literary origin than is the work of a great writer to the primer from which he learnt at school.

But a "people of the book," unlike a normal people, is a slave to the book. It has surrendered its whole soul to the written word. The book ceases to be what it should be, a source of ever-new inspiration and moral strength; on the contrary, its function in life is to weaken and finally to crush all spontaneity of action and emotion, till men become wholly dependent on the written word and incapable of responding to any stimulus in nature or in human life without its permission and approval. Nor, even when that sanction is found, is the response simple and natural: it has to follow a prearranged and artificial plan. Consequently both the people and its book stand still from age to age; little or nothing changes, because the vital impulse to change is lacking on both sides. The people stagnate because heart and mind do not react directly and immediately to external events: the book stagnates because, as a result of this absence of direct reaction, heart and mind do not rise in revolt against the written word where it has ceased to be in harmony with current needs.

We Jews have been a people of the book in this sense for nearly two thousand years; but we were not always so. It goes without saying that we were not a people of the book in the era of the Prophets, from which we have traveled so far that we can no longer even understand it. But even in the period of the Second Temple heart and mind had not lost their spontaneity of action and their self-reliance. In those days it was still possible to find the source of the Law and the arbiter of the written word in the human heart, as witness the famous dictum of Hillel: "Do not unto your neighbour what you would not have him do unto you; that is the whole Law." If on occasion the spontaneity of thought and emotion brought them into conflict with the written word, they did not efface themselves in obedience to its dictates; they revolted against it where it no longer met their needs, and so forced upon it a development in consonance with their new requirements. For example: the Biblical law of "an eye for an eye" was felt by the more developed moral sense of a later age to be savage and unworthy of a civilized nation; and at that time the moral judgment of the people was still the highest tribunal. Consequently it was regarded as obvious that the written word, which was also authoritative, must have meant "the value of an eye for an eye," that is to say, a penalty in money and not in kind.

But this state of things did not endure. The Oral Law (which is really the inner law, the law of the moral sense) was itself reduced to writing and fossilized; and the moral sense was left with only one clear and firm conviction—that of its own utter impotence and its eternal subservience to the written word. Conscience no longer had any authority in its own right; not conscience, but the book became the arbiter in every human question. More than that: conscience had no longer the right even to approve of what the written word prescribed. So we are told that a Jew must not say he dislikes pork: to do so would be like the impudence of a slave who agrees with his master instead of unquestioningly doing his bidding. In such an atmosphere we need not be surprised that some commentators came to regard Hillel's moral interpretation of the Law as sacrilegious and found themselves compelled to explain away the finest saying in the Talmud. By "your neighbour," they said, Hillel really meant the Almighty: you are not to go against His will, because you would not like your neighbour to go against your will. And if the doctrine of "an eye for an eye" had been laid down in the Babylonian Talmud, not in the Mosaic Law, and its interpretation had consequently fallen not to the early Sages, but to the Talmudic commentators, they would doubtless have accepted the doctrine in its literal meaning; Rabbis and common people alike would have forcibly silenced the protest of their own moral sense against an explicit injunction, and would have claimed credit for doing so. . . .

The Supremacy of Reason

. . .[But] it is worth while to point out that most of the early opponents of Maimonides had no clear conception of the real nature of the innovation which he had introduced into Judaism. They all felt instinctively that his teaching involved a complete revolution in the Jewish outlook; but not all of them understood where the gravamen of the attack lay. For the most part they merely fastened on heresies of detail, such as the denial of resurrection, of hell and paradise, and so forth. Only a few of them understood that what was revolutionary was not the attitude of Maimonides on this or that point of detail, but his substitution of reason for faith as the supreme arbiter of opinion, and his enunciation of the principle that "whenever a Scripture is contradicted by proof we do not accept the Scripture," but interpret it in conformity with the dictates of reason.

This emancipation of reason from its subordination to an external authority is the great and lasting achievement which has so endeared Maimonides to all those of us who have sought after knowledge and enlightenment. The theoretical system on which Maimonides expended so much labour throughout the whole of his life was swept away long ago, together with the Arab metaphysics on which it was based. But the practical outcome of that system—the emancipation of reason—remains, and has left its mark on the evolution of the Jewish mind to the present day. Every product of the traditional Jewish system who has traveled the hard and bitter road that leads from blind faith to free reason must have come across Maimonides at the beginning of his journey, and must have found in him a source of strength and support for those first steps which are the hardest and the most dangerous. And that road, after all, was traveled not only by Moses Mendelssohn, but also by Spinoza, and before and after them by a whole host of intellectuals, many of whom have achieved distinction in Jewish life or outside.

Letters

. . . In my essay *Slavery in Freedom* I have, I think, shown clearly that religion alone does not account for our survival, and that the Western Jews, who assert that it does, tie themselves up in a hopeless tangle of paradoxes and sophistries, thereby proving that they are simply driven to take this line because they are afraid that they may lose their civil rights if they admit that the Jews are a separate nation. . . . But we East-European Jews are not prevented from seeing the truth by the lure of civil rights, because we are not given rights even if we foreswear our nationality; and we remain fully conscious that we are a distinct people, and that even those of us who throw off religion do not thereby abandon their people, because they know that religion is not the only bond that keeps us together.

. . . You also overlook the distinction between state and nation. In the political sense you are an Italian and I am a Russian; but in the national sense we are both simply Jews. If you look closely I think you will find even in Italy, perhaps even in your own congregation, Jews who are so remote from Jewish religious beliefs and observance that it is impossible to suppose that they are Jews only by religion, and who yet would sacrifice their lives for their nation, though they do not know themselves what is the compelling motive. . . .

To Rabbi E. Lolli (Padua), April 11, 1898

. . . I do not agree with you that it is the religious associations of Hebrew that have preserved it to our day, and that in these days of nationalism there is no hope for Hebrew except in becoming the vehicle of a literature which will appeal to the imagination. In my opinion the survival of Hebrew is due to the love of Torah, which used to spring from religious faith, but is now the outcome of national sentiment. What we need today is not a literature of devotion, but a literature of Jewish learning and scholarship, so that anybody in search of knowledge about any aspect of Jewish life or thought will be able to find all that he needs in Hebrew.

To Dr. S. Bernfeld (Berlin), March 8, 1899

. . . Experience everywhere, and especially in America, has shown that the Synagogue by itself, as a House of Prayer exclusively, cannot save Judaism, which, unlike other religions, does not depend on prayer. Nor can the separate House of Study, which is intended for young people in search of knowledge, serve as an instrument of *popular* education. What we have to do is revert to the system which our ancestors adopted in days gone by, and to which we owe our survival: we have to make the Synagogue itself the House of Study, with Jewish learning as its first concern and prayer as a secondary matter. Cut the prayers as short as you like, but make your Synagogue a haven of Jewish knowledge, alike for children and adults, for the educated and the ordinary folk. The sermon on Sabbaths and Holy Days must give the congregants instruction in Torah, not phrases of unctuous piety. But the sermon alone is not enough. The Synagogue must be the centre to which those who want to learn about Judaism resort to every day. "Readings" on Jewish subjects can be arranged every evening, for the more and the less educated separately. That is what our ancestors did, with good results. The spirit of the teaching must be different, to suit the altered conditions; but the system itself cannot be bettered. . . . But learning—learning—learning: that is the secret of Jewish survival.

. . . Clearly, then, if you want to build and not to destroy, you must teach religion on the basis of nationalism, with which it is inseparably intertwined. But when you talk of propagating "religious nationalism," I do not know what you mean. . . . Do you really think of excluding from the ranks of the nationalists all those who do not believe in the principles of religion? If that is your intention, I cannot agree. In my view our religion is national—that is to say, it is a product of our national spirit—but the reverse is not true. If it is impossible to be a Jew in the religious sense without acknowledging our nationality, it is possible to be a Jew in the national sense without accepting many things in which religion requires belief.

To Dr. J. Magnes (New York), Sept. 18, 1910

. . . I do not agree with you as regards the subordination of ethics to religion in Judaism; on the contrary, as I have suggested in various essays, I think that religious development has followed moral development. But certainly, as you say, "Jewish ethics cannot be understood except in the light of the ideas of Judaism."

To Dr. S. Schechter (Florence), March 29, 1911

. . . The answer to the question what Judaism is depends, of course, on the meaning one attaches to the vague terms "Judaism," "religion" and "culture." In the sense in which I understand these terms, I should say that religion itself is only one of the forms of culture, and that Judaism is neither the one nor the other, but is the national creative power, which in the past expressed itself in a primarily religious culture. In what form it will express itself in the future—that we cannot foretell.

To Dr. I. Abrahams (Cambridge), March 30, 1913

Ber Borochov (1881–1917)

Introduction

Until the beginning of the twentieth century, Zionism and Marxism were poised as mutually antagonistic ideologies. Zionism was regarded as a "bourgeois" nationalism, inimical to Marxist revolutionary theory. It was the brilliant achievement of Ber Borochov, therefore, to synthesize the two by providing a Marxist rationale for Zionism, leading him to become the major theoretician of Jewish socialism.

Borochov, whose father was a supporter of Hibbat Zion (Lovers of Zion), was raised in Poltava, in the Ukraine, a town that was a favorite for revolutionary exiles. His excellent formal education came to an end after high school. Having encountered antisemitism among his teachers, he did not want to endure more of it at the university level. He embarked on a career of political activism while continuing to educate himself and to travel. Expelled from the Russian Social Democratic Party because of his Zionism, he spent his time developing his Marxist-Zionist themes in research and writing. He founded Poale Zion (Workers of Zion) in 1906. He had to leave Russia in 1907 because of difficulties with the police and traveled about Europe as a party propagandist, serving as secretary of the world union of Poale Zion for several years.

Borochov came to the United States when World War I broke out and continued to develop his political ideology, working as a writer and editor. When the Kerensky government was established in 1917 Borochov returned to Russian to participate in the Congress of Minorities. He died in Kiev several months later of pneumonia.

In addition to his work as a political theoretician, Borochov was the founder of modern Yiddish studies. He searched through the libraries of Europe for the sources which would enable him to reconstruct the history of the Yiddish language and of its literature. He wrote several seminal articles on Yiddish philology.

The selection which follows is part of the program he wrote for Poale Zion in collaboration with Yizhak Ben-Zvi, the future second president of the state of Israel. Following Marx, Borochov distinguishes between reactionary and progressive national movements, designating Zionism as the latter. Instead of revolutionary bloodshed, dictatorship, enmity to national culture and to national movements, Borochov presents a vision of a humane Marxist Zionism based on the return of an exiled nonproductive people to a normal social structure, thereby contributing to world progress by creating a just socialist society in its own ancient land.

On Questions of Zionist Theory

We must not wait.

The Jewish people has suffered so much that greater affliction is inconceivable. Regarded objectively, our situation today, compared with the suffering experienced by our forefathers, can almost be envied, and there is every reason to believe that as time goes by our troubles will diminish. This gives support to the optimists among us, who take a hopeful view of the future in their opposition to Zionist action that aims to bring about a radical change in our situation and to put an end to the *Galut* [exile] episode with all its achievements. These optimists, since they value these achievements, try to prove to us that there is no need to be alarmed by the slowness of progress, on which they pin rosy hopes.

Objectively speaking, our position is already assured in a number of respects. The Inquisition—it is safe to assume—will not be renewed. Nor will mass expulsion ever occur again. But can the same be said when the question is viewed subjectively? On the basis of numerous experiments, psychologists have laid down the so-called Weber-Fechner Law, according to which the intensity of a sensation increases as the logarithm of the stimulus. If we translate this law from the language of mathematics to the language of life, it means that sensation increases at a much slower rate than the changes that take place in the environment, that as time goes by the individual pays less and less attention to these changes. Therefore, the more one's situation improves, the greater will be his demand for further improvement, and the longer will he have to wait to feel a real improvement in his environment that he regards as satisfactory. This explains the well-known fact that the most oppressed people are the least sensitive to their plight; they are content with their lot and only rarely complain. The surest way of making a slave dissatisfied and demanding is to alleviate the harshness of his lot. Some claim that our position has improved. I agree. But this very improvement has made us more sensitive: a reed of straw oppresses us more today than did the most savage torture rack in the past. The hostility of the environment, the restriction of civil rights, the pogroms, which in the past were facts of life we learned to live with, now strike us as horrible disasters. Our optimists fail to grasp this; for them progress has the brightness of the sun. But in reality, through the hazy glass of the Weber-Fechner Law, its light is becoming ever dimmer.

We have acquired more culture; we have lost our earlier faith in the world to come, in redemption by the Messiah, in our divine election—by virtue of which we allowed ourselves to look down on other nations, ignore their humiliating attitude, and regard it as conduct of creatures greatly inferior to us; hence they were unable, even by their most barbarous deeds, to upset our composure. One does not despair or lose his self-confidence just because he has been bitten by a dog. Today it is no longer a dog but one like ourselves who bites us, and his insults injure our honor. Formerly, religion and the ghetto constituted a wall that protected us against the enemy; but that protective wall has been undermined, and like all peoples of culture we have become sensitive to every affront to our rights, while externally our situation is much more difficult than theirs. Our optimists advise us to wait, to join forces with the progressive elements among the other nations, to help them in their struggle for the universal human ideal; they promise us and them victory over the reaction that oppresses us all.

But we Jews must not wait—and we Zionists cannot wait. Some among us fear that in the course of time, as a result of our stay in the *Galut* and the destructive effects of progress, the Jews will disintegrate and lose their national selfhood and national distinctiveness. Others say the persecutions will not cease and the forces threatening us will assault us again after a short interval—half a century at the most—when they will attack with even greater ferocity. Finally, there are those who, disregarding these apprehensions and dangers, think that this is the most opportune time for the Jews in their struggle for self-expression and national distinctiveness to pass from the purely passive resistance they have practiced for eighteen centuries to concrete, territorial creation. In any event, all of us regard our position in the *Galut* as unstable and our prospect gloomy, not only from a subjective viewpoint but even from an objective-historical one.

Be that as it may, it is our deep conviction that in the *Galut* there is no salvation for the Jewish people. We do not rely on progress; we know that its overpious proponents inflate its achievements out of all proportion. Progress is an important factor in the rapid development of technology, science, perhaps even of the arts, but certainly in the development of neurosis, hysteria, and prostitution. Of the moral progress of nations, of the end of that national egoism that is destroying their best—it is too soon to speak about these. Progress is a two-edged sword. If the good angel in a man advances, the Satan within him advances too.

It is hard to say which is the more amazing in our optimists: the naiveté of their enthusiasm or the dullness of their perception. They continue to sing hymns of praise to progress at a time when "cultured" England is cruelly grabbing from the Boers their last possessions—to the thunder of cannon and the applause of all classes of the English people; when "cultured" America is guilty of wanton despoliation of the Negroes; when Germany is threatening the entire world with its arrogant militarism; when the strong nations are prepared to trample one another for a piece of land in Turkey or China; while the weak nations groan in the world of the strong, yet pass up no opportunity to steal from one another or to demonstrate their might to peoples even weaker than they are. Most important, however, is that no one has yet succeeded in proving that he is right in trusting in the saving power of progress and in its real value. The rhetoricians and the believers are naive. It has not yet been proved that the historical process, the development of nations and society, is *progress*. Is it not improper to propose to the Jewish people to wait and put its trust in progress, when no one has yet succeeded in convincing us that such a thing actually exists?

But let us assume that it is true that all of mankind—including the inhabitants of Tierra del Fuego, the Fiji Islanders, the Japanese and the Kurds, and the anti-Semites of all varieties—will all be pacified and accept the peaceful reign of progress. But even you will not deny that such happiness cannot be attained without war and battles, you know that this war, which began some time ago, has cost and will cost mankind much blood and tears. What, then, is the price that we Jews will have to pay for it?

Let us take a small community, such as the Jews of Morocco. There are 300,000 Jews there, descendants of the exiles of Spain and Portugal in the fifteenth and sixteenth centuries, of the stock which gave to Judaism generations of distinguished personalities—scholars, poets, philosophers, and rabbis. A group of such superior descent deserves particular attention. But if the achievements of your progress must be attained by rivers of blood, by the degradation and torture of those Jews, is not the price of this boundlessly cruel idol of yours too high? For whom is the progress of Morocco desired? For those very Moroccans who drank the blood of Jews with such lust in the pogroms of 1903 and who violently abused women and children? The scraps of information available from the press show that the Moroccans have proved beyond any doubt that no upheaval will take place among them without bringing catastrophe to the Jews.

Certainly, progress cannot pass Morocco by; European states have already laid their predatory hands on that primitive country. Is it conceivable that the achievements of civilization will not arouse the hostility of the Moroccan masses, who hate everything foreign or European? Will such a revolution not be the end of the Jews in that country? Will nationalist hatred not be directed against the defenseless Jews because it cannot be directed against the well-protected predators of Europe? And will the Moroccan authorities be able to prevent this bloodshed, even if they should want to come to the aid of the Jews? Will they even want to? Will they not be pleased to divert the national passions away from themselves to the line of least resistance? Remember that even during the civil war over the throne, the Jews served as an excellent lighting rod the moment popular resentment threatened to burst over the heads of the pretenders to the throne.

The same fate awaits the Jews of Persia and other Eastern countries. These Jews will pay with their lives for the first steps of militant progress. Meanwhile, the Jews of the Moslem countries are sitting on a volcano, and those wise enough to foresee the future, who have joined the Zionist movement, are well aware of the horror of the situation. This is another reason why the Zionists cannot—have no right—to wait. Certainly, let all the nations enjoy the fruits of progress, but we do not wish to be their scapegoat. Even if we leave the *Galut* mankind will pay in blood and tears for every upheaval that occurs in its history, except that Jewish blood is not taken into account—it only serves as amusement for the raging mob. There are thousands of Moslems and hundreds of thousands of Jews; let progress be content with the thousands of Moslems.

It will be said that these fears are unreal. Such fears cannot arouse or give direction to a solid national movement, first because passing phenomena are liable to give rise to spontaneous eruptions rather than to conscious activity, and second, because a solid movement cannot expect quick success when immediate rescue from danger is called for. I agree with that entirely. I will go even further and say that the Jews in the past have been saved from graver dangers; they may have lost a tooth or an eye, but they have nevertheless been capable of a new and higher development. We are experienced in the tribulations of bondage. And it is not my intention, nor that of any thinking Zionist, to tie the need for the realization of our goal exclusively to the possibility of outbreaks of anti-Semitism. I trust I have shown how little good we are promised from this much-heralded progress. Now let us examine how our fate is affected by certain laws that operate in society.

One fundamental and practically unique impulse in the life of society is egoism. If, with respect to the individual, there are grounds for arguing that man is not the miserly egoist depicted in certain ethical theories, the egoism of the group cannot be denied. For the benefit of the group, its members eschew personal gain and individual pleasure, conferring on the group's interest a supreme moral imprimatur. The individual sacrifices himself for the good of the group, and in so doing nourishes the group's crude lack of consideration. On the other hand, nothing is done in the life of the society that is not to the advantage of the dominant classes who are in full control and have the power to forbid or permit.

Aside from this, human society, by virtue of the iron laws of historical development, is divided into tribes, nationalities and nations, and that has consequently prepared the ground for dividing man's attitude toward others in a striking manner: with respect to "ours," the laws ensure equality of duties—I may not coerce, deceive, or cause unpleasantness to "mine"—while with respect to *others* there are no limitations, everything goes: the crudest infringement of rights, the most deceitful betrayal. I do not mean to say this unfair demarcation will exist forever, but no one can prove it is destined to change in the foreseeable future. For the time being it is a fact of life; although its force is gradually weakening, it still must be taken into account.

It is man's nature to try to fit others to himself. This pure desire, which has nothing to do with the seeking of advantage, the desire to spread ideas, to impart feelings or ideals, is found in every person who relates to his existence with any degree of religious feeling or awe, and who appreciates their value not for himself alone. A man scatters his spiritual treasures willingly, and in this respect often reveals a degree of generosity that borders on heroism. Those whose ideas are being persecuted, are prepared for any suffering and sacrifice that will provide them with victory. And those whose views already hold sway over the consciousness of the masses—even though they are incapable of attaining such spiritual heights—are zealous in making converts, and their generosity is tremendous.

But my advice is to avoid becoming enthusiastic about such generosity; for spiritual possessions are not expropriable, and thus not only do not perish from this prodigality but even increase and improve in the process of preaching. By letting you share in my faith I may be giving you much, but I am still not depriving myself of anything. This is not the case with material or earthly possessions, measurable or not. Here man is generally not at all a squanderer, and social groups are even less so. It follows that every group is ready and willing to assimilate outsiders so long as it does not thereby surrender anything of its own, but faced with sharing material possessions with outsiders, no social group has as yet proved itself capable of such generosity. . . .

Joseph Haim Brenner (1881–1921)

Introduction

Entering the fictional world of Hebrew novelist and editor Joseph Brenner is a move into the harsh reality of Jewish life in the Diaspora. Brenner, who was influenced as a writer by Dostoyevsky, Tolstoy, and Nietzsche, engages in an uncompromisingly critical view of society and the hypocrisies it feeds on. His pessimistic and seemingly honest stories are filled with antiheroes and the struggle to survive in a difficult age.

Brenner was born to a pious but poor family in the Ukraine and studied at a yeshiva. Although a brilliant Talmud student, he became estranged from his family and from religion, and joined the Bund, the Russian-Jewish socialist organization. Brenner served in the Russian army for two years, but on the outbreak of the Russo-Japanese War in 1904 he escaped to England. There, appalled by the harsh conditions in which the Jewish immigrants in London's East End lived, he became a Zionist. In 1909 he went to Palestine as a settler.

As a writer, editor, and literary critic, Brenner espoused moral rectitude and justice as more fundamental than ideological commitment. His depiction of Jewish life in the ghettoes of Europe and in traditional Jerusalem underscores the grim reality of entrapment in poverty leading to degradation of spirit. In his novels, plays, and stories he tries to show the morass in which Diaspora Jews found themselves, often with no real hope of solution.

Brenner's novels, plays, articles, and translations made him an important figure in secular Hebrew modern culture. He was also the founder and editor of a number of important journals to which he was passionately devoted. He was murdered during the anti-Jewish Arab riots in 1921.

And This Is Our Nationalism!

I sit amongst my people, I, the writer of these lines, a Hebrew man of free opinions, and I do not believe that it is the question of religion and faith that does not let my people have any peace. I see Jewish men of substance who take care of synagogues, sometimes out of fanaticism and out of anger, and always according to habit and because of their inertia, that will probably last many, many years. However, there is no longer in their houses of worship the same feeling of warmth, the same enthusiasm that used to be there in ancient times, but this is another matter, and let those who want to worry, worry. . . . (I, for instance, see no greatness in that kind of warmth of those good old days, that has as its foundation some kind of prostrating and begging before some father in heaven, to give sustenance.) On the other hand, I again encounter Hebrew youth, the sons of those men of substance, that indeed like to occupy themselves somewhat in problems of life. I hear them talking about relationships between man and his fellow man, and between man and woman, and between nation and nation, and social class and social class. They are talking and also taking interest in the mystery of life and existence in general, in material and spiritual worlds, in the different movement in man's poetry, like the different trends of world literature, in the poor examples of our literature. Yet none of them fathoms sitting down and occupying themselves with the foolishness of theology: which faith is better, be it the faith that teaches that the Messiah has already arrived, or that which teaches, "What you dislike, do not do to your friend," to that which says, "Whoever hits your cheek," etc. These questions do not interest our youth but not because they are so satisfied with their inner world and their world outlook. Quite the contrary, those youth know the many conflicts that tear their souls apart and the difficulty of a life without god. They know and feel that they are not whole men, that as Hebrew youth without a complete Hebrew language, without a Hebrew homeland and Hebrew culture, nothing is smooth. However, it is quite clear to them, that in spite of all those who want to teach them, there is no history of Israel without the religion of Israel, but that a Jew and a prayer shawl are not the same thing. It is not the faith and religion of their fathers that weighs on them, they know that the lack of those is not the main cause of difficulties in their life, and so they do not turn to the religion and faith of the fathers, of their friends, the members of the world community.

* * *

In life—also in the moral, spiritual life—what is preached is not the main thing, but the deed. We find this saying in our ancient literature, but its meaning still makes sense, and its flavor has not disappeared. Everything I contemplate and especially everything I do, I don't contemplate or do just because Talmudic Judaism, in which I was educated, taught me to think or do such things, but because I want to do it. Talmudic Judaism, just as it is distant from Biblical Judaism is by its nature not a solid unit, and "Jewish life according to the Talmud" can take on various forms: there are many verses in Biblical Judaism and many sayings in Talmudic Judaism which contradict each other. My friends and I were educated at the knees of all these verses and sayings and finally they grew up and became what they were, and I grew up and became what I am. . . .

* * *

The different forms of life and the individual and the nation are not nurtured and do not live by religion. Religion itself, with all its silly ceremonies and rituals, is only a part of life that people created according to their will and in spite of themselves, because of their economic-psychological, human-national conditions of reality. Religion takes on shape, takes off shape, is born, is about to die.

In the life of faiths and religions,—and I intentionally do not say in the history of faiths and religions—there is, without a doubt, just as in the rest of life, a lot of corruption, a lot of exploitation. A great deal of man's rule over man is bad for him, and there are—as far as individuals are concerned, not the masses—certain other elements which are spiritual, secret, tragic, full of content, which come to satisfy very deep needs. The masses never quite get to the essence, and they consume, at times enthusiastically and at times with a certain coolness, as it is taught to them, they consume the outer lining. For some people, the essence is within them, or they dream about it and yearn for it, and they never have a need for the outer lining. It is known that the first Greek philosophers fought against the religion of their contemporaries and they even fought our much admired monotheism, no less than our prophets of Israel. In reality, they were quite a bit more religious than the priests and those in the service of religion who excluded these first philosophers from the community. And it is also known that there is a love for man and the respect for eternal lofty values in all the holy scriptures of all the faiths and religions, where they concern individuals. But as a matter of fact, when we get to the masses, we find enslavement, superstitions, irrational laws such as bloody wars fought over gods, idols, altars, houses of worship, rituals and ceremonies and other silly rules. Historical Christianity, the Roman, pagan, inquisition-like movement that subjugated the great Greek philosophy to serve its causes, hangs on the tree of the poor Jew, Joshua of Nazareth—are there really any close ties between them? Now we have a pagan-Pravoslavic Christianity which dominates the Russians, and a Lutheran-burgeois Christianity which dominates the Germans and a few more types of Christianity. Do you believe that those have their source in the New Testament of the Jewish messengers? No. That could not be. The qualities of those nations, together with several historical external incidents, shape their historical-religious lives, their Christianity. Our Judaism of today, in all the countries it is practiced and in all manner of practice, is unconsciously influenced by the life situations of all the masses of the house of Israel in those countries, even though it still is alien and unexplainable to those forms of life which encircle it from the outside. Is there a need to mention how distant it is from Biblical Judaism, to the extent the meaning of its principal commandments has changed, and to the extent it is different in its world view from the various world views expressed in the Scriptures of the Old Testament?—

* * *

. . . It is quite a tragedy for us when they lock the gates before our wanderers, it is a tragedy for us when our workers are thrown out of the factories, it is a tragedy for us when a Hebrew cultural institution has to close for lack of funds. All of this points to the poverty of our life, to the difficulties of our survival, to our impoverished needs and the lack of their fulfillment. It is quite a joy for us when a plot of land is bought somewhere, when a Jewish school is opened in some place, when an important Hebrew book is published, when we hear about a number of Jews that entered the productive world of labor. All of these are expressions of our productive lives, all of this is a sign that there is still life in our nation and we have not yet come to the end of our lives. It is not difficult to understand the sorrow when one sees a talented person in some profession who was born among us wandering off because he cannot find a place amongst us, and thus, as his countrymen, we remain impoverished and denied of culture. But what do we have to do with the tens and hundreds of those who are assimilated Jews from childhood, who convert to Christianity for some purpose, and why does this small outer change frighten us so much more than did their lives before the change? Since their way of life was in the main not very Jewish before, what would we have gained from them if they had not taken this last step and would have remained in name only among us without taking a real part in the difficulties or our life and in our struggles for our national future? . . .

* * *

The actual and necessary assimilation of great sections of the body of our sick and ghetto-like nation will not be removed by abstractions. "Judaism" in quotes will not be able to help here, even if a thousand flowery articles are written abut it. Let's leave theology to their and our priests, who have free time to deal with the question: which of the religions is best, in which is there more beauty, sanctity, justice, love. The field is wide and there is plenty of room to define new boundaries, to innovate, to choose a few verses from the many verses and put them together—and prove something.

The question of our Jewish life is not a question of our Jewish religion; the question of "Jewish existence," this mixture has to be uprooted. Ahad Ha'Am did so once and then regretted it, but we, his free Jewish friends, we don't have anything to do with Judaism. Yet here we are amongst the community and in no way the lesser for not observing putting on tefillin [leather boxes worn for morning prayer] and wearing tzitzit [fringes on the prayer shawl]. We say: the life question is the question of a productive place of work for us Jews. We are Jews who live everywhere, we are beaten Jews, without a country, without a language and so on. . . . The environment of the non-Jewish majority does not let us be complete and whole Jews, like our free Russian, Polish, etc., friends, who are whole Russian and Polish. The environment of the majority confuses us, eats at us, dims our shape, brings in disorder in our lives. But we are far from assimilating—how far we are, the question of converting to Christianity—there is not even a thought and even a laugh. Our nation is an exile nation. It is sick. It keeps going and stumbling, falling seven times and rising. We have to build it. Its will power is weakening—we should reinforce it. Let's get strong! There is no Messiah for Israel—let's build strong soldiers who can live without a Messiah.

. . . While we are few, the members of the living Jewish nation, we will be stronger than stone, working and creating as much as is possible. We will increase our nation's labor and its material and spiritual goods. We, the living Jews, whether we are tormented on Yom Kippur and whether we eat meat and milk, whether we hold to the conventions of the Old Testament, and whether we are in our world view faithful students of Epicurus (i.e. secular), we do not stop feeling ourselves as Jews. We live our lives as Jews working and creating the life styles of Jews, speaking in our Jewish tongue, receiving our spiritual sustenance from our literature, working for our national, free culture, for defending our national respect and fighting our war of existence in all forms that such a war takes.

* * *

And again: Hypocrites! Do you really want to convince us that "all of those thousands of human victims" the Nation of Israel sacrificed on the altar of the differences between one outlook and another was not because the other was always an alien body? Do you really try to frighten us with things like, "Millions of people are remembered with holy reverence"? Do you not understand that a nation is contemptible whose "entire life is dependent on certain known holy things," and which for many generations depended only on the prayer "because of our sins"? . . .

We are nationalists. We are zealous nationalists, but in this nationalistic frame of mind we do not ever hold that because of it we'll do anything against out beliefs. Our nationalism is the improvement of our lives and the enrichment of those forms of life which we find positive. So don't look to enslave us in its name to some kind of tradition, because to that kind of nationalism we would say: not that and not its payoff! We are live Jewish people—not more—and it is important for us to have Jewish labor, the most important principle of life, and our language is dear to us, the language of our speech and writing, and our respect is holy to us, the respect of our nation, and this is our nationalism.

"If we don't have this, and don't have that—what are we fighting for?" These hypocrites! So this would be and so would that and everything that is needed. If we do not see the majority of the rabbinical literature and the Kabbala as national treasures, but as an unnecessary burden, it does not mean that we don't need to create a different kind of literature, one that is alive, humane, free, but this is also far from being the main point. The main thing is the foundation of a new life, and the essence is Hebrew villages. And for that purpose the best of our people here and abroad are fighting, and they don't believe in the Messiah and they have nothing to do with traditional theological Judaism!

Rahel (Blustein)
(1890–1931)

Introduction

Rahel holds a place of special esteem among the humanistic bards of pioneering Palestine in the twentieth century. Many of her simple, brief, and moving poems have been set to music. Rahel's unadorned, sensitive lyrics are filled with a love for the countryside and for nature.

Rahel was born in Viatka, Russia, in 1890. She graduated from a Russian gymnasium and then went to study art in Kiev. She wrote her early poems in Russian. In 1909 she went to Palestine and worked as a farm laborer, first at Rehovot, then later at at Kinneret, a cooperative colony about which she wrote one of her famous poems. Greatly influenced by the philosophy of A. D. Gordon, she went to France in 1913 to study agriculture but was forced by the outbreak of World War I to return to Russia where she taught in a school for refugee children. She returned to Palestine in 1919 to live at Kibbutz Degania on the shores of the Sea of Galilee, but had already contracted consumption and after a while was unable to continue physical labor. The last years of her life were spent in and out of hospitals, although she continued to write poetry in her isolation. Her reflections on her approaching death fill her later poems with a sense of melancholy.

HERE ON EARTH

Here on earth—not in high clouds—
On this mother earth that is close:
To sorrow in her sadness, exult in her meager joy
That knows, so well, how to console,
Not nebulous tomorrow but today: solid, warm, mighty
Today materialized in the hand:
Of this single, short day to drink deep
Here in our own land.

Before night falls—come, oh come all!
A unified stubborn effort, awake
With a thousand arms. It is impossible to roll
The stone from the mouth of the well?

MY STRENGTH GROWS LESS AND LESS . . .

My strength grows less and less.
Be good to me, be good to me. Be
my narrow bridge across a sad abyss, across the sadness of my days
Be good to me, be good to me! Something of soul.
Be my heart's prop.
In the waste places be a shade-giving tree.
Be good to me!
The night is long, the dawn is far away.
Be a small light, be sudden joy,
be my daily bread!

Saul Tchernikhowsky (1875–1943)

Introduction

Saul Tchernikhowsky was a Hebrew poet who celebrated life, protested against stifling religious orthodoxy, and was an ardent Zionist and socialist. He had a special interest in exuberant pagan themes from Greek and Canaanite mythology. His poetry is full of the emotions of love and the joy of life, and exhibit a pantheistic view of nature.

Tchernikhowsky was born in a village in the Crimea to a pious family influenced by the Haskalah. He went to Odessa in 1890 to study at a business school and then began to publish his first poems in Hebrew. Later he studied medicine at the universities of Heidelberg and Lausanne, graduating as a physician in 1907. He practiced for several years as a country doctor and served in the Russian medical corps during World War I. In 1921 he left Russia, settling in Germany for ten years and then going to Palestine, where he worked as a physician in Tel Aviv, then later as an editor. After several years of silence, he returned to creative writing. In his later years, he enjoyed high prestige as a national poet of the new Jewish settlers.

In his verse Tchernikhowsky rebelled against the didacticism of Hebrew poetry and tradition, calling for greater freedom and free rein for humankind's natural exuberance. He believed that the

Jewish spirit was originally full of life and vitality but was then bound, restricted, and deadened by the strictness and isolation of the Jewish religion. His aim was to liberate the Jewish spirit and restore its youthful energy.

In addition to poetry, he wrote the drama *Bar Kochba,* as well as stories and essays. He was also a prolific translator of European classic works into Hebrew.

I BELIEVE

Laugh, O laugh, at all my visions,
I the Dreamer, tell you true;
laugh for I believe in man still,
for I still believe in you.

For my soul still yearns for freedom
unbartered to the calf of gold:
for I still believe in mankind,
in his spirit, strong and bold.

Man shall rise to heights of glory,
vanity's fetters from him shed;
the worker then will starve no longer,
spirit—freed, and hunger—fed.

Laugh, in friendship too my faith is,
somewhere yet I'll find a heart,
one to share my very hope with,
feeling fortune, knowing smart.

I believe, too, in the future,
though the day's not close at hand,
it will come—then peace and blessing
will be borne from land to land.

My people, too, again will flower,
on the land a breed will rise,
that will cast their chains from off them,
see the light before their eyes.

Living, loving, working, doing,
on the *earth* alive indeed,
not hereafter—hope of heaven,
not content with empty creed.

A poet then shall sing a new song,
to beauty exalted heart awake;
from my grave, for him, the young one,
they'll pluck flowers, wreaths to make.

THEY SAY THERE IS A COUNTRY

They say there is a country
A land that flows with sunlight.
Where is that country?
Where is that sunlight?

They say there is a country
Where seven pillars are.
There bloom on every hilltop
Seven wandering stars.

A land where is fulfilled
All a man can hope,
Everyone who enters—
Akiba does approach.

"Shalom to you, Akiba,
Peace be with you, Rabbi.

Where are they, the Holy,
Where are the Maccabee?"

Answers him Akiba,
Says to him the Rabbi:
"All Israel is holy,
you are the Maccabee!"

Avraham Shlonsky (1900–1973)

Introduction

Israel's most important revolutionary poet, and the leader of the literary left, was Avraham Shlonsky. In addition to being a major poet, Shlonsky translated over seventy-three major works of European literature into Hebrew. He is the only Israeli poet to have founded a poetic school.

Shlonsky was born to a Hasidic family in the Ukraine who were followers of Ahad Ha'am's cultural Zionism He received a secular Hebrew as well as a religious education, and he went to Palestine in 1921 as a pioneer, working on road building and construction. After studying in Paris, he returned to Palestine to become a literary journalist for several Hebrew newspapers and periodicals. Shlonsky rebelled against classicism in verse, challenging in particular the authority of Haim Bialik. Shlonsky's greatest achievement was as a linguistic innovator, coining new words, developing fresh imagery, and experimenting with creative linguistic constructions. He also utilized the language and forms of biblical and liturgical Hebrew, combining old and new into original poetic idioms.

Shlonsky's poetry covered many themes. In some he expressed his outrage at Nazism and the Holocaust. In others, he reflects on the pain of modern inhabitants of the urban environment or, the dilemma of life and death. One of his most famous poems is

"Amal" (Toil), which illustrates his fusion of ancient vocabulary with the new Israeli landscape.

TOIL

Harness the deserts!
Stretch the roads like reins!
I ride on the driver's seat!
I am—toil!—

Like huge fists lie on the sands
Houses—Houses—Houses—

And I feel:
It is I who am caught in the morning tree top
And in my hand like a sparkling ray, the spade.
Opposite me laughs the city newly made:
Sun! Sun!

Dress me, good mother, in a splendrous coat of many colors
And with dawn lead me to toil.
My land wraps in light like a prayer shawl,
Houses stand like phylacteries,
And like bands of phylacteries glide hand-laid asphalt roads.

Thus a beautiful city offers her morning prayer to her creator.
And among the creators, your son Abraham,
Poet-roadbuilder in Israel.
And toward evening, at dusk, father returns from his labors
And like prayer whispers with pleasure:
A dear son of mine is Abraham:
Skin, sinew, and bones.
Hallelujah!
Dress me good mother, in a splendrous coat of many colors

And at dawn lead me
To toil.

EVERYTHING ORDAINED

Blessed rain of Shaddai—blessed be its name.
Moist grace from heaven.
Sing to bread, for goodly is its taste.
Sing thanks to water.

Regard the clump of earth the same inside and out,
Seeded warm soil.
Earth give thanks that all was ordained,
Give thanks for wind and rain.

You yearned for dew, your seedbed is moist
May breasts and womb be blessed in you.
Praise bread, for it is good,
Offer thanks to bread.

Sigmund Freud (1856–1934)

Introduction

Sigmund Freud's name has become synonymous with a concept in human psychology. We speak of Freudian slips of the tongue. Freud was a "godless Jew," a Viennese son of the Enlightenment, a medical empiricist, and a dedicated rationalist. He was a militant atheist who nonetheless was loyal to his Jewish roots and was disturbed by the growing antisemitism in his day. His designation as the father of psychoanalysis marks him as one of the most important figures of the late nineteenth country.

Freud grew up in Vienna in a family on the brink of poverty. His family observed Jewish holidays and customs but were not religious. By the time Freud graduated from the gymnasium, he had become a confirmed atheist and refused to celebrate the Jewish holidays his father still held sacred. Freud graduated from medical school at the University of Vienna, where he had experienced the bitterness of social rejection because he was Jewish. Although he had desired strongly to be assimilated into German society, he now replaced that desire with Jewish pride from which he drew self-confidence and courage.

Freud set up a medical practice as a neuropathologist in 1886 and began his studies of neurosis and psychopathology, treating hysteria in particular. He engaged in intense self-analysis in the next two decades, including much dream analysis. His psychoanalytic theories were the result of this study and led to the publication of two of his most important books, *The Interpretation of Dreams* in 1901 and *Three Essays on the Theory of Sexuality* in 1905. Freud regarded psychoanalysis in part as a theoretical tool to discover the determinants of human thought and behavior. He was also interested in social theory and published his most important work in that field in *Totem and Taboo.*

Gradually Freud's work attracted disciples and the weekly meetings of the psychoanalytic group (all of them Jewish) that began in 1902 developed into the International Psychoanalytic Association in 1910. While Freud's work has had some impact on European thought and psychological practice, his most lasting influence has been in the United States.

Freud remained in Vienna until 1938, when the growth of Fascism caused him to move to London. He died there the next year.

While Freud was an atheist, he remained faithful to his Jewish identity, and fostered a strong feeling of solidarity with the Jewish people in his children. He joined the Vienna B'nai B'rith in 1897 and gave many lectures to the society in the next few years. He advanced the view in that group that Jews played a primary role in affirming universal and humanitarian values and a responsible role in transmitting them to others.

THE FUTURE OF AN ILLUSION

. . . I have tried to show that religious ideas have arisen from the same need as have all the other achievements of civilization: from the necessity of defending oneself against the crushingly superior force of nature. To this a second motive was added—the urge to rectify the shortcomings of civilization which made themselves painfully felt. Moreover, it is especially apposite to say that civilization gives the individual these ideas, for he finds them there already; they are presented to him ready-made, and he would not be able to discover them for himself. What he is entering into is the heritage of many generations, and he takes it over as he does the multiplication table, geometry, and similar things. . . .

(Chapter IV)

Let us try to apply the same [scientific] test to the teachings of religion. When we ask on what their claim to be believed is founded, we are met with three answers, which harmonize remarkably badly with one another. Firstly, these teachings deserve to be believed because they were already believed by our primal ancestors; secondly, we possess proofs which have been handed down to us from those same primaeval times; and thirdly, it is forbidden to raise the question of their authentication at all. In the former days anything so presumptuous was visited with the severest penalties, and even to-day society looks askance at any attempt to raise the question again.

This third point is bound to rouse our strongest suspicions. After all, a prohibition like this can only be for one reason—that society is very well aware of the insecurity of the claim it makes on behalf of its religious doctrines. Otherwise it would certainly be very ready to put the necessary data at the disposal of anyone who wanted to arrive at conviction. This being so, it is with a feeling of mistrust which it is hard to allay that we pass on to an examination of the other two grounds of proof. We ought to believe because our forefathers believed. But these ancestors of ours were far more ignorant than we are. They believed in things we could not possible accept to-day; and the possibility occurs to us that the doctrines of religion may belong to that class too. The proofs they have left us are set down in writings which themselves bear every mark of untrustworthiness. They are full of contradictions, revisions and falsifications, and where they speak of factual confirmations they are themselves unconfirmed. It does not help much to have it asserted that their wording, or even their content only, originates from divine revelations; for this assertion is itself one of the doctrines whose authenticity is under examination, and no proposition can be proof of itself.

Thus we arrive at the singular conclusion that of all the information provided by our cultural assets it is precisely the elements which might be of the greatest importance to us and which have the task of solving the riddles of the universe and of reconciling us to the sufferings of life—it is precisely those elements that are the least well authenticated of any. We should not be able to bring ourselves to accept anything of so little concern to us as the fact that whales bear young instead of laying eggs, if it were not capable of better proof than this.

This state of affairs is in itself a very remarkable psychological problem. And let no one suppose that what I have said about the impossibility of proving the truth of religious doctrines contains anything new. It has been felt at all times—undoubtedly, too, by the ancestors who bequeathed us this legacy. Many of them probably nourished the same doubts as ours, but the pressure imposed on them was too strong for them to have dared to utter them. And since then countless people have been tormented by similar doubts, and have striven to suppress them, because they thought it was their duty to believe; many brilliant intellects have broken down over this conflict, and many characters have been impaired by the compromises with which they have tried to find a way out of it.

If all the evidence put forward for the authenticity of religious teachings originates in the past, it is natural to look round and see whether the present, about which it is easier to form judgements, may not also be able to furnish evidence of the sort. If by this means we could succeed in clearing even a single portion of the religious system from doubt, the whole of it would gain enormously in credibility. The proceedings of the spiritualists meet us at this point; they are convinced of the survival of the individual soul and they seek to demonstrate to us beyond doubt the truth of this one religious doctrine. Unfortunately they cannot succeed in refuting the fact that the appearance and utterances of their spirits are merely the products of their own mental activity. They have called up the spirits of the greatest men and of the most eminent thinkers, but all the pronouncements and information which they have received from them have been so foolish and wretchedly meaningless that one can find nothing credible in them but the capacity of the spirits to adapt themselves to the circle of people who have conjured them up.

I must now mention two attempts that have been made—both of which convey the impression of being desperate efforts—to evade the problem. One, of a violent nature, is ancient; the other is subtle and modern. The first is the *'Credo quia absurdum'* of the early Father of the Church. It maintains that religious doctrines are outside the jurisdiction of reason—are above reason. Their truth must be felt inwardly, and they need not be comprehended. But this *Credo* is only of interest as a self-confession. As an authoritative statement it has no binding force. Am I to be obliged to believe *every* absurdity? And if not, why this one in particular? There is no appeal to a court above that of reason. If the truth of religious doctrines is dependent on an inner experience which bears witness to that truth, what is one to do about the many people who do not have this rare experience? One may require every man to use the gift of reason which he possesses, but one cannot erect, on the basis of a motive that exists only for a very few, an obligation that shall apply to everyone. If one man has gained an unshakable conviction of the true reality of religious doctrines from a state of ecstasy which has deeply moved him, of what significance is that to others?

The second attempt is the one made by the philosophy of "As if." This asserts that our thought-activity includes a great number of hypotheses whose groundlessness and even absurdity we fully realize. They are called "fictions," but for a variety of practical reasons we have to behave "as if" we believed in these fictions. This is the case with religious doctrines because of their incomparable importance for the maintenance of human society. This line of argument is not far removed from the "*Credo quia absurdum.*"

But I think the demand made by the "As if" argument is one that only a philosopher could put forward. A man whose thinking is not influenced by the artifices of philosophy will never be able to accept it; in such a man's view, the admission that something is absurd or contrary to reason leaves no more to be said. It cannot be expected of him that precisely in treating his most important interests he shall forgo the guarantees he requires for all his ordinary activities. I am reminded of one of my children who was distinguished at an early age by a peculiarly marked matter-of-factness. When the children were being told a fairy story and were listening to it with rapt attention, he would come up and ask: "Is that a true story?" When he was told it was not, he would turn away with a look of disdain. We may expect that people will soon behave in the same way towards the fairy tales of religion, in spite of the advocacy of "As if."

But at present they still behave quite differently; and in past times religious ideas, in spite of their incontrovertible lack of authentication, have exercised the strongest possible influence on mankind. This is a fresh psychological problem. We must ask where the inner force of those doctrines lies and to what it is that they owe their efficacy, independent as it is of recognition by reason.

(Chapter V)

. . . let us return once more to the question of religious doctrines. We can now repeat that all of them are illusions and insusceptible of proof. No one can be compelled to think them true, to believe in them. Some of them are so improbable, so incompatible with everything we have laboriously discovered about the reality of the world, that we may compare them—if we pay proper regard to the psychological differences—to delusions. Of the reality value of most of them we cannot judge; just as they cannot be proved, so they cannot be refuted. We still know too little to make a critical approach to them. The riddles of the universe reveal themselves only slowly to our investigation; there are many questions to which science today can give no answer. But scientific work is the only road which can lead us to a knowledge of reality outside ourselves. It is once again merely an illusion to expect anything from intuition and introspection; they can give us nothing but particulars about our own mental life, which are hard to interpret, never any information about the questions which religious doctrine finds it so easy to answer. It would be insolent to let one's arbitrary will step into the breach, and according to one's personal estimate, declare this or that part of the religious system to be less or more acceptable. Such questions are too momentous for that; they might be called too sacred.

At this point one must expect to meet with an objection. "Well then, if even obdurate sceptics admit that the assertions of religion cannot be refuted by reason, why should I not believe in them, since they have so much on their side—tradition, the agreement of mankind, and all the consolation they offer?" Why not, indeed? Just as no one can be forced to believe, so no one can be forced to disbelieve. But do not let us be satisfied with deceiving ourselves that arguments like these take us along the road of correct thinking. If ever there was a case of a lame excuse we have it here. Ignorance is ignorance; no right to believe anything can be derived from it. In other matters no sensible person will behave so irresponsibly or rest content with such feeble grounds for his opinion and for the line he takes. It is only in the highest and most sacred things that he allows himself to do so. In reality these are only attempts at pretending to oneself or to other people that one is still firmly attached to religion, when one has long since cut oneself loose from it. Where questions of religion are concerned, people are guilty of every possible sort of dishonesty, and intellectual misdemeanor. Philosophers stretch the meaning of words until they retain scarcely anything of their original sense. They give the name of "God" to some vague abstraction which they have created for themselves; having done so they can pose before all the world as deists, as believers in God, and they can even boast that they have recognized a higher, purer concept of God, notwithstanding that their God is now nothing more than an insubstantial shadow and no longer the mighty personality of religious doctrines. Critics persist in describing as "deeply religious" anyone who admits to a sense of man's insignificance or impotence in the face of the universe, although what constitutes the essence of the religious attitude is not this feeling but only the next step after it, the reaction to it which seeks a remedy for it. The man who goes no further, but humbly acquiesces in the small part which human beings play in the great world—such a man is, on the contrary, irreligious in the truest sense of the word.

. . . We shall tell ourselves that it would be very nice if there were a God who created the world and was a benevolent Providence, and if there were a moral order in the universe and an after-life; but it is a very striking fact that all this is exactly as we are bound to wish it to be . . . .

(Chapter VI)

. . . Religion has clearly performed great services for human civilization. It has contributed much towards the taming of the asocial instincts. But not enough. It has ruled human society for many thousands of years and has had time to show what it can achieve. If it had succeeded in making the majority of mankind happy, in comforting them, in reconciling them to life and in making them into vehicles of civilization, no one would dream of attempting to alter the existing conditions. But what do we see instead? We see that an appallingly large number of people are dissatisfied with civilization and unhappy in it, and feel it as a yoke which must be shaken off; and that these people either do everything in their power to change that civilization or else go so far in their hostility that they will have nothing to do with civilization or with a restriction of instinct. At this point it will be objected against us that this state of affairs is due to the very fact that religion has lost a part of its influence over human masses precisely because of the deplorable effect of the advances of science . . . but the objection itself has no force.

It is doubtful whether men were in general happier at a time when religious doctrines held unrestricted sway; more moral they certainly were not. They have always known how to externalize the precepts of religion and thus to nullify their intentions. The priests, whose duty it was to ensure obedience to religion, met them half-way in this. God's kindness must lay a restraining hand on His justice. One sinned, and then one made a sacrifice or did penance and then one was free to sin once more. . . . It is no secret that the priests could only keep the masses submissive to religion by making such large concessions as these to the instinctual nature of man. Thus it was agreed: God alone is strong and good, man is weak and sinful. In every age immorality has found no less support in religion than morality has. If the achievements of religion in respect to man's happiness, susceptibility to culture and moral control are no better than this, the question cannot but arise whether we are not overrating its necessity for mankind, and whether we do wisely in basing our cultural demands upon it. . . .

(Chapter VII)

Thus I must contradict you when you go on to argue that men are completely unable to do without the consolation of the religious illusion, that without it they could not bear the troubles of life and the cruelties of reality. That is true, certainly, of the men into whom you have instilled the sweet—or bitter-sweet—poison from childhood onwards. But what of the other men, who have been sensibly brought up? Perhaps those who do not suffer from the neurosis will need no intoxicant to deaden it. They will, it is true, find themselves in a difficult situation. They will have to admit to themselves the full extent of their helplessness and their insignificance in the machinery of the universe; they can no longer be the center of creation, no longer the object of tender care on the part of a beneficent Providence. They will be in the same position as a child who has left the parental house where he was so warm and comfortable. But surely infantilism is destined to be surmounted. Men cannot remain children forever; they must in the end go out into "hostile life." We may call this *"education to reality."* Need I confess to you that the sole purpose of my book is to point out the necessity for this forward step?

You are afraid, probably, that they will not stand up to the hard test? Well, let us at least hope they will. It is something, at any rate, to know that one is thrown upon one's own resources. One learns then to make a proper use of them. And men are not entirely without assistance. Their scientific knowledge has taught them much since the days of the Deluge, and it will increase their power still further. And, as for the great necessities of Fate, against which there is no help, they will learn to endure them with resignation. Of what use to them is the mirage of wide acres in the moon, whose harvest no one has ever yet seen? As honest smallholders on this earth they will know how to cultivate their plot in such a way that it supports them. By withdrawing their expectations from the other world and concentrating all their liberated energies into their life on earth, they will probably succeed in achieving a state of things in which life will become tolerable for everyone and civilization is no longer oppressive to anyone. . . .

(Chapter IX)

Edna Ferber (1865–1968)

Introduction

Edna Ferber was a best-selling American novelist who chronicled the growth and special vitality of different regions of the United States in her novels. While her stories are not about Jews, she was intensely connected to her Jewishness all her life, and lived proudly as a secular Jew.

Ferber was born in Michigan in 1885 and was brought up in several small midwestern towns where she experienced antisemitism first hand. Her family was not religious, and as secular Jew throughout her life, the impact of antisemitism remained a consuming interest of hers. Ferber grew up a strong, precocious young woman who was determined to make her mark somehow. She read a book a day to expand her knowledge and determined she would lead a life of self-reliance.

Although she really wanted to be an actress, her family had no money to send her to college and she went to work as a reporter for her town newspaper. The job taught her to be a keen observer and a concise writer. She left her hometown of Appleton, Wisconsin, to work for the *Milwaukee Journal,* but after two years she was so fatigued she returned home and began to write short stories for magazines. These proved so successful that they were collected into published volumes starting in 1912. Some of her early stories were about saleswomen who were strong and assertive, and Ferber implied that this was why the women were successful.

As her fame grew, she moved to New York and began her career as a playwright and a novelist. Her first best-selling novel was *So Big,* which won a Pulitzer Prize in 1924. In her lifetime she published twenty-five volumes, including thirteen novels and eight plays. The theatrical musical *Show Boat,* based on a Ferber novel, is still being presented today. Ferber's strength as a novelist was the strong and ambitious women she portrayed.

In her autobiography, *A Peculiar Treasure,* Ferber discusses her pride in her Jewishness and her strong reaction to the antisemitism she encountered in her life. She never failed to confront bigots and was horrified by the experience of the Holocaust.

A PECULIAR TREASURE

I should like, in this book, to write about being a Jew. All my life I have been inordinately proud of being a Jew. But I have felt that one should definitely not brag about it. My Jewishness was, I thought, something to wear with becoming modesty, calling attention to it no more than to my two good physical points which were a fine clear skin and an abundant head of vigorous curly hair. Perhaps someone—it may have been my grandfather Neumann, but I do not remember it—had told me this. As I grew older and became a woman the feeling was intensified. This is inexplicable, because my early childhood was spent, for the most part, in an anti-Semitic Middle Western town, and mine was not and is not a religious family. But I have felt that to be a Jew was, in some ways at least, to be especially privileged. Two thousand years of persecution have made the Jew quick to sympathy, quick-witted (he'd better be), tolerant, humanly understanding. The highest compliment we can pay a Christian is to say of him that he has a Jewish heart.

All this makes life that much more interesting. It also makes life harder, but I am perverse enough to like a hard life. I like a fighting life. I like overcoming things. Maybe a psychiatrist could tell me why, and it might not prove flattering. Being a Jew makes it tougher to get on, and I like that. The highest apple on the branch is the sweetest, and the nearest to the sun. But, I hasten to add, there's such a thing as overdoing it. The Nazis' little plan has made things just a shade too tough. A joke's a joke.

It may be that being a Jew satisfied the frustrated actress in me. It may be that I have dramatized myself as a Jew. I am fond of referring, especially of late, to two thousand years of persecution. The fact remains that hundreds and thousands of years of continued ill-treatment must stamp its mark upon a people. Primarily, to be a Jew meant to belong to a religion, not a race. But a religious sect, persecuted through the centuries, takes on a certain resemblance, one to another, in countenance, in habits, in feeling, much as one often notes that a husband and wife, through years of common experience and companionship, grow to look alike. The Jewish eye is a melancholy eye, the mask is tragic. He has acquired great adaptability, nervous energy, ambition to succeed and a desire to be liked.

It irks me to hear people say that Jews are wonderful people or that Jews are terrible people. Jews are wonderful and terrible and good and bad and brilliant and stupid and evil and spiritual and vulgar and cultured and rich and poor and beautiful and ugly and gifted and commonplace. Jews, in short, are people . . .

There was no Jewish place of worship in Ottumwa. The five or six Jewish families certainly could not afford the upkeep of a temple. I knew practically nothing of the Jewish people, their history, religion. On the two important holy days of the year—Rosh Hashana, the Jewish New Year; and Yom Kippur, the Day of Atonement—they hired a public hall for services. Sometimes they were able to bring to town a student rabbi who had, as yet, no regular congregation. Usually one of the substantial older men who knew something of the Hebrew language of the Bible, having been taught it in his youth, conducted the service. On Yom Kippur, a long day of fasting and prayer, it was an exhausting thing to stand from morning to sunset in the improvised pulpit. The amateur rabbi would be relieved for an hour by another member of the little improvised congregation. Mr. Emanuel Adler, a familiar figure to me as he sat in his comfortable home talking with my parents, a quaint long-stemmed pipe between his lips, a little black skullcap atop his baldish head as protection against drafts, now would don the rabbinical skullcap, a good deal like that of a Catholic priest.

He would open on the high reading stand the Bible and the Book of Prayers containing the service for the Day of Yom Kippur; and suddenly he was transformed from a plump middle-aged German-born Jew with sad kindly eyes and a snuffy gray-brown mustache to a holy man from whose lips came words of wisdom and of comfort and of hope.

The store always was closed on Rosh Hashana and Yom Kippur. Mother put on her best dress. If there were any Jewish visitors in the town at that time they were invited to the services and to dinner at some hospitable house afterward. In our household the guests were likely to be a couple of traveling salesmen caught in the town on that holy day. Jewish families came from smaller nearby towns—Marshalltown, Albia, Keokuk.

I can't account for the fact that I didn't resent being a Jew. Perhaps it was because I liked the way my own family lived, talked, conducted its household and its business better than I did the lives of my friends. I admired immensely my grandparents, my parents, my uncles and aunt. Perhaps it was a vague something handed down to me from no one knows where. Perhaps it was something not very admirable—the actress in me. I think, truthfully, that I rather liked dramatizing myself, feeling myself different and set apart. I probably liked to think of myself as persecuted by enemies who were (in my opinion) my inferiors. This is a protective philosophy often employed. Mine never had been a religious family. The Chicago Neumann family sometimes went to the temple at Thirty-third and Indiana, but I don't remember that my parents ever went there while in Chicago. In our own household there was no celebration of the informal home ceremonies so often observed in Jewish families. The Passover, with its Sedar *[sic]* service, was marked in our house only by the appearance of the matzos or unleavened bread, symbolic of the hardships of the Jews in the wilderness. I devoured pounds of the crisp crumbling matzos with hunks of fresh butter and streams of honey, leaving a trail of crumbs all over the house, and thought very little, I am afraid, of the tragic significance of the food I was eating or of that weary heartsick band led by Moses out of Egypt to escape the Hitler of that day, one Pharaoh; or of how they baked and ate their unsalted unleavened bread because it was all they had there in the wilderness. . . .

Right here I may as well break down and confess that even at that early day in my life I had rejected the belief of a God as portrayed in conventional terms of worship. I did not then, and I do not now, accept this God. I was too young, then, seriously to evolve a spiritual belief of any kind. But out of the years has grown the only form of spiritual guidance I have ever had. It is simply, the belief that God is Good and that Good is God. . . .

. . . There lived in New York a formidable old lady named Mrs. Wolcott. Her life's business was lion hunting. She was an inveterate and almost invincible dinner-giver. *So Big, Show Boat* and *The Royal Family* had made me fair game for her. Thus far I had escaped her careful aim.

Then, one day, when I was off guard, she said that she was giving a dinner for eight. Winthrop Ames had said he would come if I would. I welcomed the thought of sitting next to him at a small dinner and having an hour of his stimulating talk and his gay glancing wit.

There was good talk and good food. Winthrop sat between the hostess and me. The conversation turned to books, someone mentioned G. B. Stern's novel, *The Matriarch,* which had been well received.

"That book!" shouted the hostess. "When I found it was about spawning Jews I threw it across the room."

A little silence fell. It was, I suppose, just about the nastiest little silence I have ever felt. I said, with laborious dignity, "It was a rich chronicle of a dramatic and cultured family. I loved it."

In leaped the gallant Winthrop. "Dramatic! That's it! I've often thought that if it hadn't been for the Jew in me I'd never have amounted to anything in the theater."

"*You,* Winthrop!" screeched Mrs. Wolcott.

"Certainly," he went on, equably. "Old Ameus, from whom we get our name of Ames. It's all in the book of the family tree in the library up at North Easton. Old Ameus, the Jew, who was thrown out of England and into Spain, and out of Spain back into England, centuries ago. Where do you suppose I get this profile, if not from him!"

"That," I put in, lamely, "is exactly the way I feel about anything I've done in the theater. We Jews, because we've been suppressed for centuries, have to express ourselves in the creative arts and sciences."

"Oh, are you Jewish—too?" faltered our charming hostess. "I didn't know—"

"Only," I replied cheerfully, "on my mother's and father's side, my grandmothers' and grandfathers', my great-grandmothers' and great-grandfathers', my great-great-grand—"

"There are Jews and Jews," interrupted Mrs. W., graciously.

"Yes, indeed. And Christians *and* Christians." With which I took my departure.

Now, that's the sort of thing that interests me, psychologically. This beldame probably never had talked to three Jews in her life, knowing they were Jews. Her resentment of them was as pathological and unsound as the fear of, say, high places. If you multiply this one woman's ignorance and prejudice by one or two millions you have a very nice little Hitler group snugly seated in your own lap.

There are, I think, many Mrs. Wolcotts in America, male and female. Unsure, they search for something upon which to establish their superiority. This woman, like many others, had fixed upon the Jews as a symbol. Unknowingly, she had worked herself into a lather to wheedle and coax to her table two people who were proud of their Jewish background.

Emma Goldman (1869–1940)

Introduction

Red Emma. Her name became a household term in the United States as the Red Scare came to this country following the Bolshevik Revolution in 1917. Emma Goldman was deported from the United States in 1919 along with some 200 others because she was portrayed as the most dangerous woman in the world, a revolutionary, an anarchist, and a believer in free love. She may have been all of those but she was also a woman of tremendous courage, honesty, humanism, and intelligence.

Emma Goldman was born in Kovno, Lithuania, then part of the Russian Empire, in 1869 to a financially insecure but observant family. Her family moved to Koenigsberg for a number of years, where she was able to obtain some secular schooling, but when they returned to St. Petersburg, the secular window closed. Her father arranged a marriage for her when she was fifteen and when she refused, he threw her French dictionary in the fire. Only after she threatened suicide did her father allow her to leave for America in 1885.

After working in upstate New York for a few years, she moved to New York City in 1889. She had been converted to anarchism and she now became the protégé of the movement's spokesman, Johann Most. She studied political theory and began her career as a speaker, at first addressing small groups of immigrant workers in Yiddish, German, or Russian, and then setting out on an independent tour across the nation. She earned her living as a seamstress or factory worker.

When the Homestead Steel Strike in Pennsylvania was quelled by armed guards, Goldman and her anarchist lover, Alexander Berkman, decided to assassinate the chairman of the steel company, Henry Frick. Berkman pulled the trigger; Goldman's role was to explain their act to the world. Frick was merely wounded and Berkman was sent to jail. But Goldman acquired her reputation as a demon. She later served a year in prison for having given a speech that allegedly incited the unemployed to riot.

In the ensuing years, Goldman continued her task of speaking across the country, usually to packed audiences, thanks to her firebrand delivery and her reputation. She traveled also to Europe and developed a reputation in international revolutionary circles. In 1906 she began publishing and editing a new radical monthly journal, *Mother Earth*. When Berkman was released from prison he joined her as co-editor, and they made the journal a sounding board for anarchist and revolutionary ideas. In 1910 Goldman published a volume of her writings, *Anarchism and Other Essays*. It included essays on education, prisons, political violence, and the oppression of women. And despite often being arrested, she continued to make cross-country lecture tours and provocative speeches.

In 1917, after Goldman and Berkman had organized antiwar rallies and a league opposed to the draft, they were arrested, found guilty of obstructing the draft, and sentenced to two years in prison with a recommendation they be deported when their prison terms were up. In 1919, Goldman, Berkman, and 247 other "Reds'" were deported to the Soviet Union. Almost from the beginning, Goldman found herself opposed to what was happening there. Totally disillusioned, she and Berkman left Soviet Russia in 1921. After some wandering, Goldman settled in England, where she supported herself by writing. She had not lost her fighting spirit, however, and threw herself into the Spanish Civil War cause in 1936, directing the Spanish anarchists' press and propaganda effort. She died in 1940 and was buried in Chicago next to the anarchists who had been killed in the Haymarket affair.

Goldman lived her life with passion, idealism, and courage, totally committed to direct action to bring about change. She was critical of those who lived with less integrity than she. While she was a universalist and social revolutionary, she was also very Jewish in her style and in her cultural persona.

The Tragedy of Woman's Emancipation

. . . A rich intellect and a fine soul are usually considered necessary attributes of a deep and beautiful personality. In the case of the modern woman, these attributes serve as a hindrance to the complete assertion of her being. For over a hundred years the old form of marriage, based on the Bible, "Till death doth part," has been denounced as an institution that stands for the sovereignty of the man over the woman, of her complete submission to his whims and commands, and absolute dependence on his name and support. Time and again it has been conclusively proved that the old matrimonial relation restricted woman to the function of man's servant and the bearer of his children. And yet we find many emancipated women who prefer marriage, with all its deficiencies, to the narrowness of an unmarried life: narrow and unendurable because of the chains of moral and social prejudice that cramp and bind her nature.

The explanation of such inconsistency on the part of many advanced women is to be found in the fact that they never truly understood the meaning of emancipation. They thought that all that was needed was independence from external tyrannies; the internal tyrants, far more harmful to life and growth—ethical and social conventions—were left to take care of themselves; and they have taken care of themselves. They seem to get along as beautifully in the heads and hearts of the most active exponents of woman's emancipation, as in the heads and hearts of our grandmothers.

These internal tyrants, whether they be in the form of public opinion or what will mother say, or brother, father, aunt, or relative of any sort; what will Mrs. Grundy, Mr. Comstock, the employer, the Board of Education say? All these busybodies, moral detectives, jailers of the human spirit, what will they say? Until woman has learned to defy them all, to stand firmly on her own ground and to insist upon her own unrestricted freedom, to listen to the voice of her nature, whether it call for life's greatest treasure, love for a man, or her most glorious privilege, the right to give birth to a child, she cannot call herself emancipated. . . .

. . . The greatest shortcoming of the emancipation of the present day lies in its artificial stiffness and its narrow respectabilities, which produce an emptiness in woman's soul that will not let her drink from the fountain of life. I once remarked that there seemed to be a deeper relationship between the old-fashioned mother and hostess, ever on the alert for the happiness of her little ones and the comfort of those she loves, and the truly new woman, than between the latter and her average emancipated sister. The disciples of emancipation pure and simple declared me a heathen, fit only for the stake. Their blind zeal did not let them see that my comparison between the old and the new was merely to prove that a goodly number of our grandmothers had more blood in their veins, far more humor and wit, and certainly a greater amount of naturalness, kind-heartedness, and simplicity, than the majority of our emancipated professional women who fill the colleges, halls of learning and various offices. This does not mean a wish to return to the past, nor does it condemn woman to her old sphere, the kitchen and the nursery.

Salvation lies in an energetic march onward towards a brighter and clearer future. We are in need of unhampered growth out of old traditions and habits. The movement for woman's emancipation has so far made but the first step in that direction. It is to be hoped that it will gather strength to make another. The right to vote, or equal civil rights, may be good demands, but true emancipation begins neither at the polls nor in the courts. It begins in woman's soul. History tells us that every oppressed class gained true liberation from its masters through its own efforts. It is necessary that woman learn that lesson, that she realize that her freedom will reach as far as her power to achieve her freedom reaches. It is, therefore, far more important for her to begin with her inner regeneration, to cut loose from the weight of prejudices, traditions, and customs. The demand for equal rights in every vocation of life is just and fair; but, after all, the most vital right is the right to love and be loved. Indeed, if partial emancipation is to become a complete and true emancipation of woman, it will have to do away with the ridiculous notion that to be loved, to be sweetheart and mother, is synonymous with being slave or subordinate. It will have to do away with the absurd notion of the dualism of the sexes, or that man and woman represent two antagonistic worlds.

Pettiness separates; breadth unites. Let us be broad and big. Let us not overlook vital things because of the bulk of trifles confronting us. A true conception of the relation of the sexes will not admit of conqueror and conquered; it knows of but one great thing; to give of one's self boundlessly, in order to find one's self richer, deeper, better. That alone can fill the emptiness, and transform the tragedy of woman's emancipation into joy, limitless joy.

Was My Life Worth Living?

I have often been asked why I maintained such a non-compromising antagonism to government and in what way I have found myself oppressed by it. In my opinion every individual is hampered by it. It exacts taxes from production. It creates tariffs, which prevents free exchange. It stands ever for the *status quo* and traditional conduct and belief. It comes into private lives and into most intimate personal relations, enabling the superstitious, puritanical, and distorted ones to impose their ignorant prejudice and moral servitude upon the sensitive, the imaginative, and the free spirits. Government does this by its divorce laws, its moral censorship, and by a thousand petty persecutions of those who are too honest to wear the moral mask of respectability. In addition, government protects the strong at the expense of the weak, provides courts and laws which the rich may scorn and the poor must obey. It enables the predatory rich to make wars to provide foreign markets for the favored ones, with prosperity for the rulers and wholesale death for the ruled. However, it is not only government in the sense of the state which is destructive of every individual value and quality. It is the whole complex of authority and institutional domination which strangles life. It is the superstition, myth, pretense, evasions and subservience which support authority and institutional domination. It is the reverence for these institutions instilled in the school, the church, and the home in order that man may believe and obey without protest. Such a process of devitalizing and distorting personalities of the individual and of whole communities may have been a part of historical evolution; but it should be strenuously combated by every honest and independent mind in an age which has any pretense to enlightenment. . . .

I consider Anarchism the most beautiful and practical philosophy that has yet been thought of in its application to individual expression and the relation it establishes between the individual and society. Moreover, I am certain that Anarchism is too vital and too close to human nature ever to die. It is my conviction that dictatorship, whether to the right or to the left, can never work—that it never has worked, and that time will prove this again, as it has been proved before. When the failure of modern dictatorship and authoritarian philosophies becomes more apparent and the realization of failure more general, Anarchism will be vindicated. Considered from this point, a recrudescence of Anarchist ideas in the near future is very probable. . . .

Anarchism alone stresses the importance of the individual, his possibilities and needs in a free society. Instead of telling him that he must fall down and worship before institutions, live and die for abstractions, break his heart and stunt his life for taboos, Anarchism insists that the center of gravity in society is the individual—that he must think for himself, act freely, and live fully. The aim of Anarchism is that every individual in the world shall be able to do so. If he is to develop freely and fully, he must be relieved from the interference and oppression of others. Freedom is, therefore, the cornerstone of the Anarchist philosophy. Of course, this has nothing in common with a much boasted "rugged individualism." Such predatory individualism is really flabby, not rugged. At the least danger to its safety it runs to cover of the state and wails for protection of armies, navies, or whatever devices for strangulation it has at its command. Their "rugged individualism" is simply one of the many pretenses the ruling class makes to unbridled business and political extortion. . . .

The fact that the Anarchist movement for which I have striven so long is to a certain extent in abeyance and overshadowed by philosophies of authority and coercion affects me with concern, but not with despair. It seems to me a point of special significance that many countries decline to admit Anarchists. All governments hold the view that while parties of the right and left may advocate social changes, still they cling to the idea of government and authority. Anarchism alone breaks with both and propagates uncompromising rebellion. In the long run, therefore, it is Anarchism which is considered deadlier to the present regime than all other social theories that are now clamoring for power.

Considered from this angle, I think my life and my work have been successful. What is generally regarded as success—acquisition of wealth, the capture of power or social prestige—I consider the most dismal failures. I hold when it is said of a man that he has arrived, it means that he is finished—his development has stopped at that point. I have always striven to remain in a state of flux and continued growth, and not to petrify in a niche of self-satisfaction. If I had my life to live over again, like anyone else, I should wish to alter minor details. But in any of my more important actions and attitudes I would repeat my life as I have lived it. Certainly I should work for Anarchism with the same devotion and confidence in its ultimate triumph.

Horace Kallen (1882–1974)

Introduction

Horace Kallen would feel right at home in the current American struggle over multiculturalism in the classroom. Kallen was an early exponent of the idea of retaining ethnic identities in order to foster cultural pluralism in American society. He advised immigrants to take pride in their national origins, and to keep their native language as a second language to English. As a philosopher, secular humanist, and Zionist, he made important contributions to Jewish life in America, yet is virtually unknown today.

Horace Kallen was born in Germany in 1882, the son of a rabbi. The family came to America when he was a child. He did his undergraduate and graduate training in philosophy at Harvard University, where he was a student of the eminent William James. After teaching at a number of American colleges and universities, he helped to found the New School for Social Research, where he then taught from 1919 to 1956. He published a study of what he regarded as philosophically contrasting theories of life in his *William James and Henri Bergson*, published in 1914.

After moving to New York, Kallen began to devote more time to Jewish affairs. He became active in the American Jewish Congress and in 1942 was appointed co-director of a newly formed board of trustees of the Institute for Jewish Affairs. He was also active in the

Society for the Scientific Study of Religion and in the International League for the Rights of Man. Following his mentor William James, Kallen sought to conciliate the claims of modern science with religion, particularly Judaism. He maintained that religion is created by people, not revealed by God, and, as an expression of the moral values of the group, is an important factor in binding groups together. His stress on the need for a pluralistic, democratic, secular society flowed from his conviction that only such a society could prevent the interests of any one group from dominating the others.

Kallen was a lifelong Zionist, believing that a Jewish state would serve both as a cultural, "spiritual" center for Jewish people as well as a place of refuge for persecuted Jews. He argued against the universalist humanists who attacked Zionism because it was nationalistic. Kallen insisted that genuine liberalism necessitated that nations have the same freedom to develop as that accorded to individuals. He never doubted that the Jews qualified as a nation based on their history. After a visit to Palestine he published *Judaism at Bay* in 1932. Some of his other chief published works are *Frontiers of Hope, Why Religion?*, and *Zionism and World Politics.*

Is There a Jewish View of Life?

Albert Einstein says that there isn't, "in the philosophic sense." He may be right. But also, he may be wrong. The question does not admit of a single, unambiguous answer.

For the Jews are an ancient people, and their history is long and varied. Their religion, Judaism, is not so old nor so varied as the history of its creators and adherents, yet its own life-history is marked with at least as many crises and alternations as the life-story of the Jewish people. And it could not be otherwise. For Judaism, like Hebraism, is an indefinite manifold. Its existence consists of the coming together and the moving apart of great numbers of diverse and contradictory items of thought, feeling and conduct.

Each and every one of these items has a claim upon the consideration of any person endeavoring to establish what Judaism is or what Judaism is not.

But this claim is hardly even honored. The definition which any citizen gives Judaism depends on his loves and hates, on his wishes and frustrations Those cause him to react selectively to the entire shifting aggregate of which living Judaism is composed. They will lead him to affirm qualities which others deny, and deny qualities which others affirm.

To this rule, Einstein is no exception. In science, a specialist in astronomical mathematics; in human relations, a democrat, an internationalist and pacifist, the loyalties and rebellions these terms imply determine in advance what items from the manifold of Judaism he will choose in order to make up an exclusive definition of "the Jewish view of life."

With Dr. Einstein's selection I have no quarrel. On the contrary, it is quite in harmony with the type of selection I myself make, as those well know who have read my works on this subject, especially my *Judaism at Bay,* where I have endeavored to show why some such view of Judaism may be held as peculiarly representative of the high place in the rise and fall of the Jewish tradition.

But demonstrating and establishing this definition call for the simultaneous recognition that there exist other opinions, other views of Jewish life, other and quite contrary definitions, each one of them an alternative demanding to be refuted and cast aside. Refuting them and casting them aside meant acknowledging that they had a place in the aggregate which is Judaism. Some of them include Maimonides and shut out Spinoza. Others include the Bible and exclude the *Siddur* [prayerbook]. Some include the *Shulhan Arukh* [code of laws], but exclude Maimonides, Spinoza, the *Siddur* and the Bible. Others combine them all with the *Shulhan Arukh.* Still others exclude the *Shulhan Arukh,* mutilate the *Siddur* and include a "mission of Israel" and "ethical monotheism" and at the same time glorify Maimonides and patronize Spinoza.

Who is right? Who is wrong? The answer does not depend on the intrinsic character of the definition nor on its historical correctness nor its religious sanctions. The answer depends entirely on its *consequences* to the strength, the enrichment of Jewish life.

Now in life, quite otherwise than in mathematics, consequences belong to an unpredictable future. They can not be established in advance. They are not foregone conclusions.

History, which can be written only by survivors in the struggle for life, is the judgment which the survivors pass upon both their struggle and their opponents. Thus, Jewish history as written by Jews embodies the judgment of the victorious Elohist upon the defeated Yahwist, the victorious priest upon the defeated prophet, the victorious Pharisee upon the lost Sadducee, the persisting rabbi upon the transient dissenter, the effortful nationalist upon the sentimental religionist, and so on. Contemporary parties in Israel employ or reverse these judgments in order to rationalize their own ends and to justify their own struggles. For example, the very reverend Dr. Cyrus Adler, President of the Jewish Theological Seminary, President of Dropsie College, President of the American Jewish Committee, etc., etc., will put together and invoke one set of historic judgments to justify his mortuary policy and attitude in Jewish life. The less reverend Drs. Albert Einstein or Stephen Wise will invoke another set to justify their vital ones. Their compositions, their invocations, their demonstrations, their arguments are not revelations of the facts. Their compositions, their invocations, their demonstrations, and their arguments are only invidious uses, special application of the facts. The facts themselves remain everlastingly neutral to all the causes that employ them, stubbornly elusive to all the meanings which are imposed on them.

We may get some inkling of the character and implications of the facts when the observer who studies them has no passionate concern about their use.

Thus, we may take it as being pretty close to the truth when George Foot Moore tells us, in his magnificent *Judaism,* that the Judaistic tradition owns no theology in the Christian or Greek sense of the term; that its dynamic essence was the rule of life or the system of observances which were finally codified in the *Shulhan Arukh* and were the same wherever in the wide world Jews could be found; but that "basic human relations are without measure or norm and left to the conscience and right feeling of the individual"; that they are *masur lalev,* committed to heart.

But Moore was writing of what has sometimes been called "normative Judaism." He had also made a selection. He paid attention to nothing outside of this traditional historic complex which the generations kept on reliving until the middle of the last century. He ignored the variant, the new, the heretical, which had arisen and struggled to establish itself within the complex. But he knew he did so, and he did not endeavor to have anyone take the part for the whole. A complete science of Jewry cannot ignore those things. A complete science must include everything that any Jew has ever identified as Jewish in life and quality. But Jews laboring in their struggle for a life and a living, are prevented from dealing with this all-inclusive total. The time and place and circumstances of their struggle, its passions and its ideals dispose them to seek one item and reject another, so that their passions may be gratified and their ideals realized.

Thus, it is Dr. Einstein's necessity and his right to select from the Jewish inheritance that which seems to him pertinent to his struggle and his ideals. His opponents have the same necessity and right to make their own selections. But both he and they would be wrong if they treated their selections as accounts of the entire Jewish reality, as descriptions of the historic content of Judaism and Hebraism. In the nature of the case, such selections can be nothing of the sort. First and last, they are personal and class valuations, special pleas made by means of data lifted thus out of their original contexts, and employed to express the feelings and to realize the ideals of those who have so lifted them. Judaism and Hebraism is not any one of them by itself. It is all of them together—and then some.

Is there, then a Jewish view of life? No. There is not *a* Jewish view of life. There are Jewish *views* of life. The views are many. Life, with all its conflicts and antagonisms and hates, indeed through them, makes itself somehow one.

JUDAISM AT BAY

. . . In history the culture of the Jews appears as no mere religion; in the world's count of it, it receives another name and a different estimate. It is called Hebraism, not Judaism, and to be a lover of Hebraism is more than to be a Judaist. A sectarian life . . . is no excuse whatever for separation. Sects and dogmas pass, ethnic groups and cultures endure. The blindness and insensibility of "reform" lies in the failure or refusal to recognize this fact and in the consequent attempt to thin the richness of Jewish existence to the verbal tenuousness of a few unproved dogmas and to substitute for concrete Jewish living the anatomical horror of their "Jewish science." Hebraism is a life and not a tradition; Judaism is a spirit, a concrete and particular mode of behavior, not a formula. They are growing and changing things, expressions of a palpable vitality, not dead unalterable "universals." The true deniers of "everything Israel has stood for in history," are those alone who would substitute the bloodless "universal" for the fecund concrete life. What really destroys the Jews is what "universalizes" them, what empties their life of distinctive particular content and substitutes void phrases to be filled with any meaning the social and religious fashion of the day casts up. Hebraism, what "Israel has stood for in history," is the life of Jews, their unique achievement,—not as isolated individuals, but as a well-defined ethnic group,—in government, in industry and commerce, in social economy, in the arts, in religion, in philosophy. Hebraism is the particular inheritance of the Jews, their tradition and their culture, potently efficacious in contemporary Jewish living, its matrix and inspiration.

The historic content of Hebraism was in metaphysics the vision of reality in flux; in morals, the conception of the value of the individual, in religion, the conception of Yahweh as a moral arbiter. That the national life in Palestine, expressed in the Scriptures, is the source of a considerable portion of the moral and religious ideas of the western world is, of course, a commonplace. What is not so clearly apprehended is the fact that the Jews, as an *ethnic group*, were the great middlemen of medieval times, and that what they disseminated was as much the wisdom of the ancients as the commodities of commerce. Related only in the most incidental fashion to the polities of Europe, they lived an organic, inner political life of their own, distinct and segregated from all others, and as its social expression, generated the basis of the present efficacious financial system, helped preserve and restore the ancient wisdom to Europe and practiced with signal distinction the art of medicine. In modern times the life of the majority of the Jews has been no less national, confined as they are to the pales of settlement, though it has been less obviously contributory to civilization—the emphasis appearing to lie on the notion of political and economic freedom. To culture Jewry has contributed a significant bi-lingual literature, Hebrew and Yiddish, just as the earlier ages saw the creation of Talmudic and Hebrew. From Amos to Karl Marx and from the singer of Deborah's song to Peretz, the vision of the world and the expression of life has been continuous yet varying for the Jews and honestly efficacious for western civilization.

That this vision and expression are rooted in ethnic solidarity and a geographical concentration, practically equivalent to nationality, any one with eyes may see. The isolation of the Jews is traditional, but the notion of the "Diaspora" as *absence from Palestine* has taken such hold of the world's imagination that the life of the Jewish mass as *presence in another region* was not thought of, the various devices that, during the Middle Ages, made a federated European Jewry were not considered. As a matter of fact, the "Diaspora" is only a partial thing; it is like the Diaspora of the English in the British Empire. The Jews always had a center of reference, a spiritual capital to look to; in the long run the *majority* of them have throughout their history lived together and lived a homogeneous national life.

In sum: Up to within a century ago the Jews of the world as a *majority,* lived an organic social life and have expressed it in a culture which has been continually efficacious in the wider world. The "Jewish problem," for the Jews the problem of the Jewish spirit, began with the external and artificial attempt to thin Hebraism down to a mere sectarian Judaism. There is every reason be believe this attempt, however well intended, dangerous to Jewish survival. . . .

(Chapter IV)

Cultures, you will see, possess a nature as organic as the physical form of life. Just as in temperament and in power you cannot separate yourself from your ancestors, from your heredity; or in health, you cannot separate the condition of one of your organs—of your lungs or heart or brain or liver—from the rest, so you cannot separate any social institution from the natural community-complex of which it is a part. To do so is to kill it, and in so far as the rabbis have detached Judaism from the total complex of *Jewish* life, they have condemned it to death. Life is organic; you cannot breed a feather without breeding a whole chicken, nor a living heart without a whole living body. You cannot convert the Jewish community into a mere sect without destroying Judaism. Judaism as Judaism can flourish only in the organic wholesomeness of Jewish communal life, with its checks and counterchecks, its conflicts, adjustments, and balancing of opposed parts. Only by reintegrating

Judaism into the wholeness can it be saved.

This is why I, as a Zionist, find something unthinking in what each theorist tries to do to the fact of Jewishness. For each lays stress on some particular part or aspect of the whole; each seeks, in fact, to substitute this part for the whole. In religion orthodoxy is more organic than reform, however, for orthodoxy is a *way of living*, while reform is only a way of talking.

As a Zionist, I am concerned about the *wholeness* of the Jewish spirit, that wholeness in which each tendency, each party, exercises a particular organic function, as the organs of the body do in the body. I welcome them all, I acknowledge them all; orthodox and radical, sectarian and nationalist. However much they may deny it, their addressing each other, their quarreling and debating with each other, diseased as this often is, is a complete acknowledgment of how dependent upon each other they are. If the Jews were really a sect, the sectarians would be at no such pains to prove it; if the Jews were as integrally a nation as they are a nationality, the nationalists would not be so ardent. In point of fact, all these parties are members of one another, dependent upon one another for their existence. Together, not in isolation, they constitute that social fact, the Jewish people. . . .

(Chapter VIII)

Erich Fromm (1900–1980)

Introduction

Erich Fromm was a major American psychoanalyst and social philosopher whose goal was to integrate psychoanalysis with the humanistic tradition in philosophy, social science, and religion. He was also determined to turn theory into practice in his work as an analyst, political activist, and social scientist. He was the author of many influential books and articles. He influenced generations of college students and gave humanistic consciousness to American intellectual debate.

Fromm was born in Germany in 1900 into a family of rabbis and was devout as a youth. He was educated in Frankfurt and attended the famous Lehrhaus of Franz Rosenzweig. After Hitler came to power, Fromm emigrated to the United States. He held teaching appointments at several American universities and at the end of his life moved to Mexico, where he died in 1980.

When Fromm abandoned Jewish ritual and practice in his late twenties, he retained his faith in the validity of religious teachings about human beings. Fromm, although a Freudian, did not share Freud's ideas about religion being an illusion. Fromm believed that religion has humanistic, liberating aspects. He maintained that human development followed a path advocated by the great humanistic religions, that of overcoming greed, hate, and intense egoism and evolving instead into compassionate, caring beings who live life fully.

Fromm's interpretation of the Bible and the Talmud was critical from the secular perspective but also affirming. In his *You Shall Be as Gods* (1966), he interprets the development of the concepts in the Bible as an unfolding struggle toward humanistic consciousness and the final overcoming of idolatry. God's total power in the beginning gives way eventually to man's power, and God rejoices in this victory of his creation.

In his influential book, *Escape from Freedom* (1941), Fromm explored humanity's unconscious fear of freedom and demonstrated why authoritarian political systems had such appeal. Later in his life Fromm was active in the peace movement, speaking out for arms control in the 1960s and voicing opposition to the Vietnam War and to the Cold War against the Soviets. While he was optimistic about human nature and its capacity for creative growth, Fromm understood the potential in humans for destructive behavior as well.

PSYCHOANALYSIS AND RELIGION

Humanistic religion . . . is centred around man and his strength. Man must develop his power of reason in order to understand himself, his relationship to his fellow men and his position in the universe. He must recognize the truth, both with regard to his limitations and potentialities. He must develop his powers of love for others as well as for himself and experience the solidarity of all living beings. He must have principles and norms to guide him in this aim. Religious experience in this kind of religion is the experience of oneness with the All, based on one's relatedness to the world as it is grasped with thought and with love. Man's aim in humanistic religion is to achieve the greatest strength, not the greatest powerlessness; virtue is self-realization, not obedience. Faith is certainty of conviction based on one's experience of thought and feeling, not assent to propositions on credit of the proposer. The prevailing mood is that of joy, while the prevailing mood in authoritarian religion is that of sorrow and of guilt.

Inasmuch as humanistic religions are theistic, God is a symbol of *man's own powers* which he tries to realize in his life, and is not a symbol of force and domination, having *power over man.*

Illustrations of humanistic religions are early Buddhism, Taoism, the teachings of Isaiah, Jesus, Socrates, Spinoza, certain trends in the Jewish and Christian religions (particularly mysticism), the religion of Reason of the French Revolution. It is evident from these that the distinction between authoritarian and humanistic religion cuts across the distinction between theistic and nontheistic, and between religions in the narrow sense of the word and philosophical systems of religious character. What matters in all such systems is not the thought system as such but the human attitude underlying their doctrines.

One of the best examples of humanistic religions is early Buddhism. The Buddha is a great teacher, he is the "awakened one" who recognizes the truth about human existence. He does not speak in the name of a supernatural power but in the name of reason. He calls upon every man to make use of his own reason and to see the truth which he was only the first to find. Once man takes the first step in seeing the truth, he must apply his efforts to live in such a way that he develops his powers of reason and love for all human creatures. Only to the degree to which he succeeds in this can he free himself from the bondage of irrational passions. While man must recognize his limitations according to Buddhistic teaching, he must also become aware of the powers in himself. The concept of Nirvana as the state of mind the fully awakened one can achieve is not one of man's helplessness and submission but on the contrary one of the development of the highest powers man possesses.

Another illustration of a humanistic religious system is to be found in Spinoza's religious thinking. While his language is that of medieval theology, his concept of God has no trace of authoritarianism. God could not have created the world different from what it is. He cannot change anything; in fact, God is identical with the totality of the universe. Man must see his own limitations and recognize that he is dependent on the totality of forces outside himself over which he has no control. Yet his are the powers of love and reason. He can develop them and attain an optimum of freedom and of inner strength.

. . . The same humanistic spirit can be found in many stories from the Chassidic folklore of more than a thousand years later. The Chassidic movement was a rebellion of the poor against those who had the monopoly of learning or of money. Their motto was the verse of the Psalms: "Serve God in joy." They emphasized feeling rather than intellectual accomplishment, joy rather than contrition; to them (as to Spinoza) joy was the equivalent of virtue and sadness the equivalent of sin. The following story is characteristic of the humanistic and anti-authoritarian spirit of this religious sect:

A poor tailor came to a Chassidic rabbi the day after the Day of Atonement and said to him, "Yesterday I had an argument with God. I told him, 'Oh God, you have committed sins and I have committed sins. But you have committed grave sins and I have committed sins of no great importance. What have you done? You have separated mothers from their children and permitted people to starve. What have I done?" I have sometimes failed to return a piece of cloth to a customer or have not been strict in the observance of the law. But I will tell you, God. I will forgive you your sins and you forgive me mine. Thus we are even.' " Whereupon the Rabbi answered, "You fool! Why did you let him get away that easily? Yesterday you could have forced him to send the Messiah."

. . . While in humanistic religion God is the image of man's higher self, a symbol of what man potentially is or ought to become, in authoritarian religion God becomes the sole possessor of what was originally man's: of his reason and his love. The more perfect God becomes, the more imperfect becomes man. He *projects* the best he has on to God and thus impoverishes himself. Now God has all love, all wisdom, all justice—and man is deprived of these qualities, he is empty and poor. He had begun with the feeling of smallness, but he now has become completely powerless and without strength; all his powers have been projected on to God. This mechanism of projection is the very same which can be observed in interpersonal relationships of a masochistic, submissive character, where one person is awed by another and attributes his own powers and aspirations to the other person. It is the same mechanism that makes people endow leaders of even the most inhuman systems with qualities of superwisdom and kindness.

When man has thus projected his own most valuable powers on to God, what of his relationship to his own powers? They have become separated from him and in this process he has come *alienated* from himself. Everything he has is now God's and nothing is left in him. *His only access to himself is through God.* In worshipping God he tries to get in touch with that part of himself which he has lost through projection. After having given God all he has, he begs God to return to him some of what originally was his own. But having lost his own he is completely at God's mercy. He necessarily feels like a "sinner" since he has deprived himself of everything that is good, and it is only through God's mercy or grace that he can regain that which alone makes him human. And in order to persuade God to give him some of his love, he must prove to him how utterly deprived he is of love; in order to persuade God to guide him by His superior wisdom he must prove to him how deprived he is of wisdom when he is left to himself.

But this alienation from his own powers not only makes man feel slavishly dependent on God, it makes him bad too. He becomes a man without faith in his fellow men or in himself, without the experience of his own love, of his own power of reason. As a result the separation between the "holy" and the "secular" occurs. In his worldly activities man acts without love, in that sector of his life which is reserved to religion he feels himself to be a sinner (which he actually is, since to live without love is to live in sin) and tries to recover some of his lost humanity by being in touch with God. Simultaneously, he tries to win forgiveness by emphasizing his own helplessness and worthlessness. Thus the attempt to obtain forgiveness results in the activation of the very attitude from which his sins stem. He is caught in a painful dilemma. The more he praises God, the emptier he becomes. The emptier he becomes, the more sinful he feels. The more sinful he feels, the more he praises his God—and the less able he is to regain himself.

YOU SHALL BE AS GODS

The Old Testament is a book of many colors, written, edited, and re-edited by may writers in the course of a millennium and containing in itself a remarkable evolution from primitive authoritarianism and clannishness to the idea of the radical freedom of man and the brotherhood of all men. The Old Testament is a *revolutionary* book; its theme is the liberation of man from the incestuous ties to blood and soil, from the submission to idols, from slavery, from powerful masters, to freedom for the individual, for the nation, and for all of mankind. Perhaps we, today, can understand the Hebrew Bible better than any age before, precisely because we live in a time of revolution in which man, in spite of many errors that lead him into new forms of dependence, is shaking himself free of all forms of social bondage once sanctioned by "God" and the "social laws." Perhaps, paradoxically enough, one of the oldest books of Western culture can be understood best by those who are least fettered by tradition and most aware of the radical nature of the process of liberation going on at the present time.

A few words must be said about my approach to the Bible in this book. I do not look at it as the "word of God," not only because historical examination shows that it is a book written by men—different kinds of men, living in different times—but also because I am not a theist. Yet, to me, it is an extraordinary book, expressing many norms and principles that have maintained their validity throughout thousand of years. It is a book which has proclaimed a vision for men that is still valid and awaiting realization. It was not written by one man, nor dictated by God; it expresses the genius of a people struggling for life and freedom throughout many generations. . . .

If it is possible to discover the seeds of radical humanism in the older sources of the Bible, it is only because we know the radical humanism of Amos, of Socrates, of the Renaissance humanists, of the Enlightenment, of Kant, Herder, Lessing, Goethe, Marx, Schweitzer. The seed becomes clearly recognizable only if one knows the flower, the earlier phase is often to be interpreted by the later phase, even though, genetically, the earlier phase precedes the later.

There is one more aspect of the radical humanist interpretation that needs to be mentioned. Ideas, especially if they are the ideas not only of a single individual but have become integrated into the historical process, have their roots in the real life of society. Hence, if one assumes that the idea of radical humanism is a major trend in the biblical and post-biblical tradition, one must assume that basic conditions existed throughout the history of the Jews which would have given rise to the existence and growth of the humanistic tendency. Are there such fundamental conditions? I believe there are and that it is not difficult to discover them. The Jews were in possession of effective and impressive secular power for only a short time, in fact, for only a few generations. After the reigns of David and Solomon, the pressure from the great powers in the north and south grew to such dimensions that Judah and Israel lived under the ever increasing threat of being conquered. And, indeed, conquered they were, never to recover. Even when the Jews later had formal political independence, they were a small and powerless satellite, subject to big powers. When the Romans finally put an end to the state after R. Yohanan ben Zakkai went over to the Roman side, asking only for permission to open an academy in Jabne to train future generations of rabbinical scholars, a Judaism without kings and priests emerged that had already been developing for centuries behind a facade to which the Romans gave only the final blow. Those prophets who had denounced the idolatrous admiration for secular power were vindicated by the course of history. Thus the prophetic teachings, and not Solomon's splendor, became the dominant, lasting influence on Jewish thought. From then on the Jews, as a nation, never again regained power. On the contrary, throughout most of their history they suffered from those who were able to use force. No doubt their position also could, and did, give rise to national resentment, clannishness, arrogance; and this is the basis for the other trend within Jewish history mentioned above.

But is it not natural that the story of the liberation from slavery in Egypt, the speeches of the great humanist prophets, should have found an echo in the hearts of men who had experienced force only as its suffering objects, never as its executors? Is it surprising that the prophetic vision of a united, peaceful mankind, of justice for the poor and helpless, found fertile soil among the Jews and was never forgotten? Is it surprising that when the walls of the ghettos fell, Jews in disproportionately large numbers were among those who proclaimed the ideals of internationalism, peace, and justice? What from a mundane standpoint was the tragedy of the Jews—the loss of their country and their state—from the humanist standpoint was their greatest blessing: being among the suffering and despised, they were able to develop and uphold a tradition of humanism.

(Introduction)

THE ART OF LOVING

Any theory of love must begin with a theory of man, of human existence. While we find love, or rather, the equivalent of love, in animals, their attachments are mainly a part of their instinctual equipment, only remnants of their instinctual equipment can be seen operating in man. What is essential in the existence of man is that fact that he has emerged from the animal kingdom, from instinctive adaptation, that he has transcended nature—although he never leaves it; he is a part of it—and yet once torn away from nature, he cannot return to it; once thrown out of paradise—a state of original oneness with nature—cherubim with flaming swords block his way, if he should try to return. Man can only go forward by developing his reason, by finding a new harmony, a human one, instead of the prehuman harmony which is irretrievably lost.

When man is born, the human race as well as the individual, he is thrown out of a situation which was definite, as definite as the instincts, into a situation which is indefinite, uncertain and open. There is certainty only about the past—and about the future only as far as that it is death.

Man is gifted with reason; he is *life being aware of itself;* he has awareness of himself, of his fellow man, of his past, and of the possibilities of his future. This awareness of himself as a separate entity, the awareness of his own short life span, of the fact that without his will he is born and against his will he dies, that he will die before those whom he loves, or they before him, the awareness of his aloneness and separateness, of the helplessness before the forces of nature and of society, all this makes his separate, disunited existence an unbearable prison. He would become insane could he not liberate himself from this prison and reach out, unite himself in some form or other with men, with the world outside.

(Chapter 1)

The most fundamental kind of love, which underlies all types of love, is *brotherly love.* By this I mean the sense of responsibility, care, respect, knowledge of any other human being, the wish to further his life. This is the kind of love the Bible speaks of when it says: love thy neighbor as thyself. Brotherly love is love for all human beings; it is characterized by its very lack of exclusiveness. If I have developed the capacity for love, then I cannot help loving my brothers. In brotherly love there is the experience of union with all men, of human solidarity, of human at-onement. Brotherly love is based on the experience that we all are one. The differences in talents, intelligence, knowledge are negligible in comparison with the identity of the human core common to all men. In order to experience this identify it is necessary to penetrate from the periphery to the core. If I perceive in another person mainly the surface, I perceive mainly the differences, that which separates us. If I penetrate to the core, I perceive our identity, the fact of our brotherhood. . . .

To love somebody is the actualization and concentration of the power to love. The basic affirmation contained in love is directed toward the beloved person as an incarnation of essentially human qualities. Love of one person implies love of man as such. The king of "division of labor," as William James calls it, by which one loves one's family but is without feeling for the "stranger," is a sign of a basic inability to love. Love of man is not, as is frequently supposed, an abstraction coming after the love for a specific person, but it is its premise, although genetically it is acquired in loving specific individuals.

From this it follows that my own self must be as much an object of my love as another person. *The affirmation of one's own life, happiness, growth, freedom is rooted in one's capacity to love,* i.e. in care, respect, responsibility, and knowledge. If an individual is able to love productively, he loves himself too; if he can love *only* others, he cannot love at all . . . .

Having spoken of the love of God, I want to make it clear that I myself do not think in terms of a theistic concept, and that to me the concept of God is only a historically conditioned one, in which man has expressed his experience of his higher powers, his longing for truth and for unity at a given historical period. But I believe also that the consequences of strict monotheism and a non-theistic ultimate concern with the spiritual reality are two views which, though different, need not fight each other . . . .

(Chapter 2)

The faith in others has its culmination in faith in *mankind*. In the Western world this faith was expressed in religious terms in the Judaeo-Christian religion, and in secular language it has found its strongest expression in the humanistic political and social ideas of the last hundred and fifty years. Like the faith in the child, it is based on the idea that the potentialities of man are such that given the proper conditions he will be capable of building a social order governed by the principles of equality, justice and love. Man has not yet achieved the building of such an order, and therefore the conviction that he can do so requires faith. But like all rational faith this too is not wishful thinking, but based upon the evidence of the past achievements of the human race and on the inner experience of each individual, on his own experience of reason and love.

While irrational faith is rooted in submission to a power which is felt to be overwhelmingly strong, omniscient and omnipotent, and in the abdication of one's power and strength, rational faith is based upon the opposite experience. We have this faith in a thought because it is the result of our own observation and thinking. We have faith in the potentialities of others, of ourselves, and of mankind because, and only to the degree to which, we have experienced the growth in ourselves, the strength of our own power of reason and love. *The basis of rational faith is productiveness;* to live by our faith means to live productively. . . .

. . . If man is to be able to love, he must be put in his supreme place. The economic machine must serve him, rather than he serve it. He must be enabled to share experience, to share work, rather than, at best, share in profits. Society must be organized in such a way that man's social, loving nature is not separated from his social existence, but becomes one with it. If it is true, as I have tried to show, that love is the only sane and satisfactory answer to the problem of human existence, than any society which excludes, relatively, the development of love, must in the long run perish of its own contradiction with the basic necessities of human nature. Indeed, to speak of love is not "preaching," for the simple reason that it means to speak of the ultimate and real need in every human being. . . .

(Chapter 4)

Marie Syrkin (1900–1988)

Introduction

Marie Syrkin was an American journalist, editor, poet, and teacher. She was one of the major figures in Jewish intellectual circles in the United States and in the American Zionist movement.

Syrkin was born in Bern, Switzerland, in 1900, to parents who had left Russia for political reasons. Her father, Nahman Syrkin, was a prominent socialist who helped found the Labor Zionist movement. Marie Syrkin, who emigrated to the United States with her parents in 1908, was raised as an atheist, but with a strong Jewish identity. After attending college she became a teacher in a New York high school, and later taught in a liberal arts college. She published *Your School, Your Children* to demonstrate her theories on education.

Syrkin's passionate devotion to the cause of Jews in Palestine was heightened after her first trip there in 1933. In 1934 she was a co-founder of *Jewish Frontier*, a Labor Zionist journal, and served as its editor for several decades. For the next half century she wrote articles and books about Jewish politics and current events. Her essays appeared in journals such as *Commentary, The Nation, Midstream*, as well as in *Saturday Review* and the *New York Times Magazine*. She wrote *Golda Meir: Woman with a Cause*, after extensive interviews with Meir in Israel, as well as a biography of her father, Nahman Syrkin.

In addition to her political writing, she also wrote poetry on personal and political themes.

LAW AND ORDER

Orderly Universe,
Lawful, radiant,
Safely we move in your strict embrace
Once we discover,
Speeding past earth rise,
Shining assurance
Of your decrees.
Light and motion,
Angelic Energies
Bear in tight bond
Turbulent man,
When obedient, piously watchful,
Measuring seconds and stellar spin,
Human he courses
Down clear-ruled space.

Disorderly earthling,
Caught in heart's chaos,
Take witness from these.
Child of Aquarius,
Learn revolution,
From the sure circling
of stars and seas.

THE COVENANT

My God has pledged me to a bitter love.
His Hand is on me; I cannot forget.
I hold the key but everywhere I move
The ghetto walls slide close around me yet.
I know no psalms. The synagogue is dust.
The worshippers' thin voices fade away.
And yet how often to my knees I'm thrust,
I who do not believe forever pray.
Swine's flesh I've eaten and my faith have broken,
And he, great God, has broken faith with me,
Yet not in vain the words of awe were spoken,
The bond remains, unwilling though I be,
And when my mind cries, "Stop, there is no need,"
My blood remembers it is Abraham's seed.

Sidney Hook (1902–1989)

Introduction

Sidney Hook was one of the important figures in contemporary American philosophy. Rather than create a philosophical system, however, Hook exemplified the role of the application of pragmatic intelligence to the solution of contemporary problems, particularly in the realm of ethical, political, and social issues. He carried on the pragmatic tradition in American philosophy as he had learned it from John Dewey, and brought his powers of philosophic analysis to what he saw as the critical issues of his time.

Hook was born in New York City and was given a traditional religious education in addition to his secular schooling. After his bar mitzvah, however, Hook abandoned any religious beliefs, and was a secular humanist for the rest of his life. He received his Ph.D. in philosophy from Columbia University, where he had studied with John Dewey, and joined the department of philosophy at New York University in 1927. He served as the chair of the department from 1934 to 1968.

Hook had read Karl Marx as a young student and later attempted to treat Marxist theory from a pragmatic perspective, particularly in his *Towards the Understanding of Karl Marx* and *From Hegel to Marx*. Hook was one of the organizers of the American Workers Party and taught one of the first American university courses on communism. By the late 1930s, however, Hook was disillusioned by what was happening in the Soviet Union and became a leading critic of the totalitarian forms of Marxism, particularly Leninism and Stalinism. In books and articles he warned against Communist attempts to dominate cultural and intellectual conferences of the left. In 1949 he organized Americans for Intellectual Freedom, which later became the anti-Communist American Committee for Cultural Freedom.

Freedom, particularly in the form of political democracy, played a central role in Hook's thinking. Democracy, he felt, was grounded on the principle that people should be afforded the opportunities to fulfill their individual needs for freedom and growth. Education had a basic role to play in a democratic state by developing the citizenry's critical intelligence. During his career, Hook devoted a great deal of energy to defining and defending academic freedom within the university. In his later years, he was the founder of the University Centers for Rational Alternatives, a faculty group that was concerned with defending the academic process from politicization, including the imposition of affirmative action policies.

Hook was a critic of theology and argued in his writings that there was a lack of evidence that God existed or that there was any intrinsic purpose to reality. He even took to task those humanists who attempted to redefine the concept of God in naturalistic terms. Humanism, for Hook, was primarily an ethical position, based on his belief that ethical judgments flow independently from human experience and require no divine validation.

Hook published many articles and over thirty books, including *Education for Modern Man* and *Religion in a Free Society.*

OUT OF STEP

My criticism of neo-Thomism and Catholic philosophy, as well as of the various expressions of Protestant neo-orthodoxy—especially the views of Niebuhr and Tillich—were not motivated by any desire to defend Judaism in any of its historic forms. I was a confirmed naturalist, who in the interest of clarity, was prepared to characterize my position as one of open-minded atheism. I had never involved myself in organized political Jewish life, but I was always sympathetic to the point of view of the European Jewish Bund and the Jewish Labor Committee in the United States.

During the thirties, I wrote an essay for the *The Menorah Journal* entitled "Promise Without Dogma: A Social Philosophy for Jews" in which I held that the desire of the Jews to survive as a group, whether it be defined in terms of religion, culture, or historical continuity, was as legitimate as the desire of any other group. I then argued that the prospects of achieving this goal would in all likelihood be strengthened by emphasizing the principles of cultural pluralism, political democracy, privatization of religion, a democratic socialist welfare state, and the supremacy of the rational or scientific method. That is to say *in addition* to other good and sufficient reasons for defending these principles, I maintained that the Jews as a special group were more likely to escape their age-old discrimination in a society whose institutions furthered these values. . . .

(p.352)

THE QUEST FOR BEING

The position of this chapter is that the philosophy of *naturalistic* humanism, which regards man as an integral but distinctive part of nature, as wholly a creature of natural origin and natural end, offers an adequate and fruitful basis for the social reconstruction which is essential for the emergence of patterns of human dignity on a world-wide scale. This view in recent years has been the object of sustained criticism from various quarters which have called into question the self-sufficiency of man. Some years ago, adopting a phrase from Gilbert Murray's account of the stages of Greek religion, I referred to this anti-naturalistic movement as "the new failure of nerve." Since then it has taken on the proportions of a tidal wave in philosophy, theology, literature and the philosophy of history. Characteristic of its views are two beliefs: (1) that our time of troubles is primarily an historical and logical consequence of the abandonment of the religious and metaphysical foundations of Western civilization and of a shift to secular life; and (2) that what gives genuine happiness to man, and relief from the multiple alienations which fragmentize both personality and society, in the words of St. Augustine "is something which does not proceed from human nature but which is above human nature." And from these beliefs the criticism follows that naturalism in any form is incapable of doing justice to the actually experienced qualities of human life, particularly the nature of man's moral experience.

Before proceeding to logical analysis of these criticisms a few historical remarks are in order. The notion that the decline of medieval supernaturalism gave rise to a secular naturalistic humanism which enjoyed the same position of authority and prestige as the philosophy it replaced is a legend that will no more bear examination than its countermyth which holds that the rise of Christian supernaturalism resulted not from the bankruptcy of pagan supernaturalism but from the alleged failure of Greco-Roman secularism. The life of a culture is expressed primarily in its institutions, and the *institutional* history of Europe nowhere reveals the presence of a unifying humanistic secular philosophy to integrate with the heritage of the past the radical changes precipitated by war, scientific technology, and the expansion of the capitalist economy. On the contrary, the new tendencies of industrialization, urbanization, and nationalism were neither predicted nor prepared for by any philosophy, either supernaturalist or naturalist. They made their way in the teeth of the old traditions which were helpless to cope with them and which ultimately were compelled by the logic of events to make uneasy compromises with the historical situations they could not exorcise. The defenders of traditional supernaturalism systematically engaged themselves not so much with the social *problems* resulting from the uncontrolled expansion of the new productive forces in Europe as in a furious polemic against the humanistic striving to find the new social forms and institutions which, without aborting the burst of creative energy unleashed by the industrial revolution, would sustain through the operating institutions of a reconstructed society, the dignity of all human beings. . . .

Nor in face of the assertion that the wars, revolutions, and bestial atrocities of our century are a consequence of the abandonment of the transcendent religious and metaphysical beliefs of the past, must we overlook the significance of the fact that those centuries when European culture rested on religious foundations were marked, once allowance is made for scale, by practices of persecution and extermination almost as inhuman as those committed by modern totalitarianism.

1. But historical consideration aside, it is demonstrable that no set of metaphysical or theological statements by themselves entail any specific empirical consequences about the life of man or the structure of human society. Without raising the questions here of the criteria of meaningfulness and verification of such statements, it is apparent that they are compatible with mutually inconsistent social beliefs and the most diverse social institutions. For example, the same set of premises about divine existence, immortality, the nature of substance and the self have been held by believers in feudalism, capitalism, and socialism, by democrats as well as by totalitarians. This indicates that belief in the first set of propositions is not a sufficient condition of belief in the second set of propositions. And we are all acquainted with principled advocates of democracy or dictatorship, capitalism or socialism who regard the metaphysical and theological propositions often offered in alleged justification of these institutions as either meaningless or false which establishes that belief in them is certainly not a necessary condition of social doctrine and action. Indeed, *logically,* with sufficient technical ingenuity, allegiance to any social system can be squared with the belief in any metaphysical system whatsoever.

This has sometimes been denied by those for whom metaphysical and theological statements are value judgments in disguise. When challenged they retreat to the position that the validity of moral judgments rests upon transcendental truths of a metaphysical or theological nature. Not only does such a position destroy the autonomy of moral experience, it is exposed to the same logical and historical difficulties that we have noted above. To the extent that transcendental beliefs are disguised value judgments, the actual relation between theology and morals is obscured. For, as we have seen in earlier chapters, it is indisputable that far from morals being historically derived from theological beliefs, men have always created their gods in their own moral image.

2. Any attempt to find a basis to improve the human estate by resort to a principle "above human nature" is doomed to failure because it cannot supply definite criteria to guide the construction of the programs of action required to meet the concrete needs, wants, and aspirations of men which are very much part of human nature and in which the most pressing problems of a domestic and international character are rooted. Ideals and ends that are out of time and so lack a natural basis can never be brought into logical and causal continuity with the means recommended to achieve them, for all such means are temporal acts with temporal consequences. The result of postulating ends that are outside of time and postulating principles above human nature is that the *choice* of means, without which ends cannot be realized or tested, is lamed at the outset. Freed from critical direction, human choice *professedly* oriented to principles above human nature, oscillates between the extremes of dogmatism and opportunism.

The proposal of naturalistic humanism is to approach the problems of men in their natural and social contexts and to test the validity of all theoretical claims, not by examining their presuppositions but by investigating their empirical consequences. In refusing to allow this concern with antecedent presuppositions to dominate intellectual activity, in pointing out that conflicting varieties of presuppositions are equally compatible with verifiable fact, the naturalistic humanists seek to give the criterion of fruitfulness the same standing in all inquiry as it has in inquiry in the natural sciences. There is no guarantee, of course, that human beings, endowed with variant as well as common needs, will agree upon consequences, but a great deal of human experience testifies that in some areas and in some periods this is possible, sometimes even normal. One of the most impressive expressions of that human experience is the existence of democratic communities in which to a large part a consensus of belief and action in respect to political institutions and processes has been established among individuals holding the most varied metaphysical and theological presuppositions. What is being suggested by this proposal to take consequences not presuppositions as a point of departure is that those processes of inquiry by which in some parts of the world idealists and materialists, atheists and theists, Catholics, Protestants, Jews, and Mohammedans have been able to reach a community of working agreement be employed to explore all the empirical problems and difficulties that beset men today. . . .

The most common objection to naturalistic humanism is not that it has no place for moral experience but that it has no place for an *authoritative* moral experience except one which rests merely on arbitrary preference, habit or force. In consequence, it is accused of lapsing into the morass of relativism despite its desire to discover inclusive and enduring ends which will enable human beings to live harmoniously together. . . .

The impression that because values are relational they are therefore subjective is the consequence of confusing two different problems. The first is whether values have objective status and validity; the second is whether in case of conflict, objective values and the interests to which they are related, can be shared, *i.e.*, whether a new value situation can be constructed which will transform the conflicting values into a satisfying integrated whole.

One can hold to the belief in the objectivity of values without *guaranteeing* that agreement among conflicting values, all of which are objective from their own point of view, can be won. How far such agreement can be won cannot be foretold until actual investigation into the conditions and consequences of value claims in definite situations is undertaken—and this is precisely what naturalistic humanists propose to do instead of taking moral intuitions as absolute fiats subject to no control. The assumption that in any particular case agreement can be won, that an objective moral resolution of value conflicts is possible, entails the belief that men are sufficiently alike to work out ways of becoming *more* alike, or sufficiently alike to agree about the permissible limits of *being different*.

Rationality or reasonableness in conduct is the ability—which men possess—to envisage alternatives of action, to apply the test of observable consequences to conflicting proposals, and to accept or reconstruct these proposals in the light of consequences. The institutional expression of this rationality is the communal process of deliberation and critical assessment of evidence which alone makes possible a *freely* given consent. The willingness to sit down in the face of differences and reason together is the only categorical imperative a naturalistic humanist recognizes. And reliance upon the rules of the game by which grounded conclusions concerning concrete value judgments are reached is the only methodological absolute to which he is committed. This places authority solely in the untrammeled processes of inquiry and any alleged humanism, whether Thomistic humanism or so-called Soviet humanism, which places primary authority in institutions or dogmas, is guilty of the most transparent kind of semantic corruption. . . .

(pages 197-207)

Hannah Arendt (1906–1975)

Introduction

Hannah Arendt was a major twentieth-century political and cultural critic. As a German Jew who fled from Hitler and saw the gradual destruction of European civilization during World War II, she was motivated as an intellectual to help us to understand the meaning and direction of events in a world of chaos.

Arendt was born in Germany in 1906 and studied philosophy under Karl Jaspers at the University of Heidelberg, where she received her Ph.D. in 1928. She published a study of Rachel Varnhagen, an early-nineteenth-century salon hostess who was tormented all her life by unhappiness about being Jewish. This topic was an important one in Arendt's own life, although she never denied her Jewishness. In 1933, with the political advent of Hitler, she went to France, where she worked with Zionist organizations. When France was occupied in 1940, she came to the United States. Arendt then worked as an editor, wrote articles, primarily on Jewish topics, taught at a number of universities, and wrote several well-known books, including *The Origins of Totalitarianism, The Human Condition*, and *Eichmann in Jerusalem*.

Arendt viewed herself as a conscious pariah, a nonobservant Jew who saw Jewishness as a given identity from which one cannot escape. She believed that to be a Jew was to be an outsider and pariah in the Gentile world. She thought that this pariah status enabled the Jew to view Gentile society more objectively. Arendt believed there was a hidden tradition of isolated Jewish individuals who affirmed their pariah status, such as Heinrich Heine, Rachel Varnhagen, Sholem Aleichem, Bernard Lazare, Franz Kafka and Walter Benjamin, with no visible links among them.

There was a bitter controversy within the Jewish community after she published *Eichmann in Jerusalem.* In this book she described the Nazi evil as "banal" and highlighted the cooperation of the German-Jewish leadership with the Nazis. Arendt tried to awaken Jews to the fact they had no realistic political understanding of their situation in Germany. Many reviewers were highly critical of her work, and she was vilified in the Jewish community itself. When she died, there were few eulogies in the Jewish press. Her pariah status followed her into the Jewish world.

Creating a Cultural Atmosphere

Culture is by definition secular. It requires a kind of broad mindedness of which no religion will ever be capable. It can be thoroughly perverted through ideologies and *Weltanschauungen* which share, though on a lower and more vulgar level, religion's contempt for tolerance and claim to "possess" the truth. Although culture is "hospitable," we should not forget that neither religion nor ideologies will, nor ever can, resign themselves to being only parts of a whole. The historian, though hardly ever the theologian, knows that secularization is not the ending of religion.

It so happened that the Jewish people not only did not share in the slow process of secularization that started in Western Europe with the Renaissance, and out of which modern culture was born, but that the Jews, when confronted with and attracted by Enlightenment and culture, had just emerged from a period in which their own secular learning had sunk to an all-time low. The consequences of this lack of spiritual links between Jews and non-Jewish civilization were as natural as they were unfortunate: Jews who wanted "culture" left Judaism at once, and completely, even though most of them remained conscious of their Jewish origin. Secularization and even secular learning became identified exclusively with non-Jewish culture, so that it never occurred to these Jews that they could have started a process of secularization with regard to their own heritage. Their abandonment of Judaism resulted in a situation within Judaism in which the Jewish spiritual heritage became more than ever before the monopoly of rabbis.

The German *Wissenschaft des Judentums* [Jewish critical social science], though it was aware of the danger of a complete loss of all the past's spiritual achievements, took refuge from the real problem in a rather dry scholarship concerned only with preservation, the results of which were at best a collection of museum objects.

While this sudden and radical escape by Jewish intellectuals from everything Jewish prevented the growth of a cultural atmosphere in the Jewish community, it was very favorable for the development of individual creativity. What had been done by the members of other nations as part and parcel of a more collective effort and in the span of several generations, was achieved by individual Jews within the narrow and concentrated framework of a single human lifetime and by the sheer force of personal imagination. It was as individuals, strictly, that the Jews started their emancipation from tradition.

It is true that a unique and impassioned intensity possessed only the few and was paid for by the fact that a particularly high percentage of Jews occupied themselves as pseudo cultural busybodies and succumbed to mass culture and the mere love of fame. But it still brought forth a remarkably great number of authentic Jewish writers, artists, and thinkers who did not break under the extraordinary effort required of them, and whom this sudden empty freedom of spirit did not debase but on the contrary made creative.

Since, however, their individual achievements did not find reception by a prepared and cultured Jewish audience, they could not found a specifically Jewish tradition in secular writing and thinking—though these Jewish writers, thinkers, and artists had more than one trait in common. Whatever tradition the historian may be able to detect remained tacit and latent, its continuance automatic and unconscious, springing as it did from the basically identical conditions that each of these individuals had to confront all over again for himself, and master by himself without help from his predecessors.

There is no doubt that no blueprint and no program will ever make sense in cultural matters. If there is such a thing as a cultural policy it can aim only at the creation of a cultural atmosphere—that is, in Elliot Cohen's words, a "culture for Jews," but not a Jewish culture. The emergence of talent or genius is independent of such an atmosphere, but whether we shall continue to lose Jewish talent to others, or whether we will become able to keep it within our own community to the same extent that the others do, will be decided by the existence or non-existence of this atmosphere. It is this that seems to me to be the problem. One may give a few suggestions on how to approach it.

There is first of all that great religious and metaphysical post-Biblical tradition which we will have to win back from the theologians and scholars—to both of whom we owe, however, a large debt of gratitude for having preserved it at all. But we shall have to discover and deal with this tradition anew in our own terms, for the sake of people to whom it no longer constitutes a holy past or an untouchable heritage.

There is on the other hand the much smaller body of Jewish secular writings—dating from all periods, but particularly from the 19th century in Eastern Europe; this writing grew out of secular folk life and only the absence of a cultural atmosphere has prevented a portion of it from assuming the status of great literature; instead it was condemned to the doubtful category of folklore. The cultural value of every author or artist really begins to make itself felt when he transcends the boundaries of his own nationality, when he no longer remains significant only to his fellow-Jews, fellow-Frenchmen or fellow-Englishmen. The lack of Jewish culture and the prevalence of folklore in secular Jewish life has denied this transcendence to all Jewish talent that did not simply desert the Jewish community. The rescue of the Yiddish writers of Eastern Europe is of great importance; otherwise they will remain lost to culture generally.

Last but not least, we shall have to make room for all those who either came, and come, into conflict with Jewish orthodoxy or turned their backs on Judaism for the reasons mentioned above. These figures will be of special significance for the whole endeavor; they may even become the supreme test of its success or failure. Not only because creative talent has been especially frequent among them in recent times, but also because they, in their individual efforts towards secularization, offer the first models for that new amalgamation of older traditions with new impulses and awareness without which a specifically Jewish cultural atmosphere is hardly conceivable. These talents do not need us, they achieve culture on their own responsibility. We, on the other hand, do need them since they form the only basis, however small, of culture that we have got; a basis we shall have to extend gradually in both directions: the secularization of religious tradition and rescue from folklore of the great artists (mostly Yiddish) of secular folk life.

Whether such a development will be realized nobody can possibly foretell. *Commentary* looks to me like a good beginning and it certainly is a novum in Jewish cultural life. The reason for some optimism, is in the last analysis a political one.

The Yishuv [Jewish settlement] in Palestine is the first Jewish achievement brought about by an entirely secular movement. There is no doubt that whatever may happen to Hebrew literature in the future, Hebrew writers and artists will not need to confine themselves to either folk life or religion in order to remain Jews. They are the first Jews who as Jews are free to start from more than a pre-cultural level.

The Jewish people of America, on the other hand, live a reasonably safe and reasonably free life that permits them to do, relatively, what they please. The central and strongest part of Diaspora Jewry no longer exists under the conditions of a nation-state but in a country that would annul its own constitution if ever it demanded homogeneity of population and an ethnic foundation for its state. In America one does not have to pretend that Judaism is nothing but a denomination and resort to all those desperate and crippling disguises that were common among the rich and educated Jews of Europe.

The development of a Jewish culture, in other words, or the lack of it, will from now on not depend upon circumstances beyond the control of the Jewish people, but upon their own will.

EICHMANN IN JERUSALEM

. . . The facts of the case, of what Eichmann had done—though not of everything the prosecution wished he had done—were never in dispute; they had been established long before the trial started, and had been confessed to by him over and over again. There was more than enough, as he occasionally pointed out, to hang him. ("Don't you have enough on me?" he objected, when the police examiner tried to ascribe to him powers he never possessed.) But since he had been employed in transportation and not in killing, the question remained, legally, formally, at least, of whether he had known what he was doing; and there was the additional question of whether he had been in a position to judge the enormity of his deeds—whether he was legally responsible, apart from the fact that he was medically sane. Both questions now were answered in the affirmative: he had seen the places to which the shipments were directed, and he had been shocked out of his wits. One last question, the most disturbing of all, was asked by the judges, and especially by the presiding judge, over and over again: Had the killing of Jews gone against his conscience? But this was a moral question, and the answer to it may not have been legally relevant.

But if the facts of the case were now established, two more legal questions arose. First, could he be released from criminal responsibility, as Section 10 of the law under which he was tried provided, because he had done his acts "in order to save himself from the danger of immediate death"? And, second, could he plead extenuating circumstances, as Section 11 of the same law enumerated them: had he done "his best to reduce the gravity of the consequences of the offense" or "to avert consequences more serious than those which resulted"? Clearly, Sections 10 and 11 of the Nazi and Nazi Collaborators (Punishment) Law of 1950 had been drawn up with Jewish "collaborators" in mind. Jewish *Sonderkommandos* (special units) had everywhere been employed in the actual killing process, they had committed criminal acts "in order to save themselves from the danger of immediate death," and the Jewish Councils and Elders had cooperated because they thought they could "avert consequences more serious than those which resulted." In Eichmann's case, his own testimony supplied the answer to both questions, and it was clearly negative. It is true, he once said his only alternative would have been suicide, but this was a lie, since we know how surprisingly easy it was for members of the extermination squads to quit their jobs without serious consequences for themselves; but he did not insist on this point, he did not mean to be taken literally. In the Nuremberg documents "not a single case could be traced in which an S.S. member had suffered the death penalty because of a refusal to take part in an execution. . . .

(Chapter VI)

As Eichmann told it, the most potent factor in the soothing of his own conscience was the simple fact that he could see no one, no one at all, who actually was against the Final Solution. He did encounter one exception, however, which he mentioned several times, and which must have made a deep impression on him. This happened in Hungary when he was negotiating with Dr. Kastner over Himmler's offer to release one million Jews in exchange for ten thousand trucks. Kastner, apparently emboldened by the new turn of affairs, had asked Eichmann to stop "the death mills at Auschwitz," and Eichmann had answered that he would do it "with the greatest pleasure" (*herzlich gern*) but that, alas, it was outside his competence and outside the competence of his superiors—as indeed it was. Of course, he did not expect the Jews to share the general enthusiasm over their destruction, but he did expect more than compliance, he expected—and received, to a truly extraordinary degree—their cooperation. This was "of course the very cornerstone" of everything he did, as it had been the very cornerstone of his activities in Vienna. Without Jewish help in administrative and police work—the final rounding up of Jews in Berlin was, as I have mentioned, done entirely by Jewish police—there would have been either complete chaos or an impossibly severe drain on German manpower. ("There can be no doubt that, without the cooperation of the victims, it would hardly have been possible for a few thousand people, most of whom, moreover, worked in offices, to liquidate many hundreds of thousands of other people. . . . Over the whole way to their deaths the Polish Jews got to see hardly more than a handful of Germans." . . . To an even greater extent this applies to those Jews who were transported to Poland to find their deaths there.) Hence, the establishing of Quisling governments in occupied territories was always accompanied by the organization of a central Jewish office, and, as we shall see later, where the Nazis did not succeed in setting up a puppet government, they also failed to enlist the cooperation of the Jews. But whereas the members of the Quisling governments were usually taken from the opposition parties, the members of the Jewish Councils were as a rule the locally recognized Jewish leaders, to whom the Nazis gave enormous powers—until they, too, were deported, to Theresienstadt or Bergen-Belsen, if they happened to be from Central or Western Europe, to Auschwitz if they were from an Eastern European community.

To a Jew this role of the Jewish leaders in the destruction of their own people is undoubtedly the darkest chapter of the whole dark story. It had been known about before, but it has now been exposed for the first time in all its pathetic and sordid detail by Raul Hilberg, whose standard work *The Destruction of the European Jews* I mentioned before. In the matter of cooperation, there was no distinction between the highly assimilated Jewish communities of Central and Western Europe and the Yiddish-speaking masses of the East. In Amsterdam as in Warsaw, in Berlin as in Budapest, Jewish officials could be trusted to compile the lists of persons and of their property, to secure money from the deportees to defray the expenses of their deportation and extermination, to keep track of vacated apartments, to supply police forces to help seize Jews and get them on trains, until, as a last gesture, they handed over the assets of the Jewish community in good order for final confiscation. They distributed the Yellow Star badges, and sometimes, as in Warsaw, "the sale of the armbands became a regular business; there were ordinary armbands of cloth and fancy plastic armbands which were washable." In the Nazi-inspired, but not Nazi-dictated, manifestoes they issued, we still can sense how they enjoyed their new power—"The Central Jewish Council has been granted the right of absolute disposal over all Jewish spiritual and material wealth and over all Jewish manpower," as the first announcement of the Budapest Council phrased it. We know how the Jewish officials felt when they became instruments of murder—like captains "whose ships were about to sink and who succeeded in bringing them safe to port by casting overboard a great part of their precious cargo"; like saviors who "with a hundred victims save a thousand people, with a thousand ten thousand." The truth was even more gruesome. Dr. Kastner, in Hungary, for instance, saved exactly 1,684 people with approximately 476,000 victims. In order not to leave the selection to "blind fate," "truly holy principles" were needed "as the guiding force of the weak human hand which puts down on paper the name of the unknown person and with this decides his life or death." And whom did these "holy principles" single out for salvation? Those "who had worked all their lives for the *zibur* [community]—i.e., the functionaries—and the "most prominent Jews," as Kastner says in his report.

No one bothered to swear the Jewish officials to secrecy; they were voluntary "bearers of secrets," either in order to assure quiet and prevent panic, as in Dr. Kastner's case, or out of "humane" considerations, such as that "living in the expectation of death by gassing would only be the harder," as in the case of Dr. Leo Baeck, former Chief Rabbi of Berlin. During the Eichmann trial, one witness pointed out the unfortunate consequences of this kind of "humanity"—people volunteered for deportation from Theresienstadt to Auschwitz and denounced those who tried to tell them the truth as being "not sane." We know the physiognomies of the Jewish leaders during the Nazi period very well; they ranged all the way from Chaim Rumkowski, Eldest of the Jews in Lódz, called Chaim I, who issued currency notes bearing his signature and postage stamps engraved with his portrait, and who rode around in a broken-down horse-drawn carriage; through Leo Baeck, scholarly, mild-mannered, highly educated, who believed Jewish policemen would be "more gentle and helpful" and would "make the ordeal easier" (whereas in fact they were, of course, more brutal and less corruptible, since so much more was at stake for them); to, finally, a few who committed suicide—like Adam Czerniakow, chairman of the Warsaw Jewish Council, who was not a rabbi but an unbeliever, a Polish-speaking Jewish engineer, but who must still have remembered the rabbinical saying: "Let them kill you, but don't cross the line."...

(Chapter VII)

Adolf Eichmann went to the gallows with great dignity. He had asked for a bottle of red wine and had drunk half of it. He refused the help of the Protestant minister, the Reverend William Hull, who offered to read the Bible with him: he had only two more hours to live, and therefore no "time to waste." He walked the fifty yards from his cell to the execution chamber calm and erect, with his hands bound behind him. When the guards tied his ankles and knees, he asked them to loosen the bonds so that he could stand straight. "I don't need that," he said when the black hood was offered him. He was in complete command of himself, nay, he was more: he was completely himself. Nothing could have demonstrated this more convincingly than the grotesque silliness of his last words. He began by stating emphatically that he was a *Gottgläubiger,* to express in common Nazi fashion that he was no Christian and did not believe in life after death. He then proceeded: "After a short while, gentlemen, *we shall meet again.* Such is the fate of all men. Long live Germany, long live Argentina, long live Austria. *I shall not forget them.*" In the face of death, he had found the cliché used in funeral oratory. Under the gallows, his memory played him the last trick; he was "elated" and he forgot that this was his own funeral.

It was as though in those last minutes he was summing up the lesson that this long course in human wickedness had taught us—the lesson of the fearsome, word-and-thought-defying *banality of evil.*

(Chapter XV)

Isaac Deutscher (1907–1967)

Introduction

Isaac Deutscher was a famed Polish Marxist theorist and a chronicler of modern Russian history. His most famous and original contribution to Jewish studies was an essay called "The Non-Jewish Jew," a category in which we might place Deutscher himself. He believed that Jews who advocated a universalistic vision of the "ultimate solidarity of man" were a natural product of Jewish life and thought and could be placed within the Jewish tradition. He contrasted them with what he believed was the narrowness of Jewish orthodoxy and nationalistic Zionism.

Isaac Deutscher was born in Cracow, Poland, in 1907, where he received a traditional Jewish education. Later, however, he attended Cracow University, became a secular Zionist, and joined the Polish Communist Party. He edited the party's semi-legal periodicals, but after he advocated that united Communist/Socialist action be taken against the rising threat of Nazism, he was expelled from the Party. In 1939 he went to London as the correspondent for a Warsaw Jewish paper, and he remained there the rest of his life as a well-known journalist, commentator, and historian. He published *Stalin: A Political Biography* in 1949, and wrote critical articles on the Stalinist regime for the *Observer* and *Economist*.

Deutscher, who visited Israel for the first time in 1953, argued that a Jewish nation-state in an age of growing internationalism was a dangerous and anachronistic step for Jewry. He was critical of some Israeli policies but positive about the state as a whole.

The Non-Jewish Jew

There is an old Talmudic saying: "A Jew who has sinned still remains a Jew." My own thinking is, of course, beyond the idea of "sin" or "no sin"; but this saying has brought to my mind a memory from childhood which may not be irrelevant to my theme.

I remember that when as a child I read the *Midrash* [biblical interpretations deriving moral lessons] , I came across a story and a description of a scene which gripped my imagination. It was the story of Rabbi Meir, the great saint and sage, the pillar of Mosaic orthodoxy, and co-author of the *Mishnah* [collection of rabbinic commentaries], who took lessons in theology from a heretic, Elisha ben Abiyuh, called Akher (The Stranger). Once on a Sabbath Rabbi Meir was with his teacher, and as usual they became engaged in a deep argument. The heretic was riding a donkey, and Rabbi Meir, as he could not ride on a Sabbath, walked by his side and listened so intently to the words of wisdom falling from his heretical lips that he failed to notice that he and his teacher had reached the ritual boundary which Jews were not allowed to cross on a Sabbath. The great heretic turned to his orthodox pupil and said: "Look, we have reached the boundary—we must part now; you must not accompany me any farther—go back!" Rabbi Meir went back to the Jewish community, while the heretic rode on—beyond the boundaries of Jews.

There was enough in this scene to puzzle an orthodox Jewish child. Why, I wondered, did Rabbi Meir, that leading light of orthodoxy, take his lessons from the heretic? Why did he show him so much affection? Why did he defend him against other rabbis? My heart, it seems, was with the heretic. Who was he? He appeared to be in Jewry and yet out of it. He showed a curious respect for his pupil's orthodoxy, when he sent him back to the Jews on the Holy Sabbath; but he himself, disregarding canon and ritual, rode beyond the boundaries. When I was thirteen, or perhaps fourteen, I began to write a play about Akher and Rabbi Meir and I tried to find out more about Akher's character. What made him transcend Judaism? Was he a Gnostic? Was he an adherent of some other school of Greek or Roman philosophy? I could not find the answer, and did not manage to get beyond the first act.

The Jewish heretic who transcends Jewry belongs to a Jewish tradition. You may, if you like, see Akher as a prototype of those great revolutionaries of modern thought: Spinoza, Heine, Marx, Rosa Luxemburg, Trotsky, and Freud. You may, if you wish to, place them within a Jewish tradition. They all went beyond the boundaries of Jewry. They all found Jewry too narrow, too archaic, and too constricting. They all looked for ideals and fulfillment beyond it, and they represent the sum and substance of much that is greatest in modern thought, the sum and substance of the most profound upheavals that have taken place in philosophy, sociology, economics, and politics in the last three centuries.

Did they have anything in common with one another? Have they perhaps impressed mankind's thoughts so greatly because of their special "Jewish genius"? I do not believe in the exclusive genius of any race. Yet I think that in some ways they were very Jewish indeed. They had in themselves something of the quintessence of Jewish life and of the Jewish intellect. They were *a priori* exceptional in that as Jews they dwelt on the borderlines of various civilizations, religions, and national cultures. They were born and brought up on the borderlines of various epochs. Their mind matured where the most diverse cultural influences crossed and fertilized each other. They lived on the margins or in the nooks and crannies of their respective nations. Each of them was in society and yet not in it, of it and yet not of it. It was this that enabled them to rise in thought above their societies, above their nations, above their times and generations, and to strike out mentally into wide new horizons and far into the future.

It was, I think, an English Protestant biographer of Spinoza who said that only a Jew could have carried out that upheaval in the philosophy of his age that Spinoza carried out—a Jew who was not bound by the dogmas of the Christian churches, Catholic and Protestant, nor by those of the faith in which he had been born. Neither

Descartes nor Leibnitz could free themselves to the same extent from the shackles of the medieval scholastic tradition in philosophy. . . .

Heine was torn between Christianity and Jewry, and between France and Germany. In his native Rhineland there clashed the influences of the French Revolution and of the Napoleonic Empire with those of the old Holy Roman Empire of the German Kaisers. He grew up within the orbit of classical German philosophy and within the orbit of French Republicanism; and he saw Kant as a Robespierre and Fichte as a Napoleon in the realm of the spirit; and so he describes them in one of the most profound and moving passages of *Zur Geschichte der Religion und Philosophie in Deutschland*. In his later years he came in contact with French and German socialism and communism; and he met Marx with that apprehensive admiration and sympathy with which Acosta had met Spinoza.

Marx likewise grew up in the Rhineland. His parents having ceased to be Jews, he did not struggle with the Jewish heritage as Heine did. All the more intense was his opposition to the social and spiritual backwardness of contemporary Germany. An exile most of his life, his thought was shaped by German philosophy, French socialism, and English political economy. In no other contemporary mind did such diverse influences meet so fruitfully. Marx rose above German philosophy, French socialism, and English political economy; he absorbed what was best in each of these trends and transcended the limitations of each.

To come nearer to our time, there were Rosa Luxemburg, Trotsky, and Freud, each of whom was formed amid historic cross-currents. Rosa Luxemburg is a unique blend of the German, Polish, and Russian characters and of the Jewish temperament; Trotsky was the pupil of a Lutheran Russo-German gymnasium in cosmopolitan Odessa on the fringe of the Greek-Orthodox Empire of the Tsars; and Freud's mind matured in Vienna in estrangement from Jewry and in opposition to the Catholic clericalism of the Habsburg capital. All of them had this in common, that the very conditions in which they lived and worked did not allow them to reconcile themselves to the ideas which were nationally or religiously limited and induced them to strive for a universal *Weltanschauung* [world view]. . . .

All these great revolutionaries were extremely vulnerable. They were, as Jews, rootless, in a sense; but they were so only in some respects, for they had the deepest roots in intellectual tradition and in the noblest aspirations of their times. Yet whenever religious intolerance or nationalist emotion was on the ascendant, whenever dogmatic narrow-mindedness and fanaticism triumphed, they were the first victims. They were excommunicated by Jewish rabbis; they were persecuted by Christian priests; they were hunted down by the gendarmes of absolute rulers and by the *soldateska;* they were hated by pseudo-democratic philistines; and they were expelled by their own parties. Nearly all of them were exiled from their countries; and the writings of all were burned at the stake at one time or another. Spinoza's name could not be mentioned for over a century after his death—even Leibnitz, who was indebted to Spinoza for so much of his thought, did not dare to mention it. Trotsky is till under anathema in Russia today. The names of Marx, Heine, Freud, and Rosa Luxemburg were forbidden in Germany quite recently. But theirs is the ultimate victory. After a century during which Spinoza's name was covered with oblivion, they put up monuments to him and acknowledged him as the greatest fructifier of the human mind. Herder once said about Goethe: "I wish Goethe read some Latin books apart from Spinoza's *Ethics.*" Goethe was indeed steeped in Spinoza's thought; and Heine rightly describes him as "Spinoza who has thrown off the cloak of his geometrical-mathematical formulae and stands before us as a lyrical poet." Heine himself has triumphed over Hitler and Goebbels. The other revolutionaries of this line will also survive and sooner or later triumph over those who have worked hard to efface their memory.

It is very obvious why Freud belongs to the same intellectual line. In his teachings, whatever their merits and demerits, he transcends the limitations of earlier psychological schools. The man whom he analyses is not a German, or an Englishman, a Russian, or a Jew—he is the universal man in whom the subconscious and conscious struggle, the man who is part of nature and part of society, the man whose desires and cravings, scruples and inhibitions, anxieties and predicaments are essentially the same no matter to what race, religion, or nation he belongs. From their viewpoint the Nazis were right when they coupled Freud's name with that of Marx and burned the books of both.

All these thinkers and revolutionaries have had certain philosophical principles in common. Although their philosophies vary, of course, from century to century and from generation to generation, they are all, from Spinoza to Freud, determinists, they all hold that the universe is ruled by laws inherent in it and governed by *Gesetzmässigkeiten* [legalisms]. . . .

All these thinkers agree on the relativity of moral standards. None of them believes in absolute good or absolute evil. They all observed communities adhering to different moral standards and different ethical values. What was good to the Roman Catholic Inquisition under which Spinoza's grandparents had lived, was evil to the Jews; and what was good to the rabbis and Jewish elders of Amsterdam was evil to Spinoza himself. Heine and Marx experienced in their youth the tremendous clash between the morality of the French Revolution and that of feudal Germany. . . .

Finally, all these men, from Spinoza to Freud, believed in the ultimate solidarity of man; and this was implicit in their attitude towards Jewry. We are now looking back on these believers in humanity through the bloody fog of our times. We are looking back at them through the smoke of the gas chamber, the smoke which no wind can disperse from our sight. These "non-Jewish Jews" were essential optimists; and their optimism reached heights which it is not easy to ascend in our times. They did not imagine that it would be possible for "civilized"Europe in the twentieth century to sink to a depth of barbarity at which the mere words "solidarity of man" would sound as a perverse mockery to Jewish ears. Alone among them Heine had the poet's intuitive premonition of this when he warned Europe to beware of the coming onslaught of the old Germanic gods emerging *"aus dem deutschen Urwald"*[from the German primeval forest], and when he complained that the destiny of the modern Jew is tragic beyond expression and comprehension—so tragic that "they laugh at you when you speak of it, and this is the greatest tragedy of all."

We do not find this premonition in Spinoza or Marx. Freud in his old age reeled mentally under the blow of Nazism. To Trotsky it came as a shock that Stalin used against him the anti-Semitic innuendo. As a young man Trotsky had, in most categorical terms, repudiated the demand for Jewish "cultural autonomy," which the *Bund*, the Jewish Socialist Party, raised in 1903. He did it in the name of the solidarity of Jew and non-Jew in the socialist camp. Nearly a quarter of a century later, while he was engaged in an unequal struggle with Stalin and went to the party cells in Moscow to expound his views, he was met with vicious allusions to his Jewishness and even with plain anti-Semitic insults. The allusions and insults came from members of the party which he had, together with Lenin, led in the revolution and civil war. After another quarter of a century, and after Auschwitz and Majdanek and Belsen, once again, this time much more openly and menacingly, Stalin resorted to anti-Semitic innuendo and insult.

It is an indubitable fact that the Nazi massacre of six million European Jews has not made any deep impression on the nations of Europe. It has not truly shocked their conscience. It has left them almost cold. Was then the optimistic belief in humanity voiced by the great Jewish revolutionaries justified? Can we still share their faith in the future of civilization?

I admit that if one were to try and answer these questions from an exclusively Jewish standpoint, it would be hard, perhaps impossible, to give a positive answer. As for myself, I cannot approach the issue from an exclusively Jewish standpoint; and my answer is: Yes, their faith was justified. It was justified at any rate, in so far as the belief in the ultimate solidarity of mankind is itself one of the conditions necessary for the preservation of humanity and for the cleansing of our civilization of the dregs of barbarity that are still present in it and still poison it. . . .

All this has driven the Jews to see their own State as *the* way out. Most of the great revolutionaries, whose heritage I am discussing, have seen the ultimate solution to the problems of their and our times not in nation-states but in international society. As Jews they were the natural pioneers of this idea, for who was as well qualified to preach the international society of equals as were the Jews free from all Jewish and non-Jewish orthodoxy and nationalism?

However, the decay of bourgeois Europe has compelled the Jew to embrace the nation state. This is the paradoxical consummation of the Jewish tragedy. It is paradoxical, because we live in an age when the nation-state is fast becoming an anachronism, and an archaism. . . .

The world has compelled the Jew to embrace the nation-state and to make of it his pride and hope just at a time when there is little or no hope left in it. You cannot blame the Jews for this; you must blame the world. But Jews should at least be aware of the paradox and realize that their intense enthusiasm for "national sovereignty" is historically belated. They did not benefit from the advantages of the nation-state in those centuries when it was a medium of mankind's advance and a great revolutionary or unifying factor in history. They have taken possession of it only after it had become a factor of disunity and social disintegration.

I hope, therefore, that, together with other nations, the Jews will ultimately become aware—or regain the awareness—of the inadequacy of the nation-state and that they will find their way back to the moral and political heritage that the genius of the Jews who have gone beyond Jewry has left us—the message of universal human emancipation.

Abraham Maslow (1908–1970)

Introduction

Abraham Maslow was a psychologist who founded what is known as the Third Force in psychology, the field of humanistic psychology. He was a university professor and the author of many influential books. While he was proud of his Jewish identity, he was a secular Jew and a committed humanist. As a utopian, he combined an unbounded faith in human beings with an underlying sadness about the human condition.

Maslow was born in New York in 1908 and received his college degree and doctorate from the University of Wisconsin, where he did his psychological research on primate behavior. From 1937 to 1951 he was a member of the faculty at Brooklyn College, but he moved to Brandeis University in 1951, remaining until 1969. In that year he became a resident fellow at a research center in California, where he suffered a fatal heart attack in 1970.

Maslow's specific contribution to humanistic psychology began with his publication, in 1950, of a paper called "Self-Actualizing People: A Study in Psychological Health." Expanding and defining the basic concepts put forth in that paper occupied him for the rest of his career. His own distinctive concept was that human needs can be separated into basic needs—security, food, shelter—and metaneeds, such as beauty, justice, goodness, wholeness and order in life. Maslow argued that these metaneeds are as instinctive as the basic needs; and when they are not fulfilled, a person is dissatisfied and unhappy. His description of self-actualizing persons establishes a common core of traits that distinguish such persons. He emphasized that self-actualization is a process of becoming or growth, not a fixed end-state.

Maslow's psychological ideas influenced the fields of education, business management, political theory, and sociology. His enthusiasm for a more positive formulation of human nature than was current at his time was infectious. He himself embodied his own ideals, as he was a man of lively warmth. He emphasized the need for psychology to move toward holism in its thinking. His basic belief that human nature is fundamentally good has had an enormous impact on thinking in the field.

TOWARD A PSYCHOLOGY OF BEING

There is now emerging over the horizon a new conception of human sickness and of human health, a psychology that I find so thrilling and so full of wonderful possibilities that I yield to the temptation to present it publicly even before it is checked and confirmed, and before it can be called reliable scientific knowledge.

The basic assumptions of this point of view are:

1. We have, each of us, an essential biologically based inner nature, which is to some degree "natural," intrinsic, given, and, in a certain limited sense, unchangeable, or, at least, unchanging.

2. Each person's inner nature is in part unique to himself and in part species-wide.

3. It is possible to study this inner nature scientifically and to discover what it is like—(not *invent—discover*).

4. This inner nature, as much as we know of it so far, seems not to be intrinsically or primarily or necessarily evil. The basic needs (for life, for safety and security, for belongingness and affection, for respect and self-respect, and for self-actualization), the basic

human emotions and the basic human capacities are on their face either neutral, pre-moral or positively "good." Destructiveness, sadism, cruelty, malice, etc., seem so far to be not intrinsic but rather they seem to be violent reactions *against* frustration of our intrinsic needs, emotions and capacities. Anger is in *itself* not evil, nor is fear, laziness, or even ignorance. Of course, these can and do lead to evil behavior, but they needn't. This result is not intrinsically necessary. Human nature is not nearly as bad as it has been thought to be. In fact it can be said that the possibilities of human nature have customarily been sold short.

5. Since this inner nature is good or neutral rather than bad, it is best to bring it out and to encourage it rather than to suppress it. If it is permitted to guide our life, we grow healthy, fruitful, and happy.

6. If this essential core of the person is denied or suppressed, he gets sick sometimes in obvious ways, sometimes in subtle ways, sometimes immediately, sometimes later.

7. This inner nature is not strong and overpowering and unmistakable like the instincts of animals. It is weak and delicate and subtle and easily overcome by habit, cultural pressure, and wrong attitudes toward it.

8. Even though weak, it rarely disappears in the normal person—perhaps not even in the sick person. Even though denied, it persists underground, forever pressing for actualization.

9. Somehow, these conclusions must all be articulated with the necessity of discipline, deprivation, frustration, pain, and tragedy. To the extent that these experiences reveal and foster and fulfill our inner nature, to that extent they are desirable experiences. It is increasingly clear that these experiences have something to do with a sense of achievement and ego strength and therefore with the sense of healthy self-esteem and self-confidence. The person who hasn't conquered, withstood and overcome continues to feel doubtful that he *could*. This is true not only for external dangers; it holds also for the ability to control and to delay one's own impulses, and therefore to be unafraid of them.

Observe that if these assumptions are proven true, they promise a scientific ethics, a natural value system, a court of ultimate appeal for the determination of good and bad, of right and wrong. The more we learn about man's natural tendencies, the easier it will be to tell him how to be good, how to be happy, how to be fruitful, how to respect himself, how to love, how to fulfill his highest potentialities. This amounts to automatic solution of many of the personality problems of the future. The thing to do seems to be to find out what one is *really* like inside, deep down, as a member of the human species and as a particular individual.

The study of such self-fulfilling people can teach us much about our own mistakes, our shortcomings, the proper directions in which to grow. Every age but ours has had its model, its ideal. All of these have been given up by our culture; the saint, the hero, the gentleman, the knight, the mystic. About all we have left is the well-adjusted man without problems, a very pale and doubtful substitute. Perhaps we shall soon be able to use as our guide and model the fully growing and self-fulfilling human being, the one in whom all his potentialities are coming to full development, the one whose inner nature expresses itself freely, rather than being warped, suppressed, or denied.

(Introduction)

A MEMORIAL VOLUME

Unpublished Notes

1979 If I had to condense this whole book into a single sentence, I think I could come close to the essence of it by saying that it spells out the consequences of the discovery that man has a higher nature and that this is part of his essence. Or, more simply, human beings can be wonderful out of their own human and biological nature. We need not take refuge in supernatural gods to explain our saints and sages and heroes and statesmen, as if to explain our disbelief that mere unaided human beings could be that good or wise.

Feb. 23, 1970 Man *can* solve his problems by his own strength. He never has, so far, because he has never yet developed to his full strength. As to the forces of "goodness" within him, neither have these ever been developed full enough to be seen as the hope of the world—except in rare moments of exaltation. He doesn't have to fly to a god. He can look within himself for all sorts of potentialities, strength and goodness.

. . . I learned later in psychoanalysis that much of my push and my change in direction came out of being the object of anti-Semitism (and also, therefore, of being especially horrified by anti-Negroism).

I can now say it (and I see it) much more clearly than I did then. I simply didn't *understand* anti-Semitism. It seemed to me like a totally mysterious, unexplainable, unpredictable, whimsical kind of ailment that seized people in a mysterious way. I simply couldn't understand it, let alone predict it or control it.

I am sure that my preoccupation with the inner intricacies of human nature, and especially of mental health and illness and of social health and illness, led me to the search for values and ethics and to an interest in psychotherapy and social therapy (Utopianism). Furthermore, I think this is peculiarly Jewish, and it may become peculiarly Negro. The whole enterprise is a kind of huge coping mechanism (rather than defense), a way of fighting depression, inferiority feelings, self-hatred, lowering of self-esteem, feelings of lovelessness and being unloveworthy.

The One-Way Membrane

One great advantage of being a Jew—an advantage that many do not appreciate or are not even aware of—is that you are automatically exempted from contact with anti-Semites.

Because I am a Jew, I carry with me always a semipermeable membrane that has the miraculous property of excluding from contact with me bores, dolts, mean people, sadists, stuffed shirts, the overconventionalized anti-Semites, Fascists, and other such undesirable people. But this does not exclude *all* non-Jews. The only Christians I ever get to know well are the decent, honorable, brotherly, and friendly people.

Coming into a new community, especially in a small town (1947), this has been of incalculable importance to me. I have been almost completely spared the whole dreary round of ceremonial visits from preachers, American Legionnaires, sewing circles, benevolent orders, fraternal orders, various dull neighbors, etc. I have not been invited to the usual tea parties, ceremonial calls, or afternoons of chit-chat that take so much of the time of the ordinary person. I have not been summoned to those formal dinners at which hours are spent making superficial comments on this and that with various strangers one will never see again.

In a word, I have been spared the worst half of the culture—the stereotyped, the dull, the boring, the ceremonial. I am exempted from routine waste of time with the worst half of the American population, the sick minds, the overtimid, the profoundly hostile, with whom, if I were not a Jew, I should have to fritter away so large a proportion of my precious hours. I have never known well a Fascist or a Nazi or even a native reactionary.

Thus it comes about that the only unpleasant or nasty or boring people I know well are Jews. My membrane doesn't work for them. This is also true for Communists. Here, too, my membrane loses its selective ability.

1967

Men are not evil; they are schlemiels. Most of the evil gets done without malice.

I think what I'm groping toward as an insight is again that evil comes less from malice and sadism than from good intentions that are stupid and low-level.

PART THREE
FRAMERS OF SECULAR JUDAISM

Sherwin Wine
(1928–   )

Introduction

Sherwin Wine is the founder and leader of the movement called Humanistic Judaism. He has not only laid out the intellectual foundations for this movement, but has also created many of its celebration rituals and educational materials. As an ordained rabbi, Wine has been a pioneer in developing a professional leadership for secular Jewish communities. As an accomplished speaker and writer, he has devoted much of his time to "spreading the word" of Secular Humanistic Judaism throughout the Jewish world.

Wine was born in Detroit, Michigan, in 1928, was raised in a traditional Jewish household, and went on to receive his B.A. and M.A. in philosophy from the University of Michigan. He attended the Hebrew Union College in Cincinnati from which he was ordained in 1956.

Wine founded the Birmingham Temple, the first congregation of Humanistic Judaism, in a suburb of Detroit in 1963. In 1969 he founded the Society for Humanistic Judaism as a national organization; and, in the next two decades, he helped to found several other related organizations, including the International Institute for Secular Humanistic Judaism and the International Federation of Secular Humanistic Jews. He serves as chairman or co-chairman of several of these organizations.

Wine has published both philosophic and inspirational materials, including *Judaism Beyond God* and *Celebration: A Ceremonial and Philosophic Guide for Humanists and Humanistic Jews*. He has written hundreds of articles on humanism, ethics and religion which have appeared in *Humanistic Judaism, Free Inquiry,* the *Humanist,* and other publications. He serves as a major spokesperson for the Secular Humanistic Judaism movement.

Believing Is Better Than Non-believing

It is not easy these days to be a Humanistic Jew. We live in a world in which the professed beliefs of most people—including most Jews—are either non-humanist or anti-humanist.

We live with the collective memories of nations that associate their roots and their ancestors with piety and religious devotion.

We live with the power of entrenched religious establishments that confer respectability upon those who join churches and synagogues and say they believe in God.

We live with the indoctrination of the past which claims that atheism and morality are incompatible and that, in a time of moral decay, only a renewed faith in traditional religion will rescue society from anarchy.

We live with the shallowness of an age of science in which countless numbers of people understand the use of machines but do not understand the method of free inquiry which gave birth to them.

We live in a world of disillusionment with modern times, in which many young people assume that the faith of the past will be the cure for their anxiety and disappointment.

We live in a world of aggressively proselytizing fundamentalists who—sensing the secularist loss of nerve—have branded secular humanists the enemies of civilization.

We live in a time of Orthodox revival, in which religious fanaticism has replaced secular Zionism as the imagined guarantor of the Jewish future.

It is not easy for humanists of any variety to survive comfortably in this new social environment. At the beginning of the twentieth century—when human self-confidence and optimism were stronger—non-humanists were on the defensive. The reigning intellectuals were solidly in the secular corner and put the religious on the defensive. But now the tables have been turned. The tone of humanist writers is less strident, more cautious, and more apologetic. We never thought 30 years ago that we would be back arguing the truth of the Biblical creation story, the merits of evolutionary theory, and the possibility of reincarnation.

If you are Jewish, to be out of step is a familiar situation. In fact, it may stimulate the emergence of survival skills which turn out to have value even in less troubled times. This new assault may be a time for humanists and Humanistic Jews to reassess their survival strategy and develop a more effective response to the outside world.

We should begin our evaluation by asking a very practical question. Why is the opposition—why are religious fundamentalists—so successful? A realistic answer turns upon the style of presentation the fundamentalists use.

The "born-again" religionists believe that they have an important message, which the world needs to hear. They believe that this message is urgent and that terrible consequences will ensue if the warning is ignored. They believe that they are the defenders of morality and that the welfare of society depends on their missionary zeal. They believe that they are surrounded by powerful enemies who want to subvert what they work so hard to create. They believe that they have the right to intrude into the privacy of citizens to share their message because the information they bring is a matter of life and death. Although they see themselves as a beleaguered minority, they believe that, in the end, they will win. They convey confidence and hope.

Above all, they present themselves as "believers," as the messengers of a positive statement about the world and its future. Their opponents (namely, we "vicious" humanists) are labeled "unbelievers," deniers of the truth, and purveyors of negativism and nihilism. In fact, the religionists have been so successful with their propaganda that many humanists consent to their label and freely refer to themselves as "unbelievers."

Unbelief is a loser's style. It is a posture of inferiority, an acknowledgment that the message of your enemies is so powerful and so positive that you must define yourself by it. It is also the posture of resignation. While the opposition has a compelling reason to speak to the outside world about its beliefs, "unbelievers" have no really significant beliefs to share. Their style is a holding operation, a defensive stance. They only want to make sure that the religious world does not intrude on their lives. They have no urgent or important message for others.

So long as we present ourselves as unbelievers—whether in the Jewish community or in the broader world—we will be losers. We will be viewed as the deniers of other people's strong convictions, not the possessors of strong convictions of our own. Especially in a free society of competing ideas, unbelief is a disastrously negative strategy.

So what does it take to turn a Humanistic Jew into a "believer," an enthusiastic messenger of a positive philosophy of life?

Not very much. After all, we do have strong positive beliefs about nature, people, and morality. The problem is how we see ourselves and how we present our convictions to others.

The following ten guidelines may be helpful.

1. *If you are a believer, you refuse to be an unbeliever.*

It is very important never to allow others to define you publicly in terms of their own attachments. Humanists not only do not believe in Biblical creation; they do believe in evolution. They not only do not believe in the efficacy of prayer; they do believe in the power of human effort and responsibility. They not only do not believe in the reality of the supernatural; they do believe in the natural origin of all experiences.

2. *If you are a believer, you focus on the positive.*

Believers tell people first what they believe, not what they do not believe. Effective humanists do not begin their presentation of personal conviction by announcing what they deny. They describe the things and the events in the universe that they think are really there. Agnosticism with regard to God may be the intellectual position of most humanists. But it is less important than our positive commitment to reason and scientific inquiry. Skepticism with regard to the divine origins of Jewish history may be the attitude of

Humanistic Jews, but it is less important than our affirmation that Jewish culture is the creation of the Jewish people.

3. *If you are a believer, you know that the message is important.*

From the fundamentalist perspective, preparing yourself for the afterlife is desperately important; from the humanist perspective, training yourself to make the most out of your life here on earth is equally important. Dignity is the power to take responsibility for your life without guarantees. Self-esteem is essential to human happiness. It is no more a trivial reward than is eternal heavenly care. In a world in which infantile behavior and infantile dependency are rampant, Humanism has something important to say to people, whether or not they are open to hearing the message.

4. *If you are a believer, you offer positive alternatives.*

Too often humanists and Humanistic Jews assault existing institutions and practices without providing adequate substitutes. Just because traditional Jewish communities were built around prayer and God does not mean that alternative Jewish communities cannot be built around a secular Jewish culture and ethical concerns. Just because the traditional Jewish puberty rite is male chauvinist and focused on Bible readings does not preclude an alternative growing-up ceremony that is discrimination-free and celebrates the child's connection to all Jewish creativity. Just because trained professional leadership in the Jewish community has been primarily religious does not mean trained leadership is bad and Humanistic rabbis, inconceivable.

5. *If you are a believer, you do not worry about being unfashionable.*

Many people enjoy unbelief when it is chic, when it is the intellectual rage. They take pleasure in tweaking the nose of authority and announcing their liberation. But when unbelief becomes less fashionable, they find their defensive posture uncomfortable. The assertiveness and drive of their opponents reminds them of their own vulnerability. They prefer to assault; they are uncomfortable being assaulted. But humanists who are believers are prepared for changes of fashion. Since they know what they do believe, as opposed to what they do not believe, they do not lose their intellectual security when the crowd stops applauding.

6. *If you are a believer, you do not resent the enthusiasm of opponents.*

Many humanists decry the efforts of fundamentalist missionaries. They despise these self-appointed proselytizers who intrude on their privacy and rudely challenge their personal beliefs. Like many classic liberals, they consider religion a tender, private area likely to be wounded by pushing. If you are convinced that your message is essential to the welfare of another human being, if you believe that the information you possess is essential for human survival and happiness, you have a moral obligation to intervene. Many liberals who think it perfectly appropriate to proselytize actively for nuclear freezes and abortion freedom resent the same enthusiasm when it is applied to religion. This attitude prevents us from being effective. If we, as humanists and Humanistic Jews, have something important to say about the path to self-esteem, we should be eager to share it. Our resentment of "intrusion" is merely a sign of our own discomfort with positive convictions. In an open society, "pushing" and sharing increase our options and make life more exciting.

7. *If you are a believer, you turn negative situations into positive ones.*

In a non-humanistic world, there are many humanistically objectionable institutions and social practices that cannot be changed. Unbelievers—because they are more comfortable with denunciation—rail against them and helplessly seek to remove them. Religious chaplains in the army, religious inscriptions on national monuments, invocations and benedictions at school and fraternal events—all these provocations move many unbelievers into futile resistance. But believers recognize that these practices and institutions exist because they are the only way in which many communities know how to celebrate their connection with their roots and their past. An invocation can as easily be a quotation from Thomas Jefferson as an appeal to Jesus. A "religious" lecturer to the Israeli army can as easily be a faculty member of the Institute for Humanistic Judaism as a Lubavitcher Hasid. Believers do not seek to destroy "misguided" institutions. They seek to use them.

8. *If you are a believer, you choose to reverse roles.*

Since unbelievers see themselves as outsiders in a community of believers, they make concessions more readily than do their opponents. If the Orthodox want to close down the Jewish Community Center on the Sabbath, if traditionalists want to insist that all community-sponsored banquets be kosher, if Conservatives want to keep Humanistic literature out of the Jewish community library, unbelievers often will yield to the opposition out of a sense that their opponents feel more strongly about these issues than they, the unbelievers, do. But believers refuse to be second-class citizens. Humanistic Jews do not reject the Sabbath. They believe that the Sabbath should be a day for family celebration, personal recreation, and Jewish cultural stimulation. Humanistic Jews do not reject dietary laws. They simply have a different set of regulations which are governed by the criteria of health and personal fitness. Humanistic Jews do not discard Jewish literature. They affirm the importance of seeing the Jewish experience through eyes that are not traditional. In most cases, their convictions are just as intense as those of their opponents. So if the other side is always making demands, Humanistic believers reverse roles. They have demands to make too.

9. *If you are a believer, you seek out other believers for mutual support.*

Unbelievers are notorious non-joiners. Because they often are refugees from authoritarian structures and authoritarian institutions that persecuted them, the idea of belonging to a group or community that supports congregations and fellowships—of developing a working network of philosophic brothers and sisters—is anathema to them. The very smell of organizations terrifies them. They prefer the safety of isolation. Even though the opposition derives its strength, power, and effectiveness from the willingness of its members to express their solidarity through group effort, unbelievers resist measures that would enable them to be equally effective. But believers know that everything the other side does is not bad. Organization is not bad if the purpose of the organization is good. Believers also know that isolation is a self-destructive strategy. It reinforces helplessness and the sense of "outsiderness," and leads to ideological impotence. A voice that cannot be heard is no voice at all.

10. *If you are a believer, you give personal testimony all the time.*

Fundamentalists are never reluctant to share their personal convictions when the opportunity arises—whether in business, in friendship, or at public celebrations. Their religious beliefs are not in some little corner of their minds, unrelated to their self-image and to their daily activity. In a real sense, what they are flows from what they believe.

One of the reasons people are so strongly aware of their existence is they talk about it all the time. For unbelievers, however, personal testimony is difficult. There is nothing to testify to, because there is nothing positive to proclaim. Humanist believers shed such inhibitions. Even when an audience is less than friendly, they are willing to speak out. They recognize that "hiding" subverts integrity and cultivates self-hate. They want other people to know who they are and what they stand for. They want humanism and Humanistic Judaism to have a public voice. They may do no more than the Holocaust survivor who, at a community Holocaust commemoration in Detroit, shared her humanistic vision of the meaning of the horror in a moving declaration that justice cannot rely on the fates but must depend on human effort and human vigilance. They may do no more than the young man in my congregation who rose to explain secular humanism in his high school class when a Christian fundamentalist student denounced it. Believers give testimony when testimony is necessary.

Believing is better than not believing. It is a strategy more conducive to self-esteem and community effectiveness. If there have to be unbelievers let those who do not believe in humanism play that role for awhile.

Humanistic Judaism, Spring 1986.

The Meaning of Jewish History

For the Jewish people, Jewish history has been more than a history. It has also been a course in philosophy.

For more than three thousand years, priests, prophets, poets, rabbis, and scholars have used the Jewish experience to "prove" their vision of the world. The events of the Jewish saga became "evidence" for certain beliefs about the nature of God and the universe. The exodus from Egypt was more than an exodus. In priestly and rabbinic hands, it became the demonstration of divine power and divine justice.

The meaning of Jewish history is the set of answers to important questions about God, the world, and people, which observers derive from the Jewish experience. Four questions, in particular, became the dominant themes of this evaluation. What does Jewish history demonstrate about:

The nature of the universe?
The power of human beings?
The evolution of human experience?
The essence of Jewish identity?

The Rabbinic View

Rabbinic Judaism, which was the establishment ideology of the Jewish people for more than two thousand years, used the events of the Jewish story to answer these four questions. The answers of the rabbis became the "official" meaning of the Jewish experience. Rabbinic literature derived its character from this unique perspective.

What were the answers of the rabbis?

From the rabbinic point of view, the existence, experiences, and survival of the Jewish people demonstrated the presence in the universe of an all-powerful, loving, and just God, who punished the wicked and rewarded the good, and who was attentive to the hopes and aspirations of all humanity. The world was a well-ordered place in which a divine intelligence was actively concerned with the moral agenda of human beings. Therefore, whatever happened in the world—no matter how seemingly unjust—happened for the good. In the end, even the suffering of the innocent would be vindicated by divine rewards.

Jewish history, according to the rabbis, demonstrated that human power was extremely limited; that human beings, relying on their own power alone, could accomplish very little. Time after time, according to the Bible and the Talmud, the Jewish people were rescued from disaster and from the embarrassment of their own inadequacy by divine intervention. The message of the priests and the prophets was that reliance on human effort and on human ingenuity was as effective as leaning on a "weak reed." The wise man recognized that human happiness was possible only with supernatural help.

Jewish history also revealed that the quality of human life was gradually declining. The present was inferior to the past, and the future would be inferior to the present. Similarly, the teachers of the present were inferior to the teachers of the past, and the teachers of the future would be inferior to the teachers of the present. The patriarchs, the prophets, and the rabbinic fathers were wiser, more saintly, and more inspired than any sages that would follow. Modern-day saints and scholars would be mental and spiritual pygmies in comparison with their ancient predecessors. God's conversations with humanity, and the time of divine revelation, had come to an end with the prophet Malachi. The world would sink into corruption and violence until only the messianic intervention of God would rescue humankind.

As to the nature and character of the Jewish people, the rabbis were very definite in their answer. The Jewish people was inseparable from the Torah and the religion it embodied. Without the Torah, the Jewish people would lose its essence and its unique personality. Without the Torah, the Jewish people would lose its motivation to survive as a distinct nation and would quickly be absorbed by the Gentile world. The Jews and rabbinic Judaism were pragmatically one.

The Humanist Critique

The meaning of Jewish history, as it was conceived by the rabbis, presents many problems for Humanistic Jews.

Supernatural guidance of natural events is not a credible idea for rational secularists. The assumption that what happens in this world is caused by decisions made in another is without valid evidence. If there are natural events, they have natural causes.

The discoveries of the past are important. But there is no evidence that the experts of the present are inferior to the experts of the past. In the world of science and technology, the information of the present is far superior to that of the past. There is no reason to assume that the development of religions and philosophic truths has been any different.

Religious personalities have been important in Jewish history. But to maintain that priests, prophets, and rabbis were the chief actors in the Jewish drama is to ignore the secular dimension of the Jewish experience. The authors of the Bible and the Talmud may not have chosen to record the achievements of the merchants, bankers, and artisans. Yet these achievements, economic and cultural, may have been just as influential in molding the Jewish character.

Traditional scholars make no distinction between the experience of the Jewish people and the descriptions of that experience that appear in the official texts of sacred literature. They simply assume that what the Bible and the Talmud claim to have happened did happen. If the Book of Exodus maintains that the Red Sea split before the fleeing Hebrews, then there was a split. If the anonymous Talmudic storyteller declares that a one-day supply of holy oil lasted for eight days, then this extraordinary event was real. There is no awareness of the fact, so amply confirmed by modern scientific criticism, that the real history of the Jews is vastly different from the saga presented by the rabbinic tradition.

In the light of these objections to the rabbinic approach to Jewish history, Humanistic Jews provide different answers to the four questions.

A Humanistic Perspective: World View

From a humanistic perspective, the existence, experience, and survival of the Jewish people hardly demonstrate the existence of a loving, just God who is compassionately involved with the moral agenda of human beings. On the contrary, the very opposite is indicated. In the century of the Holocaust, after twenty centuries of continuous, unprovoked Jew hatred, the experience of the Jewish people points to the absence of God.

A humanistic Judaism finds a totally different meaning in Jewish history from that proposed by traditional Judaism. A believer in future supernatural rewards and punishments would be hard put to justify the scenarios of Jewish sorrow and suffering from a morally divine perspective. No good God would arrange or allow a Holocaust of six million innocent victims. A thousand glorious resurrections would never provide moral compensation.

If Jewish history has any message abut the nature of the universe, it is that the universe is indifferent to our suffering or happiness, that it cares nothing about the moral concerns of the human struggle. The Jewish experience points to the absurdity of the world. Events happen in accordance with physical laws, not in accordance with ethical ones. Earthquakes and wars cannot defy the law of gravity; they can easily defy the Golden Rule.

The cosmic implication of Jewish history is that you cannot rely on the kindness of the universe. In the end, if human beings want justice, they will have to arrange for it. If they want happiness and dignity, they will have to arrange for them, too. And there is no messianic guarantee that we will achieve what we strive to achieve. Uncertainty is the stuff of an absurd universe.

In the light of four thousand years of continuous reproduction, Jewish survival is not so dramatic. Look at the Chinese, the Hindus, and the Greeks, who are equally ancient. Look at the Arabs, our Semitic rivals. Whatever gods took care of them did a far better job than Yahveh.

A Humanistic Perspective: Human Power

The rabbinic answer to the question of human power is inadequate and contrived. To assume that every human failure is due to human weakness and that every human success is due to divine assistance is to build the desired conclusion into the premise. From a naturalistic point of view, human success is the result of human effort and human ingenuity. If the achievement occasionally seems "divine," that is a tribute to human potential. Sometimes adversity evokes extraordinary results.

The Exodus from Egypt (if it is indeed a historical event) was a human happening that used human power to arrange for human freedom. The resistance of the Maccabees was a "human" rebellion that used human ingenuity to defeat the Greeks.

The survival of the Jews through fifteen centuries of unremitting persecution is no testimony to divine benevolence. It is a witness to the continuous ability of the Jews to invent new reasons for their enemies to let them live. If their religious ideas were offensive, their economic skills remained indispensable. The Zionist enterprise was a determined effort on the part of secular Jews to reject the historic passivity of the pious, with all its messianic waiting, and to assume conscious responsibility for the Jewish fate.

Jewish history testifies to the power of human ingenuity to cope with the cruelty of destiny. While Jewish suffering was more destructive than helpful, it did hone Jewish survival skills and stimulated the development of group solidarity and ambition.

A Humanistic Perspective: Progress

The rabbinic vision of human development, its answer to the question of human progress, is a distortion of reality. The belief that the best, the smartest, and the most charismatic lived long ago and that succeeding generations of religious experts and moralists can only manage to be less brilliant and less inspiring would be a charming myth if it did not have such harmful consequences.

The helplessness of modern Orthodoxy to find legal and moral relief for its overburdened adherents is the result of this doctrine. If contemporary scholars are overwhelmingly inferior to Moses and

Jeremiah, Hillel and Akiba, they have no moral authority to change what the superior ones have sanctioned. If divine revelation is confined to the distant past, nothing in the present can override its commands. Religion is reduced to the worship of the past.

Even modern liberal expressions of rabbinic Judaism such as Conservatism, Reform, and Reconstructionism, which accept some form of contemporary revelation, suffer from this view. They still vigorously seek to find sanction in the Bible and the Talmud for the changes they institute. Without the "kosherizing" of the past, present decisions lack validity.

Nostalgia for the pious past pervades the historic perspective of contemporary Jewish leaders. Most of these commentators on the Jewish scene see modern Western urban Jewry as less "Jewish" and less exciting than the pietists of earlier generations. They imagine that the age of the Secular Revolution has devastated the Jewish people through skepticism, assimilation, and intermarriage.

For Humanistic Jews, this nostalgia is deplorable. From our perspective, the Secular Revolution was the best thing that ever happened to the Jewish people. It removed the tyrannical religious monopoly of the traditional rabbis. It opened the Jewish mind to scientific inquiry and naturalism. It provided Jews with a more realistic understanding of the Jewish past and the evolution of Jewish culture. It introduced Jews to secular studies and to the intellectual pursuits that enabled them to make their mark on the revolutionary rethinking of the human condition. It provided them with a free economy and a democratic political structure that enabled them to reach unprecedented heights of prosperity and community involvement. It rescued them from religious passivity and gave them the confidence to assume responsibility for the Jewish fate.

Despite wars and massacres, the human condition and the Jewish condition have vastly improved. Few contemporary Jews, if offered the option, would volunteer to return to the Age of the Patriarchs.

Jewish wisdom and creativity in the twentieth century does not have to take a back seat to the legacy of the distant past. The Jews of this century are, probably, the most interesting, the most challenging, and the most creative generations of Jews that ever lived. Einstein was not inferior to Moses. And Freud did not have to offer reverence to Isaiah. Bialik and Tchernikhovsky are the equals of the psalmists. Herzl and Nordau are more relevant than Leviticus.

None of us need the sanction of the Torah or of the rabbis to be Jewishly valid. The worship of the past is replaced by respectful listening.

A Humanistic Perspective: Jewish Identity

The rabbinic answer to the question of Jewish identity is simply untrue. Jewish identity and Torah allegiance are not wed to one another. As the Zionist ideologue Ahad Ha'am pointed out, the Jewish people existed before Judaism, and the ethnic will to live preceded any theological formulations that justified it.

From the humanistic point of view, rabbinic Judaism did not create the national determination to survive. It provided a respectable public justification of it. In modern times, secular Zionism is an equally successful expression of the same ethnic drive.

The constant in Jewish identity is not theological conviction or Torah allegiance but Jewish peoplehood. In every age, the urge to survive—universal among nations—motivated Jews to find appropriate ways to satisfy it. In a religious age, they found religious strategies. In a secular age, they have found secular strategies.

The experience of Jewish ethnicity is the heart of Jewish identity. Even today, returnees to traditional Judaism do not first come to it out of theological conviction but out of a profound (if misleading) conviction that it is the best means of guaranteeing Jewish ethnic survival.

Conclusion

The meaning of Jewish history is radically different for Humanistic Jews from what it is for traditional or even liberal Jews.

The moral universe of the rabbis dissolves into the indifferent universe of the post-Holocaust era. The depreciation of human power and ingenuity is replaced by an appropriate tribute to the surprise of the human potential. The gloomy vision of a world declining in wisdom yields to a reassuring recognition of human progress. The rigid equating of Jewishness with religiosity gives way to recognition of the creative power of the Jewish will to live.

This new meaning is an important message we must share with the Jewish world.

Humanistic Judaism, Spring 1986.

Secular Humanistic Jewish Ideology

Addressing the Needs of the Future

There were times when ideology was very important in Jewish life, when a set of compelling ideas seized the minds and hearts of Jewish men and women and mobilized them to make dramatic changes in religion and culture.

The prophetic ideology of Amos, Hosea, Isaiah, and Jeremiah turned defeat into victory. Yahveh, the national God of the Jews, who was unable to crush the superior power of the Assyrians and their natural allies, became a world God of infinite power, who was using the Assyrians to punish his chosen people for their sins. Yahvism, rescued by prophetic ingenuity, became the foundation of a new and powerful religion. The Jewish people was thrust into the center of a divine drama of cosmic proportions.

The ideology of the Pharisees and their rabbinic leaders provided a response to the suffering and humiliation of the Jews and to the seeming injustice of God. A final judgment day would mark the end of this world and usher in the Kingdom of God. The dead would rise from their graves, stand before the seat of justice, and receive either eternal reward or eternal punishment. The powerful appeal of this scenario transformed Jewish life. Thousand of Jews flocked to the standard of the Pharisees. The rabbis assumed power. Rabbinic Judaism became official Judaism.

Other compelling ideologies have entered Jewish life from time to time, causing radical changes in Jewish behavior. A compelling ideology embraces all of life: the personal and the communal, the spiritual and the corporal. It addresses anxieties people have. It answers the questions people are asking. It is enhanced by charismatic leaders and dramatic symbols. Above all, it defines the goals of personal and social existence and identifies the source from which the power to achieve them will come.

In modern times, both Marxism and Zionism have won passionate adherents. Both have mobilized millions of people. But with these two exceptions, the past two hundred years have witnessed a decline in Jewish ideology. Fewer and fewer Jews connect their Jewishness with powerful and mind-grabbing ideas. Being Jewish and being ideological because one is Jewish no longer equate with the same intensity that they did in prophetic and rabbinic times. Most Jewish ideology today is about as passionate as the courteous statements made at interfaith banquets.

Why has this change occurred?

The old ideology, whether prophetic or rabbinic, is no longer credible. In an age of reason, science, and comparative religion, divinely chosen nations and resurrections are hardly the theological stuff of which conviction is made. What used to seem possible and real no longer seems possible or real. Political emancipation and secular education have made it difficult to believe what used to be easy to believe.

The new twentieth-century ideologies have failed to produce their promised utopias. This failure has provoked a pervasive disillusionment and cynicism. Scholars are now suspect. Rational thinking is condemned as shallow. Intuition and mystic insights are exalted. Listening to one's heart is preferred to listening to one's mind. New Age philosophy thrives on anti-intellectualism. Inconsistency becomes a virtue in an environment in which following one's feelings is accepted advice even in educated circles. Impulse rather than ideology becomes the sign of the free spirit. It is also an excuse to avoid establishing any real control of one's life.

Most modern Jews separate their Jewishness from their personal philosophy of life. The first is a cultural and nostalgic experience. The second is a private commitment—or a commitment exercised in a group other than a Jewish one. Jews *daven* [pray] and do transcendental meditation. They chant traditional blessings on Jewish holidays and oppose the encroachments of organized religion on public life. Jewishness and ideology function in separate compartments of people's lives. One has nothing to do with the other.

The power of traditional religious literature—the Bible, the Talmud, the Siddur—makes it difficult to dispense with them, especially in the absence of other Jewish writings of equal prestige. Being Jewish means using "the sources" even if you do not believe in most of what they say. The *Kaddish* is no longer a rabbinic tribute to a powerful and just God; it is a collection of Jewish sounds stripped of conceptual meaning.

In the century of racial anti-Semitism and the Holocaust, the survival of the Jewish people is an obsessive issue. Jewish survival demands Jewish activity. Prayer and worship are the most familiar Jewish activities, especially in the Diaspora, where Jewish languages have all but disappeared. Parents hire religious teachers to teach their children to recite religious words they do not believe in, because they imagine that Jewish prayer is a guarantee of Jewish identity—and Jewish identity is a guarantee of Jewish survival. For a nonideological Judaism, any synagogue will do.

Modern Jewish ideological secularism is often a sham. Most "secular" Jews define their secularism by their hostility to organized religion and the traditional rabbinate. Their secularism is not a positive philosophy of life, a new compelling vision of the world and of Jewishness. While these negative secularists resent the burden of traditional law and traditional authority, they do not mind playing traditional when it is convenient. A funeral or bar mitsva becomes an opportunity to dress up in the costumes of Orthodoxy and pretend for a moment that one is identifying with one's ancestors. People who grumble about the oppressiveness of religion, who choose to spend Rosh Hashana on a Tel Aviv beach, are often the same people who insist that all the halakhic details of *shiva* [mourning] be observed when their parents die. In their minds religion is irrelevant or worse—but: if you do it, you might as well do it "right."

Jewish nationalism—whether Yiddishist or Zionist—began with secularists. But its success brought antisecularists into the fold. Today a majority of the supporters of Zionism are followers of conventional religion. Public Zionism, therefore, has to be circumspect. It can no longer afford to offend the religious. The old secularist fervor would undermine Jewish unity, successful political campaigning, and fundraising. Public Zionism has become a set of safe nationalist clichés that offer no real guidance to Jews seeking a meaningful personal philosophy of life. A nationalism that seeks to mobilize large numbers of people of diverse opinions needs a safe ideology—which, for practical purposes, means no ideology.

The decline of ideology is manifest everywhere in Jewish life. Jewish feminists don the symbols of the halakhic system that rejects them. The Reform movement seeks to be emotionally kosherized by a return to tradition. The Conservative movement has given up trying to explain why it is neither Orthodox nor liberal and instead justifies itself by the meaningless plea of moderation. Even bold stands on female rabbis and homosexual rabbis are comfortably combined with ritual praise of the ethical traditions of the Jewish past.

Philosophical talk has been replaced by survival talk. Whatever seems to enhance Jewish survival, regardless of its effect on the quality of Jewish life, is good. Secularists give money to the Lubavitchers because Orthodox Jews stay Jewish. Reform rabbis sponsor Orthodox conversions because Jewish unity strengthens the Jewish people. Welfare federations provide support to Orthodox yeshivas—the more tradition, the more survival. At one time in the Jewish world, in the days of the prophets and the rabbis, the primary question of Judaism was, "Is it true?" Today, in a survival-obsessed Jewish society, the question of truth has vanished. The only question that remains is, "Is it Jewish?"

As we contemplate the future of the Jewish people and the future of Secular Humanistic Judaism, we need to deal with the decline of ideology.

One option is to play down ideology—to become merely a potpourri of people who have either vague or vivid grievances against organized religion. The danger in this approach is that we will give up our substance in order to improve the packaging; and the new packaging will not work in the end. Negative secularists are not the stuff of which to build a strong movement. They share no positive agenda. They are easily seduced by Orthodox tidbits when they want to feel Jewish. They can be satisfied by Reform or Conservative nostalgia as well as by secular nostalgia.

The other option is to be clearly ideological in a Jewish world that avoids ideology. The opportunity in this approach is that we can recruit people who share our positive agenda, who value our willingness to deal with ideas and with personal integrity in Jewish life. The danger is that we will turn off negative secularists who find no value in philosophy or in consistency.

Given the advantages and disadvantages of both options, I would choose the path of ideology. We are a movement committed to a radical reinterpretation of the Jewish experience. We are not a movement equipped to benefit from impulsive nostalgia. In the long run, we will serve individual Jews and the Jewish people more effectively if we enable them to link their personal beliefs with their Jewish identity. We will serve our movement more effectively if we give it a unique function in Jewish life.

What do we need to do to make our ideology a strong ideology?

We need to insist that the question "Is it true" is more important the question "Is it Jewish?" The *Sh'ma* [prayer affirming God] is Jewish, but it is not, from our perspective, true. The *Kaddish* is Jewish, but it is not consistent with what we believe. A strong ideology insists that when we celebrate who we are, we speak with conviction. New words that express our convictions are preferable to old words that do not. Nostalgia is valuable, but it is not primary.

We need to reduce our basic beliefs to four or five simple, dramatic statements—statements that address Jewish anxieties and concerns. A powerful message is a brief message. Overlong academic formulations are useless.

If I were to choose five basic statements, they would be the following:

Judaism is the culture of the Jewish people, which includes many religious and secular traditions.

A Jew is any person who chooses to identify with the fate and culture of the Jewish people.

After the Holocaust, it is clear that the meaning of Jewish history is that Jews must be responsible for their own fate.

Every person is entitled to be the master of his or her own life, subject to the final authority of his or her own conscience.

The power to achieve human survival, happiness, and dignity is a human power.

We need to be what we are and not try to be what we are not. We have deep roots in the Jewish experience. But we represent a radical break with the rabbinic tradition. We can use the literature of the past when it expresses humanistic sentiments. But we do not need to be kosherized by it. Quotations will not make us more legitimate. The ultimate vulnerability of the Reform and Conservative movement is the need to find authority in the literature of rabbinic Judaism. Orthodox clothing does not fit non-Orthodox people.

We need to take seriously our commitment to reason. Old liberal beliefs that no longer conform to the evidence should be discarded. Unyielding loyalty to a humanistic tradition can be as reactionary as unyielding loyalty to the halakhic tradition. We should not burden ourselves with embarrassing falsehoods. Old humanistic clichés like "All people are basically good," or "Human ethical progress is constant and inevitable," or old Marxist slogans like "The laws of history dictate ultimate human liberation" are, in the light of the twentieth century experience, simply silly. They are about as credible as the Lubavitcher messiah or the Reform vision of the messianic age.

We need to answer questions that Jewish people are asking. The power of the prophetic and rabbinic traditions lay in their responsiveness to deep concerns. The quest for spiritual experience is a Jewish quest. It demands an answer—and not the dismissive answer of the old secular tradition, which was deeply suspicious of the very word *spirituality.* Today many Jews who seek a spiritual dimension in their lives are fully humanistic. But they have no vocabulary to describe what they want and need. A Secular Humanistic Judaism that lacks a strong, clear, and positive answer to the question of spirituality will not be effective.

We need to reconnect Jewish identity with a strong personal philosophy of life, a philosophy that enables people to cope more adequately with the adversities and opportunities of individual existence. Jews are more than Jews. They are human beings, with all the fears and anxieties of the human condition. Prophetic and rabbinic Judaism addressed the human condition as well as the question of Jewish survival. Modern Judaism, by and large, does not. Jews do their Judaism in the synagogue and their personal philosophy of life in universities, friendship circles, professional work, private readings, marathon weekends, or psychotherapy. They do not expect the message of the synagogue to be a personal guide for effective living. They expect it only to reinforce their Jewish identity. An effective ideology addresses Jewish issues in the context of broader human issues: How are Jewish identity and self-esteem related? What does Secular Humanistic Judaism have to say about the search for personal dignity and fulfillment? In what way is Jewish liberation connected to general human liberation?

We need to speak in a language that people understand. Intellectual formulations appeal to some people, but others can better understand principles imbodied concretely in the lives of real people. Biography becomes philosophy. Heroes become role models. All successful ideologies have vivid personalities who serve as living examples of appropriate behavior; even children can comprehend the values they represent. Who are our unique heroes? What literature do we have to tell their stories to adults and children? There are many biographies of Spinoza and Einstein. But we do not have a biographic literature written from a Secular Humanistic Jewish point of view.

We need appealing symbols. The most effective ideology is never found in dry formulations. It is expressed in songs, holiday celebrations, and body decorations. The ideology of halakhic Judaism is better expressed by the Siddur than by the Maimonidean creed. The principles of Jewish Marxism were better dramatized by May Day and the Yiddish "Internationale" than by public readings of *Das Kapital*. What are the songs of our movement? What are the unique celebration formats we all share? What are the symbols of our commitment that we would choose to wear? It is not enough that each community is creative. There has to be a set of shared symbols, songs, and formats that uniquely dramatize the ideology and membership of our movement. At some time or other we all need to sing the same song and know that other Secular Humanistic Jews are singing it too.

We need to be pluralistic with conviction. A successful Judaism needs to be a pluralistic Judaism, in which all Jewish options have their place. But it does not need to be a mushy pluralism that seeks to avoid confrontation and gloss over differences. Ideological competition is real—and it is good for Judaism. No single ideology, or lack of ideology, can possibly serve the needs and temperaments of all Jews. Only the give and take of competing views of Jewish identity can produce the vitality and variety that a healthy Judaism requires. Strong convictions, strongly expressed, are essential to meaningful internal debate. As long as they do not degenerate into absolute and self-righteous convictions, they give substance to Jewish commitment. A strong ideology needs to find the balance between offending nobody and rejecting everybody else.

Humanistic Judaism, Winter 1991

What Could Be More Humanistic Than Jewish Humor?

Jewish humor. Most everybody admits that it exists. But not everybody agrees on what it means. Is it simply ordinary humor with a slightly distinct ethnic touch? Or is it more significant—a folk culture assault on the establishment ideology of rabbinic Judaism?

For most secularized Jews in North America, Jewish humor is a more important part of their lives than the Torah. It speaks more powerfully to them than the priestly piety of the Pentateuch. Long after traditional religion virtually vanished from the lives of many Western Jews, Jewish jokes remain a standard part of Jewish conversation.

Despite its universal presence, Jewish humor is rarely taken seriously. To the scholars of Judaism, Jewish belief and conviction lie in the texts of the rabbis, the Talmud, and the Siddur. Religion is a very serious business. What most people believe is what official texts tell them they believe. Since almost none of these texts is very funny, humorous observations about the human condition do not play a part in any elementary discussion of basic Judaism.

Traditional religion and humor are opposite ways of responding to the human condition. The heart of religion is worship, a recurrent surrender to the will of God. Worship rests on the profound conviction that all is well with the world even though the world appears to be sick. God is loving, just, and orderly even though we do not seem to be experiencing a lot of love, justice, and moral order. From the human perspective, life is crazy. From the divine perspective, the world, with all its supernatural rewards and punishments, is a wonderful place.

Philosophic humor starts with the absurdity of life. The world is not fair. The good are punished more than they ought to be. The wicked are rewarded more than they ought to be. Kindness gets you *bubkes* ["beans"]. Cruelty gets you power. The nicest thing you can say about God, if you believe that he exists, is what Woody Allen said: "God is an underachiever." (Mordecai Kaplan, founder of the Reconstructionist movement, and Harold Kushner, author of *When Bad Things Happen to Good People,* really say the same thing as Allen. But they are so caught up in the worship mentality that they don't understand how funny they are.)

Humor, unlike worship, is neither friendly nor reverent. It is usually hostile. In human evolutionary history (as Desmond Morris suggested in *Manwatching*), laughter did not begin as a friendly gesture. Displaying teeth was generally the prelude to biting, not caressing. In philosophic humor, our words do what our teeth are no longer permitted to do.

A simple story by Sholem Aleichem from *Tevyeh the Milkman* will illustrate my point. Tevyeh is talking to God.

". . . Blessed are they that dwell in Thy house (Good! But I take it, O Lord, that Thy house is somewhat more spacious than my hovel!). . . . I will extol Thee, my God, O King (What good would it do me if I didn't?). . . . Every day I will bless thee (on an empty stomach, too). . . . The Lord is good to all (And suppose He forgets somebody now and again, good Lord, hasn't He enough on his mind?). . . . The Lord upholdeth all that fall, and raiseth up all that are bowed down (Father in Heaven, loving Father, surely it's my turn now, I can't fall any lower). . . . Thou openest Thy hand and satisfiest every living thing (So You do, Father in Heaven, You give with an open hand—one gets a box on the ear, and another roast chicken, and neither my wife nor I nor my daughters have even smelt a roast chicken since the days of creation). . . . He will fulfill the desire of them that fear Him; He will also hear their cry and will save them. (But when, O Lord? When?. . .)"

With worship like that you don't need blasphemy. And with theology like that you don't need religion. Sholem Aleichem is a folk philosopher. He says more in ten lines than most formal philosophers say in volumes. What he says, although formally couched in reverence, is profoundly irreverent.

Tevyeh is the voice of the counter-establishment in Jewish life. While the rabbis and pietests weave tales of divine love and divine justice, the folk culture is more honest. After two thousand years of undeserved persecution and murder, the appropriate response to all this misery is not "thank you." It is *"oy gevalt!"* The rabbinic establishment preached denial and came up with faith. The folk culture paid attention to experience and came up with skepticism.

The skepticism was never openly proclaimed. To do so would have filled the ambivalent souls of the common people with guilt. It also would have been very risky, inviting repression and excommunication. Skepticism generally was dressed up in tradition and piety. But the tongue was in the cheek.

Both prophetic and rabbinic Judaism are filled with a powerful sense of divine justice. In the end goodness will triumph and evil will be defeated. It is this conviction that made them such powerful ideologies, able to win the allegiance of the Jewish people. But they run counter to the experience of everyday life, especially the experience of oppressed people.

The ideological enemy of these humorless ideologies is Jewish humor, which is actually philosophy, albeit folk philosophy. Jokes may not be considered a respectable way to communicate philosophy, but they are usually more effective than tedious theological prose. Woody Allen and Sholem Aleichem are part of a long, largely unpublished, skeptical tradition, a tradition filled with anger and a sense of outrage.

Jewish humor is the chief "traditional" voice of this skepticism. It is distinct from humor not specific to the Jewish condition, which is the common possession of both Jews and non-Jews. Conventional humor rests on the absurdity of surprise. It ranges from slipping on banana peels to taboo sex. It makes you laugh because you are caught unaware.

Jewish humor has the element of surprise. But it has more: a philosophic bitterness that ranges in degree from the safe commentary of Sam Levenson to the cruelty of Lenny Bruce.

Jewish humor is more than the humor of an oppressed people. African-American humor is the humor of an oppressed people. But it is the humor of an oppressed servile people. Slave peoples mock themselves and their masters. They do not mock their religion. Jews are an oppressed pariah people. They were persecuted and rejected. But even though they were social outcasts, they retained their own community structures. Slaves are integrated into the lives of their masters. Pariahs are marginal, existing on the fringes of established society. They have enough distance to develop a healthy skepticism toward all authority, even divine authority.

There are two characteristics of traditional Jewish humor. Both are present in the words of Tevyeh. Both reflect the necessity to speak skepticism in a world that was officially pious. There is a false reverence, a false deference to authority. Tevyeh pretends to be pious, but his words are taunting. There is also deliberate denial. Disasters are called successes; defeats are labeled victories; absurdity is called justice. The implication is clear: "With friends like this, you do not need enemies."

Jewish humor was just as important as Jewish piety in preserving the Jewish people. Without the catharsis of laughter, the Jews would have choked on their own rage. The philosophy of Jewish humor was an antidote to the philosophy of faith, with all its passive acceptance and passive waiting. The Jewish personality that emerged out of the Jewish experience relied heavily on Jewish skepticism. Jewish ambition and self-reliance did not come from piety. They arose out of the deep-felt conviction that the fates were not as reliable as the rabbis made them out to be.

The nervous, ambitious, skeptical, good-humored Jew has always been the Jew that appealed to me. Laughing has always seemed to me more Jewish than praying.

Humanistic Judaism, Summer 1991

Intermarriage

Should Jews marry only Jews?

Most Jews think that they should. Even the most sophisticated prefer the perils of atheism to the trauma of mixed weddings. The prospect that their children will be doing their reproducing with Gentiles arouses the deepest dread that their unconscious can conjure up.

Outspoken liberals, who are big on brotherhood, open pot, and female liberation, often turn hysterical when they learn that their Jewish son intends to cohabit in a legal way with a non-Jewish woman. Infamous Jewish anti-Semites, who are turned off by all forms of organized religion and find Jewish culture depressing, are known to become violent when their daughter announces her intention to marry a Gentile man.

Why this overreaction to what appears to be decent love?

The answer is important because no issue in Jewish life is as explosive as the question of intermarriage. Even the Reform rabbinate, the so-called paragons of religious liberalism, are deeply divided on the issue. We are witnessing the ironic spectacle of radical egalitarians and libertarians turned into fanatic inquisitors eager to expel erring rabbis from the rabbinic fold for the unspeakable sin of officiating at mixed marriages.

The reason for this behavior is no mystery. Tribal loyalty is an old and respected human emotion. Although it is not uniquely Jewish, it has been strengthened among Jews by centuries of exile and homelessness. Jews have had to make a special effort to survive as a group. Without the dramatic differences in their rituals, food, language, and dress, they would have had great difficulty resisting the religious onslaught of their hostile neighbors.

Throughout the centuries, Jews worked very hard to maintain these differences. As a result, their descendants feel very guilty when they give them up. Even when they no longer believe in the viability of traditional customs, even when the tyranny of outmoded practices violates their individual integrity; they often consent to do them. The guilt of repudiating what so many of their ancestors died to preserve is too much for them to bear.

The most effective technique for group survival in an alien environment was social segregation and compulsory inbreeding. The ban on intermarriage followed logically from the overwhelming desire to preserve Jewish identity. People who reproduce together, stay together. As a technique for the maintenance of dispersed minorities, this prohibition is both universal and familiar. The Aryan conquerors of India used it well when they devised the caste system. And the English colonials found it useful in the preservation of Anglo-Saxon identity in the colonial environments.

The Jewish ban on intermarriage dates from the sixth century B.C.E. When the Jewish aristocracy were taken by the Chaldeans to a Babylonian exile, they found themselves a small minority in a sea of Semitic strangers. Too snobbish to assimilate and too affluent to forego the new luxuries of Babylon for the rural poverty of Judea, they turned to rigid inbreeding as a way of enjoying the best of two worlds. Under the leadership of fanatic priests, they elevated their new custom into divine law. The Zadokite priests inserted this prohibition into the text of the Torah, which they were writing, giving it a divine aura.

When some of the Babylonian Jews returned to Jerusalem in the fifth century, they brought with them both the Torah and the ban. Their charismatic leader Ezra forced the native Jews to accept the authority of the Torah and to divorce their non-Jewish wives.

In the contemporary world, the prohibition against outmarriage is of crucial importance to Jewish survivalists. With the rapid disappearance of many unique Jewish forms of behavior and with the quick assimilation of Jews to the cultures of Western nations, the only barrier that seems to stand between group identity and the ethnic melting pot is segregated reproduction.

Since group survival for the sake of group survival is no longer publicly respectable, Jewish professionals are driven to find "noble" reasons for this parochialism. Jews and Gentiles are annually inundated by a variety of books that make the old claim that without Jewish exclusiveness, mankind would enjoy less brotherhood, justice, and intellectual greatness. A world without Jews, they claim, would almost be a world not worth having.

Threatened minorities do not survive unconsciously (like the Russians and the Chinese). They often survive only by becoming obsessed with the problem of their own survival. Everything in

Jewish life today is seen from the perspective of group survival, from the perspective of group identity. For many Jewish professionals, synagogue social action, experimental services, and the updating of Jewish philosophy are not avenues for individual fulfillment. They are gimmicks for involving Jews in Jewish institutions. Their value is a function of their ability to promote Jewish identity.

Even most liberal rabbis who consent to officiate at mixed marriages are often apologetic about their own activity. Embarrassed by their natural empathy for two individuals who love each other, they feel impelled to justify their action. Maintaining that if they refuse to officiate, the couple will choose to get married in a purely secular or Christian setting, they opt for the lesser of two evils. Intermarriage is bad. But losing a Jew forever is worse.

So great is the fear of the vanishing Jew that the moral worth of individual happiness and personal love is lost in timid and defensive arguments about group survival. Irrational comparisons between the European Holocaust and assimilation crop up in the reasoning of the self-proclaimed liberal theologians. How can we complete the work of Hitler, they cry, by allowing the Jew to disappear? As though the physical extermination of individuals were equivalent to the opportunity of individuals to freely choose their marriage partners!

In the midst of all this anxiety and exaggeration, the factual and moral realities remain.

Since Jewish identity is not a belief identity, two Jews marrying each other may be further apart ideologically and morally than a Jew and a Gentile marrying. A truly orthodox Jew may share his Jewish identity with his humanist Jewish wife. But they will share little else. The negative critics of Jewish-Gentile intermarriage often complain about the loss of ideological and moral consistency for children, even though the "mixed" couple may share a secular approach to life and values, but they rarely discuss the "intermarriage" problems of two totally incompatible Jews. For traditionalists, a Jewish atheist is better than a Bible-believing Gentile.

Most Jews who intermarry value their Jewish identity. Their choice of a non-Jewish partner is not a rejection of their Jewishness. It is merely an expression of their power to love people who share their ideas and values, even though their lovers are not Jews. Jewish identity is an important commitment. But it is not their *only* commitment or their *chief* value. To elevate Jewish identity to a supreme position is to violate the basis of a humanistic ethics. It is to deprive the individual of personal identity and to narrow the exploration for personal dignity.

If the most important Jewish enterprise is the promotion of Jewish identity, then the ban on intermarriage is perfectly rational as a means to that end. If the most significant thing for a Jew to be is to be Jewish, then denouncing the immorality of outmarriage is a logical consequence.

If, on the other hand, the primary goal of life for all Jews is to secure their own happiness and dignity, then the ban on intermarriage is an unethical interference. If the purpose of a group, whether kinship, ethnic, religious, or professional, is to serve the welfare of its individual members, then the refusal of rabbis to place personal love above Jewish identity is a form of moral negligence.

Certainly, it would be wrong to pretend that rabbinic ethics is neutral to these options. As a group-oriented conventional morality, it makes the same demands on the individual that the morality of any insular minority makes. The rabbis of old would have found an individualist ethic abhorrent and subversive of the divine will. A humanistic morality, which affirms the ultimate value of the individual, has never been a part of any national religion—least of all the rabbinic variety.

A consistent humanist maintains the right of individuals to pursue their own dignity in the way that their personal needs and temperament requires, so long as they do not harm the dignity of others. The consistent humanist maintains the right of all Jews to marry whomever they choose and is happy to assist them in exercising this choice. Recognizing the value of personal love and respect to human happiness, the consistent humanist welcomes the fact that two people have discovered these positive experiences in their new relationship. If the value of Jewish identity for humanistic Jews lies in its message of human self-reliance, how can this value be maintained if Jewish identity is used to promote its very opposite?

The children of Jewish parents are Jews whether they want to do anything about their Jewish identity or do not. Since the Jewish connection is a kinship connection—especially in the eyes of the Gentile world—intermarriage does not deny this birthright to the child of a Jewish father or mother. The protests of the traditionalists who claim that a Jewish mother is necessary for Jewish identity go against the practices of social reality. Just as who is black is determined not only by blacks but also by the majority whites, so who is a Jew is determined not only by Jews but also by the Gentile world. In the eyes of most Jews and Gentiles, Jewish descent becomes a sufficient reason for conferring Jewish identity. In fact, Jewish fathers, because they give their children Jewish surnames, are more powerful in determining the kinship labels of their descendants than Jewish mothers. If Cohen is not Jewish, he has to explain why.

Secular Gentiles who marry Jews may freely choose a secular Jewish identity for themselves if they are not treated as rejects. Unlike the demands of those Jews who insist on the public disavowal of past belief systems as the price of conversion, the approach of humanistic Jews is to make Jewishness an addition, not a repudiation. Since humanistic Gentiles are already humanistic, the assumption of Jewish identity does not negate what they believe. It merely reinforces it.

On the other hand, humanistic Jews who marry fundamentalist Christians have a serious problem. It is the same problem of incompatibility that they face when they marry fundamentalist Jews.

The Jewish people of the future will be different from the Jewish people of the past. Except for a small minority, it will be more open in an open society. Intermarriage will make Jewish identity less intense. But it will also make it more widespread and more significant to secular people in a secular world.

This change is not unwelcome. The rabbinic segregation that led to bigotry and to the rejection of the Gentile world is subversive of the values that individual Jews should cultivate in themselves.

The Jewish identity of the future will depend not only on the children of Jewish mothers. It will also be a kinship option for born Jews and for those who choose to marry Jews. Unless we want a Lubavitcher redoubt—where the saving remnant lives in self-righteous isolation from the Gentile world—the boundaries of the future between Jew and non-Jew need to be less formidable and more accommodating.

Humanistic Judaism, Winter 1990

Daniel Friedman
(1935–)

Introduction

Daniel Friedman is rabbi of Congregation Beth Or, a Humanistic Jewish community in Deerfield, Illinois. He is one of the leading philosophers of Humanistic Judaism. In 1968 he transformed his congregation from a conventional Reform temple into a community of Humanistic Jews.

Friedman was born in Denver and received his B.A. degree from Brandeis University in 1957. He attended Hebrew Union College in Cincinnati and was ordained in 1962.

Friedman has a special interest in the fields of ethics and human rights. He was one of the founding members of the Society for Humanistic Judaism and is a frequent contributor to its quarterly journal, *Humanistic Judaism*. His lucid commentary has brought clarity to many important issues.

Reason and Spirituality

Ever since I began to investigate this matter, I have been amazed at the dearth of information available on spirituality. There has been virtually no research into the nature of spirituality; what little literature is available deals not with what spirituality is, or whether it is, but with its consequences. The literature is largely in the form of anecdotal testimony concerning how important spirituality is, how much it is needed in our day, and how profoundly it has influenced certain lives. Rarely is the word defined in a clear, coherent manner.

So, let me begin by suggesting my own simple definition. The word *spirituality* is, of course, derived, from *spirit*, which, in its most basic meaning signifies that which is non-material. Matter and spirit are opposites. We could spend many hours discussing the classical philosophical understandings and arguments surrounding the matter-vs.-spirit dichotomy. But for the purposes of our discussion, it will be sufficient to suggest that the most useful way of understanding the word *spirit*, as it has come to be understood, is to contrast it with matter; to contrast the spiritual with the material. It is alleged that there are two kinds of reality: the ordinary, material, physical world, which can be experienced by means of the five senses; and another realm, the spiritual, which cannot be touched, tasted, seen, heard, or smelled but can be experienced by means of other, non-sensory "faculties," such as intuition or faith, or by means of "consciousness-raising" techniques, such as meditation or the use of mind-altering chemicals.

Furthermore, it is said that this non-material world not only exists but transcends the material world; is deeper than, more profound than, more beautiful and significant than—and even explains and gives purpose to—the physical world. Not to have access to the spiritual, therefore, is to be cut off from that which is more meaningful and beautiful in life—indeed, beyond life. For, since life is itself a function of the physical world, only in the spiritual realm can one find immortality—life beyond death. So, not only is life explained by the spiritual, but death and what lies beyond death is, by its very nature, confined to the spiritual. It is impossible even to believe in a hereafter without first believing in the spiritual.

Spirituality partakes of the non-material, the other-worldly, of that which lies beyond the world of sensation; underlies it, explains it, gives it purpose and meaning, and even transcends it in time—which makes it very, very important. It is supremely important—to know about, to study, and, surely, to connect with, to communicate with.

The word *spiritual* is commonly used in describing such persons as Jesus, Gandhi, perhaps Einstein, and Martin Luther King, Jr. These people are generally regarded as spiritual types. Gandhi, yes; Iacocca, no. Abraham Heschel, Buber, Elie Wiesel, yes; Don Rickels, no.

It would generally be agreed that, on the whole, poets and composers are, and typical businessmen are not, spiritual persons. Meaning that a predominant interest in material things such as the pursuit of wealth and power is not characteristic of spiritual persons. It is attention to non-materialistic interests that defines spiritual people and, therefore, spirituality.

Spirituality can be said to be a kind of attitude. A direction, a focus not so much on immediate, physical, mundane matters—especially not on the petty, routine concerns of the day—but rather a direction toward the larger, transcendent qualities of life; toward the eternal as opposed to the temporal.

We may visualize a spiritual person gazing upward—beyond the horizon—not at things here at hand, but gazing, as it were, at eternity.

There is the sense that spiritual people partake of the spiritual (realm); that they not only have access to it, but are themselves part of it. A kind of respect and even reverence is accorded them even by people who are not spiritually inclined. It is presumed that such people have achieved—the best word I can think of to describe what they seem to have achieved is *serenity.* They seem to have achieved a status that is admired, even by those who are not "into" spirituality. That is, they (spiritual people) have about them the aura of being in touch with, and being touched by, a larger, more important, more profound power than the rest of us.

And this, of course, brings us to God. Since God is typically understood to be the invisible, untouchable, non-material power underlying the material world—preceding it, transcending it, indeed, creating it—it is also widely assumed that the spiritual is the divine; that the realm that we have been discussing is precisely what God is, or, where God is located, rather than right here in this material world; that if one would contact God, one must do so by developing spiritual talents, such as prayer and meditation.

In other words, the spiritual and the religious are very closely related in many minds. The two words are even used interchangeably, as are other words and concepts, such as *mystical, supernatural*. The realm of religion has become identified, in the minds of many people, with the realm of the spiritual.

Inasmuch as even "non-spiritual" people, secular people, may offer token respect to "the spiritual," religion is accorded a certain status by many people who are themselves non-religious. Let me expand on this point a bit.

Many people have a yearning for what is called *transcendence*—for the ability to rise above the petty concerns and mundane problems of the day. They may also have experienced moments of deep meaning or emotion, say, upon viewing the Grand Canyon or other natural wonders, or listening to a beautiful concerto, or giving birth to a child, or making love, or in a thousand different ways. People glimpse possibilities of meaning, feeling, and appreciation—of nature, of other people, of themselves—that they cannot explain rationally—that is, that they think they cannot explain rationally. They experience what they perceive to be a different order, a higher, more significant order, than that of the here-and-now-world, the world that can be analyzed in a laboratory. Because religions have for millennia talked about non-rational understanding (called faith) and recommended ways of achieving it (such as prayer, meditation, and fasting), many people interpret the aforementioned spiritual experiences as religious experiences—indeed, as glimpses of the divine. These experiences and interpretations then feed into conventional religious propaganda, which insists that reason is inadequate, that underlying and transcending our world is the divine, that beyond this life is a hereafter. People find themselves saying: "Maybe there is something to what religion teaches."

To sum up: 1) The very common human need or yearning to transcend reality as we know it with its problems, disappointments, pain, frustration, death—especially death—and to find solace, comfort, joy, meaning in another realm; and 2) the presence in the popular imagination of such figures as Jesus, Buddha, Gandhi, and Buber, who seem to have achieved a much-to-be-desired serenity, a sense of peace that transcends worldly concerns; plus 3) occasional glimpses in common human experience of such a realm; plus 4) a long history of respected religious teachings that confirm the existence and supreme importance of "the spiritual"—all provide a powerful context that conventional religion exploits and from which it derives a great deal of respectability. Acknowledgment of that respectability comes, not only from devoutly religious people, but even from rather unreligious, secular people who, while not committed to God, see some truth and value in the religious message, if only because there seems to be no other way of making sense out of the occurrence of the spiritual in their lives.

So religion has come to have a monopoly on the spiritual market. And we Humanistic Jews are left with an enormous problem and challenge. Our commitment to reason (rather than faith) and our tendency to be relatively untraditional, not to mention non-mystical, give us the appearance of being also non- or unspiritual. Humanism can be, and usually is, misunderstood to mean a concern with only the material world—that which is accessible to science; and we are accused of overlooking, or of being too narrow-minded to see, the spiritual.

This is one of the most serious misunderstandings of humanism and of Humanistic Judaism that has developed. We must address ourselves to it and clarify our message, or we will risk excluding from our community many actual humanists who see themselves as non-humanists by virtue of their recognition of the spiritual dimension of life.

In order to move toward this clarification, I propose that we distinguish between two kinds of spirituality: the first, I'll call supernatural or theistic spirituality; and the second, natural or humanistic spirituality.

Theistic, mystical religion does not have a monopoly on spirituality. Far from it! There are such things as love, compassion, integrity, meaning, purpose, beauty, joy, exhilaration, wonder—and appreciation thereof. Awareness of the grandeur of nature and of human creativity. The sense of wonder at the birth of a child. The thrill of achievement. The glory of Beethoven. There is an infinite variety of experiences that are spiritual—in the natural, humanistic sense. These experiences cannot be reduced to physical sensation, to material functions. They are the very experiences that make life beautiful, rich, adventurous, significant. We do not deny them. We affirm them. We celebrate them.

Secondly, we should acknowledge clearly that not only are these spiritual experiences possible without reference to a supernatural being, because they are no more apart from nature than is the Law of Gravity, but they are, potentially, more significant to a humanist than to a theist!

To a theist, everything is an aspect of divinity, the only ultimate reality. Human creativity, for example, is just a pale imitation of supernatural power. Human love is a mere reflection of divine love. Inasmuch as divine power and love are beyond human understanding, they are beyond human appreciation. If human love merely reminds us of God's love, it is less important, less profound, than God's love.

For humanists, human love is not a reflection of something else; human achievement is not a pale imitation. These are reality—they are, in and of themselves, valuable and precious. No human experience is but a reflection of a power other than ourselves to whom we owe gratitude; all experiences are the expression of ourselves. How much the more, therefore, to be cultivated, appreciated, enjoyed!

Religions undercut the inherent value of experience by insisting that what is truly real is not what you're experiencing but is the source of what you're experiencing—namely, God. Humanism says: what you are experiencing is real. You need not look for validation beyond the experience itself—for something ineffably more wonderful than the experience, more authentic than human experience. For us, there is nothing more authentic than human beings.

Our challenge, then, is to articulate and communicate our humanistic understanding of spirituality so that our reputation will accurately reflect the reality of what we are. We are not cold, unfeeling rationalists, who refuse to acknowledge the richness of life—who ignore the spiritual, the emotional dimensions, of human experience.

On the contrary, it is precisely our humanism that enables us to feel all the more deeply—knowing that we, not a distant deity, are responsible for our feelings. We, not a mystical force, are the agents of creativity, of love, of joy—and yes, of sadness and tragedy.

It is human responsibility, not divine authority, that ultimately gives us the most authentic access to the sources of spirituality, which are not outside human experience or beyond nature but right here in our heads and in our hearts.

Humanistic Judaism, Autumn 1986.

Defining Our Jewish Heritage

What is "our Jewish heritage"? The phrase is used endlessly in sermons, articles, and classrooms. Children are sent to Sunday schools to learn it. Rabbis urge us to preserve it. Rarely is it defined clearly and precisely.

To answer the question, "What is our Jewish heritage?" I suggest that there are two different ways of viewing and understanding *Judaism*. The first is the popular, conventional approach, which views Judaism as either a religion or an ideology—a system of beliefs, practices, and rituals or a system of ideas and values. Accordingly, the Jewish people are defined as a religious community bound together by the beliefs of the religion, Judaism; or they are defined as an ideological community united by shared "Jewish" values.

If Judaism is viewed as a religion or an ideology, certain distinctive beliefs, ideas, or values are taken to be the basis for the existence of the community. They are prior to the people and are the reason for their peoplehood. They are inherited, preserved, and passed on from generation to generation.

It is commonly asserted that "our Jewish heritage" includes the Ten Commandments; a commitment to such values as family cohesiveness, learning, *tzedakah* (charity, generosity), justice, peace; and, for theists, God. There are, then, two versions of this understanding of Judaism—the theistic and the secular: the one including God in the collection of essential elements constituting "our Jewish heritage" and the other excluding God but still maintaining that there are specific and distinctive ideas or values that constitute "our Jewish heritage."

I propose that this understanding of Judaism is in error. It is not empirically verifiable. There is no idea, belief, or value that Jews always have accepted that constitutes and causes their Jewishness.

An alternative way of viewing and understanding Judaism—and I believe, a more valid one—is the historical approach that views Judaism not as a belief system or ideology but as the experience of the Jewish people. Judaism is what happened to those people, what they did, created, thought, believed, wrote, affirmed, denied, suffered, and enjoyed during their 4,000-year history. Judaism includes what Jews have believed, but it is not defined by nor limited to what they believed. Just as the life of every person includes beliefs that are accepted, then changed or abandoned, so the life of the Jewish people is a dynamic process of acceptance and rejection. Jews are an evolving historical (not ideological) people. There is no single idea or list of ideas more "Jewish" than another. All ideas are equally "Jewish" because all are part of the Jewish experience. They are to be judged not by whether or to what degree they are "Jewish" but by how true they are. Whether a belief is old or new, whether attributed to Moses or Jesus or Meir Kahane, is of no relevance to its truth or falsity. If it is true, it is as true for non-Jews as it is for Jews. Truth occupies a universal, not an ethnic, domain.

According to this historical view of Judaism, Jewish people are Jewish not by virtue of their beliefs, values, or commitments, but by virtue of their presence within Jewish history. They may be born into it or they may choose to participate in it. In either case, Jewishness is not a religious or ideological identity. Nor is it a national, racial, or cultural identity. It is a historical identity.

From the standpoint of this understanding of Judaism, "our Jewish heritage" *is the totality of the Jewish experience.* It includes whatever meaning and wisdom that experience reveals. That is, each of us must examine that experience and decide what, if anything, it means; what values, if any, it demonstrates; what beliefs, if any, it documents. Each of us decides what the significance of Judaism is. There is no official, objectively true meaning, any more than the experience of an individual person can be said to have this rather than that meaning.

Judaism includes authoritarians and libertarians, priests and prophets, socialists and capitalists, rationalists and mystics, Zionists and anti-Zionists, theists and humanists. None is more "authentic" and more "Jewish" than another. All are equally present in the Jewish experience. And so is each of us

Each person is free to derive from the Jewish experience that which he or she finds true in it and about it. This freedom is, in itself, the principal value of "our Jewish heritage." Whatever we say, we have the freedom to say it without fear of official censure or excommunication. Such freedom is not available to Christians or Moslems, who are bound by and to a doctrine that takes precedence over the people.

Christian doctrine (that Christ is the savior) is prior to the possibility of there being Christian persons. Thus, the essence of Christianity precedes the existence of Christians.

There being no "Jewish" doctrine, Jews exist prior to their beliefs. "Existence precedes essence." Our beliefs follow, flow out of, our experience. As such, they are subject to change as our experience changes.

This historical view reveals Judaism as an emancipatory experience, inasmuch as it frees individuals from all prior doctrine, from inherited dogma, from authoritarian strictures—to be themselves.

We are most true to "our Jewish heritage" when we are most true to ourselves.

Humanistic Judaism, Spring 1986

Saul Goodman
(1901–)

Introduction

Saul Goodman is a writer, educator, and lecturer who has been a passionate campaigner for a secular Jewish identity and culture based primarily on Yiddish. He has promoted the idea that the younger generation of Jews must be made aware of the spiritual richness of their heritage.

Goodman was born in Bodzanow, Poland, into a family that was Hasidic but also followers of Haskalah. As a consequence he received both a traditional Jewish and a secular education. He came to the United States in 1921, where he received a B.S. in social science from Boston University, and an M.A. in philosophy from the New School for Social Research. He worked for a doctorate in philosophy with Professor Horace Kallen and did further studies at Harvard and Columbia universities.

Goodman became active in the Yiddish cultural movement, and served as the executive director of the Sholem Aleichem Folk Institute, with its network of Yiddish schools, for twenty-four years. He then served as professor of Jewish thought and Yiddish literature on the graduate faculty of Herzliah Jewish Teachers Seminary for several decades.

Goodman wrote *Traditsye un Banayung* (Tradition and Innovation), for which he received the Zvi Kessel Literary Prize in 1968.

He edited *Our First Fifty Years,* a survey of the Sholem Aleichem *shulen* (schools), and an educational journal in English and Yiddish, *Deredkh.* He contributed to the development of a secular and humanistic Judaism by publishing a number of essays which presented a new interpretation of Jewishness and the ancient texts. He also edited *The Faith of a Secular Jew,* an anthology of the writings of many well-know Jewish secularists.

Jewish Secularism in America

. . . Jewish secularism in the Diaspora, for modern Jews who cannot affirm theistic religion—and Judaism is God-centered—aims at underlining that Jewishness is complex, profound, unique and comprehensive, that every Jewish individual may find in that symphony the melody which captivates him and those motifs which find the deepest echo in his personality. And if secular Jews, on occasion long for the values which gave meaning and sustenance to the existence of their ancestors; if they are sensitive to their ancestors; if they are sensitive to the beauty and to the insights of the religious creativity of their people, they are not thereby contradicting their secularist professions, but they manifest rather that both terms in the expression *secular Jew* are of equal importance; they confirm thereby that Jewish secularism bears the imprint of the collective Jewish experience, and that it looks upon the world, in the words of Peretz, through Jewish eyes.

Jewish humanists or secularists realize that their most precious ideals and values, if they are to answer their need for solace and sustenance in times of crisis, must spring from their people's unique experience, must be rooted in the spiritual soil of their ancestry. For secularism, like Judaism, if it is to give the Jew a sense of belonging to his group, must draw its inspiration from the people's sages, martyrs, traditions, hopes and aspirations. A secularism that is meaningful to the modern Jewish individual must be the result of an organic development and the fruit of a particular climate. Only secularism with deep roots in the culture and history of the group can give the modern Jew the mooring that he seeks. Otherwise we will, as in the case of Esperanto, add a new ism competing with other isms for its survival, instead of helping in the survival and spiritual enrichment of its adherents, for whom it was devised.

To the secular Jew, the chief characteristic of religion in general, and of Judaism in particular, lies in a personal faith, in a divine power, that rules the universe; and he cannot impose upon himself that faith by virtue of being born of Jewish parents. However, this does not imply that he is a complete stranger to the loftiness, the poetry, the universal insights, which his ancestors have woven into historic Judaism. And if he ever experiences moments of exaltation and yearns to transcend the limitations imposed on the spirit by its material nature, in the words of Henri Bergson, then the God of the prophets, of the Kabbalists and the Pietists (Hassidim) may come closer to him. But the Jewish faith cannot be normative to him as it is to an Orthodox Jew. Jewish secularism suggests a philosophy which perceives all that is good and valuable in non-Jewish cultures, but through the prism of Jewish history which shaped both, the Jewish collectivity and the Jewish individual. It recognizes that the modern Jewish secularist is bound *to* Jewish tradition but not bound *by* it. For as long as all traditional observances and customs are not obligatory for him, but are rather of a voluntary nature—for his own sake, for the sake of an anchorage for his children, or because they give him an esthetic experience—then they do not contradict his secularist philosophy.

Were we to give an American twist to the concept of Jewish secularity we could designate it as *religious secularism.* This apparent contradiction is easily resolved when one remembers John Dewey's definition of the adjective *religious.* John Dewey, in his *A Common Faith* differentiated between the noun *religion* and the adjective *religious.* Religion, he emphasized, signifies dogmas, institutions, rituals, precepts and practices, but the adjective religious denotes an attitude, a disposition, a commitment. "Any activity pursued on behalf of an ideal and against obstacles and in spite of threats of personal loss because of conviction of its general and enduring values is religious in quality."

In view of this definition, it follows that when a Jew bets his life on the survival of his people; when he makes an effort to inculcate his own child with Jewish values, or when he is deeply involved in Jewish cultural or spiritual activities—all of these experiences are then religious in character. Jewish secularism in America at the present time is then, in the *Deweyan* sense, *religious secularism*, for this Jewishness obligates one to foster Jewish values and ideals—the values that are reflected in Jewish literature, in Jewish history and in all emanations of the Jewish ethos.

The Jewish secular conception is an attempt by all those who are seeking to identify themselves with the Jewish group through modern means; it is an attempt to harmonize the prevalent ideas of modern culture with the historic Jewish heritage. It is confluent with the mainstream of Jewish thought explored and deepened by Philo, Maimonides, Moses Mendelssohn, Ahad Ha'am, Peretz, Zhitlovsky, Dubnow,—all these and many more Jewish thinkers who laid the cornerstones in the edifice of Jewish secularism, which if renovated in each generation may serve as a satisfactory rationale for modern Jews in America.

Morris Schappes
(1907–   )

Introduction

Editor, historian, and educator, Morris Schappes has been the editor of *Jewish Currents,* the journal of the Association for the Promotion of Jewish Secularism, since 1958. Schappes, an avowed socialist, has endeavored to bring Jewish ideas and culture to the American left, and to bring the left into the Jewish community.

Morris Schappes was born in the Ukraine in 1907, but his family emigrated first to Brazil and then arrived in New York in 1914. After obtaining an M.A. in English, Schappes taught in the English department of the City College of New York. In 1941, dismissed from his position as one of the faculty members accused of belonging to the Communist Party, he refused to be an informer and served fourteen months in prison. Upon leaving prison, Schappes retrained himself as a scholar in American Jewish history and has published several works, including *A Documentary History of the Jews in the United States, 1654–1875.* He is also an expert on the poet Emma Lazarus, and has edited collections of her writings.

In 1958 Schappes assumed the editorship of *Jewish Currents,* a post he still retains. He has written many articles, essays, and books and has received many honors for his work.

A Secular View of Jewish Life

Currently, a great debate is coursing through American organized Jewish life on the nature of "Jewish values" and their meaning for the continuity of American Jewish life.

To face this problem is as vital for secularist (non-religious) Jews as for any other trend in the Jewish community. Yet, as Dr. Sanford Goldner remarked:

"the secular way of life for the Jewish people has never been worked out as a meaningful alternative" to the religious way of life.

Perhaps one reason for the lag is a certain uneasiness felt by many Jewish progressives in the face of the very term, "Jewish values." Knowing the phrase is often used by religionists in a mystical sense that "Jewish values" are derived from God and by chauvinists in the sense that Jewish values are somehow superior to those of other peoples, Jewish progressives have disdained the concept of Jewish values altogether. By doing so, however, they have merely abandoned the field to the religionists and the chauvinists and perpetuated the weakness Dr. Goldner deplored.

Are there Jewish values? Or are there only "universal values" or "human values" or "progressive values"?

Well, are there American values, Russian values, Cuban, Chinese or French values? When recently some leaders in American public life debated the nature of American goals, American ideals, American values, progressive Americans had no hesitation in getting into this debate with their view of these values. Why are Jewish progressives inhibited from studying the nature of Jewish values and formulating their views on this subject?

Every group, people, nationality and nation develops its values in terms of its experience in the course of its history. What has the people, in terms of its historical experience, learned to prize, to need, to want, to fight for? These are the people's values, and they are expressed in its culture, religious and secular, its traditions, its ideals.

The Jewish people, like all others, has in its long and diversified history developed its values. Can there be any question of that? Or are we to assume that the Jewish people are the only people in world history that has not expressed its experiences in terms of ideals, goals, values?

Now the Jewish people, like all others, has, since tribal days, been divided in various ways along class and social lines, with conflicts among them. These conflicts gave rise to two historic traditions, two sets of values. In a challenging monograph, *Social Work and Jewish Values,* Alfred J. Kutzik has defined this as a conflict between the democratic and the anti-democratic tradition in Jewish history and life .

This conflict is best known in ancient Jewish history in terms of the Hebrew prophets, who cried out against social evil, oppression and injustice, who denounced those Jews who grind the face of the poor, who fought for social good, social equality and social justice. It is also part of Jewish history that these prophets were ignored or persecuted. Hence the saying about "a prophet without honor in his own country" or in his own time. The prophets were decidedly in a minority when they announced programs and ideals for the benefit of the majority.

The conflict between democratic and anti-democratic values runs all through history, including Jewish history. Out of the people's struggles against non-Jewish enemies and against anti-democratic classes and forces inside the Jewish communities have come the people's values, Jewish values, democratic values. Among the most obvious I should like to note: social justice; the need for peace; the right to be different; moral idealism; self-sacrifice for the common good; group solidarity in the face of the anti-Semitic enemy; the social responsibility of art and the artist; the desire for group continuity.

What we are reflecting, incidentally, is a *secular* approach to values. To the religionist, values derive from God. To us, values derive from the needs and experiences of a people—any people—all peoples, moving down the centuries, striving for civilization and progress, not only for a better living but for a better life.

To the extent that various peoples have similar experiences, they will tend to develop similar values. But the values they develop will be *their own,* born of their own needs and experiences, and cast in their own specific forms of expression.

Now it may well be that the values that have been truly helpful to one people will be truly helpful to all peoples. In that sense, what is truly national (in the best interests of the masses of the nation) in this *one world* becomes truly international. But it is a false issue to pose "Jewish values" as against "universal values" or "human values." Democratic Jewish values are a part of "universal," "international" values, but they are a Jewish part, born of Jewish historic experience.

No one lives in The Universe. There is no address that reads 175 Fairview Boulevard, The Universe. Even the Universal Postal Union could not deliver mail to such an address. You live in a country, a state, a nation. There is no history of The Universe. Universal history is the sum total of group (tribe, people, nationality, national group, national minority, nation) histories, seen in their interconnections. Similarly, there is no *simply* "human" experience that can give rise simply to "human values." For all these thousand of years all human experience has been cast in the form of the limited group. An "internationalist," thus, is not one who lives in an "internation" in outer space, far far out. He is an American internationalist, a Polish internationalist, A Ghanaian or an Indian internationalist. They may converge, but they converge from different points. We here may be American Jewish internationalists. But to omit the American or the Jewish is to strip the "internationalist" of vital, concrete meaning.

Traditionally, secularism has been progressive (and progressivism has been internationalist).

For secularism as a movement in Jewish life was historically associated in one way or another with workers' movements and trends. This political progressivism is still a necessary part of our secularism.

There are those who would stress the secularism as a *bridge* to all non-religious Jews who seek an alternative way of Jewish living and tend to make the progressivism secondary. But we may also point out that progressivism is a *bridge* to religious people who are, on one or another or all issues, progressive. The platform of progressive secularism is not exclusive and welcomes all who wish to stand on any part of it.

The secularist *movement*, with its built-in progressivism, had its main origin in Eastern Europe towards the end of the 19th century. In the United States there were secularist Jewish individuals but no *movement* until the East European Jewish immigrants developed it. (Even before the term was born, Ernestine L. Rose was a Jewish secularist in the USA in the 1840's, but had no influence on the Jewish community directly because she was completely disaffiliated from it by her atheism and by the absence of a secular trend. In the 1880's, Emma Lazarus was a secularist who for a time had a considerable influence on the Jewish community through her passionate defense of the Jews against anti-Semitism and her espousal of the cause of the East European immigrants. Yet she too could develop no secular trend.)

Now in Eastern Europe, the secular movement had to fight bitterly against hidebound Orthodoxy, superstition and fanaticism. Secularists often waged this fight with an atheism that was sometimes primitive, vulgar and anarchistic. In a certain sense, every religion begets the atheism it deserves. Secular progressivism, with its internationalism, also fought, with the moral and social idealism of the working class movement, against the narrow, reactionary, separatistic nationalism of the Jewish bourgeoisie.

Although it was always preferable to the reactionary ideas of its opponents, this internationalism sometimes had its flaws. When it was not rooted in reality, this internationalism covered over what was really a national nihilism.

What is national nihilism? It reduced the group, the people, the nation, to *nihil*—to nothing. It downgrades and degrades the nation and the people to a thing of no value. National nihilism expressed itself in indifference to or contempt of the history of a people, including its history of struggle; the traditions, including the progressive traditions and values, of a people; to the customs and culture of a people. Such indifference to the past and the culture of a people feeds and breeds indifference to its future.

Today progressive secularism is not thus indifferent to the past, present or future. We are internationalists who are concerned with the past, present and future of the Jewish people everywhere in the world and particularly, of course, in our own country.

In the United States, we foresee Jewish group life for generations to come. We are concerned with the organized Jewish community and with its relation to the general American community. We want organized Jewish life to be more liberal, more active and more progressive than it is now—on all issues facing the American people.

Finally, there is the question: is there room for progressive Jewish secularism in American Jewish life today, amid the growth of extensive Jewish congregational and synagogue affiliation? There is not only room for but a need for such secularism.

We strive to express and serve the secular progressive Jewish trend in American life. A trend grows in terms of organized affiliation. The unaffiliated secular Jew is helpless.

The distinctive feature of American Jewish life today is that it is more highly organized than ever before in its 300-year-old history. To the secular unorganized Jew we seek to offer a meaningful alternative to Jewish congregationalism or to helplessness. There are cultural clubs, fraternal organizations, women's groups, schools and *shules* with their parents' associations—or they need to be built where they are inadequate or do not exist. It is time for the unorganized Jewish progressive to get his organizational bearings.

Abridged version.

Max Rosenfeld (1913–   )

Introduction

Max Rosenfeld was born in Philadelphia in 1913. Currently he teaches courses in Yiddish language and culture at Gratz College and at the Jewish Community Center of Greater Philadelphia. From 1963 to 1977 he was director of the Philadelphia Jewish Children's Folkshul. He is presently working on a new collection of stories by American-Yiddish writers.

Rosenfeld has been a Yiddish translator for some forty years. Many of his translations from Yiddish literature have been published in *Jewish Currents* magazine. Among the books he has translated are *Pushcarts and Dreamers: Stories by Ten Noted American-Yiddish Writers,* published by the Sholem Aleichem Club of Philadelphia, of which he was a founder. Through his work Rosenfeld celebrates the secular dimension of Yiddish culture.

What is Secular Jewish Education?

The English word "secular" is an inadequate translation of the Yiddish word *veltlich,* which means *this*-worldly as opposed to *next*-worldly, profane as opposed to sacred, rationalism as opposed to supernaturalism. The concept "secular" also contains elements of philosophical humanism as opposed to belief in a Deity or Divine Being who governs the affairs of men. The word-combination "secular-humanism" better expresses the ideas contained in the word *veltlich.*

This view of Jewish history and tradition holds that the Jews are a *people* and that Judaism (their religion) is only one aspect of Jewish culture. It recognizes the historic importance of Judaism as a cementing force in the existence of the Jewish people, but does not consider this the sole reason for Jewish existence or the sole explanation for Jewish survival.

There are other views, going from certain orthodox beliefs which maintain that it is the Jewish religion alone that distinguishes the Jews from other peoples, to the extreme "sociological" view which explains Jewish existence exclusively on the basis of the "social function" of the Jews in society, and predicts their disappearance when that function is no longer needed. (This "function" has to do mainly with the activities of Jews as merchants, financiers and middlemen in the development of modern industrial society.)

Then there are views which combine both concepts and regard the Jews as a "religious people" or Judaism as a civilization. Obviously, this is a topic which defies compression into two paragraphs.

The secularists among the Jews (which would include also most Zionists, especially those who pioneered and built Israel) base their views on the premise that the Jews are more than a religious group; that they constitute a world people; and that as with every modern people there is room in Jewish life for a diversity of opinion, including the secular-humanist view which does not subscribe to the tenets of religion or organized religious (congregational) affiliation.

At this point, a definition of humanism would be helpful. It is a word that is apt to get fuzzy. Dr. Corliss Lamont, one of America's leading humanist philosophers, has worked out a ten-point definition in his book *The Philosophy of Humanism.* For our purposes I have condensed these ten points to five:

1. Humanism considers all forms of the supernatural as myth which man has developed in his long history to explain things he could not understand or control. It regards Nature as a constantly changing system of matter and energy which exists outside of any mind or consciousness.

2. Humanism believes that man is an evolutionary product of Nature, of which he is a part.

3. Humanism believes that human beings possess the power of solving their own problems; that they have a freedom of choice, although within certain objective limits.

4. Humanism holds as its highest goal the *this*-worldly happiness, freedom and progress of all mankind.

5. Humanism believes in applying reason and scientific method to society—which means the full use of democratic procedures throughout all economic, political and cultural life.

This definition, in addition to its de-emphasis of supernaturalism, contains an emphasis upon the ethics and ideals of brotherhood and social justice. These ideals and values, *as they have found Jewish expression,* are a basic ingredient of secular Jewishness, and they permeate secular Jewish education. This is not to say that religious education does *not* contain these values. It does. But religious education bases its reason for the socially-conscious values on God; humanism bases it on Man.

It should be noted particularly that the secular approach does not rule out the indispensable role of tradition and folklore in Jewish life and education. *Without these aspects it could hardly be considered Jewish education.* The holidays, therefore, are an integral part of our curriculum. The Bible stories, moreover, cannot be taught without an explanation of the important place which the idea of God held in the thinking of the ancient Hebrews.

Hershl Hartman
(1929–   )

Introduction

Hershl Hartman is the education director and former principal of the Sholem Community Organization of Los Angeles and a certified *vegvyzer* (lay leader) of the Secular Humanistic Movement. He serves on the executive board of the Congress of Secular Jewish Organizations and is a member of the faculty of the International Institute for Secular Humanistic Judaism.

Hartman was born in New York in 1929 into a radical, secular Jewish household. Both of his parents had been active in the labor union movement. Along with his education in the public schools of New York, he attended Yiddish secular schools through high school. He went to the City College of New York as well as the School for Teachers and Higher Jewish Education and received a degree in Yiddish education and Yiddish journalism in 1948.

Hartman pursued a career in journalism for a number of years. He was a reporter and feature writer for *Morgn Frayhayt*, a left-wing Yiddish daily, and an editorial assistant at *Jewish Currents*. In 1957 he was appointed principal of the Center Island, New York, Jewish School and has been involved in Jewish education ever since.

Hartman has translated many works from Yiddish, including Itzik Manger's *Megille Songs*. He has also written secular guides to many of the Jewish holidays.

Using the Tradition

When my wife was a little girl, she came home one day in tears because a neighbor child had assured her that "if you don't have chicken on Friday nights, you're not Jewish!"

When our eldest daughter was approaching puberty, I was informed that Jewish tradition "celebrated" the onset of menstruation by slapping the young woman's face. When the day arrived, I brought home a bottle of champagne instead.

When I began developing the concept of a secular bar/bas mitzvah ceremony—and that was almost thirty years ago, by the way—the owners of catering halls on the Grand Concourse in The Bronx (still somewhat grand, then) were solemnly informing parents that "the bar mitzvah boy always wears a gold lamé tuxedo!"

I rake these memories from my personal past to stress the potential danger that lies in the amorphous concept of "the Tradition." When secular humanists talk about "the Tradition," it is usually thought of as a largely benign, slightly outdated set of practices and beliefs that we may have outgrown but that it would be nice to cling to, if we could only find a way to do it without feeling uncomfortable. Before we start figuring ways of "using the Tradition," we need to be fairly clear about just which "Tradition" we're talking about—and what guidelines we apply in selecting the traditions that enhance the human face of Jewish identity.

. . . There is not *one* "Tradition." There are many, many traditions among the Jewish people—and we had better be clear about *which* traditions we choose to adopt or to adapt, and about *why* we make our choices.

At this juncture, I should acknowledge a tension between what can be (and has been) characterized as a patriarchal or masculine-oriented approach to traditions—absorbed with demonstrable facts and rigorous logic—and a more feminist approach that tends to consider emotional content with less or no regard to whether the relevance or irrelevance of the traditions can be precisely articulated.

That I am aware of the tension does not mean I know how to alleviate or resolve it, nor that I agree with the gender-based designations. I can understand, for instance, how someone can feel that "you can't celebrate Hanukka without the miracle of the oil." By the same token, I am helpless to share that feeling because I know that the "miracle of the oil" was deliberately invented centuries after the Maccabean victory, that there is no mention or hint of it in the Book of Maccabees, that there were specific socio-political reasons that led the Talmudic rabbis to convert a celebration of victorious national self-determination into a mystical, religious celebration of a "miracle" that never happened—that has not a shred of basis in any kind of fact, physical or poetical.

I am unable to suppress that knowledge in order to join, emotionally, in celebrating a tradition I find repugnant—and not only because it is based on pure myth. By the same token, however, I have no difficulty with lighting the candles of the *khanekeh lempl,* which the Reform temple taught me to call a *menorah,* which some Israelis now want me to call a *hanukiah,* but which, if it's all right with all concerned, I think I may go back to calling by its name before it became assimilated: *ah poshet khanekeh lempl.*

How can one reject the "miracle of the lights" while accepting the *khanekeh lempl?* That apparent contradiction leads to the next stage of this discussion. Close readers of the work of Theodor H. Gaster can detect a definite pattern in the development of all Jewish holidays and of most other Jewish customs and events. At the root of Jewish festivals and observances are *primitive, nature-based customs* that explain and celebrate recurring events in humanity's annual cycle and common events in the life cycle of individual human beings. In large part, those roots of Jewish observances are common to human experiences that, therefore, find their echoes in the festivals and observances of many other peoples. Let's call this the *primitive,* or *anthropological* foundation of Jewish tradition.

The next stage is the association of the primitive customs with one or more specific events in Jewish history. It is in this way that the general human experience receives the specific physiognomy that makes it meaningful to specific peoples. This state can be called the *historic component* of traditions.

A third stage is the *collection of folkways,* superstitions, myths, legends, and customs that accumulate around festivals and events in the course of a couple thousand years or so, give or take several centuries.

Finally, there is a fourth stage that Gaster approaches gingerly, but which secular humanistic Jews must face fully and totally: How can we—informed by an understanding of an event's human roots, its Jewish historical associations, and the customs that have given it its specific color and aroma, its *Yiddish tam*—how can we, so informed, devise ways of celebrating and observing that are meaningful to us, that have relevance to our lives, that strike healthy emotional chords? Let's call this the *folk-cultural, secular humanistic* stage.

So that you may better understand the analytical approach I have described, let me try to apply it specifically to *khanekeh*, or Hanukka.

A) Primitive human origins

Most primitive peoples mark the winter solstice, when the sun almost dies, with magical ceremonies designed to revive the dying sun or to comfort human beings with the hope that the sun will indeed be reborn. In Northern Europe, primitive humans worshipped the one element in nature that hadn't died as the sun weakened: the evergreen fir tree. The trunk of that tree, the Yule log, was set ablaze as a form of imitative magic—an example to the sun of what was expected of it. The Grecian rites of Dionysius involved young men running through the hills with torches. A more direct form of imitative magic involved encouraging the sun to grow stronger, day by day, by lighting a growing series of fires: first one, then two, then three, and so forth. In Scandinavia, young women with candles in their hair came together in the village square, creating a blaze of light.

In all these primitive customs, there is apparent the general human need to take action with nature to assure further human survival. While there is recognition of the superior power of natural forces (and, of course, of the gods controlling them), there is not a fatalistic acceptance of the vagaries of nature and nature's gods. While the sun was "reborn" at the previous year' solstice, humans couldn't *rely* on nature to repeat the event: nature and its gods needed to be encouraged, taught, reminded, cajoled, praised—and that was the job, not of other gods, but of *human beings*.

Hanukka means initiation or dedication of something new, as the reborn sun is new. The ninth candle on the *khanekeh lempl* is called shammes, but that might be a corruption of the word *shemmesh*—sun.

B) Historical component

I won't take the time to review the history of the Maccabean revolt in the years 168 to 165 B.C.E., except, perhaps, to challenge some of the typical Sunday school coloring book mythology. First, let's be clear that Antiochus IV, emperor of the Syrian portion of the former Grecian empire of Alexander the Great, was mainly interested in conquering the Egyptian portion of Alexander's empire, from which his father had already seized a little border area, which the Romans would later call Palestine. Antiochus IV needed "national unity on the home front" before he launched his war. Any ruler, ancient or modern, can understand that. Antiochus IV was *not* a follower of the mythical Haman or a precursor of Hitler. He was not a representative of classic Greek philosophy: The Greco-Syrian Seleucid empire and the Greco-Egyptian Ptolemaic empire, between which sat Palestine, were both a far cry from the golden age of Hellenic culture.

So the victory of the Maccabean-led revolt was not a Jewish victory over an arch anti-Semite, nor was it a victory of superior Hebraist monotheism over corrupt Hellenistic materialism, as almost every rabbi's Hanukka sermon would have you believe.

Nor does Hanukka celebrate "the world's first successful struggle for religious freedom," as the editorial writer in your local newspaper insists every year. That issue was settled at the time, in and around Jerusalem. The Pietists who were part of the coalition led by Judah Maccabee were, indeed, ready to settle for the freedom to "follow the ways of our fathers." The Maccabees, on the other hand, insisted on full national independence—far more than mere "religious freedom." Their view prevailed.

Nor were the Maccabees simply the "heroic leaders of a people's uprising." Once in power, the Maccabees set about building a Jewish empire no less despotic than the Greco-Syrian; uncircumcised Jews were forcibly corrected and young men were impressed into armies of conquest.

The myth that is most important to shatter is the one that ascribes the Maccabean victory to the Jewish people alone. Antiochus' program of eliminating all ethnic and religious differences within his empire produced resistance not only in Palestine but in many other parts of the empire. Were it not for these simultaneous revolts, Antiochus would have had little trouble putting down the handful of partisan brigades in the hills of Judah.

C) Folkways, legends, customs

According to the Second Book of Maccabees, Hanukka was to be "the Festival of Booths in the month of Kislev"; that is, a second version of the eight-day Sukkos festival, to be celebrated beginning with the 25th of Kislev, coinciding approximately with December. Gaster sees this as an attempt by the Maccabees to make the rededication of the Great Temple as significant as the two previous dedications, in the days of Solomon and in the Prophetic era. Other scholars see it as a means of tying the Maccabean victory to the widespread primitive practices we just talked about—making Hanukka as important in its time as the rebirth of the sun had been in earlier days. In any event, there is no doubt that the lighting of successively larger and larger flames over eight nights is a custom that has its roots firmly in primitive concepts and that is no less firmly wedded to the historical facts of the Maccabean victory.

Hanukka, like Purim, is considered a minor holiday in the rabbinic tradition. The only rabbinic recognition of Hanukka is to convert its history—with no foundation whatsoever,—into one of the supernatural "miracles and wonders" for which God, not the Maccabees and their partisan brigades, must be praised. But for the people, the folk, Hanukka and Purim were not minor; they were major occasions for celebrating and merry-making. One can only wonder if it is the very lack of religious rituals that added to the popularity of Hanukka and Purim among the common folk.

Another impact of Hanukka was on the generation that came of age in Eastern Europe at the turn of this century. When the historical writing of Heinrich Graetz and especially of Simon Dubnow rescued the historical facts of Hanukka from the "miracles and wonders" on which Jewish generations had been fed for some seventeen centuries, the effect was unbelievably liberating. The "Maccabean spirit" inspired a whole generation toward self-emancipation whether in rebuilding Zion or in building a new Socialist society. It is nor exaggeration to say that the uprisings in scores of ghettos and death camps, the extensive Jewish participation in partisan and underground movements, the organization of the Haganah and especially of the Palmach are linked directly to a tradition of Hanukka that is not expressed in synagogue sermons or in "brotherhood Christmas/Hanukka" editorials.

D. Folk-cultural observance

Now, the challenge: How can secular humanistic Jews celebrate Hanukkah in a meaningful, moving way? Notice that the question is *not*: How is Hanukka celebrated in Israel? Nor is it: What are the *traditional* ways of celebrating Hanukka? Not yet: What are the aspects of Hanukka that I, personally, am most nostalgic about? These may all be legitimate questions, but they do not help us determine what aspects of the traditions associated with Hanukka we can adopt or adapt to a meaningful, moving celebration for secular humanistic Jews.

A secular humanistic Hanukka has at its center the Maccabees and the *khanekeh lempl* or *menorah* or *hanukiah.* The Maccabees—for their role as leaders of a radical struggle for national self-determination in opposition to both the assimilationist and the pietist paths. The self-delusion of the Hellenists in Jerusalem is still among us—that denial of one's own identity, stripping oneself of one's own cultural uniqueness, somehow brings one closer to others (who have their own identities) or somehow brings closer the day when all humanity will be bereft of distinctive identities—and that that is somehow "A Good Thing." And still among us is the self-delusion of the Pietists; the concept that all wisdom, all knowledge, all virtue is assigned to the anointed of G-dash-D, and if the rest of us would but follow blindly, then *Moshiakh* would surely arrive.

Certainly the Maccabees must be at the center of our Hanukka. And the *khanekeh lempl,* too. The lights of the *khanekeh lempl* are rooted in rites common to much of humanity and are tied, as well, to a moment in real, not mythical, Jewish history.

And yet there are secular humanistic Jews who find that a ceremonial lighting of candles is too close to religious ritual for their comfort. Not only on Hanukka. On Shabbes, too. Perhaps especially on Shabbes.

It is not candles, *per se,* that are objectionable. Candles on a dining table are acceptable, charming, beautiful, even romantic. It is the *ceremonial* kindling of candles that is the problem. Does this stricture apply to the candles on a birthday cake? And if not, then is the problem only with Jewish ceremonial candles? If that is so—and I fear it is—then intellectual honesty and consistency demand rejection, as well, of fireworks on July 4th and Bastille Day and in the skies over Moscow in celebration of victory in the Great Patriotic War.

Jewish ceremonial candles are the fireworks of a small people, oppressed for much of its recent history, in exile of one kind or another for much of its existence, and never accorded the right of national/cultural self-determination, not even on these shores, not even to this day. Those candles are our fireworks. But they are more than that: they are a link with the common human foundation on which every people's culture grew and developed. There is no rational reason to break that link and certainly no humanist reason to do so.

What do we do when we light those candles? Can't bless them. Don't want to say prayers about "miracles and wonders"—especially since we've placed the Maccabees in the center of our Hanukkah. In family settings and in secular schools, we've gotten a lot of mileage out of having the children dedicate each candle to a worthwhile idea or person. Trouble is, it gets a bit repetitive after the twenty-eighth candle on the seventh night, if not sooner. Dedicating candles to Peace and to the memory of Martin Luther King, Jr. is meaningful. Moving? I'm not so sure.

How about finding thirty-six readings: some brief, some not-so-brief, some funny, some moving, some heart-rending, some soul-lifting—but all expressing what we think and feel about the whole, rounded, profound meaning of Hanukka in our past, distant and recent, in our present, and in our future, not overlooking what must be overcome if we are to have a future at all. We might even try our hands at writing one or two of those readings. But where to find the rest?

Where we find appropriate readings for Hanukka depends on where we look, and where we look depends on our outlook as to the fundamental nature of secular humanistic Jewishness. Of course, we will be "using the tradition," but *which* tradition or, more accurately, *which part* of the tremendously varied and frequently contradictory tradition?

For some, "Using the tradition" means turning automatically to religious rituals, customs, *aggadot*, sayings of the sages, and mechanically eliminating direct references to the deity. That way—one, two, three, presto!—we have certifiably "secular" material. No matter that the ethos of such material is unremittingly non- or anti-humanistic. Little concern that this newly-secularized wisdom dates from no later than the tenth century C.E. and does not reflect more than a thousand years of relevant Jewish experience. It's easy. It's all laid out. It's comfortingly familiar. . . .

Without access to the treasure-trove of Yiddish culture, which is secular humanist at its very core, in its very marrow, we cannot hope to develop secular humanistic celebrations, observances, and life cycle events that are both meaningful and moving. Without access to the scores of thousands of poems . . . the volumes full of pithy, profound, and funny folk expressions . . . the historical, cultural, anthropological. and social insights of scores of thinkers . . . the hundreds upon hundreds of songs created both by and for the folk . . . the thousands of personal memoirs that can keep an army of historical researchers going on grants for decades . . . and, yes, the twenty-eight volumes of Sholem Aleichem's works . . . and whole libraries of novels, plays, and short stories . . . overflowing archives of thousands of newspapers and periodicals from every continent on earth—without access to these "cultural tidbits," we cannot create a meaningful, viable secular humanistic expression in Jewish life.

Humanistic Judaism, Spring 1988

Isaiah Berlin (1909–)

Introduction

Isaiah Berlin is a distinguished British philosopher and historian of ideas. As an intellectual historian, occupied all his life with the world of ideas, he has made a career not only in academia but also in public service.

Berlin was born in Latvia in 1909 but his family later moved to Petrograd where he witnessed the revolutions of 1917. He settled in England in 1919, where he was educated at St. Paul's school and then at Corpus Christi College, Oxford. His genius was recognized early and he began lecturing in philosophy at Oxford when he was just twenty-three. In 1938 he became the first Jew to be elected a fellow of New College, where he remained until 1950, when he was appointed a fellow at All Souls College. Through the years Berlin has had a major impact on several generations of students.

During World War II he was asked to serve in the British Ministry of Information and later in the Foreign Service, where he was posted to Washington, D.C. and Moscow.

After the war he resumed his academic career, being appointed Chichele Professor of Social and Political Theory at Oxford and then the first president of Wolfson College. He was elected to the British Academy in 1957 and served as its president from 1974 to 1978. He became a Knight of the British Empire in 1957 and was awarded the Order of Merit in 1971. Berlin has earned many prizes, among them the Jerusalem Prize for lifelong defense of civil liberties.

Berlin's principal contribution as an historian of ideas was to demonstrate how the emergence of a related group of basic ideas has transformed sensibilities in the West since the eighteenth century. Proponents of some of the new values which accompanied these ideas were bound to conflict among themselves as they chose from the vast variety available. These conflicts, according to Berlin, dramatize the need for the largest possible freedom of choice and a constant devotion to pluralism in society. The necessity for a minimum of interference with choice and the central value of freedom have been two of his constant themes.

Berlin has always been involved with the Jewish community and its leaders, and has been a strong advocate of Zionism and Israel. He has offered his support to the international movement for Secular Humanistic Judaism.

The Pursuit of the Ideal

. . . There is a world of objective values. By this I mean those ends that men pursue for their own sakes, to which other things are means. I am not blind to what the Greeks valued—their values may not be mine, but I can grasp what it would be like to live by their light, I can admire and respect them, and even imagine myself as pursuing them, although I do not—and do not wish to, and perhaps could not if I wished. Forms of life differ. Ends, moral principles, are many. But not infinitely many: they must be within the human horizon. If they are not, then they are outside the human sphere. If I find men who worship trees, not because they are symbols of fertility or because they are divine, with a mysterious life and powers of their own, or because this grove is sacred to Athena,—but only because they are made of wood; and if when I ask them why they worship wood they say "Because it is wood" and give no other answer; then I do not know what they mean. If they are human, they are not beings with whom I can communicate—there is a real barrier. They are not human for me. I cannot even call their values subjective if I cannot conceive what it would be like to pursue such a life.

What is clear is that values can clash—that is why civilizations are incompatible. They can be incompatible between cultures, or groups in the same culture, or between you and me. You believe in always telling the truth, no matter what; I do not, because I believe that it can sometimes be too painful and too destructive. We can discuss each other's point of view, we can try to reach common ground, but in the end what you pursue may not be reconcilable with the ends to which I find that I have dedicated my life. Values may easily clash within the breast of a single individual; and it does not follow that, if they do, some must be true and others false. Justice, rigorous justice, is for some people an absolute value, but it is not compatible with what may be no less ultimate values for them—mercy, compassion—as arises in concrete cases.

Both liberty and equality are among the primary goals pursued by human beings through many centuries; but total liberty for wolves is death to the lambs, total liberty of the powerful, the gifted, is not compatible with the rights to a decent existence of the weak and less gifted. An artist, in order to create a masterpiece, may lead a life which plunges his family into misery and squalor to which he is indifferent. We may condemn him and declare that the masterpiece should be sacrificed to human needs, or we may take his side—but both attitudes embody values which for some men or women are ultimate, and which are intelligible to us all if we have any sympathy or imagination or understanding of human beings. Equality may demand the restraint of the liberty of those who wish to dominate; liberty—without some modicum of which there is no choice and therefore no possibility of remaining human as we understand the word—may have to be curtailed in order to make room for social welfare, to feed the hungry, to clothe the naked, to shelter the homeless, to leave room for the liberty of others, to allow justice or fairness to be exercised. . . .

These collisions of values are of the essence of what they are and what we are. If we are told that these contradictions will be solved in some perfect world in which all good things can be harmonized in principle, then we must answer, to those who say this, that the meanings they attach to the names which for us denote the conflicting values are not ours. We must say that the world in which what we see as incompatible values are not in conflict is a world altogether beyond our ken; that principles which are harmonized in this other world are not the principles with which, in our daily lives, we are acquainted; if they are transformed, it is into conceptions not known to us on earth. But it is on earth that we live, and it is here that we must believe and act.

The notion of the perfect whole, the ultimate solution, in which all good things coexist, seems to me to be not merely unattainable—that is a truism—but conceptually incoherent; I do not know what is meant by a harmony of this kind. Some among the Great Goods cannot live together. That is a conceptual truth. We are doomed to choose, and every choice may entail an irreparable loss. Happy are those who live under a discipline which they accept without question, who freely obey the orders of leaders, spiritual or temporal, whose word is fully accepted as unbreakable law; or those who have, by their own methods, arrived at clear and unshakable convictions about what to do and what to be that brook no possible doubt. I can only say that those who rest on such comfortable beds of dogma are victims of forms of self-induced myopia, blinkers that may make for contentment, but not for understanding of what it is to be human.

So much for the theoretical objection, a fatal one, it seems to me, to the notion of the perfect state as the proper goal of our endeavours. But there is in addition a more practical socio-psychological obstacle to this, an obstacle that may be put to those whose simple faith, by which humanity has been nourished for so long, is resistant to philosophical arguments of any kind. It is true that some problems can be solved, some ills cured, in both the individual and social life. We can save men from hunger or misery or injustice, we can rescue men from slavery or imprisonment, and do good—all men have a basic sense of good and evil, no matter what cultures they belong to; but any study of society shows that every solution creates a new situation which breeds its own needs and problems, new demands. The children have obtained what their parents and grandparents longed for—greater freedom, greater material welfare, a juster society; but the old ills are forgotten, and the children face new problems, brought about by the very solution of the old ones, and these, even if they can in turn be solved, generate new situations, and with them new requirements—and so on, for ever—and unpredictably.

We cannot legislate for the unknown consequences of consequences of consequences. Marxists tell us that once the fight is won and true history has begun, the new problems that may arise will generate their own solutions, which can be peacefully realized by the united powers of harmonious, classless society. This seems to me a piece of metaphysical optimism for which there is no evidence in historical experience. In a society in which the same goals are universally accepted, problems can be only of means, all soluble by technological methods. That is a society in which the inner life of man, the moral and spiritual and aesthetic imagination, no longer speaks at all. Is it for this that men and women should be destroyed or societies enslaved? Utopias have their value—nothing so wonderfully expands the imaginative horizons of human potentialities—but as guides to conduct they can prove literally fatal. Heraclitus was right, things cannot stand still.

So I conclude that the very notion of a final solution is not only impracticable but, if I am right, and some values cannot but clash, incoherent also. The possibility of a final solution—even if we forget the terrible sense that these words acquired in Hitler's day—turns out to be an illusion; and a very dangerous one. For if one really believes that such a solution is possible, then surely no cost would be too high to obtain it: to make mankind just and happy and creative and harmonious forever—what could be too high a price to pay for that? To make such an omelette, there is surely no limit to the number of eggs that should be broken—that was the faith of Lenin, of Trotsky, of Mao, for all I know of Pol Pot. Since I know the only true path to the ultimate solution of the problems of society, I know which way to drive the human caravan; and since you are ignorant of what I know, you cannot be allowed to have liberty of choice even within the narrowest limits, if the goal is to be reached. You declare that a given policy will make you happier, or freer, or give you room to breathe; but I know that you are mistaken, I know what you need, what all men need; and if there is resistance based on ignorance or malevolence, then it must be broken and hundreds of thousands may have to perish to make millions happy for all time. What choice have we, who have the knowledge, but to be willing to sacrifice them all?

Some armed prophets seek to save mankind, and some only their own race because of its superior attributes, but whichever the motive, the millions slaughtered in wars or revolutions—gas chambers, gulag, genocide, all the monstrosities for which our century will be remembered—are the price men must pay for the felicity of future generations. If your desire to save mankind is serious, you must harden your heart, and not reckon the cost.

The answer to this was given more than a century ago by the Russian radical Alexander Herzen. In his essay *From the Other Shore,* which is in effect an obituary notice of the revolutions of 1848, he said that a new form of human sacrifice had arisen in his time—of living human beings on the altars of abstractions—nation, church, party, class, progress, the forces of history—these have all been invoked in his day and in ours: if these demand the slaughter of living human beings, they must be satisfied. These are his words:

> If progress is the goal, for whom are we working? Who is this Moloch who, as the toilers approach him, instead of rewarding them, draws back; and as a consolation to the exhausted and doomed multitudes, shouting "morituri te salutant," can only give the . . . mocking answer that after their death all will be beautiful on earth. Do you truly wish to condemn the human beings alive today to the sad role . . . of wretched galley slaves, who, up to their knees in mud, drag a barge . . . with . . . "progress in the future" upon its flag?. . . a goal which is infinitely remote is no goal, only . . . a deception; a goal must be closer—at the very least the labourer's wage, or pleasure in work performed.

The one thing that we may be sure of is the reality of the sacrifice, the dying and the dead. But the ideal for the sake of which they die remains unrealized. The eggs are broken, and the habit of breaking them grows, but the omelette remains invisible. Sacrifices for short-term goals, coercion, if men's plight is desperate enough and truly requires such measures, may be justified. But holocausts for the sake of distant goals, that is a cruel mockery of all that men hold dear, now and at all times.

. . . The first public obligation is to avoid extremes of suffering. Revolutions, wars, assassinations, extreme measures may in desperate situations be required. But history teaches us that their consequences are seldom what is anticipated; there is no guarantee, not even, at times, a high enough probability, that such acts will lead to improvement. We may take the risk of drastic action, in personal life or in public policy, but we must always be aware, never forget, that we may be mistaken, that certainty about the effect of such measures invariably leads to avoidable suffering of the innocent. So we must engage in what are called trade-offs—rules, values, principles must yield to each other in varying degrees in specific situations. Utilitarian solutions are sometimes wrong, but, I suspect, more often beneficent. The best that can be done, as a general rule, is to maintain a precarious equilibrium that will prevent the occurrence of desperate situations, of intolerable choices—that is the first requirement for a decent society; one that we can always strive for, in the light of the limited range of our knowledge, and even our imperfect understanding of individuals and societies. A certain humility in these matters is very necessary.

. . . But, in the end, it is not a matter of purely subjective judgment: it is dictated by the forms of life of the society to which one belongs, a society among other societies, with values held in common, whether or not they are in conflict, by the majority of mankind throughout recorded history. There are, if not universal values, at any rate a minimum without which societies could scarcely survive. Few today would wish to defend slavery or ritual murder or Nazi gas chambers or the torture of human beings for the sake of pleasure or profit or even political good—or the duty of children to denounce their parents, which the French and Russian revolutions demanded, or mindless killing. There is no justification for compromise on this. But on the other hand, the search for perfection does seem to me a recipe for bloodshed, no better even if it is demanded by the sincerest of idealists, the purest of heart. No more rigorous moralist than Immanuel Kant ever lived, but even he said, in a moment of illumination, "Out of the crooked timber of humanity no straight thing was ever made." To force people into the neat uniforms demanded by dogmatically believed-in schemes is almost always the road to inhumanity. We can only do what we can: but that we must do, against difficulties.

Of course social or political collisions will take place; the mere conflict of positive values alone makes this unavoidable. Yet they can, I believe, be minimized by promoting and preserving an uneasy equilibrium, which is constantly threatened and in constant need of repair—that alone, I repeat, is the precondition for decent societies and morally acceptable behavior, otherwise we are bound to lose our way. A little dull as a solution, you will say? Not the stuff of which calls to heroic action by inspired leaders are made? Yet if there is some truth in this view, perhaps that is sufficient. An eminent American philosopher of our day once said, "There is no *a priori* reason for supposing that the truth, when it is discovered, will necessarily prove interesting." It may be enough if it is truth, or even an approximation to it; consequently I do not feel apologetic for advancing this. Truth, said Tolstoy . . . is the most beautiful thing in the entire world. I do not know if this is so in the realm of ethics, but it seems to me near enough to what most of us wish to believe not to be too lightly set aside.

Albert Memmi
(1920–   )

Introduction

Albert Memmi, honorary president of the International Federation of Secular Humanistic Jews, is one of the most highly respected writers in France. He was born in Tunis in 1920 in the poor Jewish section. He was, however, able to study at an exclusive French secondary school. During World War II he was arrested and interned in a forced labor camp but managed to escape. After the war he went on to study at the University of Algiers and then the University of Paris. He became a professor of sociology at the University of Paris as well as a prize-winning writer.

Early in his life, Memmi began to experience a sense of separateness from the groups in which he found himself. Although his family was observant, he became secular. And, while in Tunisia he was a Jew in a Muslim nation, when he moved to France, he was an Arab among Europeans. His autobiographical novel, *Pillar of Salt*, published in 1953, dealt with these paradoxes. He was awarded several literary prizes for this work. Memmi has written sociological works as well as additional novels, works of criticism, and political commentaries. His most influential sociological work was *The Portrait of the Colonized*, published in 1957, in which he analyzed the dilemmas of both the colonized and the colonizer. He has explored the subject of human oppression in many of his writings. Memmi has contributed to Algerian literature as both critic and author. He founded a research group on North African literature at the École Pratique des Hautes Études in Paris. He has lectured in the United States as well as throughout Europe, Israel, and Africa.

Memmi has examined his Jewish heritage in *Portrait of a Jew,* published in 1962, and *The Liberation of the Jew,* published in 1966, and has written about the situation in Israel in *Jew and Arab*, published in 1974.

PORTRAIT OF A JEW

I recall a time when I, too, repeated arrogantly to anyone who would listen: "To be a Jew is a choice!" By that I meant: "Admire my courage; against wind and tide and, without being forced to, I have made up my mind to be a Jew!" Like most young animals, I believed for a long time that I had, to begin with, a great and marvelous freedom at my disposal. When I discovered that the Jewish fate was restrictive, curbed, I began to rebel. I hesitated between systematic revolt and an impassioned claim; I fluctuated between not being a Jew at all or being one insolently and provocatively. With the result that I maintained whatever role I chose, and apparently, my freedom.

Now all that was fairly false. That puerile pride was based on an optical illusion. Neither the Jewish will to live, nor the solidarity, nor belonging to Jewry, are the results of a free choice. A man is not a Jew because he decided to be one; he discovers that he is a Jew, then he either consents or refuses . . . without ceasing to be one. Of course he is a Jew in a different way depending upon his refusal or his approval, but in any case he is still a Jew. It is a matter of age, perhaps. Since those days I have discovered, rightly or wrongly and even before those impassioned decisions, that the important thing was to take stock of what I really was in relation to the world and to other Jews. Only then, after I had admitted the essential facts, made up my mind and recognized my duties towards my own people and towards other men, would I perhaps be able to find a moderate if not a definitive peace.

Now it is clear that one always feels a close kinship with one's own people, even if they repel you, even if they irritate you. For, after all, it is not the same thing to have had a long history, a rich, cultural tradition, and not to have had one. As a Jew, I am heir to a powerful tradition and culture. Traditionalists are right to speak of a "Legacy of Israel": as Jews we are rich heirs.

I can fail to recognize the extent of the lands of that heritage, the number of horses, the geography and the importance of the wells; the invader has often ridden roughshod over the frontiers, carried off cattle, uprooted trees. But I know that the heritage is great and almost inexhaustible; and above all that it is there, within reach of my hand. That has not prevented me, and very often, from rebelling frequently against the supremacy of the Tribe, from mocking the words of the ancients. Would I even say that, in my opinion, it is the best way to live a culture? The other way, that scrupulous and obedient submission to detail, is a way of embalming. But in discussing the teaching of my fathers, in debating against the written and the oral word, I nevertheless am nourished by it. I can even reject completely the riches of my people, give it away, dissect their teaching bit by bit, exorcise it of all false prestige. Explained, rationalized, humanized, restored to its place in the perspective of all the cultures in the world, it still occupies a considerable space. And it is always mine in some fashion, since at least it once was mine: "It is always on me," as they used to say in the ghetto. Goetz von Berlichingen, Sartre's hero in *The Devil and the Good Lord,* discovers it is one thing to be poor after having been rich, and another never to have known riches. At least I have been rich: it is not true that one can forget that.

I am not even sure that I seriously wish to forget it. If my people had not had so much trouble in other respects, why would it have occurred to me to forget who I am, I who am so rich with such ancient riches? And when, in a burst of pride, I try to remember who I am, I turn instinctively to that heritage. After all, I say to myself, it is a fabulous heritage! The next moment, it is true, I laugh at myself for that proprietary reflex, the reflex of the prodigal son, tempted to go back home, to receive his father's blessing and the advantages of life in a community. But though I can make fun of details, at heart I do not find it ridiculous to belong to the "People of the Book," as they all call themselves; my people and non-Jews in agreement on this point. And in moments of distress, too, why not admit it? I know that this at least is left me: that culture and that tradition, that extraordinary age-old refuge of all Jews that stands unscathed through so many storms and all the firmer because they themselves have strengthened it against the tempests. That refuge is still surprisingly habitable precisely because they themselves have fashioned it throughout the ages with their own bones which history has gathered, burned and pulverized; with their own ingenuity, with their own spirit which is always on guard. All his life my Uncle Khailou, a poor silk weaver, never failed to gather all his friends together every Saturday. Bending over their huge books from the midday coffee till the first stars shone out, they sought, with marvelous confidence, the answer to all problems, the most commonplace and the most metaphysical, their own problems and the problems of their families, of the community and of the world. They argued, examining line for line, word for word; and if the text did not seem to give them the answers they needed, they added their own commentaries so vividly that they made it vibrant with their own life.

"In exile," writes David Ben-Gurion, the President of the Israelian Council, "we have continued to live, in heart and mind, within our Biblical heritage." ("Ethics, Science and the Pioneer Spirit," speech made at Boston University.)

Let us set aside at least for the moment a philosophical examination of those Jewish values or even the question of their compatibility with the world in which we live. Not that I have nothing to say on this subject; nor that I am intimidated by postures of respect or a guilty and paralyzing modesty. I have shown that enough, I hope. But I must make it clear that the problem is greater than an ideological discussion. At the level of the experience lived, a cultural tradition is not only a culture in the bookish sense of the word, a concatenation of ideas or even a coherent system of truths that one can shrug off after proving that it contains serious errors, prejudices and even lies. A cultural tradition, is also a sum total of ways of living, of mental attitudes, of confused riches in which the best, the mediocre and the worst rub elbows with the marvelous and the striking, with solid virtues and vulgar waste, the whole so well blended, assimilated and incorporated that it constitutes a collective way of being which, as a matter of fact, is transmitted by inheritance. One can, of course, try to carry the analysis farther and I have suggested elsewhere distinguishing sanctuary values and defensive institutions in the heritage. By those words which have since had some success, I meant all that ideological social machinery slowly constructed by the Jewish will to live to preserve the Jew during the terrible vicissitudes of his history. But institutions, like family or religion, like ethical, religious or social values, apparently all tend toward the same end: the Jew's heritage is also a concrete organization of his life and of his relations with other people in the world. Whence probably their extraordinary perenniality, both positive and negative, coercive and protective, so rigid and yet supple enough to persist through so many vicissitudes.

I mean, in short, that my heritage as a man and as a Jew is essential to me, above any discussion, above any problematical issues. More precisely, it embraces and comprises those problematical issues and that reflection as a part of itself. No doubt that my hesitations, my misgivings, my revolt, my shifts, stem directly from my uneasy attachment to that Jewish heritage. When I would launch into a long, critical, detailed and impassioned examination of a certain point of doctrine, my Uncle Khailou would listen to me indulgently and conclude:

"I have hopes for you: you argue well."

That is why, paradoxically, no matter how helpful Jewish values may be in gaining a true understanding of Jewishness, those values would themselves seem mystifying and even incomprehensible if they were viewed in complete isolation, apart from the concept of Jewishness. In any case, if I may venture to say so, the lot of the Jew would not be fundamentally altered by his Jewish values, as they fail to account for his destiny. It is that specific Jewish destiny which must first be accounted for and comprehended before we reconsider those values in the light of that destiny as a whole.

The above statement can be easily proved in the case of religion. Religion is certainly the most notable and the most effective defense institution of the Jew, as it is among colonized people—which is not accidental. I have gone to some length to point out exactly what concerns the religion of my people and perhaps I have not quite finished. I thought I had practically disposed of religious magic; I rejected the irrational and mythical opportunities that systems of religious thought offer. My case was not exceptional for that matter; a great many, if not most young Jews showed the same mistrust. And yet, in that respect, my dealings with the Jewish religious fact were based on an ambiguity. Because the dogmatic content of Judaism did not seem to us on a par with modern science and philosophy, which we held henceforth to be the sole truth, we wanted to believe that the Jewish religious factor no longer interfered in any way with our lives. Because traditional religious attitudes no longer seemed to us compatible with our professions, our ambitions, our desire to be integrated in the non-Jewish city, we pretended to believe that those attitudes belonged to a sort of familial museum, which we visited from time to time but which did not influence to any extent our daily conduct, our spirits and our thoughts.

Then one day we had to admit that this religious factor, a complex mixture of beliefs more or less quiescent, of diffused values, of traditions more or less supple, of institutions more or less altered, continued surprisingly to govern our lives either directly or indirectly. More or less inwardly perhaps, often in opposition to it, but we lived it constantly; our every action was conditioned by it. Whether we decided to fast or not to fast on the Day of Atonement, we had to stop our activities out of respect for the tradition; whether we ate properly or not at Passover, whether we organized or refused to organize a certain ceremony. Was it necessary or not to have the prayer for the dead said at our uncle's funeral or in memory of our father? Was it necessary or not to send for the rabbi, accept or reject his presence at the birth of our children? We decided first one way, then the other. But, in any case, we took into account that fact which cropped up insistently on every solemn occasion in Jewish existence. In short, I have long confounded a philosophic doubt with a practical void, a doctrinal decision with the actual absence of a social fact and a behavior pattern which, more or less impatiently, more or less willingly, I have continued to live.

Besides, I now see clearly that this practical divorce has never been as complete and as virulent with me as my theoretical impatience sometimes was. Perhaps because they did not seem to me so closely connected. In agreeing to sing the Haggadah at Passover or to celebrate Purim, I did not think I was confirming the existence of God or the miracle of the Red Sea or of the fall of Haman. Simply, I was returning to my own people, to my father, my mother, my brothers and sisters, and to the ghetto, in a half-serious, half-childish collective game which either irritated or amused me according to my mood; an almost obligatory game, however, if I wanted to be one with them again or merely not to hurt them. The truth or the falsity of the traditional dogmas, the post-reasonings of apologists as to the presence of God or the rejection of God which by the very violence of my refusal would confirm it, and other theological juggling, had truly nothing to do with it. This hiatus must also have contributed to that mistake in perspective I mentioned farther back among well-meaning non-Jewish authors. Their Jewish friends have often declared—and sincerely I believe—that they do not know if they themselves can be called Jews. Traditional beliefs had no theoretical value for them or rather they scarcely knew them; they had never read a line of the great Jewish books, the Talmud for example, and sometimes not even the Bible! Are not those authors therefore right in concluding that there are Jews without Judaism and without Jewishness? . . .

"If you want to know, I myself have lost faith in God. If you want to know, I am a Marxist, but nevertheless I believe I am part of the community of Israel. No one can live without his family name . . . The God of Israel is absent, undoubtedly He does not exist, and yet He is the rallying point of our dispersion. One day a year men and women from New York to Helsinki, from Paris to Tashkent, from Johannesburg to Buenos Aires can commune in the same thought, can bear witness to their fundamental communion of destiny with the aid of an identical mask formed by hunger. In speaking to their God-Symbol, they are speaking to one another no matter what the diversity of their tongues and of their language." (A. Mandel, *The Burnt Vessel*.)

The religion of the oppressed person is not only a religion; it is a cement and a dike, an opportunity and a powerful means of reunion. Whence that fact, paradoxical only in appearance, that in those transition periods in which the oppressed person begins to free himself, in which he tries to go forward and to leave his accursed past behind, he reverts to his old rites, the most ancient and sometimes the most hidebound in which he has ceased to believe for a long time.

My students among the colonized, who had often affirmed their atheism, used to fast on the day of Ramadan. When I would ask them why, they would answer, "To be with the people who believe in it and who fast." In the same way, when we were young Zionists, we organized demonstrations to explain to the still skeptical ghetto the meaning of Zionism, the need to guarantee our collective future, we took care to make use of our common past and the traditional solemnities. We organized meetings on Purim, excursions on Passover, and the sale of lapel buttons for pilgrimages. Of course, we gave all this a new meaning, we minimized the mystical dimensions, we made fun of ourselves a bit, but in the end we had reaped the heritage.

DOMINATED MAN

One can maintain that laicization is perhaps the only way of saving Jewish tradition. Such an adaptation alone would permit the Jewish heritage to be taken up once again and henceforth continued by the Jew. . . . The laicization of Jewish tradition is to be found first of all in its negation, in the way that it is understood and lived by its believers, and in the way that it proposes itself to them. This negation is much needed, because Judaism, which for so long helped the Jews to live, has become impossible to live with today. The Jew, who today wants to make advances in the field of knowledge and of liberty, who wants to live together with the others, must begin with this rebellion, or must at least show indifference to the law and its institutional manifestations. There is a certain ingratitude to be found here. Just as the father protected the child during its early youth, so the law protected the people during their threatened childhood. But just as the father must stand aside for the child to become a man, so the tyranny of Moses must be overcome for the modern Jew to be liberated.

. . . *Self-rejection is the first step on the path of revolt and liberation.* In any case, the denial of himself as a traditional Jew is the necessary price that the modern Jew must pay if he is to escape from oppression, both interior and exterior.

. . . One can, indeed one must, reject Judaism, but one cannot reject Jewry, of which one is part, at least because one is not part of the others. It is not for a lack of courage or only for solidarity. . . . Without talking of pride, it is an almost therapeutic necessity, a degree of mental hygiene. One cannot reject oneself completely without the risk of destroying oneself. When one is already part of a minority and banned by society, one cannot allow oneself to break with one's own people as well. Rejected by others and rejecting one's own kind, what would become of one? The ground would slip away under one's feet. There is no doubt that those who are a part of a minority can better withstand separation and desertion by feeling that they belong to their own group. This is their only reliable trump-card: *Jewishness becomes a positive force once again*. This is the meaning of the important advice that Freud gave to Graf who asked him whether he should convert his son; no, because he would lose everything, and he would not even be able to defend himself anymore.

. . . To the question that history asks the modern Jew Freud replies: Jewishness is both negative and positive; the Jewish condition must be both rejected and accepted. Is it not obvious that most great modern Jews, each in their own way, have made the same reply? And that it is probably the only possible reply? Whether it be Herzl, the founder of the State of Israel, who had suddenly thought of a collective conversion, or Spinoza, whose position was clouded by the hatred of the devout, basically they both made the same proposal: one must cut off the old branch for new buds to blossom forth. At first it is only by rejecting Judaism that one can better assume one's Jewishness. There is no contradiction here, unless it be the very contradiction of Jewish existence.

Haim Cohn
(1911–   )

Introduction

Justice Haim Cohn is known as a great legal scholar, public figure, and humanist. He served in a number of legal positions in modern Israel: attorney general, minister of justice, judge and deputy chairman of the Israel Supreme Court, member of the United Nations Commission on Human Rights, Judge of the Permanent Court of Arbitration at the Hague, member of the board of governors of the International Institute of Human Rights in Strasbourg, etc. He is also honorary president of the Israel Association for Citizens' Rights and of the Israel Association for Secular Humanistic Judaism.

Cohn was born in 1911 to a religious family in Luebeck, Germany. He received a religious and secular education. Early in his life he became a Zionist and insisted on going to study in Eretz Israel. In 1930 he went to study at the famous Rabbi Kook Yeshiva in Jerusalem. He practiced law and joined the Legal Council of the Jewish authorities in Palestine (1947). Parallel to his official positions in the legal system of Israel he served as professor of law at the Hebrew University of Jerusalem and later at the Hebrew Union College in Jerusalem. He also worked as a scholar of law, publishing many articles and books, such as *The Trial and Death of Jesus* and *Human Rights in Jewish Law.*

Through his variegated life-long activities Haim Cohn has had a decisive influence on the shaping of the high standards of Israel's legal system, and of the liberal-humanistic trend in its legal philosophy and practice.

Who Is a Jew?

It is one of the fundamental tenets of the modern doctrine of human dignity that no status may be imposed on a human being against his or her will. Where a status is acquired by birth or by operation of law, human dignity requires that it should be repudiable at will—subject only to the prior discharge of obligations voluntarily incurred by virtue of that status, or to possible formal requirements of administrative procedure.

The status of Jew is traditionally acquired either by birth or by conversion. Both modes of acquisition have this in common—that they confer membership both in the Jewish religion and in the Jewish peoplehood. The proselyte, however, adopts and acquires Jewish religion, and his membership in the Jewish peoplehood is being conferred on him incidentally, as if by way of an automatic gratuity. The natural-born Jew, on the other hand, is by birth endowed with all aspects and features of Jewishness and, whether or not he wishes to believe in the Jewish God and practice the Jewish religion, he is halakhically held to be not only a member of the Jewish peoplehood but also a Jewish religionist. It is this apparent indivisibility of Jewishness from Jewish religion that renders their separation by the secularization of Jewishness so incongruous in the eyes of the traditionalists.

The fact is that Jewish religion is no longer a common denominator for all Jews; the majority of Jews in Israel, and a very substantial part of the Jews in the Diaspora, nowadays are non-religious. They do not regard themselves bound by Jewish religious law, and the halakhic tests of Jewishness bear for them only historical meaning but no normative character. Where a person is born of Jewish parentage, he will usually regard himself, and commonly be regarded, as a Jew; but where only one of his parents was Jewish, he (or his parents) will generally be called upon to make a choice. That the status of Jew is halakhically imposed on him if his mother was a Jewess, will not relieve him of having to choose: if he chooses to follow the halakhic rule of matrilineage, no legal conflict is likely to arise; and if he chooses to opt for patrilineage, his choice may have to be deemed irrelevant for halakhic purposes, but is none the less valid: he does not have to regard himself bound by halakhic norms, as a Jew, but may well regard himself, and be regarded by others by virtue of his paternal descent—and thus be a Jew by birth and by choice and by repute.

. . . A natural-born or converted Jew who desires to cease being a Jew, ought not to be required or expected to convert to another religion: he may well remain as irreligious as he was before and scorn all other religions no less than the Jewish; or he may wish to renounce Judaism regardless of his existing or future religious beliefs. It is true that in the State of Israel it rarely happens that a Jew wishes to cease being a Jew except when embracing another religion—not necessarily from religious motivations, but mostly in contemplation of matrimony. But we speak of his right to disengage himself from Jewishness if and when and from whatever motives he so desires—and this right cannot be taken away from him.

Outside the State of Israel it is a matter of common experience that Jews cease to regard themselves as Jews, and often enough also cease to be regarded as Jews by others, not because they embraced another religion, but because they actually and consciously severed all ties with Jews and shook off all emotional, religious, familiary or other relationship with Jews and Judaism; these people resent being reminded of their Jewish origins and emphatically insist on being and remaining wholly and definitively emancipated from them. Then there are natural-born Jews who are halakhically perfectly qualified, and who by their lives and deeds demonstrate outright hostility to everything Jewish, or who are actively engaged in violent efforts to destroy and eliminate the Jewish State: that they should, against their own better judgment and without any objectively reasonable cause, be accorded the status of Jew—borders on suicidal aberration.

It is self-evident that any futurology of Jewishness, whether from the conceptual or from the demographic point of view, cannot be made dependent on "Jews" who are Jews only by halakhic definition, but have detached themselves from Jewish life. Not only will they, as a matter of course, intermarry and have their children intermarry with non-Jews, but their descendants will naturally be brought up without allegiance to, or any personal or direct involvement with, Jewish concerns. To indulge in the illusion that it might be possible to reverse this development and to "save" some of those people for Jewry, is nothing but self-deception, so long as Jews live outside Israel and undergo assimilatory processes. Even if it were feasible to undertake such reversionary efforts, it would certainly not be compatible with fundamental human rights.

There are, on the other hand, those Jews whose self-identification as Jews is as honest and sincere as their exclusion from Jewry by halakhic rule is unwarranted and self-defeating. Their conscious choice of Jewishness and Jewish identity—though they may not profess and practice Jewish religion—is entitled to the same respect and recognition as other people's choices of persistent and uncompromising assimilation. To inquire of anybody whether his mother or grandmother or great-grandmother was Jewish, or whether the proselytizing minister had orthodox credentials, amounts to an inexcusable violation of their human rights.

Humanistic Judaism, Winter 1985

Some Basic Concepts for Secular Humanistic Jews

Religion

In its original, literal meaning, *religion* (in Hebrew, *dat)* is synonymous with the concept of judgment (law, custom/manner). Its modern meaning stems from the fact that in Hebrew there was no term to signify the concept of religion. This caused a confusion between religion and faith in Judaism.

The first and foremost commandment (*mitsva*) of religion is belief in God. Since we do not keep the commandment of belief in God, we are labeled nonreligious or anti-religious. But, at the same time, we are not religious because we do not keep the commandment forbidding the eating of leavened bread during Passover. The two are interdependent; since we cannot believe in God (the Torah from Heaven, sin and punishment, the Next World), we regard ourselves exempt from keeping "godly" commandments. It does not follow, however, that these commandments do not exist. They need to be studied, at least as part of our cultural history.

Belief

There is a prevalent opinion that if we do not believe in God, we don't "believe" at all. Not only are we "atheists," but "anarchists."

God forbid!

Whoever it was who said atheism is also a kind of religion was right. It is even more right to say that everyone is free to believe in the God that exists in the heart. Spinoza denied the existence of the God of Israel but believed that humanity, beauty, and the universe are godly.

A belief such as this, however, is outside the "Judaism" that was transmitted to us from generation to generation. It is a matter that is personal—belonging to each person to decide between him and his conscience or his taste or his romanticism.

Choice

Each person chooses a way of life—not only we, the "nonreligious," but also the very Orthodox and pious. Nobody keeps all 613 commandments and laws to the letter, with all the minute details. Everyone has his or her own "set table" (*Shulkhan Arukh*), as the differences between the various sects show. However, this selection process is not so apparent when we observe the various Orthodox groups, especially if one is not really familiar with their ways. The selection process is clear in the Conservative and Reform movements. These movements keep the basic *mitsva* of belief in God, and they pick from all God's commandments those that they wish to follow and others that they are not going to keep.

Our choice is not different in principle from those other choices, but it goes further, reaching to the limit of free human choice. We choose humanistic values not because we are commanded to choose something but because we chose to choose. There isn't any choice that binds anybody other than the person who makes the choice. And a humanistic association that demands one choice or another is itself an instant contradiction.

Humanism, including Jewish humanism, opens gates and lifts up those that are bent down; its only requirement is freedom of choice for everybody.

Judaism

It is true that humanism, with all its values, requirements, and achievements is not the "property" of Judaism. It is universal. We have no title to it. We hope that all humanity will claim ownership of it.

Judaism is our cultural, religious, and legal history. It is not a matter for belief but for knowledge and research. It is not a matter of ritual and practical commandments but a matter of national pride and intellectual satisfaction.

Humanistic Judaism, Spring 1989

Yehuda Bauer
(1926–)

Introduction

Professor Yehuda Bauer is the outstanding Israeli scholar on the history of illegal aliya (Berikha), on the Holocaust, and on anti-semitism today. He is a leader of the Movement for Secular Humanistic Judaism, chairman of the Israeli Association, Co-chairman of the International Institute and co-chairman of the International Federation of Secular and Humanistic Jews.

Born in 1926 in Prague, Bauer joined the Hashomer Hatzair movement and settled in Kibbutz Shuval in the south of Israel. He obtained his Ph.D. at the Hebrew University in 1960, became a lecturer in 1961 and a full professor in 1977. He served as director of the Division of Holocaust Studies at the Institute of Contemporary Jewry at the University and is presently head of the Sassoon Center for the Study of Anti-Semitism. He is a well-known participant in conferences, research projects and publications related to these subjects. He also serves as chairman of the President of Israel's Continuous Seminar on Jewish Studies.

Among his well-known books are *A History of the Holocaust* and *Historical Aspects of the Holocaust.* His most recent publication is *Jews for Sale? Nazi-Jewish Negotiations, 1933–45.*

Yehuda Bauer is one of the major leaders and spokespersons for the international movement of Secular Humanistic Judaism. His ideas have helped to shape the intellectual framework of the movement.

The Holocaust, Religion and Jewish History

How then, should a Jew respond to the Holocaust? Elie Wiesel has stated the dilemma many times. Faced with the impossibility of genuine transmission of the experience, the survivor's only response can be silence. But it is chiefly from the survivor that our knowledge, such as it is, of the Holocaust derives; silence is self-defeating, un-Jewish in the extreme, and the only hope for the future is to speak, possibly to find new forms of language that will transmit, not the reality, but that reflection of it that will not falsify and yet will be understandable to us who were not there.

More than that: as the Israeli literary expert Dr. Sidra de Koven Ezrahi has pointed out recently, Jewish suffering between the destruction of the First Temple and the nineteenth century has always been expressed, in the final resort, in biblical imagery. The many references to the destruction of the Second Temple in talmudic and post-talmudic literature notwithstanding, the classical response was in terms of Eichah (Lamentations), and many were its imitators throughout the centuries. Yet the Holocaust cannot be expressed in those terms; new forms of expression must be found.

We find ourselves caught in a tension between continuity and break of continuity, and in this all the religious interpretations are no help at all. All Jewish religious interpretation of catastrophic events is basically magical: human deeds or misdeeds cause the reaction of divine forces, which cause the disaster. It is this primitive interpretation that Schneerson, along with all of extreme Orthodoxy, adopts, and which modern Orthodox thinkers then try, not very successfully, to overcome.

Much has been written about the uniqueness of the Holocaust and its universality. I contend that the Holocaust was unique because of the uniqueness of the motivation of the perpetrator, who saw the Jews as a satanic force out to control the world, and who believed that the Jews had to be destroyed to save a racially ordered, hierarchical "humanity." Essentially, Nazism was a pseudo-religion, indeed a Manicheic religion, because it sought to contrast an absolutely good Nordic "race" with an absolutely evil

Jewish "race." Nazis, including Hitler, were Deists. They believed in a god that was both nature and the universe, and also somehow personalized. Their god was absolutely good, except that the good in Nazi eyes was on a number of rather important counts very different from the Judeo-Christian good. From Judaism and Christianity, Nazism accepted the ideas of salvation and the messiah; except that for them the messiah was here and now, and his name was Hitler. They used Christian terminology to speak of the Father of the Nation and the Son of the Race, and many of them believed this.

The Holocaust was unique also because of the victim—a peculiar, individualistic people exercising, mostly unconsciously, the most human right there is: that of being different, free to develop their own culture in their own manifold ways. The concentration camp system was designed to destroy all individual human existence. Nazism was an attempt, not really successful, at totalitarianism; its only considerable success was with the Jewish "problem," and the only place where a full-scale totalitarian approach was attempted—and almost succeeded—was in the camps. The total destruction of the individual was to be achieved by the denial of the necessities of life: food, drink, cleanliness. It was, in the last resort, excremental control; the latrine, or lack of it, was the fundamental means of dehumanization and humiliation. You had no name, no clothes, no food, no drink, no bed of your own, no water to wash, and you were controlled through your basic physiological needs. There was no parallel to this in Jewish history, no precedents to be followed, no halachic or humanistic rules that could be applied. This, despite previous mass murders and persecutions, was completely new. But there was a built-in weakness; the control to which the Nazis aspired was total, which meant that if it failed in only one case, the system had failed.

Now, it is true that the system succeeded in many cases. Yes, there were many Kapos who identified with the aggressors and exercised control in their name. Yes, there were cases of inmates stealing bread from each other in the struggle to survive. Yes, there were betrayals of friends and relatives. Survivors have told us these facts because they wanted to tell us the unadorned truth. But this was against the background of the attempt at total dehumanization by the dehumanized perpetrators. What is amazing is not that they succeeded in many cases but that they failed in so many others. To have withstood the most terrible temptations to yield to depersonalization is what really needs explaining. And we are not dealing here with individual cases, but with very large numbers. In fact, there is scarcely a testimony of a survivor that does not tell of mutual help, of self-sacrifice, of care and encouragement amid the throes of hell. The system, therefore, failed, because we know for certain of many thousands of cases in which it did. And we must remember that we know of only a fraction, because many of those who survived have not yet told their stories, and most inmates did not survive. Their tale of struggle is scattered with their ashes all over Europe.

The system was unique in its total pretensions; the suffering was unique; so was the reaction. Our religious contemporaries try to determine in what ways religious life was observed in the ghettoes and camps. That, indeed, was one element of continuity. In the face of these sudden and new terrors, people tried to preserve, as best they could, continuity with their past; it was another, very important, means of survival. Religious observance was a path of resistance, as were other forms of ideological or intellectual self-preservation. Bundists, Zionists, Communists, liberals believing in the essential goodness of humans, all relied on their respective ideologies to keep their sanity and their humanity. Nobody will deny that continuity; indeed, without it nothing can be explained. Only a dialectical approach can help us: the situation demanded both continuity and its opposite, and there is no contradiction between them.

Two opposing arguments are frequently heard regarding the issue of the Holocaust's uniqueness. Both stem from religious sources and both are wrong. One puts the Holocaust outside of human and Jewish experience, as a totally new and inexplicable event. The other says that it is "simply" another, harsher form of anti-Jewish persecution.

The first is the argument mainly of writers and poets with a religious bent; in a form that shows how little thought out it is, it is often advanced in Reform and Conservative circles in North America and among traditionally inclined Jews elsewhere. It is understandable, because the Holocaust indeed is a "tremendum," a quasi-unique horror. But the elements that composed the Holocaust, other than the motivation of the murderers and the uniqueness of the victim's situation, are not really outside of past human experience at all. Sadism, including the burning of children and mass murder, has been practiced by humans from time immemorial. The destruction of the town of Beziers by Catholic armies of the French king in the early thirteenth century, the mountains of human skulls accumulated by the Mongols in what is now Iran, the destruction of Carthage, the Armenian massacres—the list is literally interminable. The Bible, too, contains such cases: for instance, the mass murder by the Israelites of all the Midianties with the exception of virgin girls (Numbers 31). It does not matter whether or not this crime was actually committed, the point is that it was thought to be perfectly justifiable and normal behavior (at God's command, of course; without that "moral" support it would have been at least questionable). It is the brutality, the government-induced mass murder, and the organized, bureaucratic way it was done that caused people to look for extra-historical explanations for the Holocaust. But it is not only the brutality that has plenty of precedents; all the above examples (except for that of the Midianites, for which we have no available materials) and many more were well-planned and executed by orders from above.

It is a very understandable deviation from simple facts when writers, musicians, artists, and their critics express their justified shock at the horrors perpetrated during the Hitler era by escaping into mystical explanations, which may help them put their emotions into artistic form. The emotions evoked are real, and one can and should identify with them. Which does not mean that the Holocaust is not perfectly explicable. It is part of world history and Jewish history, explicable because it was done by humans to humans for reasons that, in all their irrationality, can be rationally explained. It had antecedents not only in the history of the perpetrators, but in the peculiar situation of the victims that made them candidates for victimization.

But the second interpretation, that the Holocaust is merely a continuation of similar disasters in the past, is equally wrong. There are definite and crucial differences between the events of the past and those of the Holocaust. The destructions of the Jerusalem Temples were political-cultural events that did not endanger the physical existence of the Jews as a collectivity. The Holocaust did. The Crusades and the pogroms were not and could not be aimed at the total physical annihilation of the Jews. In most cases the individual Jew could escape by submitting to conversion, and often could afterwards return to Jewish identity. In most cases, one of the aims of the persecutors was to chase the Jews away; in the Nazi case they were forbidden to flee so they could all be murdered.

The desire to go to one of these two extremes—to take the Holocaust out of Jewish history or to make it into just one of the many persecutions—is understandable. It seems to originate in the insecurity that the remembrance of the Holocaust inevitably produces. If it was a totally unique event, then it will not be repeated; it is then somehow parallel to the Flood and the promise to Noah contained in the story of the rainbow. If it is part of known Jewish experience, its horrors parallel to those of the Crusades or the Chmielnicki riots of 1648–9, it also becomes less frightening. But if it is indeed part of Jewish experience and its uniqueness lies not only in the motivation of the murderer but also in the existential situation of the victim, then we have a problem of our own identity and a difficult task of confronting the Holocaust as something that has to be woven into life.

In this task, religion is quite useless both as an attempt at explaining the event and as a facilitator in working through it. Religion does not and cannot explain a thing; its attempts at doing so are convoluted and often lead (as with Schneerson) to anti-Semitic, murderous conclusions. It is, however, important and useful as a balm for people who are hurt and who look for an irrational, mystical explanation because they are incapable of looking the thing in the eye.

In the end, there is a truthful and respectable religious answer to the Holocaust. It has been expressed to me many times, and I respect it and those who make that statement: "I have a problem with the God of Auschwitz, I cannot explain it, it bothers me, but I believe it nevertheless." It is a totally irrational response, but religion is irrational, after all; it is a projection of the internal life of human beings onto an abstraction, which then becomes personified as God. I don't have to share religious beliefs to respect them and their believers.

Actually, you don't need the Holocaust to arrive at this position; you can take the case of any child run over by an automobile. The religious person's escape, if she or he is honest, is into irrationality, or into a statement that there is no answer.

The answer is, however, palpably there: humans are capable of Holocausts, just as they are capable of goodness. The gods and the Satans that they create out of their troubled imaginations are really within themselves and may be acted out in bloody murder or in unlimited goodness.

Humanists have to confront the fact that the Holocaust was committed not by "beasts" or "animals" (what an insult to the animal kingdom!) but by humans for very human reasons. But the same Holocaust also contains shining examples of human heroism, self-sacrifice, altruism, and simple good in the most impossible situation. Which means that Holocausts can be prevented by human effort. No god or Satan told the Nazis to do what they did. Hence, human action is possible.

Paradoxically, then, there is a case for a positive interpretation of the major tragedy in all of Jewish history. The purpose, after all, of non-Jews and Jews alike, it to prevent its recurrence.

Humanistic Judaism, Spring 1991

Zev Katz
(1924–   )

Zev Katz is a teacher, writer and activist in the movement for Secular Humanistic Judaism. He is a cofounder of the Israel Association for Secular Humanistic Judaism and an active participant in the International Institute for Secular Humanistic Judaism.

Katz was born in Poland and spent the World War II years in the Soviet Union (Siberia and Kazakhastan). In 1946 he returned to Poland and soon left illegally for the American occupation zone of Germany, where he lived in a displaced persons camp. He became a teacher and a leading member of Hanoar Hatzioni (the Zionist Youth Movement). In the spring of 1948 he left for Israel as a volunteer for the Haganah and he participated in the War of Independence on the central and southern fronts. In autumn of 1949 he began his studies at the Hebrew University of Jerusalem. In 1954 he went to the University of London on a scholarship to pursue his studies for the doctorate. After obtaining his doctoral degree, he returned to Israel in 1957. There he served as foreign editor and diplomatic correspondent for the leading Hebrew daily newspaper, *Haaretz*.

In 1967 Katz was invited to teach and do research abroad at the universities of Glasgow and Essex and in 1969 he went to teach at Harvard University and the Massachusetts Institute of Technology where he remained until 1973. Since 1974 he has been teaching at the Institute of History and at the School of Overseas Students at the Hebrew University of Jerusalem. He has also done some teaching and research at Stanford university, Eton College, and Spiro Institute in London.

Together with Yehuda Bauer, Katz founded the Israel Association for Secular Humanistic Judaism. He is one of the founders of the International Institute and of the International Federation of Secular Humanistic Jews. Katz served as deputy chairman of the Israel Association and dean of the Institute until 1993. During the last few years he has made a number of trips to the former Soviet Union, where, together with Simeon Augustevich, he founded the Association for Humanistic Judaism of the Former USSR.

Katz is editor and author of a number of books and publications and served as coeditor of this volume.

Jewish History—Theistic or Humanistic?

We, secular and humanistic Jews, should try to build for ourselves a true understanding of Jewish history, distinct from the mythologies and the editing of the religious. This is fundamental for our own understanding and can become a basic source for the teacher who transmits the Jewish heritage to our children.

Religious institutions rarely teach history. If at all, they teach the periods from the Old Testament until Maimonides. Further Jewish history is not taught systematically—no Holocaust, no rebirth of the State of Israel, no Jewish national movement, no Jewish socialist Yiddish movement. People finish 10–15 years of Jewish study in yeshivot and religious institutions without an inkling of the true history of their folk.

What is our understanding of Jewish history? There is a basic difference between the religious and the academic understanding of it. Either Jewish history has been predetermined by a supreme transcendental being and the Jews are merely an instrument for the purposes of this divine being; or Jewish history is of this world, and whatever has been achieved in it is the work of human beings, of our people and its great leaders. They were both religious leaders and secular leaders and the latter often presented in a religious garb. Jewish history was the work of human beings, some of them great geniuses, others great military leaders and national heroes of their people.

Moses—Hero or Instrument?

The example of Moses is notable. According to Jewish tradition, Moses is possibly one of the greatest heroic figures in any history. A liberator of his people from bondage in Egypt. Raised in the court of Pharaoh, he was a prince, who risked his life by defending a Jew who had been beaten by an Egyptian in the street. He had to flee and became a refugee in the desert. He could have continued to live as a prince of Egypt. But he came back to liberate his people, became a law-giver, a liberator, a national leader. In short, a great historical personage.

In his great essay Ahad Ha'am writes that it doesn't matter whether Moses existed or not. Moses exists in the historical memory and conscience of the Jewish people and of many in the world who have taken this heritage for themselves. Simon Dubnow and the school of the spiritual essence of peoples, rather than the material one, has always said that it is the spiritual heritage that matters. The same for Ahad Ha'am.

There have been peoples that lived somewhere, were mighty in numbers, had immense territories, awesome power, great riches, but didn't create anything. What do we know about such peoples thousand of years later? Nothing, because nothing remains. Yet a small people without riches, empire, numbers, or great lands, but spiritually creative, a people that left great ideas and literary works, profound philosophical treatises and great works of art, so that thousands of years later we find the products of their creativity—we know a lot about this small people.

Moses, as the major figure in the creative saga of the Jewish people, whether historically real or not, represents a national leader, a religious leader and a political leader. There can be only two ways of interpreting Moses. One is that Moses was the loudspeaker who spoke for God. Called in front of the burning bush, Moses found all kinds of excuses to refuse this role, but was forced by God to accept it. The conclusion is that all Moses ever said to the Jewish people and left as a legacy to the world, was what God put in his mouth.

This approach denies the creativity of Moses. It ignores the Jewish people and the impact of their culture. Moses ceases to be a great genius capable of creating what he did and becomes a mere jukebox, a relay station for the Supreme Being.

Secular humanists view the same story differently. We reject the transcendental origins of the achievements of human beings, of the Jewish people in those times. Whether Moses was real or a mythical creation of someone from a later era is of less importance than the story of a great leader who led one of the very few successful attempts at liberation of an enslaved people from Egypt. The Jewish people began its proud independent existence, created a system of values, philosophical and religious beliefs and thus Moses left his imprint for millennia on the Jewish people and the world.

The same can be said about the Jewish people coming out of Egypt. Either this was a revolt of our forefathers who were slaves and who liberated themselves from Egyptian bondage, or it was the ten plagues, the Egyptian first-born dying, and all the other "miracles done by the strong arm" of the Divine Being, with the Jews actually opposing and protesting. We can look at this historical event one way or the other. There is no in-between.

The Hasmoneans and the Holocaust

Later events can be viewed in the same way, such as the deeds of the Hamoneans. The story about the little oil lamp which had enough oil for one day and lasted eight days, which the rabbinical religious establishment places as the central event which is marked by the Chanukah celebration, is described as this miracle. We do not seek to denigrate the traditions of a religious person in his sincere belief But from the critical secular humanistic point of view the true meaning of Chanukah does not lie in miracles about an oil lamp.

The great revolt of the Jewish people for independence, this deed of an entire family, the Hasmoneans, almost all of whom fell in the defense of the Jewish people, recreated a Jewish independent existence for a long period of time under the most difficult conditions of ancient empires. This is the real meaning of Chanukah. The religious blessing on the Chanukah candles reads: "Blessed art Thou, Lord of the Universe, who made miracles for our forefathers then and in our own time." God does it all.

There remain two ways of looking at Jewish history. Today a new generation of scholars, young people in Israel and elsewhere, Jewish and some non-Jewish, are at work on Jewish history. These scholars are seeking to reshape our conception of Jewish history. The example of how to interpret the Holocaust becomes a sharp dividing line. The religious approach says that God punished the people for their sins. What looked to us like a purgatory and a terrible catastrophe was the punishment, due to the murdered in the next world, but given to them here. Now after the Holocaust, they can go straight to the Garden of Eden!

Let us hope that some years from now a volume that will present Jewish history in its true historical dimensions will be before us. For the religious, the removal of the Supreme Being from Jewish history leaves it denuded of any meaning. Without God, Jewish history is merely the work of human beings. From the humanistic-secular point of view that is precisely the case. It is our forefathers who have struggled, suffered, created, revolted,—sometimes successfully, sometimes not. It is this man-made history that can be a rock of strength for our further survival.

There were thinkers who turned the religious thesis on its head. It is interesting that such Zionist leaders as Ahad Ha'am, Jabotinsky and Ben-Gurion agreed in this matter. It was not the Jewish religion that preserved the Jewish people, but the Jewish people who realized that their national survival depended on adopting the form of a religious sect. At that time this was the only method which under the prevailing conditions enabled them to survive. When survival was no longer dependent on religion, the Jews adopted what we call peoplehood as the framework of continuity in recent times.

Many of the proscriptions of our sages were intended"l'havdil et ha-Yehudium min ha-goyim"—(in order to differentiate the Jews from the others). It was not that God "commanded," but in order to maintain Jewish separateness. Much of the Jewish religious commandments can be interpreted in this way. This approach has another basis. From earliest times, the Jews lived as a nomadic people between the desert and the settled areas of the ancient Middle East. Under those conditions they developed a unique ability for survival, and adopted the religious form necessary for survival in the world in which they lived.

In the last few hundred years the Jewish religion has not been the central force for Jewish survival. When one deals with survival, it is necessary to add "Survival for what and in what form?" If, for example, the only way to survive would be for all to put on "ka-po-tehs" (long black coats) and "shtreimlech" (fur hats) and act like an outlandish sect that doesn't eat this or doesn't do that, and this would be the only content of Jewish survival, would we want such survival? If Israel should become a ghettoized, backward, reactionary, racist society—and one must always remember that such a possibility may occur—would it be worth sacrificing our strength, our life, our emotions; ourselves, for the survival of such an Israel?

We believe that the form and content of secular humanistic Judaism is the means of Jewish survival. The other kind of ghettoized survival would not succeed—and will create a chasm between Jews and entire world of Gentiles. Such an Israel will not survive. Only an open, highly developed, progressive, scientific and humanistic Israel will survive. Our secular humanistic content is also the secret for survival of the entire Jewish people.

Secular Humanistic Judaism, no. 2 (August 1987)

Theories About Jewish Survival

How did the Jewish people survive? This is a major problem for which historians and thinkers have offered varied explanations. At first sight it looks like a mystery: how could the Jews alone among so many peoples and cultures of the ancient world continue their existence—through so many centuries of wars, occupations, persecutions, exile, minor and major holocausts? Why and how did the Jews survive all those great kingdoms and empires—the Egyptians, Babylonians, Assyrians, Greeks, Romans, Franks, the medieval empires and so on? A small, fragile people, on a little piece of land between the desert and the sea, and then a dispersed, wandering people tossed on the great ocean of world events—how did it survive? Ultimately the Jewish people was able to launch a veritable national renaissance; a mighty national movement of repatriation, the rebirth of an independent state in its ancient homeland, the resurrection of a "dead" language, a new culture. What is the secret, what is the nature of force and dynamism that made this unprecedented case in history possible?

The problem was naturally of great interest to many thinkers and a number of explanatory theories were put forward. Here we shall briefly discuss the following:

1. the religious explanation

2. the Ahad Ha'am and Jabotinsky theory about the inborn "national will for survival"

3. Dubnow's theory about multiple "national-spiritual centers"

4. Prof Rivkin's "Darwinian" explanation of "mutations"

I shall then propose an application of some of these theories to the issue of Secular Humanistic Judaism.

The "religious" explanation of Jewish survival can be formulated in two basic versions. The first is as follows: "The Jewish religion was and still is a major force for Jewish strength and survival." The second asserts: "The Jewish religion is the sole force for Jewish survival—throughout the history of the Jewish people, from its inception to this very day and as long as the Jewish people will exist." From the positive, one can also learn the negative: "Weakening or disappearance of the Jewish religion also means the weakening and disappearance of the Jewish people."

Although they may look similar, these two assertions are profoundly different in substance and meaning. To the best of my knowledge, all major thinkers and historians accept the validity of the first assertion. Even a totally irreligious, "secular" person can agree that at certain stages of history when the entire world "lived by religion," the Jewish religion was a major and indispensable force for Jewish survival. This is still very much so under certain special circumstances. For example, when in Moscow I attended services at the Great Synagogue although I am entirely "secular." This is so because, paradoxically, there is no other place in the Soviet capital where Jews are allowed to congregate, engage in some traditional Jewish activity, and meet with Jews from all over the world.

However, the "religious theory" about Jewish survival in its second formulation can hardly withstand a critical examination, even from the point of view of a religious person. It has many problems. Here we shall indicate a few of them. One is the survival of the Jewish people during the period of exile and persecution (a mini-holocaust—"Throw every new-born Hebrew boy into the river . . . kill him")—some 430 years (Exodus 2:16-22). The sojourn in Egypt was obviously before the Sinai revelation, so the Jewish religion could not fulfill the function of "the sole force for survival"—how did the Israelites survive? Moses went out and "saw an Egyptian strike a Hebrew, one of his brethren" (Exodus 2:1). How did Moses know that the smitten fellow was a Hebrew? The Hebrews had Elders of their own (God sent Moses to them), they knew precisely who was an Israelite and who was not (for example, when they marched out of Egypt), and so on. So the Jews obviously were a distinctive people before Sinai and they survived hundreds of years in a Diaspora situation which entailed enslavement and persecution.

There is equally a major problem with the entire period until the destruction of the First Temple. Even a first-hand perusal of the evidence of the Bible itself clearly indicates that during that entire period idolatry was widespread in Judea and Israel. King Solomon did not build a Temple to Yahweh; he built altars and temples for "Chemosh, the abomination of Moab . . . and for Molech, the abomination of Ammon . . . for Ashtoreth, the goddess of the Zidonians, and Milcolm, the abomination of the Ammonites," and so on (1 Kings 11:5-8). Pillars, statues and symbols of various gods were even placed within the Temple of Solomon and idolatry was practiced there.

"And the King [Josiah] commanded to remove from the Temple of the Lord all the vessels that were made for Baal. . . and for all the host of heaven. . . He pulled down the houses of the male prostitutes attached to the House of the Lord. . . He destroyed the horses that the kings of Judah had set up in honor of the sun[-God] at the entrance to the House of the Lord (2 Kings 23:4-11).

So, during the entire formative period of the Jewish people—for more than four centuries in the first exile in Egypt and then during some six centuries in their own land—for more than one thousand years—the Jews survived as a separate people with their own language, culture, tribal and monarchical structure, at first without the Jewish religion at all (in Egypt) and then without the Jewish religion being the sole or even the dominant factor in their survival. We also have little evidence of how the Jews survived after their return from the Babylonian exile between 480 and 165 B.C.E.—the revolt of the Maccabees.

There is no doubt that during the Babylonian exile and from the destruction of the Second Temple until the beginning of the modern era—and especially during the Middle Ages—when the entire world was dominated by religion, it was the Jewish religion that was the great force for Jewish survival. During that long period the very notion of "Jew" meant "a believer in the Jewish faith."

However, during the last few centuries a new breed of Jew appeared, "the non-believing (secular) Jew." Spinoza, early in the 17th century, was the first outstanding example. In the modern era, almost all great Jews who made an impact on the Jews and the world—thinkers, creators, scientists, statesmen—were either secular Jews or not accepted by the religious Orthodoxy (even if they were believers of some kind). Spinoza, Mendelssohn, Freud, Buber, Einstein, Marx, Herzl—all were such. Moreover, almost all great new movements and ideologies in Jewish life, such as the great cultural achievements in modern times, were created by non-religious Jews: the Haskalah, modern Jewish literature, poetry, theater (in Hebrew, Yiddish and other languages), modern Jewish historiography, Jewish socialism (Bundism), and finally the great Jewish national renaissance (Zionism) and the miracle of revived Jewish sovereignty— the State of Israel. Was it the Jewish religion that motivated Sholem Aleichem, Mendele Mocher-Sforim, Bialik and Goldfaden, Graetz and Dubnow, Agnon and Bashevis-Singer to create a new, great, modern Jewish culture? Was it Jewish Orthodoxy that motivated generations of pioneers and fighters to resettle the ancient land and fight victoriously in the Wars of Israel? Is it the Halachah that inspired Soviet Jews in our times to undertake a heroic struggle for opening the gates and repatriation to Israel? In modern times, for several centuries, it was secular ideas held by secular people that brought a new efflorescence to the Jewish people, created a modern Jewish culture, a national movement, the State of Israel—and thus sustained the existence of the Jewish people.

A theory which is the complete opposite of the "religious" explanation was offered by Ahad Ha'am and, paradoxically, by Jabotinsky. The former, the father of "spiritual Zionism," and the latter, the founder of "Revisionism," were at opposite poles in almost everything. But they proposed the same basic explanation for Jewish survival. It turned the religious thesis "on its head," religion was not the force for the survival of the Jewish people, but the will for survival of the Jewish people "used" religion for this purpose, when other means were not effective. This thesis can be expressed as follows: since earliest times the Jewish people developed an innate and very powerful "will for survival." When the normal existence of the people in its own land, with its own political structure and separate culture could not continue, e.g. with the destruction of the Second Temple, their will for survival put all its effort into religious forms and structures and made them an instrument for further existence. Actually, not all Jews survived, only a minority with the strongest attachment to their Jewish identity, which in those times was identical with the Jewish faith. There were 5 to 8 million Jews at the time of the Roman empire, yet sometime in the 15th–17th centuries there were only 1.2 million Jews in the world. However, with the advent of emancipation, secularization and modernization, when religion weakened, the old national essence came again to the fore, shedding the old religious shell—the modern secular Jewish identity and culture broke through and flourished.

Another approach to the problem was presented by the great Jewish historian Simon Dubnow. The Jewish people survived because it developed a unique capacity for creating ever new "national-spiritual" centers, instead of those that had been destroyed or that had vanished. When the old national center in Eretz Israel was destroyed, there rose a great new center in Babylon (4th–10th centuries). Again, when this center lost its strength, there arose just about that time another great center—Spanish Jewry, with great Talmudic sages, philosophers, and poets (11th–15th centuries). Then followed, in succession, the Rhineland and South Germany center, the Polish-Lithuanian and the Russian center, and parallel with it, the Mid-European center (Germany). Dubnow died a martyr's death at the age of 82 at the hands of the Nazis. But it is possible to project his thesis for the post World War II situation. After the destruction of the Central-East European center, two parallel centers arose: the national cultural center in reborn independent Israel, and the great center of Jewish scholarship and learning in North America. The importance of the latter should certainly not be disregarded, today it has major rabbinical academies, a great number of departments and institutes for Jewish studies, some of the most significant Jewish writers and thinkers, and so on. The two centers are now mutually influencing and enriching each other, and their contributions are giving new content to Jewish life everywhere.

Finally, we arrive at the theory of Professor Ellis Rivkin; which I called here "Darwinian:"

"The answer lies in three modes of problem solving which the Jews developed. . replication, when the Jews solved the problem in exactly the same way it had previously been solved; variation on a theme (or adaptation); and mutation or quantum jump when replication or variation on a theme do not work. . . (and when) innovative solutions (were necessary)" (E. Rivkin, in *Humanistic Judaism,* Spring 1983, pp. 39-4 1). According to Prof Rivkin, such mutations of Judaism occurred at a number of crucial turning points in Jewish history—and it was due to these that not only the Jewish people but also Judaism itself survived. Such mutations happened when prophetic Judaism which depended on revelation changed into "Judaism of the Book" with the promulgation of the Five Books of Moses. Instead of the prophets came priests and scribes. The next change was from written law only to oral law, "from a belief that all reward and punishments occur in this world to a belief in eternal life and resurrection." The final quantum jump or mutation, according to Rivkin, came when "the rise of capitalism and scientific thinking" made a new change necessary. Reform Judaism was the answer to this need. Reform Judaism started among a portion of German Jewry, a small minority of the Jewish people. Yet today it is a major stream in American Jewry, much larger than the orthodox. It is by a constant process of replication, adaptation, and mutation that Judaism and the Jewish people survived. As a result, the very essence of Judaism changed on a number of occasions—and Judaism today is essentially very different from what it was in the past.

The theories presented above provide insight into the variety of approaches relating to the "secret" of Jewish survival. I would like to add a comment to some of these theories—and a coda to that of Rivkin. Secular Jews would certainly reject the "extreme" religious theory, much like almost all who take a rational attitude. There is much that can be learned from the other theories—the "moderate" religious theory, the "national will to survive" theory or the "spiritual centers" theory of Dubnow. The Rivkin theory is especially valuable since it borrows its notions from the world of science and clearly demonstrates the mutability of Judaism at its various stages.

Humanistic Jews will agree with Rivkin that Reform Judaism is a mutation in response to modernization and emancipation. We live, however, in an age of change so rapid that the one and a half centuries which have passed since the inception of Reform are comparable to the passing of many centuries. "Scientific thinking" and modernization have progressed so much since the mid-19th century that a new mutation is imperative—going beyond Reform or anything known hitherto in Judaism. As a result of all these developments a new phenomenon has appeared in the Jewish people: a secular Jew, educated, given to scientific thinking, Zionist or pro-Israel, who wants to remain a Jew and link the Jewish heritage with the great positive ideas of Universal Humanism. This Jew does not accept any ideas about a supernatural being and it not inclined to participate in prayers and religious ceremonies. This is so especially among the young generation of Jews—in Israel and in the Diaspora. This portion of the Jewish people will continue growing—as the world and Israel pass further into the highly industrialized and post-industrial stage. The Jewish people are presently becoming the first "post-industrial" people in the world.

The survival of the Jewish people and of Judaism now calls for a new mutation: Secular Humanistic Judaism.

Secular Humanistic Judaism, no. 1
(February 1986)

Shunya Bendor
(1916–   )

Introduction

Shunya Bendor was born in Romania and as an adolescent, became a leader of the Hashomer Hatzair youth movement in that country. In 1936 he made aliya and was one of the founders of Kibbutz Dahlia. Bendor became secretary of the Hashomer Hatzair movement in Palestine and in Europe and also served as leader of the Kibbutz Artzi organization in Israel.

Bendor's career in education began when he became a teacher at his kibbutz. He went on to become a lecturer at Oranim, the Kibbutz Educational College near Haifa, and later became its director.

Bendor's research activities were concentrated in the field of biblical studies. With the late Mordechai Razin he co-authored *Origins of the Institution of Kingdom in Ancient Israel,* and his doctoral thesis, *The Structure of Society in Ancient Israel,* which will soon be published in English.

Bendor is one of the founders of the Association for Humanistic Judaism in Israel, and is now retired from academic life.

The Ideological Basis of Secular Humanistic Judaism

The secular concept does not find, and does not need to find, good beyond man, and it does not rely on a Divine good. By itself, the universe is neither good nor evil in the moral or animate world. There is neither good nor evil in the struggles for existence between animals. Man distinguishes between good and evil within the framework of human society. To the great distress of the "good" man, historic human experience does not prove the good of providence. According to the secular concept, transcendence towards the "sublime good" is embodied in the ascent from the individual towards the greater humankind, at the same time that men struggle individually and collectively.

No contemporary secular person would be self-conscious at the title of "apikoros" [nonbeliever]. He would agree that ethics and justice are given to the autonomous man, derive from him, and are granted him without specific reason. The disbeliever is not obligated to relate to the question, "Is there a God?" or "Did God create the world?" The subject about which he takes a position is the question of Providence: a personal and historical God, a judging God; God the leader who imposes His precepts; the judge, the provider of reward or punishment.

The concept of disbelief contradicts the concept of religion, not in the cosmic area but in that of Providence. This contradiction is expressed by Rabbi Elazar Ben Arach, "One should know for whom he toils; he will thus be faithfully rewarded." And, with reference to the apikoros, "One should learn Torah well enough to answer the apikoros." The approach of the apikoros contradicts religion in the crucial aspect of theodicy, justifying the judgment of God. ("He is the Rock, his word is perfect; for all his ways are just" Deuteronomy 32:4; and "As for God, His way is perfect" Psalms 18:31.) The justification of judgment refers to judgment inherent in the history of an individual as well as the history of a nation, in one generation as well as in others.

This generation has experienced the worst tragedy of the Jewish nation, and the religious man who wants to establish justification of Divine judgment suffers tremendously. Some claim justification by saying the punishment was deserved. There is another rationalization: In consequence of the Holocaust we were granted our own state.

The approach of the apikoros neither consoles itself with justification nor suffers. It relies neither on judgment nor on a judge beyond the human realm of good and evil between human beings, between the individual and humanity.

Adam sinned, ate from the tree of knowledge, and became a human being: he was capable of distinguishing between good and evil, and he was doomed to struggle for the sake of this distinction throughout all his days and throughout the generations.

The apikoros takes this responsibility only upon himself. The religious person expects God's help, praying, "Help us refrain from sin, teach us to love Torah, teach us to eschew evil. . . ."

Secular humanism . . . tries to fulfill the words found in the Psalm, "Depart from evil and do good; seek peace and pursue it and not because of the fear of God, but because of the love of man." The aim of these words is not to suspend the function of religion in the process of the humanization of man and the development of civilization. Human society would not have forged the capability of choosing between good and evil without expecting God's blessing or fearing His curse, without accepting that the choice between good and evil is the choice between life and death. The possibility of doing good for the love of man is greater today than in the past. Generation after generation people have been oppressed by the force of religious rule, compelled to accept norms and values which they would not otherwise have accepted.

The idea of secular humanism is daring because the alienation noted earlier is not an external pressure but rather one of existential human need. Moreover, it is not simply alienation but an interweaving of man in his social existence. That inner need, that set of rules, make it difficult for the monotheistic notion to remain pure. Many who look for answers to the dilemmas of good and evil, ordeals, dualism between God and Satan, diverse beliefs and customs are very far from a pure monotheism. The idea of secular humanism is therefore more respected, as a daring human adventure, on the path towards overcoming powerful and deeply rooted alienation.

The secular humanist concept does not ignore the existential human need for hope, belief, and meaning. According to this concept, meaning derives only from man himself, and only he can give meaning to life. In this aspect he differs from the beast, "That which befalleth the sons of men befalleth beasts . . . as one dies, so the other dies. . . so that a man has not preeminence above a beast . . ." (Eccles. 3:19).

Death is common to both man and animal. But in his life, man is disadvantaged. It is his consciousness; it is the quality out of which the need for meaning in life derives. It is the source of his "weakness" and his power. The same applies to worship and hope; belief and hope are an essential need. The more man suffers and is perplexed, the greater is the need. Man is not satisfied with "knowledge." In order to hope, he needs belief. He does not need "knowing," but "supposing and expecting"; expectation stems from the human soul.

Expressions typical of the language of prayer are used by the secular humanist ("Good God!" when he's surprised; "God knows" when he's perplexed) though he does not believe he is talking to God who hears his prayers. Secular humanism, its hope and worship, is embodied in man and his spirit only: man can be good, and can distinguish between good and evil only by his rational power, and according to his morality. For the secular humanist hope and belief are much more complex because he is always confronted with reality, and he can never give up rational criticism and reality itself. It must be admitted that expecting things to improve in socialist society is based on belief—not on scientific certainty—which assumes the evolutionary necessity of history as unavoidable "progress."

With respect to man's striving for the world beyond, secular humanism regards Transcendentalism as the transcendence of the individual out of himself towards the universal human being, towards humanism. This transcendence occurs in any human being, either in reality, or in history. This is also the Transcendence of the secular humanist Jews: they belong to the Jewish people, they choose to belong to the Jewish people, they are responsible for the people's continuation; they live according to the cultural norm of the people, they maintain it and they change it, they make it real.

Uri Rapp
(1923–)

Introduction

Uri Rapp is a lecturer in the sociology of the theater at Tel Aviv University. He was born in Germany in 1923 and went to Israel in 1936. He received his M.A. at the Hebrew University in Jerusalem and his Ph.D. at Constanze University in Germany.

Parallel to his academic work, Rapp has served for many years as theater critic for a number of Israel's foremost newspapers. In 1991, he published *Humanism: The Concept and Its History*, based on lectures he gave for the Israel Army's Radio University of the Air.

Rapp is a member of the executive of Tekhila, the Israeli Association for Secular Humanistic Judaism, as well as a member of the board of governors of the International Institute for Secular Humanistic Judaism.

HUMANISM: THE CONCEPT AND ITS HISTORY

Humanism and Religion

An understanding of this struggle may be sharpened by examining a radical saying: A religious man thinks that God created man; a humanist thinks that man created God. The statement may seem exaggerated (for there are humanists who believe in God, even though they do not believe in Divine providence or in God-given commandments, or said differently, do not ascribe the rules of nature and ethical values to a Supreme Being) but it enables us to say that the humanist thinks that just as man created art, science, and other works, so he created religion—historically, a very great creation. The problem with fundamentalism is that it turns a creation that has great, sometimes even imperative historical value, into a present-day force that demands obedience to each and every written word.

We use the Decalogue as an illustration. Ethically, this is an extremely important document. At one time it was a definitive document even though there were similar laws among other nations of the ancient world. Today, those who see the Ten Commandments as literally the central ethical document must carefully read the commandments, particularly the descriptive passage "A jealous God visits the iniquities of the fathers onto the children," or, as another example, the last commandment: "Thou shalt not covet." First of all, it is written, one should not be envious of the house of a friend, and only afterwards, the friend's wife, along with his manservant, his maidservant, his ox and his mule. In other words, the wife is considered to be property, property of a lesser importance than a house. It is, therefore, impossible to accept the Ten Commandments, even with all its ethical values, as a document that is fully applicable today. A consistent humanist would say that the first commandment—"I am the Lord your God"—turns all ten of the commandments into orders from on high, whereas humanist values must flow from moral awareness and the strength of will of man himself.

The humanist approach holds that there is an ethical world view which has moral values of its own, and that this ethical world view demands certain conditions that the religious establishment is, in fact, unable to agree to. These are a) open debate; b) abolishing priorities based on sectoral power, thereby ensuring that no one group can impose its ideas on another; c) forbidding the use of violence when there is disagreement—the struggle against violence has not come to an end in the modern world where even among enlightened nations people behave violently, indeed killing one another in the name of their own religious sect—and lastly d) pluralism, the multiplicity of religious groups that makes possible the variety which leads to genuinely free discussion.

Religious people who are convinced that they are responsible for the ethical behavior of their fellow man are unable to accept this approach. Therefore, in a dialogue between religious and secular persons the religious man wants to bring the secularist closer to religion; basically, he neither intends to listen to explanations of humanism nor to relate to it.

Here a certain weakness of Humanism becomes apparent. The current return to religion is, among other things, an outgrowth of man's search for meaning. Men and women want meaning and value in their lives, though they may not always articulate it in this way. Human beings also require communality, relationships with others, a group in which they can find their place. . . .

The weakness of Humanism lies in its inability to win over those who are searching for absolute answers to their questions. I saw the following saying written on the wall of a school in the United States, "It is not our job to answer the questions, but to question the answers." This is the basic principle of Humanism, according to which everything is open to question; questions may be asked about everything and it is possible to challenge everything—nothing is final. This is a principle of science but in the present context, it is the principle of a world outlook. Humanists have principles, but they must always stand up to renewed review. This rule was formulated in its full and definitive form by John Stuart Mill, and it is still the formula that underlies the humanistic approach. Many people, particularly the young, do not require examination, study or debate, but authority. It is this longing for authority that leads them to join groups that are primarily religious.

For a certain period of time, Marxism offered some sort of answer to people who were searching for meaning in their lives, and for ethnicity or communality in their social lives. Marxism does not supply the requisite answer, at least not for people in the more developed countries. Indeed, one contemporary humanist defined the basic duty of humanists in this way: To live a responsible life, without God or Marx. This ethic of accountability to others, of opposition to exploitation, and of responsibility for the future of mankind founders on one of the sharpest arguments against Humanism heard in our time. The argument is that men are unable to stand up before this ethical imperative because of their own weakness and self-involvement. Their need to receive instructions and guidelines from others is stronger than their ability to take on personal responsibility and to think independently. It is also argued that people don't want to stand up to such an ethical demand: group fanaticism, identification with one's own sect, and emotions of revenge and hatred toward others are too strong to permit men to talk to one another truthfully—without subterfuge—about common values. From the humanist's point of view the most unethical phenomenon that can be imagined is collective revenge.

Humanism and the Jewish People

Nationalism began as part of the humanist tradition, particularly as formulated by Johann Herder, around the year 1800 in Germany. Herder claimed that the identification of a man with the nation into which he is born and in whose traditions he lives constitutes his identity, even his honor as a man. Nationalism became an antihumanist cause only when it imposed itself on other nations whose people it did not respect. This process was defined in the middle of the 19th century by the great playwright Grillparzer as "the development from humanism to nationalism to animalism," a development to which recent generations have been both witness and victim.

Allegiance to the nation to which one belongs is not necessarily rational, but is it to one's discredit? It is not unlike the relationship of a man to his parents, a relationship into which rationality does not enter. If it were rational, we would certainly undertake a market survey before selecting our parents or before selecting the nation to which we would wish to belong. In modern society a man may secede from his nation. Those people, however, who are loyal to their nation, who belong with an internal essence to a specific culture and social environment, see in this belongingness a value that should be nurtured. . . .

The Jewish people owe a great deal to the values that may be called humanistic, and therefore the problem of Orthodox Haredi Judaism has taken on great significance today. The claim of Haredi Judaism that it was halakhah which preserved the Jewish people throughout the generations, is—from the humanistic view—flawed for a number of reasons. First, this argument exploits the Torah as though it were an instrumentality, as though the belief in God and the devotion to God's commandments exist solely for the purpose of keeping the Jewish people alive rather than for the purpose of worshipping God. This argument—which enslaves religion to national survival—appears for the first time in the 17th century. In a polemic against Uriel Acosta, Rabbi Yehudah Aryeh of Modena poses the question where would we be if everyone could develop his own point of view (as Uriel Acosta did); he argues that the unity of the Jewish nation demands adherence to halakhah and to the halakhic establishment. The rabbi's seemingly innocent argument was used continually to the 20th century as the justification for religious faith and subservience to the religious establishment.

Second, the argument is historically incorrect. Indeed the Jewish people adhered to halakhah through all the generations, until about 200 years ago. However, this phenomenon was actually caused by the fact that Jews who did not adhere to the halakhah were forced to leave the community. In other words, the leaders of the Jewish people did not countenance pluralism. Pluralism has prevailed from the onset of the Emancipation enabling today's Jews who live in the United States, for example, to practice "American Judaism," or "World Judaism." The word Judaism is used here to mean Jewry in the sense of the general Jewish public, not in the sense of a particular "ism." In those matters that touch upon the interests of the Jewish nation and the principles that enable it to live, all the various religious communities, the Orthodox, Reform, Conservative and atheist, are partners in a struggle against any attempt to subvert citizens' rights. Even so, a dilemma exists in the Western world: the Jewish public is conceived of (in its own eyes and in the eyes of others) as both a religious community and an ethnic group. The ways of history are strange: precisely in the USSR the Jewish people was considered a national unit in its own right and not in order to justify the wrongs that Russia committed against the Jews.

The attempt of the Jews to leave Russia was a struggle of principle. Many people in the world saw it as a struggle for the basic right of every man to move freely from any land in which he found himself. Jews, more than any other people, were forced to adopt this principle. It is one of the principles of Humanism recognized from the time of the Magna Carta to the present day, according to which a man always has the option of moving to another place if he feels himself oppressed in the land where he lives, if he is prevented from struggling against this oppression, and if he does not have the option of changing his situation.

The option of migrating to another place was cited in the Talmud in the words: "God favored the people of Israel when he spread them out among the nations." The fact that in the past it was always possible to move to a place free of oppression was the decisive factor in the continued existence of Jewish life and the right to do so has remained one of the basic principles of Humanism throughout the generations. . . .

Yaakov Malkin
(1926–   )

Introduction

Yaakov Malkin is one of the leaders of the Israeli Secular Humanistic movement. Since 1993, he has been editor of its journal, *Free Judaism*, and chairman of its Academic Council. He is also the co-chairman of the International Institute for Secular Humanistic Judaism.

Malkin was born in Warsaw, Poland, in 1926, then moved with his family to Palestine in 1934 and attended school in Tel Aviv. He went on to study at the Hebrew University of Jerusalem, the University of Paris, and Tel Aviv University, and was appointed lecturer in rhetoric at the Hebrew University of Jerusalem.

Malkin has been a theater, film and literary critic since 1946. In the years before Israeli statehood, he was director and broadcaster of the Hagana Underground Radio. He has worked as director, screenwriter, translator, and literary adviser for several theater and film productions, was a founder-director of community art and culture centers, and in 1971 won the M. Katz Adult Education Award.

As founder of the community center movement in Israel, Malkin has explored ways to create viable secular Jewish communities within the urban centers of Israel.

The Beliefs of the Secular Jew

3. Jewish Pluralism Since Mount Sinai

The perceptions of Judaism current among those working within a narrow field of specialization—be it talmudic or scientific, professional or commercial—are distorted by several fallacies. One of the most damaging is the suggestion that Judaism is a uniform culture, an exclusive path rejecting all who stray from it as idol worshippers, and demanding that all identify with one narrow definition of it. Judaism is a changing, multifaceted and dynamic national culture. It allows for many ways of implementing its principles, leaves room for conflicts between the old and the new, features a variety of religious rituals and a myriad of secular cultural expressions. These processes of diversification and pluralization have intensified in modern times due to secularization, mass waves of immigration, and the concentration of a third of the Jewish people in the state of Israel, in which Jewish traditions and cultures from over one hundred countries now converge. In the Diaspora, groups affiliated with different trends of Judaism can lead separate lives and need not engage in social or political contact: there is no need to foster links between Lubavitcher or Satmar Hasidim, members of Temple Emanu-el, and the secular circles associated with the Society for Ethical Culture in New York. In Israel, the dense togetherness forces all to mingle, at times in the same city, or the same neighborhood, or even the same building. This encounter takes place within a democratic political culture, where governments depend on coalitions, and where every group is, either willingly or unwillingly, influenced by everyone else. These sustained contacts between various groups and trends of Judaism, as well as the growing number of marriages—now about a fifth—between members of different Jewish ethnic groups living in Israel, have increased the awareness of pluralism among secular and religious Jews. A secular educational policy that strives to develop awareness of all forms of Jewish experience and resists attempts to negate certain traditions or to favor one over another, has also contributed to this endeavour.

4. "Judaism" Versus "Judaisms"

. . . Yeshayahu Leibowitz is right in his claim that there is no "Judaism says," but only "it is said in Judaism." It is impossible to speak in the name of "Judaism," which lacks a centralistic structure or leading authority, and one can only quote different spokespersons representing different groups within the Jewish people. There is no binding credo that could turn anyone denying it into a non-Jew or a nonreligious Jew. Observant Jews who do not believe in God as a separate entity, or in a certain image of God, are still religious Jews because they observe His commandments. Nonobservant Jews can faithfully believe in the existence or the roles of God, but their opinions do not turn them into religious Jews. Hence, there is no exhaustive definition of either religious or secular Judaism nor a lifestyle typical of all Jews, or even of most Jews. There is no approach shared by all Jews per se, and therefore, it makes no sense to speak in the name of Judaism, but only in the name of people within Judaism. Understanding the culture developed by the Jewish people over the last three thousand years demands acquaintance with all its hues, a grasp of the pluralistic essence of Judaism as a whole, and an understanding of all its trends throughout its history. This pluralism is as old as Judaism itself, and in fact begins with it. The refugees of Egyptian slavery, who gathered under Moses' leadership to launch the first slave rebellion in history, were a "mixed multitude," that included tribal groups and many others who decided to join them. The constitutive assembly of the "children of Israel" was meant as an expression of unity, showing their commitment to one Jewish religion. At this gathering, a covenant was struck between a one and only God and a unique and special people, who chose to believe that they had been chosen by the God of the cosmos. But bitter disputes erupted even at this early stage, and the echoes of these strifes resound throughout Jewish history. Instead of one, two totally different and radically opposed religions emerged. One is a religion of worship and sacrifice to a god shaped in the image of a calf from the believers' own jewelry. The other is a religion of moral commandments, in which instructions concerning the proper behavior of human beings toward one another appear as part of the covenant between God and the people. This God is abstract and shapeless, a power which, in Moses' view, can only be defined as a potential for the future—"I shall be what I shall be." The one religion, led by Aaron the priest, is a religion of ritual and ecstasy, of dance, song, and sacrifices offered to a concrete, calf-like god. The other, led by Moses the prophet, is a religion of vision and of a written covenant with God, a covenant stating that the behavior of human beings is determined by rules and laws written down in a book. At the center of this religion is a book, containing unique and special commandments, rather than a calf that can be created or found in any temple devoted to any god. The historicity of this account, describing the foundation of the nation as a constitutive assembly, is obviously hard to ascertain. But two fundamental beliefs stamped the Jewish national consciousness: the collective memory of the foundation of the Jewish nation as a covenant of general moral principles that extend beyond the Jewish people, and the notion that, from the outset, the nation was marked by cultural, social, and religious splits, that would culminate later in the division of the Jewish kingdom into two separate realms, differing in their religion and their practices. In the national memory, this constitutive assembly is an historical event that marks the birth of the Jewish people as a distinct national, political and religious entity, different from other nations. The features of this event became the defining features of Judaism: the relentless struggle between priest and prophet and between ethics and cult, determined the pluralistic character of Judaism. The Egyptian Pharaoh Amenhotep IV who, in the second millennium B.C. engraved in stone the account of his victory over "Israel" and proclaimed he had destroyed them forever, recognized a unique national entity named "Israel." A copy of this stone is found in the Israel Museum in Jerusalem. The Jewish people also linked the foundation of their nation to a struggle against the Egyptians, describing the crushing defeat of the Egyptian army. Although the "historicity" of the biblical narrative may be hard to determine, it is highly symbolic that the pluralistic character of Judaism is already part of its earliest historical memories.

5. Cultural and Ideological Splits in Judaism

Like variations on a theme, echoes of the basic conflict between the priests of ritual and the prophets of justice resound throughout the history of Jewish culture. During the period of the First Temple, the prophets admonished the members of the religious and political establishment for their tolerance of oppression and for their exploitation of the poor and destitute. Shortly after King Solomon inaugurates the First Temple, Jeroboam erects other competing temples in another Jewish kingdom. Jerusalem becomes the capital of the smaller Jewish realm. The larger realm, the kingdom of Israel, returns to the cult of the golden calf, whereas the hub of the Jerusalem Temple is the book containing the ethical commandments. But the "true" prophets, who themselves were a minority within the prophetic community in both kingdoms, tell us that the Jews not only worship the God of Israel but also many other local gods, from the Baal and Astarte family. Jews visit ritual prostitutes in the temples of other nations, erect altars "on every high hill and under every leafy tree,' host the prophets of other gods and allow them to join the courts of their own kings. The testimony of the biblical prophets, which we have no reason to doubt, shows that Canaanization preceded Hellenization, and was certainly more dangerous than the latter, as it also included the secular exploitation of children and their sacrifice to the Moloch. The picture emerging from the biblical description emphasizes the splits and the divergences that characterize Jewish culture since the beginnings of Jewish settlement in Canaan. Ever since, most Jews have tended to absorb the cultures of the nations among whom they dwell. Immediately after the destruction of the First Temple, the vast majority of Jews begins to show a preference for life among other nations and in faraway lands. Cyrus' edict, like the Balfour Declaration two and a half thousand years later, inspires only a small minority of the Jewish people to settle in the land of Israel, although, in both cases, the land was promised to the Jews as a national home. The founding of the Hasmonean kingdom during the Second Temple intensified pluralization in Jewish society and Jewish culture, in the land of Israel as well as outside it. Jews who were considered Hellenizers, and thus idol worshippers in the eyes of their opponents, view themselves as loyal to the laws and the spirit of Judaism. This loyalty does not prevent them from enjoying the rich pleasures offered by Hellenic culture, such as bathhouses like the one in Acre flaunting a statue of Aphrodite, which Rabban Gamaliel visited claiming: "She came into my purview, not I into hers." Greek culture also offered theatres built in the center of Jewish Jerusalem next to the gymnasium and the stadium, a rich literature that includes Philo and Josephus, new artistic achievements in the field of music and visual arts, inspiring the creation of mosaics and statues in synagogues such as those found in the Galilee and in Nehardea. The contact with Greek philosophy and literature also included an encounter with the atheistic trends that appealed to a great Torah scholar like Elisha ben Avuyah, whose steadfast friendship with R. Meir remained unaffected by Elisha's intellectual stirrings. The basic contradictions between the tendency toward integration into Hellenistic culture and that of seclusion within traditional Jewish culture crystallized in the variety of trends and groups which made up Judaism during and after the Second Temple: differences between Pharisees and Sadducees, Essenes, Jewish Christians, radical zealots and supporters of compromise with the foreign rulers, Jews seeking to ensure Jewish continuity in centers such as Yavneh, and others willing to die for freedom at Masada. Josephus epitomizes this pluralism, in his life as well as in the attitude which Judaism has evinced toward his memory and his writings. His figure unites conflicting strands—a loyal freedom fighter, a wise politician who knows when to admit defeat and shrewdly estimate the balance of power, a Roman writer who devotes his work to the history and the wars of the Jewish people and to the struggle against Hellenistic anti-Semitism, the self same anti-Semitism that Christianity was to inherit and develop. Josephus defines himself as a Pharisee, but before choosing his own path within Judaism he became acquainted with all its main trends—he studied Essene, Sadducee and Pharisee doctrines, and chose the latter. Christianity, which split away from Judaism in Paul's times and became a separate culture with a distinct religion, began as one of many Jewish sects. This was certainly the case during the time of Jesus and of the Jewish-Christian synagogue in Jerusalem. After Jesus' death, this synagogue was led by his brother Jacob, and not even the Sanhedrin excluded it from the community of Israel.

Shulamit Aloni
(1928–   )

Introduction

Shulamit Aloni is a lawyer, feminist, an outstanding defender of civil rights in Israel, a member of the Knesset, and a minister in the cabinet of Prime Minister Rabin since 1992.

Shulamit Aloni was born in Israel in 1928. She graduated from the Teacher's Seminary and began her career in education but later matriculated at the Hebrew University, from which she obtained a law degree in 1956.

Aloni became active in Israeli politics and was first elected to the Knesset in 1965. In 1973, she formed a new party, the Citizens Rights Movement (Ratz), and was elected to represent it in the Knesset. In 1974 she served as minister without portfolio. In 1992, she won reelection as the head of a new coalition party, Meretz. Prime Minister Rabin appointed her minister of education in his government, but her attempts to secularize education led to her being shifted to a less sensitive cabinet post.

Aloni has been a columnist for the newspaper *Yediot Ahronot*, and has written articles for the magazine *L'ishah* as well as other publications. In 1980, she received a Leadership Award from the Society for Humanistic Judaism, and was instrumental in helping to found the Israeli section of the Society.

Defending Human Rights

We must determine that the universal legal concept of the rule of law is not merely a formal matter concerning the obeying and enforcement of one law or another, but is related to the spirit of the law. In the democratic world, the rule of law means justice and fairness, human liberty and the restraint of authority, the universality of laws and the equality of all before the law.

Similarly, it is important to remember what most Israelis are unaware of—that democracy is not only the will of the majority or majority rule. Even though everyone knows that Italian Fascism and German Nazism enjoyed the support of the vast majority of their countries' population, and although their leaders made no claim for democracy, the politicians and journalists and opinion-makers of Israel accord legitimacy in the name of "the will of the majority" to any deviant and anti-democratic law passed by the Knesset, under pressure by one party or another or for the speculative needs of staying in power.

Any jurist knows that there can be no rule of law and justice without restraints upon the capricious will of the majority and without the subordination of the ruler to a supreme normative system. The Jewish legal heritage recognizes the principle of going along with the majority, but alongside this rule is one that is no less clear and obligatory: "You shall not be led into wrongdoing by the majority" (Exodus 23:2). The supreme normative system which every well-ordered society needs must follow both these principles.

The tragedy of Israeli democracy is that it lacks a system of overriding norms, according to which the government and the Knesset are required to guide and to restrain acts of legislation. We have no constitution, no bill of human rights, no history of democratic life.

The Jews came here from 102 countries, most of them from Eastern Europe or Islamic nations where they were a defensive and seclusive minority, fearful of the authorities and far removed from carrying the burden of sovereign responsibility for service, security and their neighbors. When the state was established, we did not undergo the necessary revolution from a defensive minority, seclusive and fearing for itself and its remnants. We instantly became the government, the legislature, the judiciary, the army and the police—and thereby took upon ourselves the reponsibility for the rights of every person, every group and every minority.

The only transformation we underwent with the establishment of the state is that we now have the power to impose our authority on others: to collect taxes, to conscript, to give out land, to confiscate land, to impose order. But on the other hand, we have not limited ourselves, our leaders or our legislators by the kind of restraint called for by the very power and authority given them. Because we in the past lacked the authority and power to impose our will upon others and to coerce them according to our needs, today we have an irresistible impulse to exploit our power and authority in the legislature and the government to anchor any caprice and any religious demand, national or factional, in the framework of the law.

The Knesset has had many opportunities to pass a "Basic Law: Human Rights" as well as a "Basic Law: Legislation" that would have enabled the Supreme Court to serve as a constitutional court and strike down as illegal any laws that violated the foundations of the rule of law in its enlightened and universal sense. The big parties did not do so because they did not want to give up their bargaining power nor restrain by an overriding law the various nationalist, factionalist, economic, partisan, or religious impulses.

The Knesset even refused to adopt the principles set down in the Declaration of Independence in May 1948—which the High Court of Justice determined to be our collective credo—as an overriding law by which subsequent legislation would be tested. When the Knesset debated the foundations of a justice bill, even the Labor Party—then in opposition—decided to relinquish the principles of the Declaration of Independence and sufficed with "laws according to the Jewish heritage," in the hope of buying the support of the National Religious Party—then in the coalition—in a matter of power politics.

The faith in Israeli democracy just because we are a pluralistic society with many parties and hold elections from time to time, is exaggerated. The government always has a majority in the Knesset, and this majority can—and does—decide anything that one of the coalition's components wants. This rule applies to matters of clearly individual concern, as well as to matters of coercion and discrimination regarding certain groups such as women, minorities, secularists, members of other religions, etc.

Similarly, the Knesset majority can legislate extra-territorial laws in defiance of international law. And create different legal systems for Jews and Arabs—and it does so particularly in the occupied territories. We must remember—and be reminded—that the recognition of the natural, inalienable respect and equality of rights due all mankind are the foundations of freedom, justice and peace. We must remember that our people has been among the most oppressed and unfortunate victims of the contempt for human rights.

Only in a society that assures every human being freedom of speech and belief, freedom from fear and want, and defends these freedoms from the rule of arbitrary law, can the rule of law be said to exist in practice. Only in such a society will a person not be forced, as a last resort, to risk rebelling against injustice and oppression.

Israel has not yet reached this level. In light of the political reality in which we live, and given the satisfaction of the prevailing governmental system with Israeli democracy and the despatch with which laws are enacted by the power of the disciplined ruling majority, we can expect long years of struggle until we attain the rule of law; both in its universal sense and in the sense of an enlightened Judaism upholding justice, fairness, truth and peace.

The hope that we shall succeed in doing so rests absurdly on the growth of religious coercion and nationalist extremism. It is a law of nature that every action creates a reaction. Today democracy is under such fierce attack that there exists the hope that its adherents will wake up and respond with the same degree of power, and free us from the dark age of tribalism descending upon us.

Jerusalem Post, May 5, 1986

Gershon Weiler (1926–1995)

Introduction

Gershon Weiler was born in Szeged, Hungary, in 1926. He survived the Holocaust and after the war made aliya to Israel, where he studied at the Hebrew University of Jerusalem. When Weiler graduated in 1954 he received a fellowship to Oxford University and completed his doctoral studies there in 1957. He then held teaching positions at the universities of Dublin in Ireland, and at Canberra and Melbourne in Australia. In 1973 Weiler returned to Israel, where he was appointed professor of philosophy at the University of Tel Aviv.

Weiler became well known in Israel as a proponent of the separation of religion and the state, and published widely. Among his most important books are *Jewish Theocracy, Philosophy of Everyday,* and *State and Education.*

JEWISH THEOCRACY

It is strange to recall that in the great debate between secularists and anti-secularists that agitated the young Jewish settlement in Palestine in the first decades of this century, Gordon entered the field as an anti-secularist, in defense of tradition, against Brenner and Berdichevski, the chief secularist spokesmen of the day. It is strange, because from the vantage point of the present we see only too clearly that what makes a doctrine secularist is not its readiness or lack of it to accord respect to religious tradition but its refusal to accept that tradition on its own terms. Re-interpretations of the *halakha qua* national culture contribute far more toward robbing it of its obligatory content than frontal attacks upon its historical and/or theological foundations. The attack of the early secularists had to fail for it was aiming at the impossible: a sudden and conscious rejection of the past and its patterns of thought. But secularization itself has become an undeniable fact. It was accomplished with the aid of those thinkers who, like Achad Ha'am and Gordon, re-interpreted the theocentric past in ethnocentric and anthropocentric terms, suggesting thereby that it is this new reading of tradition that correctly expresses what it had always really meant. When Ezra and his successors effected their dramatic reversal in the thinking of the Jewish people about itself, they too had built upon a new reading of the national past. They succeeded in incorporating *their version* of the history of the kingdom into the official history of the religious community; being thus incorporated the kingdom gave no further trouble. The same thing happened now to the *halakhic* conception of Jewish history. Those secularizers who won the day did not reject *halakha* outright but came to terms with it in the shape of tradition. They incorporated it into something else, they made it possible to look at it with affection and yet from the outside and thereby pulled the ground from under its claim to unconditioned supremacy and obedience. From then to this day, *halakha* must fight for itself amidst conditions that are inimical to its very essence. Although the Jewish people have become secular for historical, religous and mainly sociological reasons, it is still concerned with *halakha*, but this concern is neither exclusive nor overriding. The practice of the *halakha* is just one consideration, even if an important one, but still one among many others. The Jewish people *qua* a religious community whose sole *raison d'etre* is obeying the will of God as expressed in *halakha,* apart from a few surviving pockets of the extreme orthodox, no longer exists.

The process of secularization has been completed by the destruction of European Jewry during World War II and by the subsequent success of political Zionism. The first event not only destroyed the centres of population where life was lived, by and large, within the framework of *halakha* but it also shook to its foundation the faith of the survivors and their respect for the rabbinic establishment. Just as the spiritual ancestors of this establishment, the Pharisees, were the only cohesive group capable of coming to terms with the destruction of the last vestiges of nationhood some nineteen centuries ago, so now the Zionists were the only Jews who needed no conceptual re-orientation to be able to cope with the disaster. It is not surprising therefore that the survivors accepted quite naturally the basic Zionist attitudes. Zionism was ready; it had the doctrine of Achad Ha'am on hand. It also had a programme of action. The survivors spoken of here are not the actual survivors of the camps of Poland and Germany but the whole Jewish people. For even those who had watched the horror of Europe from the other shore knew that they were survivors. Had the fortunes of war gone the other way, they too would have shared the fate of those whom they could now mourn. While before World War II the synagogue was, generally speaking, anti-Zionist, after the war it adopted Zionism to such an extent that it sometimes seems that it has taken the place of religion. True enough, synagogues are still attended and during High Holidays much attended; Jewish parents still impart a kind of Jewish education to their children, the content of this is inevitably religious. But synagogue affiliation and attendance or Jewish education are now motivated by the secular ideal of group cohesion and not by the *halakhic* ideal of doing what is right in the eyes of God. That the affirmation of the ideal of cohesion takes a religious form is inevitable in a culture that developed nothing but its religious dimension. But the content is manifestly missing. It cannot be doubted today that the rabbinic establishment was right when it sounded alarm at the first approach of enlightenment and Zionism; these movements were indeed secularist and as such destructive of *halakhic* authority. The rabbis realized then what many still refuse to accept viz. that the new ideas constitute a radical break in the continuity of that Jewish history which begins with the reforms of Ezra.

The Jewish state was ultimately established by people who no longer saw themselves as instruments of a divine will, who no longer thought of themselves as the spectators of history, as Abravanel would have had it, but as active participants in the shaping of their own fate. This is the fact of the secularization of the Jewish people. Nevertheless it is not yet recognized for what it is. Here too consciousness is lagging behind the facts of history. The fact is that the life conditions of the Jewish people presuppose a secular approach to life. This is not the same, however, as an open avowal of such an approach. It is not so surprising, after all, that a generation which lived through changes on a scale that can be compared only to the experience of the generation of Ezra and Nehemiah, should still be attached to its earlier patterns of thought and that it should try to articulate the new reality in the concepts of the old. It is this condition, so typical of transit generations, that explains the very possibility of a slogan like "Jewish state according to the *Torah.*" We have seen how the *Torah,* as *halakhically* understood, emerged at the precise moment when the very idea of statehood was rejected. So the intellectual labour necessary to make the fundamental conflict between *halakha* and statehood understood, is not yet complete. There is still much reluctance to discuss openly the fundamentals of the religion/state problem, as contrasted with the day-to-day issues which emerge as a consequence of its permanent presence. It is perhaps functional to pretend that there is no incompatibility, only accidental breakdowns. This is not our conclusion. A *halakhic* conception of life, whether anti-state or ambitiously aiming at total control of the state, cannot live in peace with the democratic state of Israel.

Lastly, brief mention should be made of the phenomenon of "return," of orthodox revivalism. It is not something which changes anything in the analysis offered here. Neo-orthodoxy is to be understood as an offspring of American revivalism and Oriental dissatisfaction with the modern world, rather like Islamic revivalism. It is not a new response to the modern world but a rejection of it. The strongest claim that can be made for Jewish neo-orthodoxy is that it has perhaps the potential of destroying the state from within. It is certainly not the answer to the genuine problem set by its existence and by the need to maintain it.

(Chapter 9).

Amos Oz
(1939–   )

Introduction

Amos Oz holds an acclaimed place among the new generation of Israeli-born writers. In addition to being a prize-winning novelist, he is also a journalist and a major public figure who is often referred to as a "man of conscience." In his works of fiction and his essays, he explores the human condition with rare empathy, with an appreciation for the fine line that often exists between comedy and tragedy.

Oz was born in Jerusalem and was sent by his parents to an elementary school with strong religious tendencies. But at age fourteen, Oz left Jerusalem to become a member of Kibbutz Hulda, which was antireligious and socialist. He studied philosophy and literature at the Hebrew University and was a visiting fellow at Oxford. As an adult he declared himself a secular Jew.

Oz's first two novels were published before he was thirty. The first is set on a kibbutz and the second in Jerusalem. These have continued to represent the two major foci of Oz's literary universe. Another theme of his writing is the problem of bereaved parents who lose a child during wartime. Many of Oz's stories show that primitive, irrational behavior is part of humanity's fate, as if the gods were laughing at the human illusion of a purely sane, rational existence.

After the Six-Day War, Oz was one of a team which produced a volume of soul-searching discussions with combatants, *The Sixth Day.* Oz is well-know as a dove and has used his talent as a writer to pursue peace through the airing of competing extremist views.

Oz was awarded the German Publishers Peace Prize in 1992. His most recent novel, *Fima,* is a comedy of ideas in which he again presents characters who are fascinated by ethical and moral dilemmas, and who are full of compassion. He lives in the desert, in Arad, and teaches literature at Ben-Gurion University.

THE SLOPES OF LEBANON

The real problem is that there are some religious Jews who do not and cannot accept any law except rabbinic law. The heart of the problem is a question of the source of authority: Are the people sovereign, through the Knesset and its laws, or is there no sovereign other than the Sovereign of the Universe, no law other than the law of Torah?

The problem can be papered over for the sake of domestic peace. It can be delayed. It can be repressed. But it cannot be eliminated. The problem is solely for the religious public to tackle, inasmuch as virtually all secular Jews have accepted, and will continue to accept, sometimes with clenched teeth, all the laws enacted by the Knesset—including laws passed due to coalition pressure and shady deals. At most, some of them will be pushed to a sense of internal exile.

The religious public, however, stands at a crossroad. They will have to make up their minds: either the messianic era has already arrived and the time has come to shove rabbinic law down the throat of a majority that does not want it, or else the messianic era has not yet arrived, and they will have to go on praying, believing, and waiting.

If widespread sectors of the religious community believe that the Messiah is at the gate, then no compromise is possible and there is, from their point of view, no room for tolerance and forbearance. In that case, there is no choice for the secular Zionist majority but to grant full autonomy to the religious people and to the limited territories in which there is such a messianic majority: the right of self-determination to the point of secession, for both the ultranationlist religious Jewish settlers in Hebron and the anti-Zionist ultra-Orthodox Jews in Mea Shearim and some other neighborhoods. Messianic logic leads to a partition of the land, not just between Jews and Palestinians, but between libertarian Zionist Jews and those Jews who cannot accept the people as the source of authority, sovereignty, and law. Thus let there be a Zionist state for the Zionists, and alongside it—under conditions of peace and security—a Palestinian state for the Palestinians, an ultra-Orthodox state for the ultra-Orthodox, and a settlers' state for the settlers of Gush Emunim. In the words of American poet Robert Frost, "Good fences make good neighbors."

The option of separation and secession is infinitely better than the danger of continuous civil strife. The reality of partition is preferable, in every respect. The secular Zionist public which is ready to separate peacefully from the Palestinians should not be frightened by the idea of establishing one or two ultra-Orthodox Jewish "Vatican Cities," a few dozen acres each, nor by the idea of autonomy for Gush Emunim settlers within a zone of Palestinian autonomy. The division is a sad fact, and the separation will be no more than an honest expression of this division: We will not obtrude ourselves on anyone who is unwilling or incapable of being Israeli because Israel is too Jewish for him, or not Jewish enough—in short, anyone who feels that a Zionist, democratic Israel conflicts with his principles. A Zionist, democratic Israel will be able, under certain conditions, to exist and even to flourish alongside an independent Palestine, an autonomous Torahland, and an autonomous settlerland. We are not thinking, heaven forbid, about dispossession, exile, deportation, or ghettoization. We are talking about granting a piece of land for self-determination and self-fulfillment to whoever feels he has not attained self-determination and fulfillment within the State of Israel: to the Palestinian who will not settle for anything less than the total actualization of his nationalism, and to the Jew who will not settle for anything less than a total reign of Torah. It is fascinating to contemplate that if Israel were to disappear suddenly, the Palestinians might immediately jump at one another's throats even as the various Orthodox Jewish sects would be drawn into ferocious confrontation over the form of the rabbinic government they so fervently desire. Nevertheless, there is no reason for a Zionist state to take upon itself the role of bouncer in a hall full of groups that unanimously wish the bouncer would disappear. Thus, the question lies before the religious public: Do you want a theocratic government ruling over tiny, scattered pieces of territory, or coexistence at the price of giving up the realization of a rabbinic regime? Messiah Now at the price of severance from the House of Israel, or acceptance of the secular democratic principle by which the people are the ultimate sovereign, the source of law and authority through the instruments of Knesset and legislation?

The question is a religious, a theological one. Let us not relate to it as if it were a question of policing. Let the religious public and its spiritual leaders give us their answer, one way or another.

Yehuda Amichai (1924–)

Introduction

Yehuda Amichai is a major Hebrew poet, novelist, and playwright. Many believe that he is modern Israel's greatest poet. He helped to create a new style of Hebrew poetry, changing the language to include the terms of common speech. In his novels and plays, he explores the nature of Jewish identity in the late twentieth century.

Amichai was born in Germany in 1924 to an Orthodox family but was greatly influenced by German writers and German culture. His father, Amichai says, was disappointed that he left religious practice, but "love won over condemnation." The family arrived in Jerusalem in 1935, but Amichai is regarded as a "native" Israeli poet and writer. Amichai volunteered to serve in the British army during World War II and later served in the Israeli army. He started publishing his poems in the early 1950s. His major work, *Not of This Time, Not of This Place* appeared in 1963. Some of his themes were love, war, the passage of time, and memories of his father.

Amichai's poetry and stories have a unique style, breaking with a realistic tradition in Israeli literature. In his later poetry, he gives expression to the difficulties Israelis face living in a land racked by wars and insecurity. Much of his poetry is centered on Jerusalem, where he now lives. His writing is expressive of profound sensitivity and humanism. When Israeli Prime Minister Rabin was awarded the Nobel Peace Prize, Amichai was invited to read four of his poems at the ceremony, and was also quoted by Rabin in his Nobel address.

MY HEAD, MY HEAD

When my head got banged on the door, I screamed,
"My head, my head." And I screamed, "Door, door."
And I did not scream, "Mother," and not, "God."
Nor did I speak of the vision of the End of Days
of a world where there will be no heads and doors anymore.

When you stroke my head I whispered,
"My head, my head," and I whispered, "Your hand, your hand."
And I did not whisper, "Mother," and not, "God."
And I did not see wonderful visions
of hands stroking heads in the opening heavens.

Whatever I scream and speak and whisper is
to comfort myself: My head, my head.
Door, door. Your hand, your hand.

AN ARAB SHEPHERD LOOKS FOR A KID ON MOUNT ZION

An Arab shepherd looks for a kid on Mount Zion,
And on the hill across I am looking for my little son.
An Arab shepherd and a Jewish father

In their temporary failure.
Our two voices meet above
The Sultan's Pool in the valley between.
We both want them to stay out
The son and the kid, out of the process
Of that terrible machine:—of Had Gadya.

Later we found them among the shrubs,
And our voices returned to us crying and laughing inside.
Searches for a kid or for a son
Were always
The beginning of a new religion in these hills.

THE MILL AT YEMIN MOSHE

This mill never ground flour
It ground sacred air and birds
Of Bialik's longings, it ground
Milled words and milled time, it ground
Rain and even bomb shells
But it didn't grind flour. Ever.

Now it has discovered us,
And grinds our lives day by day,
To make us into peace flour
To bake us into peace bread
For the coming generations.

I FEEL GOOD IN MY TROUSERS

If the Romans hadn't glorified their victory
With the Arch of Titus, we wouldn't know
The shape of the Menorah from the Temple.
But we know the shape of Jews
Because they multiplied unto me.

I feel good in my trousers
In which my victory is hidden
Even though I know I'll die
And even though I know the Messiah won't come,
I feel good.

I'm made from remnants of flesh and blood
And leftovers of philosophies. I'm the generation
Of the pot-bottom: sometimes at night
When I can't sleep,
I hear the hard spoon scratching
And scraping the bottom of the pot.

But I feel good in my trousers,
I feel good.

SABBATH LIE

On Friday, at twilight of a summer day
While the smells of food and prayer rose from every house
And the sound of the Sabbath angels' wings was in the air,
While still a child I started to lie to my father:

"I went to another synagogue."

I don't know if he believed me or not
But the taste of the lie was good and sweet on my tongue
And in all the houses that night
Hymns rose up along with lies
To celebrate the Sabbath.
And in all the houses that night
Sabbath angels died like flies in a lamp,
And lovers put mouth to mouth,
Blew each other up until they floated upward,
Or burst.

And since then the lie has been good and sweet on my tongue
And since then I always go to another synagogue.
And my father returned the lie when he died:
"I've gone to another life."

GREAT TRANQUILITY: QUESTIONS AND ANSWERS

People in the painfully bright hall
spoke about religion
In the life of modern man
And about God's place in it.

People spoke in excited voices
Like at airports.
I left them:
I opened an iron door over which was written
"Emergency" and I entered into
A great tranquillity: questions and answers.

A. B. Yehoshua
(1936–   )

Introduction

A. B. Yehoshua is an Israeli novelist, playwright, and social critic. Many of his novels have been translated into English and other languages, and he has become one of the most widely read of Israeli authors in the United States and elsewhere.

Yehoshua was born to a Sephardi family in Jerusalem in 1936. After spending some time in his youth in Paris, he returned to Israel and received a B.A. in philosophy and Hebrew literature from Hebrew University in 1961. He then settled in Haifa, where he taught at the University of Haifa, beginning in 1972, and served as dean of students for a time.

He began writing novels and short stories and is regarded as the foremost representative of the "new generation" of Israeli literature. His symbolic and psychological short stories, written in a surrealistic style, explore the moral dilemmas and problems of the young Israeli. His short story "Facing the Forests" is considered a minor classic and is included in almost every collection of the new Israeli literature. It reflects the dilemmas of the humanistic young Israeli with a sensitive conscience and a tendency for reflection who is caught up by the moral problems of the Arab-Israeli conflict. His novel *The Lover,* which takes place during the 1973 Yom Kippur War, exhibits his movement toward realism, balancing the real and the grotesque which mirrored Israeli society at its nadir. Later novels, including *Five Seasons, A Late Divorce,* and the more recent *Mr. Mani,* have won him critical acclaim in the United States.

BETWEEN RIGHT AND RIGHT

The ideological conception I shall try to present is but one such conception, but in my view it is the only one by which a Jew can continue to live after the Holocaust.

First of all, I view the Holocaust as part of history. I say part of history because attempts have been made to describe it as being somehow outside the course of history, an exception to the rules of history that operated until then, a disruption of normal comprehensible processes. I do not see it that way. The Holocaust, it is true, was the nadir, but it is part of a chain of events following a set pattern ever since we went into exile. It marks the climax of a conflict that has always been going on, without ceasing, between the Jewish people and the world. That is why, despite its awesome scope and intensity, the Holocaust was not a onetime occurrence. Based on historical facts that still obtain, it can recur.

The Holocaust Is the Final Decisive Proof of the Failure Diaspora Existence

If anyone had illusions about our ability to find our place in the world as a people scattered among the nations, the Holocaust provided the final proof of where this form of existence is likely to lead us.

To all believers that it is the mission of the Jewish people, by this form of existence, to disseminate some spiritual message among the world's nations, the Holocaust demonstrated the nations' true response to this calling. And what could be more symbolic than that it was precisely the Germans, among whom we had such a sublime sense of spiritual vocation accompanied by elaborate theories of spiritual symbiosis (witness Hermann Cohen and others, and the place the Jews occupied in German cultural and intellectual life on the eve of the Holocaust), that it was they of all people who presented us with this resounding reply.

But most horrendous of all is that the situation into which we were cast by the Holocaust came about with no "choice" whatsoever on our part. In the Crusades or the Inquisition, for example, we could say that we brought persecution upon ourselves out of steadfastness to our faith and to sanctify our world view. Faced with the choice of conversion, we chose to remain Jews, and paid the price of death. In the Holocaust even this "choice" was denied us and we cannot say that by our deaths we sanctified the name of God, for we had no alternative. We were not even given the freedom to choose death. Death was forced on us. It was forced on those who believed in God and on those who did not believe in God; it was forced on those who identified as Jews and on those who did not want to identify as Jews. Our death was decreed for the absurd reason of our being a race, which of course we never were. The Holocaust made an absurdity of our existence and beliefs.

The Jewish people's terrible sacrifice in the Holocaust was for no purpose. The Hebrew word *shoah,* with its echoes of utter devastation, expresses the nature of this sacrifice immeasurably better than the word *holocaust,* a Christian term for a whole burnt offering, a sin offering by someone for something. Those whom the concentration camp flames consumed did not die for any idea, for any world view; they did not meet their deaths for the continued existence of the Jewish people or for its imminent redemption. There are some who say, or at least try to console themselves by saying, that it was the Holocaust that, as it were, begat the State of Israel. This assertion I reject totally, on both factual and moral grounds. The State of Israel could also have been established had there been no Holocaust. In fact, the State of Israel would today be much, much stronger had a third of its people not been wiped out. And on moral grounds, the Holocaust simply cannot be accepted by virtue of the later establishment of the State of Israel. If we were confronted with the choice: no Holocaust and therefore no State of Israel, I doubt that any of us would dare say: Let there be a Holocaust so that the State of Israel can be established.

The Holocaust proved to us the danger of our abnormal existence among the nations, the danger of the nonlegitimacy of our presence among the nations. It was easy for the Nazis to destroy us and to get other peoples to participate in our destruction, either actively or by acquiescence, because our status in the world was not legitimate. We were outside of history, we were not "like all the nations." Because by our way of life we were "other," different from all others, it was easy to regard us as subhuman, and as subhuman our blood could be spilled freely. The first to be seized upon in any national shock, in any instance of social unrest, were the Jews.

The Nazi madness was only an extreme manifestation of the collective psychopathology that emerges, or is liable to emerge, in response to the ambiguity of the Jews' existence among the nations. The unclear identity of part of the people, our dual loyalty to the nation among whom we live and to the Jewish people scattered among many countries, our attachment to another homeland—all these are always potential foci of conflict in times of national crisis, and over them we have no control. Tolerance, humanism, religious pluralism are all thin protective layers that quickly crumble when national interest or social crisis presses upon them.

The essential lack of clarity of our situation in the world, the lack of clarity also about our intentions (our own lack of clarity about them), bring out pathological aggression from those historical forces unable to endure ambiguity.

The Holocaust bared the profound hazards of the Jew's situation in the world. The solution is not to change the world, to bring it into line with the special nature of our existence, but to change the nature of Jewish existence, to bring it into line with the world. The solution is normalization of Jewish existence.

All those who try to present the Holocaust as another expression of Jewish destiny are in fact asserting that this pattern of relations is irremediable, that we have no control over our destiny, that we move on a course without exit. This conception sought, for example, to unite in one memorial day both Holocaust Day and the Ninth of Av (a day of fasting in memory of the destruction of the Second Temple and the exile from Spain). That is to obfuscate the essential difference between, on the one hand, the destruction of the Temple and the loss of independence and, on the other, the Holocaust as the failure of Diaspora existence. These are two totally different events. The destruction of the Second Temple represents the failure of our way of conducting our independence, the failure of our excessive activism as a nation among nations. The Holocaust represents the failure of the terrible passivity of our scattered exilic existence among the nations. Between these two colossal failures we must find a third, more proper way to exist among the world's peoples.

The Challange of the Holocaust

But the Holocaust, while laying a heavy burden on us, also confronts us with challenges. As the sons of the victims, it is our duty to be the bearers of several clear lessons. These we must bring to the world.

The first lesson is profound rejection of racism and chauvinism. Having experienced in the flesh the price of racism and extreme nationalism, we must reject their manifestations not only in the past, not only among ourselves. We must reject them everywhere and among all peoples. We must be the standard-bearers of opposition to racism in all its forms and manifestations. Nazism was not only a German phenomenon. It is a general human phenomenon, and no people, and I stress *no people,* is immune to it.

After World War II it was asked how such a cultured and developed people as were the Germans, a people that had produced geniuses of intellect and artistic creation, degenerated to a level of such execrable crime. A number of historians and German "experts" advanced the proposition that Nazism has always been present, potentially, in the Germans, that the Nazi view of the world is rooted in the German spirit and mentality. This theory tried to prove that the nature of the German people is such that it is potentially criminal, that the unique German combination of powerful nationalism, a sense of order, and blind obedience is itself capable of breeding Nazism. In this view the Germans cannot be other than what they are and are always foredoomed to criminality. For that reason they must always be kept under close watch and on a short leash to prevent another outburst of mad violence. What is more, on the basis of this argument, the Germans cannot possible be held morally responsible for their deeds. What they did is part of their nature from birth.

The years that have elapsed since World War II, it seems, have proved theories of this sort wrong. Present-day Germany (I refer to democratic Western Germany) is a different Germany. It is a country of freedom, democracy, and strict respect for individual rights. As such, it is conclusive proof that Nazism is not inevitable for the Germans but is an outlook and way of life that they *chose.* Hence they are morally responsible for it. Let it not be forgotten that Hitler was elected by great numbers of the German people and they cooperated with him along his entire course. That Germany can in fact be different indicates that Nazism was not imposed on it but was chosen by it. And therefore the Germans are historically and morally responsible for what happened.

But the years that have elapsed have also demonstrated, to our deep sorrow, that the phenomenon of Nazism is possible among other peoples as well. True, the horrors have not yet reached the heights of World War II, but events in Biafra, Bangladesh, and Cambodia are not so distant from the scale of Nazi butchery.

We, as victims of the Nazi infection, must be the bearers of the antibodies to this horrible disease which is liable to attack any people. And as the bearers of these antibodies we must first of all be careful regarding ourselves.

At the same time we must also be careful not to lose a sense of proportion and not to measure everything by comparison with the Holocaust. Having suffered such a horrendous experience, we are liable to grow indifferent to any lesser suffering. He who has suffered greatly may become inured to the suffering of others. That is completely natural. But as the bearers of the anti-Nazi message we must whet our sensitivity, not dull it. We must bear in mind that our having been victims does not accord us any special moral standing. The victim does not become virtuous for having been a victim. Although the Holocaust inflicted a horrible injustice on us, it did not grant us a certificate of everlasting righteousness. The murderers were amoral; the victims were not made moral. To be moral you must behave ethically. The test of that is daily and constant.

I have already noted that the Holocaust can lead an individual to despair of the world. After the experience of the Holocaust it is natural to be left with no faith in man or his actions. We, the sons of the victims, have a redoubled right to express our profound disappointment with the world. But this, too, we should remember, that despair of the world is a Nazi stance, that Nazism also was born of a feeling that by its nature the world is valueless, that good cannot be expected of man, that the only valid values are might and cunning. Whoever arrives at a nihilistic stance in wake of the experience of the Holocaust paradoxically deeply confirms an implicit Nazi thesis. To be bearers of hope and faith in man is not easy after the Holocaust, but if we wish to be consistent in our anti-Nazism we must take up this challenge as well.

When we study the Holocaust and wonder how it was at all possible, we come to realize how meager was our knowledge of the horrors during the war itself. We sometimes ask ourselves how it is possible that large parts of the people (including the Jewish community in Eretz Israel) had no knowledge of what was going on in occupied Europe. And had we had more knowledge of what was happening, would we have found a way to help more? The problem of blocked channels of communication is not only an objective problem, a situation imposed by the iron hand of a totalitarianism which made sure that the horrors would be concealed from the world's view. It also stemmed from an inner refusal to know what was happening, a refusal to search for every crumb of information that could provide a clearer picture of what was going on. The importance of human communication, the opening of channels of communication, the fostering of the press and other modes of communication are one of the clear lessons of this period. It seems to me that the world after the Holocaust, the Western world, has understood this and is doing what it can to ensure that concealment will no longer be possible. The struggle for unrestricted communication is one of the most important efforts being made to prevent a recurrence of such horrors. We have seen this in our struggle for the fate of Soviet Jewry; we see it in other struggles. Again, as the bearers of the anti-Nazi and antitotalitarian message we must be in the forefront of the fight for the free flow of information and ideas. Whoever tries to silence expression, even for reasons of security and solidarity, in the final analysis sows the seeds of calamity. An open society with a roily flow of information is preferable to denial, concealment, and obfuscation.

And in the final analysis, although the Holocaust is a distinctly Jewish experience, it has eternal meaning for mankind as a whole. Even after many years have passed, man will return to study this period, for the events of this terrible war enlarged the concept of man, expanded the horizon of human possibilities. It taught us things we did not know about man's nature. The concept of man, for good or for evil, after the Holocaust is not the same as the concept of man prior to the Holocaust. We understand man better after the Holocaust. True, we always knew that man was capable of both the most awful evil and the most wondrous good; still, the Holocaust revealed a new depth of evil to which man is capable of descending. But it also revealed man's ability to endure. Walking skeletons in the concentration camps, who biologically were deemed virtually "dead," still made moral decisions and shared their last crust of bread with others. Thus, alongside the most awful despair, hope, too, can be born. We who were there and came out from there can, and in my view must, raise the banner of faith in man.

APPENDIX

Statements and Proclamations of the International Federation of Secular Humanistic Jews

A STATEMENT OF PRINCIPLES

We are secular Jews.

We are a unique and significant trend in modern Jewish life.

In a time of resurgent fundamentalism both in Israel and in other countries of the world, it is important for us to affirm our commitments publicly.

What are these commitments?

We believe in the value of human reason and in the reality of the world which reason discloses. The natural universe stands on its own, requiring no supernatural intervention.

We believe in the value of human existence, and in the power of human beings to solve their problems both individually and collectively. Life should be directed to the satisfaction of human needs. Every person is entitled to life, dignity, and freedom.

We believe in the value of Jewish identity and in the survival of the Jewish people. Jewish history is a human story, Judaism, as the civilization of the Jews, is a human creation. Jewish identity is an ethnic reality. The civilization of the Jewish people embraces all manifestations of Jewish life, including Jewish languages, ethical traditions, historic memories, cultural heritage, and especially the emergence of the state of Israel in modern times. Judaism also embraces many belief systems and lifestyles. As the creation of the Jewish people in all ages, it is always changing.

We believe in the value of a secular humanistic democracy for Israel and for all the nations of the world. Religion and state must be separate. The individual right to privacy and moral autonomy must be guaranteed. Equal rights must be granted to all, regardless of race, sex, creed, or ethnic origin.

We have come together, from Israel and many countries of the world, to affirm and defend these commitments.

We establish this International Federation of Secular Humanistic Jews so that we may do together what we cannot do alone and so that we may enjoy the strength of solidarity and unity. We give voice to an important constituency in the Jewish world. We have an important message for the Jewish people.

October 24, 1986
Detroit, Michigan

WHO IS A JEW?

Preamble

Who is a Jew? After more than thirty centuries Jews continue to debate this question.

At stake is the integrity of millions of Jews who do not find their Jewish identity in religious belief or religious practice, but who discover their Jewishness in the historic experience of the Jewish people. At stake also is the Jewish identity of thousands of men and women, in Israel and in other countries of the world, who want to be Jewish, but who are rejected by the narrow legalism of traditional religious authorities.

We, the members of the International Federation of Secular Humanistic Jews, believe that the survival of the Jewish people depends on a broad view of Jewish identity. We welcome into the Jewish people all men and women who sincerely desire to share the Jewish experience regardless of their ancestry. We challenge the assumption that the Jews are primarily or exclusively a religious community and that religious convictions or behavior are essential to full membership in the Jewish people.

The Jewish people is a world people with a pluralistic culture and civilization all its own. Judaism, as the culture of the Jews, is more than theological commitment. It encompasses many languages, a vast body of literature, historical memories, and ethical values. In our times the shadow of the Holocaust and the rebirth of the State of Israel are a central part of Jewish consciousness.

We Jews have a moral responsibility to welcome all people who seek to identify with our culture and destiny. The children and spouses of intermarriage who desire to be part of the Jewish people must not be cast aside because they do not have Jewish mothers and do not wish to undergo religious conversion. The authority to define "who is a Jew" belongs to all the Jewish people and cannot be usurped by any part of it.

Resolution

In response to the destructive definition of a Jew now proclaimed by some Orthodox authorities, and in the name of the historic experience of the Jewish people, we, therefore, affirm that a Jew is a person of Jewish descent or any person who declares himself or herself to be a Jew and who identifies with the history, ethical values, culture, civilization, community, and fate of the Jewish people.

October 1, 1988
Brussels, Belgium

THE FUTURE OF THE JEWISH PEOPLE

Preamble

The survival of the Jewish people is a compelling issue for the Jewish world. For millennia, the Jewish will to survive has been steadfast and resolute. In the century of the Holocaust, the establishment of the state of Israel, and the creation of significant Jewish communities in the Western Hemisphere, that resolve continues to be vigorous and unshaken.

How can we best ensure the survival and strength of the Jewish people?

The freedom and equality of an open society have challenged the traditional structures of the Jewish community. Jewish emancipation, both individual and collective, has enabled many Jews to resist the orthodoxies of the past and to develop alternative expressions of their Jewishness. This new freedom has radically altered the character of the Jewish people.

Many representatives of Orthodox Judaism, and especially its fundamentalist adherents, claim that freedom and diversity are bad for the Jews. They resist pluralism in Jewish life and reject the right of Jews, both as individuals and as communities, to express their Jewish identity in accordance with their own conscience.

Statement

We, the members of the International Federation of Secular Humanist Jews, affirm our commitment to the survival of the Jewish people. Pluralism is not a threat to that survival, but its guarantee.

Secular Humanistic Judaism, which embraces pluralism, has an important role to play in Jewish continuity. No single belief system or lifestyle can win the allegiance of all Jews. Jewish history is witness to the positive force of diversity. Where diversity and personal freedom exist, there is more Jewish creativity and more opportunity for Jews to find their place within the Jewish people.

The issue of pluralism and individual freedom goes beyond mere survival. The quality of Jewish survival is as important as the fact of survival. That quality demands the guarantee of human rights to all people, including the right of personal and cultural freedom.

Rigid and narrow views about the nature of Jewish identity are dangerous, especially now, when we are experiencing the liberation of Soviet Jewry, its cultural renaissance and the emigration to Israel and other countries.

We support the struggle for pluralism and for equality for all expressions of Judaism throughout the Jewish world. We support the struggle in Israel against orthodox coercion which threatens democracy in the Jewish homeland and the very survival of the State.

We commit ourselves to a Jewish future that guarantees pluralism, religious and secular, within one civilization.

The freedom and dignity of the Jewish people must go hand in hand with the freedom and dignity of every human being.

October 21, 1990
Chicago, Illinois

EURASIAN JEWRY

Preamble

The Jews of the former Soviet Union are now free. They are not free from economic hardship and instability. Nor are they free from anti-Semitism. But they are free to remain or leave.

The Jews of Eastern Europe are the heirs to the great national tradition of Yiddish culture and Zionist aspiration. But their inheritance was destroyed by the oppression of years of Communist tyranny and the devastation of the Holocaust. Today they are struggling to recapture their inheritance and to reconnect to the Jews of Israel and the world.

Surveys have confirmed that the overwhelming majority of Jews are not religious. In connecting to their Jewish identity, they are seeking ways to affirm their Jewishness in a secular, humanistic, and cultural way.

Both in Israel and in the former territories of the Soviet Union, they are being confronted by ultra Orthodox and Orthodox missionary activity. Their vulnerability and non-familiarity with Jewish options is being exploited. They are being manipulated, misinformed and denied information about the many Jewish ways to be a Jew.

Statement

We, the members of the International Federation of Secular Humanistic Jews, acknowledge our responsibility to serve the needs and integrity of the Jews of the former Communist Empire.

We urge the national institutions of Israel and the leadership of Jewish communities throughout the world to respect the right of freedom of choice and the integrity of former Soviet Jews wherever they may reside. We urge that they provide a pluralistic approach and guarantee equal access to all Jewish options.

We believe that Secular Humanistic Judaism is a positive option for former Soviet Jews.

We stand ready to serve the needs and the future of Russian Jewry.

October, 1992
Israel

WHAT DOES IT MEAN TO BE JEWISH?

Preamble

In 1988, at its Second Biennial Conference in Brussels, the International Federation of Secular Humanistic Jews declared:

". . . a Jew is a person of Jewish descent or any person who declares himself or herself to be a Jew and who identifies with the history, ethical values, culture, civilization, community, and the fate of the Jewish people."

The worldwide Secular Humanistic Jewish Movement has grown to include many individuals and communities that wish to participate in building a contemporary form of Jewishness and to define more precisely the meaning of their identification with the Jewish people.

There is no single way to be Jewish. Jewish identity is a developing historical phenomenon. Jews in many places throughout history have developed varied ways to affirm and express their identity. Secular Humanistic Judaism recognizes this pluralism, both within the Jewish people as a whole and among Secular Humanistic Jews, as an essential feature of Jewish life. An integral part of Jewish identity is a deep attachment to the State of Israel, its culture, and its people.

Secular Humanistic Jews seek to make their words and actions reflect their convictions. Accordingly, the International Federation affirms that:

Declaration

1. Secular Humanistic Jews make no distinction of any kind among Jews who, regardless of parentage, have chosen to identify with the Jewish people.

2. Secular Humanistic Jews derive inspiration, appreciation, and enlightenment from Jewish experience and creativity, both past and present, as well as from the experience and creativity of other cultures.

3. Secular Humanistic Jews encourage and support activities that promote the continued development of Jewish identity.

4. Secular Humanist Jews, by forming and joining Secular Humanistic Jewish communities, organizations, and schools, gain the opportunity to reinforce their group identity, to enrich their Jewish experience, to learn more about the meaning of Jewishness, and to cultivate Jewish identification among children and youth.

5. Secular Humanistic Jews actively explore ways to make Jewishness a meaningful part of their daily existence and to strengthen their solidarity with Jews everywhere. *These ways may include:*

A. Studying Jewish history, literature, and culture as a means of understanding the full scope of the Jewish experience, and particularly its secular and humanistic dimensions.

B. Celebrating Jewish holidays and life cycle ceremonies as cultural expressions of the cycles of nature and human life and of events in Jewish history. Secular Humanistic Jews feel free to adopt aspects of traditional observances that they find meaningful and to adapt others, or to create new forms that meet the needs of present and future generations.

C. Learning and using one or more Jewish languages, particularly Hebrew, the historic language of the Jewish people and the modern language of the State of Israel, as well as Yiddish, Ladino, and other Jewish languages. Each of these languages adds its unique contribution to Jewish and human culture, and each provides intimate contact with the memories, creativity, and values of the Jewish people.

D. Following ethical standards that rest on such humanistic values as personal autonomy, dignity, justice, and resistance to tyranny, exploitation, and oppression—values that flow from the experience and literature of the Jewish people.

E. Participating in the work of the wider Jewish community and defending the human rights of all people everywhere.

September 23, 1994
Moscow

Index

For Further Reading

by Adam Chalom

The selections printed in this anthology are just the beginning of a bottomless well of secular, cultural and Humanistic Jewish thought. Many of the contributors to *Judaism in a Secular Age* have been very prolific, and only a small portion of their other works are listed here. The works from which contributions to this anthology were selected are listed separately in the "sources" bibliography on page 408.

In this selected list "for further reading," I have only listed works in English for the audience of this English-language anthology, though for authors in Yiddish, Hebrew, or European languages there are many more primary and secondary works in their original languages, and in some cases there were no English language works available. I have only listed significant volumes, though several authors were prolific in pamphlets and other media as well. I have chosen only a few primary and secondary sources for each figure, though many others could have been listed – in fact, the bibliographies of some contributors have been compiled as their own books. And I tried to select the most recent editions, so that they would be more readily available to the interested reader.

Most important, I have focused on the works relevant to secular, cultural, and Humanistic Jewish exploration. It is odd to see a bibliography for Sigmund Freud that omits his *Interpretation of Dreams*, or one for Albert Einstein that has nothing of his scientific writing. Yet the perspective of this anthology is to highlight their contributions to the evolution of Judaism in a secular age, not simply their contributions to humanity. In some cases, their fiction or their intellectual exploration was their contribution to both, while in others their Jewish connections were important but not their primary focus.

In any event, I hope that you find this list for further exploration useful. If one reads one page of the Babylonian Talmud a day, it would take seven years to complete. How many more years than that to complete the library of *Judaism in a Secular Age*?

THE PRECURSOR

Spinoza, Baruch
Complete Works: Spinoza (tr. Samuel Shirley, ed. Michael Morgan) (Indianapolis, IN: Hackett Publishing, 2002)
The Letters: Spinoza (tr. Samuel Shirley, introduction and notes by Steven Barbone, Lee Rice, Jacob Adler) (Indianapolis, IN: Hackett Publishing, 1995)
Ethics: Spinoza (ed. and tr. G.H.R. Parkinson) (New York: Oxford University Press, 2000)
A Spinoza Reader: the Ethics and Other Works (ed. and tr. Edwin Curley) (Princeton, NJ: Princeton University Press, 1994)
Goldstein, Rebecca. *Betraying Spinoza: The Renegade Jew Who Gave Us Modernity* (Schocken: 2006)
Norris, Christopher. *Spinoza and the Origins of Modern Critical Theory*. (Cambridge, MA: Basil Blackwell, 1991)
Smith, Steven. *Spinoza, Liberalism, and the Question of Jewish Identity* (New Haven, CT: Yale University Press, 1997)
Yovel, Yirmiahu. *Spinoza and Other Heretics* (Princeton, NJ: Princeton University Press, 1989).

KINDRED SPIRITS

Aleichem, Sholem
The Best of Sholem Aleichem (ed. Irving Howe & Ruth Wisse) (Jason Aronson: 1989)
From the Fair: the Autobiography of Sholom Aleichem (tr. Curt Leviant) (New York: Viking, 1985)
The Letters of Menakhem-Mendl and Sheyne-Sheyndl; and Motl, the Cantor's Son (tr. Hillel Halkin) (New Haven, CT: Yale University Press, 2002)
Selected Works of Sholem Aleichem (ed. Marvin Zuckerman & Marion Herbst) (Malibu, CA: J. Simon, Pangloss Press, 1994)
Some Laughter, Some Tears: Tales from the Old World and New (sel. & tr. by Curt Leviant) (New York: Putnam, 1968)

Tevye the Dairyman and the Railroad Stories (tr. Hillel Halkin) (New York: Schocken Books, 1987)

Butwin, Joseph and Frances. *Sholom Aleichem* (Boston, MA: Twayne Publishers, 1977)

Miron, Dan. *The Image of the Shtetl and Other Studies of Modern Jewish Literary Imagination* (Syracuse, NY: Syracuse University Press, 2000)

Samuel, Maurice. *The World of Sholem Aleichem* (New York: A. A. Knopf, 1969)

Ben-Gurion, David

Ben-Gurion Looks at the Bible (Middle Village, NY: Jonathan David Publishers, 1972)

Memoirs (compiled by R. Bronstein) (New York: World Publishing Co., 1970).

Rebirth and Destiny of Israel (tr. Mordekhai Nurock) (New York: Philosophical Library, 1954).

Israel: A Personal History (tr. Nechemia Meyers & Ury Nystar) (New York: Funk & Wagnalls, 1971).

Bar-Zohar, Michael. *The Armed Prophet: a Biography of Ben Gurion* (tr. Len Ortzen) (London: Barker, 1967).

Goldberg, Giora. *Ben-Gurion Against the Knesset* (tr. Chaya Naor) (Portland, OR: Frank Cass, 2003)

Bialik, Haim Nachman

Bialik Speaks: Words from the Poet's Lips, Clues to the Man (tr. A. El-Dror, ed. Mordecai Ovadyahu) (New York: Herzl Press, 1969).

Random Harvest: The Novellas of Bialik (tr. David Patterson, Ezra Spicehandler) (Boulder, CO: Westview Press, 1999)

Revealment and Concealment: Five Essays (Jerusalem: Ibis Editions, 2000)

Songs from Bialik: Selected Poems of Hayim Nahman Bialik (tr. Atar Hadari) (Syracuse, NY: Syracuse University Press, 2000).

Aberbach, David. *Bialik* (New York: Grove Press, 1988).

Breslauer, S. Daniel. *Creating a Judaism without Religion: a Postmodern Jewish Possibility* (Lanham, MD: University Press of America, 2001).

Miron, Dan. *H.N. Bialik and the Prophetic Mode in Modern Hebrew Poetry* (Syracuse, NY: Syracuse University Press, 2000).

Brandeis, Louis

Brandeis on Zionism (Washington, DC: Zionist Organization of America, 1942 – reprint by Lawbook Exchange, 1999)

Letters of Louis D. Brandeis, Volume III: Progressive and Zionist (Albany, NY: SUNY Press, 1973)

The Brandeis Reader (ed. Ervin Pollack) (New York: Oceana Publications, 1956)

Baskerville, Stephen. *Of Laws and Limitations: an Intellectual Portrait of Louis Dembitz Brandeis* (Rutherford, NJ: Farleigh Dickinson University Press, 1994)

Gal, Allon. *Brandeis of Boston* (Cambridge, MA: Harvard University Press, 1980)

Strum, Philippa. *Louis D. Brandeis: Justice for the People* (Cambridge, MA: Harvard University Press, 1984)

Buber, Martin

A Believing Humanism: My Testament (tr. Maurice Friedman) (New York: Simon & Schuster, 1967)

Between Man and Man (tr. Ronald Gregor Smith) (New York: Macmillan, 1965)

Hasidism and Modern Man (tr. Maurice Friedman) (New York: Horizon Press, 1958)

A Land of Two Peoples: Martin Buber on Jews and Arabs (ed. Paul Mendes-Flohr) (New York: Oxford University Press, 1983)

On Judaism (ed. Nahum Glatzer) (New York: Schocken Books, 1996)

Friedman, Maurice. *Encounter on the Narrow Ridge: a Life of Martin Buber* (New York: Paragon House, 1991)

Mendes-Flohr, Paul (ed.). *Martin Buber: A Contemporary Perspective* (Syracuse, NY: Syracuse University Press and Jerusalem: the Israel Academy of Arts and Sciences, 2002)

Moore, Donald. *Martin Buber: Prophet of Religious Secularism* (New York: Fordham University Press, 1996)

Schaeder, Grete. (tr. Noah Jacobs) *The Hebrew Humanism of Martin Buber* (Detroit, MI: Wayne State University Press, 1973)

Einstein, Albert

About Zionism (London: Soncino Press, 1930)

Essays in Humanism (New York: Philosophical Library, 1983)

Brian, Denis. *Einstein: a Life* (New York: J Wiley, 1996)

Fösling, Albrecht. *Albert Einstein: a Biography* (New York: Viking, 1997)

Goldman, Robert. *Einstein's God: Albert Einstein's Quest as a Scientist and as a Jew to Replace a Forsaken God* (Northvale, NJ: Jason Aronson, 1997)

Holten, G. & Yehuda Elkan. *Albert Einstein, Historical and Cultural Perspectives: The Centennial Symposium in Jerusalem.* (Princeton, NJ: Princeton University Press, 1982)

Gordon, Aaron David

Selected Essays (tr. Frances Burnce) (New York: Arno Press, 1973 – reprint of 1938 League for Labor Palestine edition)

Rose, Herbert. *The Life and Thought of A.D. Gordon: Pioneer, Philosopher, and Prophet of Modern Israel* (New York: Bloch Publishing Company, 1964)

Herzl, Theodor

Old-New Land (tr. Lotta Levensohn) (New York: Bloch Pub. Company, 1960)

Complete Diaries (New York: Herzl Press, 1960)

Zionist Writings, Essays and Addresses (tr. Harry Zohn) (New York: Herzl Press, 1973)

Kornberg, Jacques. *Theodor Herzl: From Assimilation to Zionism* (Bloomington, IN: Indiana University Press, 1993)

Robertson, Richie & Edward Timms (eds.). *Theodor Herzl and the Origins of Zionism* (Edinburgh: Edinburgh University Press, 1997)

Elon, Amos. *Herzl* (New York: Holt, Rinehart & Winston, 1975)

Kaplan, Mordecai

Dynamic Judaism: the Essential Writings of Mordecai M. Kaplan (New York: Schocken Books and Reconstructionist Press, 1985)

The Greater Judaism in the Making: a Study of the Modern Evolution of Judaism (New York: Reconstructionist Press, 1960)

Judaism without Supernaturalism: the Only Alternative to Orthodoxy and Secularism (New York: Reconstructionist Press, 1958)

The Meaning of God in Modern Jewish Religion (Detroit, MI: Wayne State University Press, 1994 – reprint from Reconstructionist Press 1962 edition)

Breslauer, S. Daniel. *Mordecai Kaplan's Thought in a Postmodern Age* (Atlanta, GA: Scholars Press, 1994)

Caplan, Eric. *From Ideology to Liturgy: Reconstructionist Worship and American Liberal Judaism* (Cincinnati, OH: Hebrew Union College Press, 2002)

Goldsmith, E., M. Scult and R. Scltzer (eds.). *The American Judaism of Mordecai Kaplan*. (New York: New York University Press, 1990)

Gurock, Jeffrey and Jacob Schacter. *A Modern Heretic and a Traditional Community: Mordecai M. Kaplan, Orthodoxy, and American Judaism* (New York: Columbia University Press, 1997)

Scult, Mel. *Judaism Faces the Twentieth Century: a Biography of Mordecai Kaplan* (Detroit, MI: Wayne State University Press, 1993)

Peretz, Yitzhak Leib
The Book of Fire: Stories (tr. Joseph Leftwich) (New York: Yoseloff, 1960)
The I. L. Peretz Reader (New York: Schocken Books, 1990)
My Memoirs (tr. Fred Goldberg) (New York: Citadel Press, 1964)
Selected Stories (ed. I. Howe, E. Greenberg) (New York: Schocken Books, 1974).
Freiden, Ken. *Classic Yiddish fiction: Abramovitsh, Sholem Aleichem, and Peretz* (Albany, NY: SUNY Press, 1995)
Wisse, Ruth. *I. L. Peretz and the Making of Modern Jewish Culture* (Seattle, WA: University of Washington Press, 1991).

Sforim, Mendele Mocher
Fishke the Lame (tr. Gerald Stillman) (New York: Thomas Yoseloff, 1960)
The Parasite (New York: Thomas Yoseloff, 1956)
Selected Works of Mendele Moykher-Sforim (ed. Zuckerman, Stillman, Herbst) (Malibu, CA: Joseph Simon/Pangloss Press, 1991)
The Wishing Ring: a Novel (tr. Michael Wex) (Syracuse, NY: Syracuse University Press, 2003)
Aberbach, David. *Realism, Caricature, and Bias: the Fiction of Mendele Mocher Sefarim* (London: Littman Library of Jewish Civilization, 1993)
Freiden, Ken. *Classic Yiddish Fiction: Abramovitsh, Sholem Aleichem, and Peretz* (Albany, NY: SUNY Press, 1995)
Miron, Dan. *A Traveler Disguised: the Rise of Modern Yiddish Fiction in the Nineteenth Century* (Syracuse, NY: Syracuse University Press, 1996)

PATHBREAKERS

Arendt, Hannah
Essays in Understanding (ed. Jerome Kohn) (New York: Harcourt, Brace & Co., 1994)

Rahel Varnhagen: the Life of a Jewess (tr. Richard & Clara Winston, ed. Liliane Weissberg) (Baltimore, MD: Johns Hopkins University Press, 1997)

The Jew as Pariah: Jewish Identity and Politics in the Modern Age (ed. Ron Feldman) (New York: Grove Press [Random House], 1978)

The Origins of Totalitarianism (New York: Harcourt Brace Jovanovich, 1973)

Bernstein, Richard. *Hannah Arendt and the Jewish Question* (Cambridge, MA: Polity Press, 1996)

Barnouw, Dagmar. *Visible Spaces: Hannah Arendt and the German-Jewish Experience* (Baltimore, MD: Johns Hopkins University Press, 1990)

Kristeva, Julia (tr. Ross Guberman). *Hannah Arendt* (New York: Columbia University Press, 2001)

Ring, Jennifer. *The Political Consequences of Thinking: Gender and Judaism in the Work of Hannah Arendt* (Albany: SUNY Press, 1997)

Villa, Dana (ed.). *The Cambridge Companion to Hannah Arendt* (New York: Cambridge University Press, 2000)

Berdichevsky, Micah Joseph

Miriam: a Novel about Two Townships (tr. A.S. Super) (Tel Aviv: Hakibbutz Hameuchad Publishing House, Institute for the Translation of Hebrew Literature, 1983)

Mimekor Yisrael: Classical Jewish Folktales (tr. I.M. Lask) (Bloomington, IN: Indiana University Press, 1976).

Mintz, Alan. *Banished from Their Father's Table: Loss of Faith and Hebrew Autobiography* (Bloomington, IN: Indiana University Press, 1989).

(Blustein), Rahel

Flowers of Perhaps: Selected poems of Ra'hel (tr. Robert Friend & Shimon Sandbank) (London: Menard Press, 1995)

Selected Poems of Rachel (tr. Elias Pater) (Tel Aviv: Eked, 1974)

Borochov, Ber

Nationalism and Class Struggle: Essays in Zionism and Socialism (New York: Radical Zionist Alliance, 1971)

Nationalism and the Class Struggle: a Marxian Approach to the Jewish problem (New York: Poale Zion Zeire Zion of American & Young Poale Zion Alliance of America, 1937).

Brenner, Joseph Haim

Breakdown and Bereavement: a Novel (Ithaca, New York: Cornell University Press, 1971)

Out of the Depths (Boulder, CO: Westview Press, 1992)

Mintz, Alan. *Banished from Their Father's Table: Loss of Faith and Hebrew Autobiography* (Bloomington, IN: Indiana University Press, 1989).

Fleck, Jeffrey. *Character and Context: Studies in the Fiction of Abramovitsh, Brenner, and Agnon* (Chico, CA: Scholars Press, 1984)

Deutscher, Isaac

Marxism in Our Time (ed. Tamara Deutscher) (Berkeley, CA: Ramparts Press, 1971).

On Socialist Man (New York: Pathfinder Press, 1986)

Isaac Deutscher: the Man and His Work (ed. David Horowitz) (London: MacDonald and Co., 1971).

Dubnow, Simon

History of the Jews in Russia and Poland from the Earliest Times until the Present Day (tr. I. Friedlander) (New York: Ktav, 1975)

Jewish History: an Essay in the Philosophy of History (Philadelphia, Jewish Publication Society, 1903)

An Outline of Jewish History (New York: M.N. Maisel, 1929)

Dubnova-Erlikh, Sofia. *The Life and Work of S.M. Dubnov: Diaspora, Nationalism, and Jewish History* (Bloomington, IN: Indiana University Press, 1991)

Weinberg, David. *Between Tradition and Modernity: Haim Zhitlowski, Simon Dubnow, Ahad Ha-Am and the Shaping of Jewish Identity* (New York: Holmes and Meier, 1996)

Ferber, Edna

Fanny Herself (Urbana, IL: University of Illinois Press, 2001)

One Basket: 31 Short Stories (Garden City, NY: Doubleday, 1957).

Show Boat (Garden City, NY: Doubleday, Doran & Co., 1936)

Three Comedies: The Royal Family, Dinner at Eight, Stage Door (by George Kaufman & Edna Ferber) (NY: Applause, 1999).

Gilbert, Julie Goldsmith. *Ferber: A Biography* (Garden City, NY: Doubleday, 1978).

Shaughnessy, Mary Rose. *Women and Success in American Society in the Works of Edna Ferber* (New York: Gordon Press, 1977)

Freud, Sigmund

The Basic Writing of Sigmund Freud (New York: The Modern Library, 1938)

Freud and Judaism (ed. David Meghnazi). (London: Karnac Books, 1993)

Civilization and its Discontents (tr. and ed. James Strachey) (New York: W. W. Norton, 1989).

Gay, Peter. *A Godless Jew: Freud, Atheism, and the Making of Psychoanalysis* (New Haven, CT: Yale University Press, 1987).

Gresser, Moshe. *Dual Allegiance: Freud as a Modern Jew* (Albany, NY: SUNY Press, 1994)

Yerushalmi, Yosef Hayim. *Freud's Moses: Judaism Terminable and Interminable* (New Haven, CT: Yale University Press, 1991)

Fromm, Erich

The Art of Being (New York: Continuum, 1992)

The Erich Fromm Reader (Atlantic Highlands, NJ: Humanities Press, 1994)
Escape from Freedom (New York: Discus Books, 1968)
On Being Human (New York: Continuum, 1994)
Burston, Daniel. *The Legacy of Erich Fromm* (Cambridge, MA: Harvard University Press, 1991)
Funk, Rainer. *Erich Fromm: The Courage to be Human* (New York: Continuum, 1982)
Knapp, Gerhard Peter. *The Art of Living: Erich Fromm's Life and Works* (New York: P. Lang, 1989)

Goldman, Emma

Anarchy!: an Anthology of Emma Goldman's Mother Earth (ed. Peter Glassgold) (Washington, DC: Counterpoint, 2001)
Anarchism and Other Essays (New York: Dover Publications, 1969)
Living My Life (New York: Dover Publications, 1970)
Falk, Candace (ed.). *Emma Goldman: a Guide to Her Life and Documentary Sources* (Alexandria, VA: Chadwyck-Healey, 1995)
Moritz, Theresa. *The World's Most Dangerous Woman: A New Biography of Emma Goldman* (Toronto: Subway Books, 2001)
Morton, Marian. *Emma Goldman and the American Left: "Nowhere at Home"* (New York: Twayne Publishers, 1992)
Wexler, Alice. *Emma Goldman: an Intimate Life* (New York: Pantheon Books, 1984)

Ha'am, Ahad

Nationalism and the Jewish Ethic: Basic Writings of Ahad Ha'Am (New York: Herzl Press, 1962)
Selected Essays (New York: Atheneum, 1970)
Ten Essays on Zionism and Judaism (New York: Arno Press, 1973)

Simon, Leon. *Ahad Ha-am, Asher Ginzberg: a Biography* (Philadelphia, PA: Jewish Publication Society, 1960)
Weinberg, David. *Between Tradition and Modernity: Haim Zhitlowski, Simon Dubnow, Ahad Ha-Am and the Shaping of Jewish Identity* (New York: Holmes and Meier, 1996)
Zipperstein, Steven. *Elusive Prophet: Ahad Ha'Am and the Origins of Zionism* (Berkeley, CA: University of California Press, 1993).

Hook, Sidney
Convictions (Buffalo, NY: Prometheus Books, 1990)
Education for Modern Man, a New Perspective (New York: Knopf, 1963)
Religion in a Free Society (Lincoln: University of Nebraska Press, 1967)
Sidney Hook on Pragmatism, Democracy, and Freedom: the Essential Essays (Buffalo, NY: Prometheus Books, 2002)
Kurtz, Paul (ed.). *Sidney Hook: Philosopher of Democracy and Humanism* (Buffalo, NY: Prometheus Books, 1983)
Phelps, Christopher. *Young Sidney Hook: Marxist and Pragmatist* (Ithaca, NY: Cornell University Press, 1997)

Kallen, Horace.
Cultural Pluralism and the American Idea: an Essay in Social Philosophy (Philadelphia, PA: University of Pennsylvania Press, 1956)
Frontiers of Hope (New York: Horace Liveright, 1929)
Secularism is the Will of God: an Essay in the Social Philosophy of Democracy and Religion (New York: Twayne Publishers, 1954)
"Of Them Which Say They are Jews," and Other Essays on the Jewish Struggle for Survival (Judith Pilch, ed.) (New York: Bloch, 1954)
What I Believe and Why—Maybe: Essays for the Modern World (Alfred Marrow, ed.) (New York: Horizon Press, 1971)
Why Religion (New York: Boni & Liveright, 1927)

Zionism and World Politics: A Study in History and Social Psychology (Garden City, NY: Doubleday, Page & Co., 1921)
Schmidt, Sarah. *Horace M. Kallen: Prophet of American Zionism* (Brooklyn, NY: Carlson Pub., 1995)

Maslow, Abraham
The Farther Reaches of Human Nature (New York: Viking Press, 1971)
Motivation and Personality (New York: Harper & Row, 1970)
Religions, Values, and Peak Experiences (Penguin Books, 1994)
Goble, Frank. *The Third Force: the Psychology of Abraham Maslow* (New York: Grossman, 1970)
Hoffman, Edward. *The Right to be Human: a Biography of Abraham Maslow* (Los Angeles: J.P. Tarcher, 1988)
Lowry, Richard. *A.H. Maslow: an Intellectual Portrait* (Monterey, CA: Brooks/Cole Publishing Co., 1973)

Nordau, Max
The Interpretation of History (New York: Willey, 1910)
Max Nordau to His People: A Summons and a Challenge (New York: Scopus Publishing Co., 1941)
Morals and the Evolution of Man (New York, Cassell & Co., 1922)
Ben-Horin, Meir. *Max Nordau, Philosopher of Human Solidarity* (New York: Conference on Jewish Social Studies, 1956)
Nordau, Anna & Maxa. *Max Nordau: a Biography* (New York: Nordau Committee, 1943)
Stanislawski, Michael. *Zionism and the Fin de Siècle: Cosmopolitanism and Nationalism from Nordau to Jabotinsky* (Berkeley, CA: University of California Press, 2001)

Rahel. See "(Blustein), Rahel."

Shlonsky, Avraham
{No English collections of Shlonsky poetry, though selections often appear in general collections of modern Hebrew poetry}

Shoham, Reuven. *Poetry and Prophecy: the Image of the Poet as a "Prophet", a Hero, and an Artist in Modern Hebrew Poetry* (Boston, MA: Brill, 2003)

Syrkin, Marie
An Evolving Account of the Jewish Experience since the Holocaust (Washington, DC: Herzl Press & New Republic Books, 1980)
Blessed is the Match: the Story of Jewish Resistance (New York: A.A. Knopf, 1947).
The State of the Jews (Washington, DC: New Republic Books, 1980)
Nachman Syrkin, Socialist Zionist: a Biographical Memoir and Selected Essays (New York: Herzl Press, 1961).
Gleanings: A Diary in Verse (Rhythms Press, 1979)
Omer-Sherman, Ranen. *Diaspora and Zionism in Jewish American Literature: Lazarus, Syrkin, Reznikoff, and Roth* (Waltham, MA: Brandeis University Press, 2002)

Tchernikhowsky, Saul
Saul Tschernichovsky [selected poems] (tr. David Kuselewitz) (Tel Aviv: Eked, 1978).
Silberschlag, Eisig. *Saul Tschernichowsky. Poet of Revolt* (Ithaca, NY: Cornell University Press, 1968).

Zhitlovsky, Haim
Weinberg, David. *Between Tradition and Modernity: Haim Zhitlowski, Simon Dubnow, Ahad Ha-Am and the Shaping of Jewish Identity* (New York: Holmes and Meier, 1996)

FRAMERS OF SECULAR JUDAISM

Aloni, Shulamit

{No collections of essays by Aloni available in English}

Amichai, Yehuda

Even a Fist Was Once an Open Palm with Fingers: Recent Poems (tr. Benjamin & Barbara Harshav) (Perennial, 1991).

Open Closed Open (tr. Chana Bloch & Chana Kronfeld) (Harcourt, 2000)

Yehuda Amichai: A Life of Poetry 1948-1994 (tr. Benjamin & Barbara Harshav) (New York: HarperCollins, 1994).

Abramson, Glenda (ed.). *The Experienced Soul: Studies in Amichai* (Boulder, CO: Westview Press, 1997).

Bauer, Yehuda.

A History of the Holocaust. (New York: Franklin Watts, 1982)

The Holocaust in Historical Perspective (Seattle, WA: University of Washington Press, 1978).

Jewish Reactions to the Holocaust (Tel Aviv: MOD Books, 1989)

Out of the Ashes: the Impact of American Jews on Post-Holocaust European Jewry (New York: Pergamon Press, 1989).

Rethinking the Holocaust (New Haven, CT: Yale University Press, 2001).

Bendor, Shunya

The Social Structure of Ancient Israel: The Institution of the Family from the Settlement to the End of the Monarchy (Jerusalem: Simor, 1996).

Berlin, Isaiah

The Crooked Timber of Humanity: Chapters in the History of Ideas (London: Jon Murray, 1990)

Four Essays on Liberty (New York: Oxford University Press, 1969)
Jewish Slavery and Emancipation (New York: Herzl Press: 1961)
Karl Marx: His Life and Environment (New York: Oxford University Press: 1996)
Gray, John. *Isaiah Berlin* (Princeton, NJ: Princeton University Press, 1996)
Ignatieff, Michael. *Isaiah Berlin: a Life* (New York: Metropolitan Books, 1998)

Cohn, Haim
Human Rights in the Bible and Talmud (tr. Shmuel Himelstein) (Tel Aviv: MOD Books, 1989)
Human Rights in Jewish Law (New York: Ktav, 1984)
The Trial and Death of Jesus (New York: Harper & Row, 1971)

Friedman, Daniel
Jews without Judaism (Buffalo, NY: Prometheus Books, 2002)

Goodman, Saul
Editor of *The Faith of Secular Jews* (New York: Ktav, 1976)

Hartman, Hershl
The Hanukah Festival: A Guide for the Rest of Us (Los Angeles, CA: The Sholem Community)
The Hidden History of Hanukah for Kids (And Grownups Too) (Los Angeles, CA: The Sholem Community)
A Secularist's Guide to the Jewish New Year Festival (Los Angeles, CA: The Sholem Community)

Katz, Zev
From the Gestapo to the Gulags: One Jewish Life (Portland, OR: Vallentine Mitchell, 2004).

Malkin, Yaakov
*Secular Judaism: Faith, Values, and Spirituality (*Portland, OR: Vallentine Mitchell, 2004)
What Do Secular Jews Believe? (Milan Press, 1998)

Memmi, Albert
The Liberation of the Jew (tr. Judy Hyun) (New York: Orion Press, 1966)
Jews and Arabs (tr. Elanor Levieux) (Chicago: J. P. O'Hara, 1975)
Roumani, Judith. *Albert Memmi* (Philadelphia, PA: Celfan Edition Monographs, 1987)

Oz, Amos
In the Land of Israel (tr. Maurie Goldberg-Bartura) (San Diego: Harcourt Brace Jovanovich, 1983)
The Story Begins: Essays on Literature (tr. Maggie Bar-Tura) (New York: Harcourt Brace, 1999)
Where the Jackals Howl, and Other Stories (tr. Nicholas de Lange & Philip Simpson) (New York: Harcourt Brace Jovanovich, 1981)
My Michael (tr. Nicholas de Lange) (New York: Vintage Books, 1992)
Balaban, Abraham. *Between God and Beast: an Examination of Amos Oz's Prose* (University Park, PA: Pennsylvania State University Press, 1993)
Mazor, Yair. *Somber Lust: the Art of Amos Oz* (Albany, NY: SUNY Press, 2002)

Rapp, Uri
{No collections of essays by Rapp available in English}

Rosenfeld, Max
Festivals, Folklore and Philosophy: A Secularist Revisits Jewish Traditions (Philadelphia, PA: Sholem Aleichem Club, 1997)

Editor & translator of *A Union for Shabbos, and Other Stories of Jewish Life in America* (Philadelphia, PA: Sholem Aleichem Club Press, 1967)
Editor & translator of *Pushcarts and Dreamers* (Philadelphia, PA: Sholem Aleichem Club Press, 1993)
Editor & translator of *New Yorkish and other American Yiddish Stories* (Philadelphia, PA: Sholem Aleichem Club Press, 1995)

Schappes, Morris
Editor of *A Documentary History of the Jews in the United States, 1654-1875* (New York: Schocken Books, 1971)

Wine, Sherwin
Celebration: a Ceremonial and Philosophic Guide for Humanists and Humanistic Jews (Buffalo, NY: Prometheus Books, 1988)
The Humanist Haggadah (Farmington Hills, MI: Society for Humanistic Judaism, 1994)
Humanistic Judaism (Buffalo, NY: Prometheus Books, 1978)
Judaism Beyond God (Hoboken, NJ: Ktav & Milan Press, 1995)
Staying Sane in a Crazy World: A Guide to Rational Living (Birmingham, MI: Center for New Thinking, 1995)
A Life of Courage: Sherwin Wine and Humanistic Judaism (ed. Dan Cohn-Sherbok, Harry T. Cook, Marilyn Rowens) (Farmington Hills, MI: International Institute for Secular Humanistic Judaism, 2003)

Yehoshua, A. B.
The Continuing Silence of a Poet: the Collected Stories of A.B. Yehoshua (New York: Penguin Books, 1991)
Diaspora: Exile and the Contemporary Jewish Condition (Shapolsky, NY: Steimatzky, 1986)
Mr. Mani (tr. Hillel Halkin) (San Diego, CA: Harcourt Brace, 1993)

Hakak, Lev. *Equivocal Dreams: Studies in Modern Hebrew Literature* (Hoboken, NJ: Ktav, 1993)
Horn, Bernard. *Facing the Fires: Conversations with A.B. Yehoshua* (Syracuse, NY: Syracuse University Press, 1997)

Sources

Aleichem, Sholem. *The Old Country*, translated by Frances and Julius Butwin. New York: Crown Publishers, 1946.

Amichai, Yehuda. *Great Tranquillity: Questions and Answers*, translated by Abramson and Parfitt. New York: Harper & Row, 1983.

Love Poems. New York: Harper & Row, 1981.

Arendt, Hannah. *Eichmann in Jerusalem.* New York: Penguin Books, 1963.

"Creating a Cultural Atmosphere," from a symposium, "Jewish Culture in this Time and Place." *Commentary*, 1947.

Ben-Gurion, David. "The Imperatives of the Jewish Revolution," in *The Zionist Idea.* Edited by Arthur Hertzberg. New York: Atheneum, 1969.

Berdichevsky, Micah Joseph. "Wrecking and Building," in The Zionist Idea, edited by Arthur Hertzberg. New York: Atheneum, 1969.

Berlin, Isaiah. *The Crooked Timber of Humanity.* New York: Alfred Knopf, 1990.

Bialik, Haim Nahman. "On the Slaughter," in *Modern Hebrew Poetry,* edited & translated by Bernhard Frank. Iowa City, IA: University of Iowa Press, 1980.

(Blustein), Rahel. "Here on Earth," in *Modern Hebrew Poetry,* edited & translated by Ruth Mintz. Berkeley, CA: University of California Press, 1965.

Borochov, Ber. "On Questions of Zionist Theory," in Ber Borochov, *Class Struggle and the Jewish Nation*, edited by Mitchell Cohen. New Brunswick, NJ: Transaction Books, 1984.

Brandeis, Louis. *The Social and Economic Ideas of Mr. Justice Brandeis*, collected by Alfred Lief. New York: Vanguard Press, 1930.

Buber, Martin. *I and Thou.* Translated by Ronald G. Smith. New York: Charles Scribner & Sons, 1958.

Deutscher, Isaac. *The Non-Jewish Jew and Other Essays.* London: Oxford University Press, 1968.

Dubnow, Simon. "The Doctrine of Jewish Nationalism," "The Teachings of Jewish History," "The Sociological View of Jewish History," and "In Haman's Times," in Simon Dubnow, *Nationalism and History.* Philadelphia, PA: Jewish Publication Society, 1958.

Einstein, Albert. "Jewish Ideals" and "Just What is a Jew?" in *The Faith of Secular Jews*, edited by Saul Goodman. New York: Ktav, 1976.

"The Laws of the Laws of Ethics," in Albert Einstein, *Out of My Later Years.* Secaucus, NJ: Citadel Press, 1956.

Ferber, Edna. *A Peculiar Treasure.* Garden City, NY: Garden City Publishing, 1940.

Fromm, Erich. *The Art of Loving.* New York: Harper & Row, 1956.

Psychoanalysis and Religion. New Haven, CT: Yale University Press, 1950.

You Shall Be as Gods. New York: Holt, Rinehart & Winston, 1966.

Freud, Sigmund. *The Future of an Illusion*. edited by James Strachey. New York: W.W. Norton, 1961.

Goldman, Emma. *Red Emma Speaks: Selected Writings and Speeches*, edited by Alix K. Shulman. New York: Vintage Books, 1972.

"Was My Life Worth Living?" in *American Jewish Women: A Documentary History*, edited by Jacob Marcus. New York: Ktav, 1981.

Goodman, Saul. "Jewish Secularism," in *Judaism*, IX, No. 4, 1960.

Gordon, Aaron David. "Labor," "The Immortality of the Soul," and "The Nation," in *Contemporary Jewish Thought,* edited by Simon Noveck. Washington, D.C.: B'nai Brith, 1964.

Ha'am, Ahad. *Ahad Ha'am, Essays, Letters, Memoirs*, translated and edited by Leon Simon. Oxford: Phaidon Press, 1946.

Herzl, Theodor. *The Jewish State.* New York: Dover Publications, 1988.

Hook, Sidney. *Out of Step: An Unquiet Life in the 20th Century.* New York: Harper & Row, 1987.

"Nature and the Human Spirit," in Sidney Hook, *Quest for Being*. New York: St. Martin's Press, 1961.

Kallen, Horace. *Judaism at Bay.* New York: Bloch Publishing Co., 1932.

"Is There a Jewish View of Life?" in *The Faith of Secular Jews,* edited by Saul Goodman. New York: Ktav, 1976.

Kaplan, Mordecai. *Judaism as Civilization.* New York: Schocken Press, 1967,

Maslow, Abraham. *Toward a Psychology of Being.* New York: Van Nostrand, 1968.

A Memorial Volume. Belmont, CA: Brooks/Cole Publishing Co., 1972.

Memmi, Albert. *Dominated Man*. New York: Orion Press, 1968.

Portrait of a Jew, translated by E. Abbott. New York: Orion Press, 1962.

Nordau, Max. *The Conventional Lies of Our Civilization.* New York: Arno Press, 1975.

Oz, Amos. *The Slopes of Lebanon,* translated by M. Goldberg-Batura. New York: Harcourt Brace Jovanovich, 1989.

Peretz, Isaac Leib. "A Woman's Wrath," in *Yiddish Tales*, translated by Helena Frank. Philadelphia, PA: Jewish Publication Society, 1948.

Rahel. See "(Blustein), Rahel."

Schappes, Morris. *Jewish Currents Reader.* New York: Jewish Currents Press, 1966.

Shlonsky, Avraham. "Toil." In *Modern Hebrew Poetry*. Edited and translated by Ruth Mintz. Berkeley, CA: University of California Press, 1965.

Spinoza, Baruch. *Tractatus Theologica Politicus,* edited by A. G. Werham. Oxford: Clarendon Press, 1958.

Tchernikhowsky, Saul. "I Believe," in *Saul Tschernichowsky: Poet of Revolt*. New York: Cornell University Press, 1968.

Weiler, Gershon. *Jewish Theocracy*. Leiden: E.J. Brill, 1988.

Yehoshua, A. B. *Between Right and Right*, translated by A. Schwartz. Garden City, NY: Doubleday & Co., 1981.